MATERIALS ON TORT REFORM

Second Edition

■ ■ ■

Andrew F. Popper

Bronfman Professor of Law and Government
American University Washington College of Law

AMERICAN CASEBOOK SERIES®

WEST
ACADEMIC
PUBLISHING

American Casebook Series is a trademark registered in the U.S. Patent and Trademark Office.

© 2010 Thomson Reuters
© 2017 LEG, Inc. d/b/a West Academic
    444 Cedar Street, Suite 700
    St. Paul, MN 55101
    1-877-888-1330

West, West Academic Publishing, and West Academic are trademarks of West Publishing Corporation, used under license.

Printed in the United States of America

ISBN: 978-1-68328-754-4

To Dante, Payton, and Jackson and all those that follow

PREFACE TO THE SECOND EDITION

The goal for this edition is very much the same as it was for the First Edition: a presentation of essays, articles, cases, and other materials allowing for consideration of all sides of the tort reform debate. My hope is that students, lawyers, policy makers, and others in the field find this book useful in their research and in their quest to cut the Gordian knot of tort reform.

Those fighting for various changes (mostly limitations on liability or tightening of the civil liability system) believe they are in a quest for justice. They represent large segments of the GNP including retailing, wholesaling, manufacturing, healthcare, insurance, and more. Their contention is that tort law, as currently practiced, produces uncertain and unfair results. Their goal is to change the civil justice system, limiting liability, and arguably liberating resources to be used to create better services and safer and more efficient products.

Those fighting against tort reform contend that its proponents have but one goal: the reduction or elimination of accountability. They assert that this is a struggle to preserve the rights of injured consumers to a fair and just system legal system. They seek to preserve a level playing field for all parties where meaningful monetary damages are imposed on those who produce dangerous products or fail to provide reasonable professional services. Such damages, they argue, are essential not only to compensate those injured but to deter others from engaging on similar misconduct.

Both positions have multiple glimmers of legitimacy, a fact that seems obvious to all except those involved in the fight.

On opinions or points of view expressed in this text: All opinions and positions in this text represent the perspectives of the individual essayists and authors who agreed to have their work replicated in this work. The comments and notes surrounding those works reflect my best effort to explain various points in the field or, in some places, my perspective on tort reform. However, this work does not represent the point of view (nor use the resources of) American University or the Washington College of Law.

On sources: While the materials in the text are fully attributed, in the interest of ease and simplicity of use, most internal footnotes have been deleted. The user of this material would be well-advised to go to the original source for footnotes or other documentation before quoting the work of the authors or languages in the cases in this text.

AFP
Washington, DC, 2017

PREFACE TO THE FIRST EDITION

The text:

This material began as a supplemental handout for my first-year Torts course. Over time, it took on a life of its own. The more tort reform edged its way into my class, the longer the handout became until it was about twice the size of this book. At some point in the last year or so, several things became clear:

(a) Students in the fall semester of the first year are not about to read a 600-page handout for a topic not central to a final exam.

(b) Although the field is fascinating, the materials were not; edited articles alone, I'm afraid, are not quite as interesting as academicians believe.

(c) Those students who did read the materials (or some part thereof) certainly understood the basic doctrine. However, they did not have a sense of the most potent dynamic in the field: the effect on plaintiffs when wrongs are not redressed, and the effect on defendants ordered to pay damages when they believe they were not at fault or to pay damages wildly disproportionate to compensatory damages.

(d) I questioned the objectivity of my presentation. I have strong feelings about this field—a "position" if you will—we all do. Students should have the chance to make up their own minds. Since I prepared this text, you are entitled to know my position on tort reform. To that end, I included excerpts of my legal writing as well as the text of the narratives. Students of this field are equally entitled to information and arguments that support other positions in the field.

My goals with this material involve the four points mentioned above. Accordingly:

(a) This is a relatively short book.

(b) This book has edited articles, essays, statements of interest groups, public documents, conventional notes and questions, tasks students might undertake, and a simulation.

(c) This book has a fictional narrative that develops five characters—a plaintiff, a defendant, a lawyer, a lobbyist, and a U.S. Senator. My hope is that the narrative provides insight into the client side of this discourse in ways that articles, testimony, position papers, and studies cannot achieve.

(d)   I invited and received essays from a number of lawyers, interest group representatives, and other scholars. They cover many of the varying positions in the field and are presented with no substantive editing. It is my best shot at objectivity.

Editorial matters:

I recommend strongly reference to the original scholarship and full text of all cases and articles to get a better sense of the material. Most of the materials in this book are available in full through Westlaw or other online sources. I took the liberty of consolidating language and editing aggressively. I relied on ellipses and square brackets to denote omitted materials instead of using asterisks.

I dropped many concurring and dissenting opinions and *omitted completely almost all footnotes, references, and citations.*

I cut multiple case references within articles and opinions to streamline the presentation and allow you to focus on the issues in play.

Every effort has been made to identify all sources from which this material is drawn. In compiling and editing many documents (including cases and scholarship) errors will be made for which, in the end, I am responsible.

———

These materials are designed to provide insight and information to anyone interested in tort reform. I wish you the best in your study of this field

AFP
Washington, DC

ABOUT THE AUTHOR

Andrew F. Popper is the Bronfman Professor Law and Government and teaches torts, administrative law, government litigation, and advanced administrative law. In 2016 he was elected law faculty member of the year. He is the recipient of American Bar Association awards for excellence in both tort and administrative law and has received American University's highest faculty award, Scholar/Teacher of the Year. He has served as Associate Dean for Academic Affairs and for nearly two decades has chaired the law school admissions committee. He has served as chair of the Administrative Law Section of the Federal Bar Association and has been a site visitor for the ABA and AALS, participating in the accreditation review of twelve other law schools, chairing four of those visits.

Professor Popper is the author of more than 100 published books, law review articles, papers, and public documents. He is lead author of the West casebook, *Administrative Law: A Contemporary Approach* (3rd Edition, 2016). His law review articles are in journals at a number of law schools including Harvard, Northwestern, Marquette, and DePaul.

Since 2009, he has published three legally-themed novels, *Sunrise at the American Market* (2015), *Rediscovering Lone Pine* (2010) (for which he received the Maryland Writer's Association First Place Award for mainstream fiction), and *Bordering on Madness: An American Land Use Tale* (2009).

Professor Popper has served as a consumer rights advocate and pro bono counsel for the Consumers Union of America, testified before more than 40 state and federal congressional committees, and authored *amicus curiae* briefs before the United States Supreme Court. Prior to coming to the Washington College of Law, he held an endowed chair at the University of Denver, School of Law, and before that practiced law in Washington, DC.

REACTIONS TO THE FIRST EDITION OF POPPER'S MATERIALS ON TORT REFORM

For the first time in one volume is the full rainbow of views about tort reform. What is unique is the selection of authors with pro, con, and "middle of the road" perspectives about tort reform. They include both the top academic icons on the subject of tort law and leaders of the political and practical world of tort law who deal with the impact of tort law on our society. Anyone who addresses the public policy challenges of this vital subject will benefit from the wise editor's (Professor Popper's) carefully written and constructed anthology.

—Victor Schwartz, Partner, Shook Hardy & Bacon, Chair, The Public Policy Group, formerly Professor and Acting Dean, University of Cincinnati College of Law, Co-author PROSSER, WADE, AND SCHWARTZ'S CASES AND MATERIALS ON TORTS (12 ed. 2010) and Author, COMPARATIVE NEGLIGENCE (5th ed., 2010)

This book addresses the important and controversial topic of tort reform. By assembling competing views across a range of tort reform issues, it has done an enormous service in furthering public discussion of issues that should be of concern to all those interested in the legal system.

—Theodore Eisenberg, Henry Allen Mark Professor of Law, Cornell Law School

I applaud this important compilation of essays and articles covering divergent perspectives in the field of tort reform. For years, I have heard powerful testimony from people all over the country describing the urgency and importance of the complex and competing issues addressed in this book. Professor Popper's book continues the public discussion to better understand and improve the process for ensuring fair and efficient compensation to victims.

—John Conyers, Jr., Member of Congress

Professor Popper's compilation of essays and other valuable materials presents a balanced approach to the tort reform discussion. By viewing a serious personal injury case through the eyes of the participants and then carrying those perspectives over into the political arena, Professor Popper makes a unique contribution to the tort reform literature. Professor Popper's unique approach allows a glimpse of what it means to be an injured person in a tort case as well as a view from the perspective of the allegedly at fault party. Thoughtful readers will be in a better position to make rational choices about the future of the civil justice system after completing this book.

—Joseph Harbaugh, Professor of Law and Dean Emeritus, Nova Southeastern Law School

For the first time, a comprehensive and balanced look at tort reform, one of the most volatile issues of our time. Professor Popper takes us into the real world of tort reform as seen through the eyes of families, small business owners, physicians, lawyers, lobbyists, and legislators—all brought to life by a man who knows, and has lived with, the full impact of this issue on all concerned.

—Richard Warren Mithoff, Esq., Former President, American Board of Trial Advocates, Houston, Texas

Tort reform has enormous ramifications for the nation, yet even law schools generally give it short shrift. Maybe that's partly because some fear the topic is too politically-charged for the classroom, and partly because there was no text up to the task. Andrew F. Popper has now solved both of those problems. His concise anthology of key materials illuminates the many perspectives on the topic. It does so efficiently while being fair to both sides. All of the color and drama of the debate are here, along with pertinent data. This book will be a boon to schools of law and public policy, as well as interested individuals.

—Professor Carl T. Bogus, Roger Williams University, School of Law

Professor Popper has compiled a treasure trove of perspectives on the ongoing and evolving tort wars. This book is an essential resource for anyone interested in all sides of this dynamic debate, especially students of public policy.

—Linda Lipsen, Executive Vice President, American Association for Justice

Every student in Torts comes with conceptions and misconceptions about tort reform that interfere with true understanding of both the law of torts and what is at stake in the tort reform debate. To date, there has been little accessible material to provide students with accurate and thorough information from both perspectives of the debate. Andy Popper's collection fills that void, enabling students to understand based upon information and stories, using materials from those most engaged on the front lines.

—Elizabeth A. Reilly, C. Blake McDowell, Jr. Professor of Law, University of Akron, School of Law

SUMMARY OF CONTENTS

PREFACE TO THE SECOND EDITION V

PREFACE TO THE FIRST EDITION VII

ABOUT THE AUTHOR IX

REACTIONS TO THE FIRST EDITION OF POPPER'S MATERIALS ON TORT
    REFORM XI

TABLE OF CASES XIX

TABLE OF AUTHORITIES.. XXI

An Introduction to the Text and to Tort Reform.................................... 1

Part I. Tort Reform Narratives and Essays 9
A.   An Introduction to the Narrative and Essays—and More Tort Reform
    Issues.. 9
B.   The Essays 18
C.   The Narratives 122

**Part II. Select Articles, Statements, and Related Materials from
Academicians, Interest Groups, and Others** 163
A.   A Brief Look at the Background and General Goals of Tort Reform 164
B.   Is the Civil Justice System in Crisis? The Basic Dispute and the
    Nature of the Fight 186
C.   What Should Change—If Anything: the Content of the Tort Reform
    Discourse.. 224
D.   Caps and Other Tort Reforms Disputes 245

Part III. A Very Brief Look at the Caselaw 267

Conclusion... 309

INDEX.. 311

TABLE OF CONTENTS

PREFACE TO THE SECOND EDITION V

PREFACE TO THE FIRST EDITION VII

ABOUT THE AUTHOR IX

REACTIONS TO THE FIRST EDITION OF POPPER'S MATERIALS ON TORT
    REFORM XI

TABLE OF CASES XIX

TABLE OF AUTHORITIES XXI

An Introduction to the Text and to Tort Reform................................. 1

Part I. Tort Reform Narratives and Essays 9
A.   An Introduction to the Narrative and Essays—and More Tort Reform
     Issues.. 9
B.   The Essays 18
    Group One: Tort Reform: Great Issues, Choices, and Political
       Challenges.. 18
       Victor E. Schwartz, The Dynamics of Tort Law: Its Capacity for
          Change—It Can Help or Harm Society 20
       Erwin Chemerinsky, The Politics of Tort Reform 27
       Ronen Avraham, Tort Reform May Reduce Healthcare Costs, but
          It's No Silver Bullet—So Let's Think Outside of the Box 29
       Neil Vidmar, Medical Malpractice Tort Reform 33
       Joan Vogel, The Tort Reform Movement as a Teaching Vehicle 35
       Todd J. Zywicki and Dr. Jeremy Kidd, Public Choice and Tort
          Reform 39
       Michael Rustad, The Endless Campaign: How the Tort Reformers
          Successfully and Incessantly Market Their Groupthink to the
          Rest of Us.. 42
    Group Two: Tort Reform: Who Is Affected? Who Decides?...................... 51
       Stephen D. Sugarman, The Transformation of Tort Reform........... 52
       Pamela Gilbert, The Human Face of Tort Reform 55
       Mark Behrens, Who Should Decide Tort Law? A Fundamental
          Issue in the Public Debate Over Civil Justice Reform 59
       Frank J. Vandall, Tort Reform, A Power Play 61
       Jeffrey O'Connel and Christopher Robinette, Tort Law's Flaws 64
       Carl T. Bogus, Introduction: Genuine Tort Reform 66
       George Priest, The Economic Case for Tort Reform........................ 69

Group Three: Tort Reform: A Personal, Public, and Institutional
    Discourse 71
    Lisa A. Rickard, Matthew D. Webb, and Mary H. Terzino,
        American Tort and Civil Litigation—Still at a Crossroads?.... 73
    Paul Taylor, Strengthening Democracy through Tort Reform 83
    Sue Steinman, Tort Reform: A Personal Reflection 90
    Aaron D. Twerski, Musings of a So-Called Tort Reformer 92
    Joseph A. Page, An Excerpt from: Deforming Tort Reform, a
        Book Review of Liability: The Legal Revolution and Its
        Consequences (Basic Books, 1988) 95
    Corrine Parver, Health Courts: A Modern-Day Solution for
        Medical Malpractice Litigation.. 97
    Marshall Shapo, The Product Liability Reform Act, Statement of
        Marshall S. Shapo, before the Senate Committee on the
        Judiciary on S.1400, July 31, 1990 99
Group Four: Tort Reform: Justice Delayed, Denied, or Enhanced?...... 101
    Sherman Joyce, New Issues in "Tort Reform" 103
    Joanne Doroshow, Access to Justice 106
    Martha Chamallas, Civil Rights and Civil Wrongs 108
    Donald G. Gifford, Tort Reform as a Two-Way Street 111
    Richard L. Cupp, Jr., Tort Reform or Tort Restriction: Rhetoric
        as Scorekeeper 113
    Paul Figley, Calls for Justice & "Joint and Several Liability" 115
    Lucinda M. Finley, What is Tort Reform Really About?................. 117
C. The Narratives 122
    Narrative 1: The Restaurant, the Accident, Miranda and Simon
        Daine 123
    Narrative 2: Simon Daine.. 125
    Narrative 3: Richard and Simon, Through Miranda's Eyes.................. 127
    Narrative 4: Daine v. Armstrong Industries 129
    Narrative 5: Daine v. Armstrong Ends... 135
    Narrative 6: Devon Armstrong, CEO, Armstrong Industries and the
        Birmingham Case Through the Eyes of Miranda Daine 138
    Narrative 7: Devon Armstrong and the Consequences of the
        Birmingham Trial.. 140
    Narrative 8: Senator Horace Voltman, Through the Eyes of Miranda
        Daine 142
    Narrative 9: A Tort Reform Hearing Through the Eyes of Miranda
        Daine 144
    Narrative 10: Marty Correll, Through the Eyes of Miranda Daine...... 148
    Narrative 11: Marty Correll's Discussion with Senator Horace
        Voltman.. 150
    Narrative 12: Lunch with Marty Correll 154
    Notes, Questions and a Simulation.. 155

Part II. Select Articles, Statements, and Related Materials from Academicians, Interest Groups, and Others 163

The Articles 164

A. A Brief Look at the Background and General Goals of Tort Reform 164

Notes and Questions 164

James A. Comodeca, Margaret M. Maggio, Philip J. Truax, and Joshua M. Bilz, Killing the Golden Goose by Evaluating Medical Care Through the Retroscope: Tort Reform from the Defense Perspective 165

Christopher J. Roederer, Democracy and Tort Law in America: The Counter-Revolution 167

Rachel M. Janutis, The Struggle Over Tort Reform and the Overlooked Legacy of the Progressives 170

Julie Davies, Reforming the Tort Reform Agenda 175

F. Patrick Hubbard, The Nature and Impact of the "Tort Reform" Movement 178

B. Is the Civil Justice System in Crisis? The Basic Dispute and the Nature of the Fight 186

CJD Item I, "We The Plaintiffs"—A Retort 188

CJD Item II, Federal Preemption of Tort Law: No Recourse for the Injured; Immunity for the Wrongdoer 193

CJD Item III, Glossary of "Tort Reforms" 196

Larry Lyon, Bradley J.B. Toben, James M. Underwood, William D. Underwood and James Wren, Straight from the Horse's Mouth: Judicial Observations of Jury Behavior and the Need for Tort Reform 199

American Tort Reform Association: Commentary, Press Releases, and a White Paper 207

C. What Should Change—If Anything: the Content of the Tort Reform Discourse 224

Notes and Questions 224

Congressional Budget Office, 2003, The Economics of U.S. Tort Liability: A Primer 225

Nancy C. Marcus, Phantom Parties and Other Practical Problems with the Attempted Abolition of Joint and Several Liability 230

Victor E. Schwartz and Cary Silverman, The Case in Favor of Civil Justice Reform 232

D. Caps and Other Tort Reforms Disputes 245

Lee Harris and Jennifer Longo, Flexible Tort Reform 245

Lee Harris, Tort Reform as a Carrot-and-Stick 251

Joanna M. Shepherd, Tort Reforms' Winners and Losers: The Competing Effects of Care and Activity Levels 258

Richard C. Gross, Caps on Medical Malpractice Damages Cut Doctors' Insurance Costs May 2007 261

Center for Justice & Democracy, Snapshot of Justice 2008: "Caps" Do Not Cause Insurance Rates to Drop 262

The Honorable Richard Posner, United States Court of Appeals for the 7th Circuit Professor of Law, University of Chicago Law School, Posner on Tort Reform 264

Part III. A Very Brief Look at the Caselaw 267
BMW of North America, Inc. v. Gore 268
Notes, Comments, and Questions 270
State Farm Mut. Auto. Ins. Co. v. Campbell 271
Notes, Comments, and Questions 276
Wyeth v. Levine 277
Notes, Comments, and Questions 284
Oneok v. Learjet 286
Notes and Questions 289
PLIVA, Inc. v. Mensing 290
Notes and Questions 293
Zeier v. Zimmer, Inc. 294
Notes and Questions 298
Murphy v. Russell 300
Notes and Questions 301
Coleman v. Maxwell Shoe Company, Inc. 303
Notes and Questions 307

Conclusion 309
INDEX 311

TABLE OF CASES

Adams v. Meijer, Inc., 304
Altitude Nines, LLC v. Deep Nines, Inc., 81
Arizona v. United States, 287
Best v. Taylor Mach. Works, 43, 103
BMW of North America, Inc. v. Gore,
  15, **268,** 273, 274, 276
Browning-Ferris Industries of Vermont, Inc.
  v. Kelco Disposal, 11, 15
California v. ARC America Corp., 287
Campbell v. State Farm Mut. Auto. Ins. Co.,
  272
Cole v. Texas, 269
Coleman v. Maxwell Shoe Company,
  Inc., 303
Cooper Industries, Inc. v. Leatherman Tool
  Group, Inc., 15, 273, 276
Diversicare General Partner, Inc. v. Rubio,
  302
Escola v. Coca Cola Bottling Co. of Fresno,
  62
Exxon Shipping Co. v. Baker, 15, 277
Ferdon v. Wisconsin Patients Compensation
  Fund, 104
Florida Lime & Avocado Growers, Inc. v.
  Paul, 294
Garlock Sealing Technologies, In re, 76
Geier v. American Honda Motor Co., Inc.,
  281, 294
Greenman v. Yuba Power Products, Inc., 63
Hastings Mut. Ins. v. GMC, 305
Hines v. Davidowitz, 281, 283
Hollister v. Dayton Hudson Corp., 305, 306
Howell v. Hamilton Meats & Provisions,
  Inc., 23
Huck v. Wyeth, Inc., 24
Johnson v. Rockwell Automation, 298
Li v. Yellow Cab Co., 116
Liebeck v. McDonald's Restaurants, P.T.S.,
  Inc., 29, 36
Lockyer v. Andrade, 27
MacPherson v Buick Motor Co., 61, 114
McIntyre v. Balentine, 116
McMillan v. City of New York, 110
Mealer v. 3M Co., 22
Medtronic, Inc. v. Lohr, 278, 281
Murphy v. Russell, 300
Nabors Well Services, Ltd. v. Romero, 22
Northern Natural Gas Co. v. State Corp.
  Commission of Kan., 289
Ohio Academy of Trial Lawyers, State ex
  rel. v. Sheward, 103
Oneok v. Learjet, 286
Pacific Mut. Life Ins. Co. v. Haslip, 15, 269,
  274, 275
Panhandle Eastern Pipe Line Co. v. Public
  Serv. Comm'n of Ind., 288
Piercefield v. Remington Arms Co., 303, 305
Pierson v. Ray, 83

PLIVA, Inc. v. Mensing, 23, **290**
Rice v. Santa Fe Elevator Corp., 278
Riegel v. Medtronic, Inc., 285
Romo v. Ford Motor Co, 27
Sanzone v. Board of Police Commissioners,
  307
Schneidewind v. ANR Pipeline Co., 286
Silkwood v. Kerr-McGee Corp., 17
Sprietsma v. Mercury Marine, 286
State Farm Mut. Auto. Ins. Co. v.
  Campbell, 15, 187, **271**
Strickland v. Medlen, 21
TXO Production Corp. v. Alliance Resources
  Corp., 15, 269, 274
Viera v. Cohen, 307
Western States Wholesale Natural Gas
  Antitrust Litigation, In re, 288
Wyeth v. Levine, 24, 225, **277**
Wyeth, Inc. v. Weeks, 24
Zeier v. Zimmer, Inc., 294

TABLE OF AUTHORITIES

Abaray, Janet G., *Déjà Vu All Over Again: Ohio's 2005 Tort Reform Act Cannot Survive a Rational Basis Challenge*, 31 DAYTON L. REV. 141 (2006), 18

Abel, Richard L., *Questioning the Counter—Majoritarian Thesis: The Case of Torts*, 49 DEPAUL L. REV. 533 (1999), 157

Abel, Richard, *The Real Torts Crisis—Too Few Claims*, 48 OHIO ST. L.J. 443 (1997), 48

Abraham, Kenneth S., *Individual Action and Collective Responsibility: The Dilemma of Mass Tort Reform*, 73 VA. L. REV. 845 (1987), 4

Abrams, Kathryn, *Hearing the Call of Stories*, 79 CAL. L. REV. 971 (1991), 122

Addair, Michael P., *A Small Step Forward: An Analysis of West Virginia's Attempt at Joint and Several Liability*, 109 W. VA. L. REV. 831 (2007), 51

Allen, Michael P., *Of Remedy, Juries, and State Regulation of Punitive Damages: The Significance of Philip Morris v. Williams*, 63 N.Y.U. ANN. SURV. AM. L. 343 (2008), 186

Alliance for Justice, JUSTICE FOR SALE: SHORTCHANGING THE PUBLIC INTEREST FOR PRIVATE GAIN (1993), 47

American Tort Reform Foundation, *Private Consumer Protection Lawsuit Abuse* (2006), 223

Anderson, Richard E., *Effective Legal Reform and the Malpractice Insurance Crisis*, 5 YALE J. HEALTH POL'Y L. & ETHICS 343 (2005), 159

Apelbaum, Perry H. & Samara T. Ryder, *The Third Wave of Federal Tort Reform: Protecting the Public or Pushing the Constitutional Envelope*, 8 CORNELL J. L. & PUB. POL'Y 591 (1999), 157

Ausness, Richard C., *Preemption of State Tort Law by Federal Safety Statutes: Supreme Court Preemption Jurisprudence Since CIPOLLONE*, 92 KY. L. REV. 913 (2003–2004), 16

Avraham, Ronen, *An Empirical Study of the Impact of Tort Reform on Medical Malpractice Settlement Payments*, 36 JOURNAL OF LEGAL STUDIES S183 (2007), 32

Avraham, Ronen, *Putting a Price on Pain-and-Suffering Damages: A Critique of the Current Approaches and a Preliminary Proposal for Change*, 100 NORTHWESTERN UNIVERSITY L. REV. 87 (2006), 32

Avraham, Ronen, *Tort Reform May Reduce Healthcare Costs, but It's No Silver Bullet—So Let's Think Outside of the Box*, 29

Avraham, Ronen, *Tragedy of the Human Commons*, 29 CARDOZO L. REV. 15 (2008), 32

Baker, Tom, *Reconsidering the Harvard Medical Practice Study Conclusions about the Validity of Medical Malpractice Claims*, 33 J.L. MED. & ETHICS 501 (2005), 9

Bargren, Paul, *Joint and Several Liability: Protection for Plaintiffs*, 1994 WIS. L. REV. 453, 15

Barton, Benjamin H., THE LAWYER-JUDGE BIAS IN THE AMERICAN LEGAL SYSTEM 162 (Cambridge Univ. Press: 2011), 85

Bebchuk, Lucian A., *Suing Solely to Extract a Settlement Offer*, 17 J. LEGAL STUD. 437 (1988), 4

Beck ("Bexis"), James M., *Litigation—Has The Process Become The Purpose?*, 74

Bell, Peter A. & Jeffrey O'Connell, ACCIDENTAL JUSTICE: THE DILEMMAS OF TORT LAW 58 (1997), 156

Bennett, Andy D., *State Constitutional Issues Arising from Tort Reform*, 40 TENN. B.J. 27 (2004), 157

Berger, Mitchell S., *Following the Doctor's Orders—Caps on Non-Economic Damages in Medical Malpractice Cases*, 22 RUTGERS L.J. 173 (1991), 267

Bloom, Anne, *The Radiating Effects of Torts*, 62 DEPAUL L. REV. 229 (2013), 3

Bocchino, Anthony J. & Samuel H. Solomon, *What Juries Want to Hear: Methods for Developing Persuasive Case Theory*, 67 TENN. L. REV. 543 (2000), 122

Bogus, Carl T., *Fear-Mongering Torts and the Exaggerated Death of Diving*, 28 HARV. J.L. & PUB. POL'Y 17 (2004), 66

Bogus, Carl T., *Rescuing Burke*, 72 MO. L. REV. 387 (2007), 66

Bogus, Carl T., *The Hidden History of the Second Amendment*, 31 U.C. DAVIS L. REV. 309 (1998), 66

Bogus, Carl T., WHY LAWSUITS ARE GOOD FOR AMERICA: DISCIPLINED DEMOCRACY, BIG BUSINESS AND THE COMMON LAW (NYU, 2001), 66

Bradford, Michael, *Tort Reform Proponents See Boost From Bush Plan*, BUS. INS., February 17, 1992, 47

Brook, Peter & Paul Gewirtz, LAW'S STORIES: NARRATIVE AND RHETORIC IN THE LAW (1996), 122

Browne, Steven A., *The Constitutionality of Lobby Reform: Implicating Associational Privacy and the Right To Petition the*

Government, 4 WM. & MARY BILL RTS. J.
717 (1995), 156

Budetti, Peter P., *Tort Reform and the
Patient Safety Movement: Seeking
Common Ground*, 293 J. AM. MED. ASSN.
(No. 21) 2660 (2005), 72

CAPITALISM AND FREEDOM (1962), 5

Carroll, Joseph, *Pet Owners Not Worried
That Their Pets Will Get Sick From Pet
Food,* GALLUP NEWS SERVICE, Apr. 3,
2007, 223

Chalos, Mark P., *Successfully Suing
Foreign Manufacturers*, TRIAL, Nov. 2008,
299

Chamallas, Martha, INTRODUCTION TO
FEMINIST LEGAL THEORY (2d ed. 2003),
108

Chamallas, Martha, THE MEASURE OF
INJURY: RACE, GENDER AND TORT LAW
(N.Y.U. Press 2010), 108

Chamallas, Martha & Jennifer Wriggins,
THE MEASURE OF JUSTICE: RACE, GENDER,
AND TORT LAW, (New York University
Press, 2010), 45

Chavkin, David F., *Fuzzy Thinking: A
Borrowed Paradigm for Crisper
Lawyering,* 4 CLINICAL L. REV. 163 (1997),
122

Chemerinsky, Erwin, CONSTITUTIONAL LAW:
PRINCIPLES AND POLICIES, (Aspen Law &
Business 2d ed., 2005), 27

Chemerinsky, Erwin, CONSTITUTIONAL LAW:
PRINCIPLES AND POLICIES, (Aspen Law &
Business 3d ed., 2006), 27

Chemerinsky, Erwin, CRIMINAL PROCEDURE
(Aspen Law and Business 2008), 27

Chemerinsky, Erwin, EMPOWERING
GOVERNMENT: FEDERALISM FOR THE 21ST
CENTURY (Stanford University Press,
2008), 27

Chemerinsky, Erwin, FEDERAL
JURISDICTION (Aspen Law & Business 5th
ed., 2007), 27

Chemerinsky, Erwin, INTERPRETING THE
CONSTITUTION (Praeger 1987), 27

Christensen, Roland, *Comment: Behind the
Curtain of Tort Reform,* 16 B.Y.U.L. REV.
261 (2016), 102

Cohen, Henry, CRS REPORT TO CONGRESS:
FEDERAL TORT REFORM LEGISLATION:
CONSTITUTIONALITY AND SUMMARIES OF
SELECTED STATUTES 1 (2003), 87

Comodeca, James A., Margaret M. Maggio,
Philip J. Truax, and Joshua M. Bilz,
*Killing the Golden Goose by Evaluating
Medical Care Through the Retroscope:
Tort Reform from the Defense Perspective,*
31 DAYTON L. REV. 207 (2006), 14, 165

Conference, Center for Democratic Culture
at UNLV, *The Law and Politics of Tort
Reform,* 4 NEV. L.J. 377 (2003), 158, 307

Connolly, Ceci, *Obama to Speed Up Tort
Reform Tests, but Doctors Want More,*
WASHINGTON POST [ON-LINE], September
18, 2009, 160

Conrad, Robin S., *The Roberts Court and
the Myth of a Pro-Business Bias,* 49
SANTA CLARA L. REV. 997 (2009), 286

Copland, Jim, *The Tort Tax,* WALL ST. J.,
June 11, 2003, 86

Crane, Daniel and Adam Hester, *State-
Action Immunity and Section 5 of the
FTC Act*, 115 MICH. L. REV. 365 (2016),
289

Cupp, Richard L., *A Dubious Grail: Seeking
Tort Law Expansion and Limited
Personhood as Stepping Stones Toward
Abolishing Animals' Property Status,* 60
SMU L. REV. 3 (2007), 114

Cupp, Richard L., *Believing in Products
Liability: Reflections on Daubert,
Doctrinal Evolution, and David Owen's*
PRODUCTS LIABILITY LAW, 40 U.C. DAVIS L.
REV. 511 (2006), 114

Cupp, Richard L., *Moving Beyond Animal
Rights: A Legal/Contractualist Critique,*
46 SAN DIEGO L. REV. 27 (2009), 114

Cupp, Richard L., *Paint by Numbers,* L.A.
DAILY JOURNAL, July 14, 2008, 114

Cupp, Richard L., *Symposium: The
Products Liability Restatement: Was It a
Success?: Preemption's Rise (and Bit of a
Fall) as Products Liability Reform Wyeth,
Riegel, Altria, and the Restatement
(Third)'s Prescription Product Design
Defect Standard,* 74 BROOKLYN L. REV.
727 (2009), 285

Daniels, Stephen & Joanne Martin, *Myth
and Reality in Punitive Damages,* 75
MINN. L. REV. 1 (1990), 6, 44

Daniels, Stephen & Joanne Martin, *The
Impact That It Has Had Is Between
People's Ears: Tort Reform, Mass Culture,
and Plaintiffs' Lawyers,* 50 DePaul L.
Rev. 453 (2000), 11

Daniels, Stephen & Joanne Martin, *The
Strange Success of Tort Reform,* 53
EMORY L.J. 1225 (2004), 11

Daniels, Stephen & Joanne Martin, *Where
Have All the Cases Gone? The Strange
Success of Tort Reform Revisited,* 65
EMORY L.J. 1445 (2016), 103

Davies, Julie, *Reforming the Tort Reform
Agenda,* 25 WASH. U. L. J. & POL'Y 119
(2007), 175

Davis, Mary J., *Symposium The Products
Liability Restatement Was It a Success?
On Restating Products Liability
Preemption,* 74 BROOKLYN L. REV. 759
(2009), 285

Denemark, Howard A., *Seeking Greater
Fairness When Awarding Multiple
Plaintiffs Punitive Damages for a Single*

Act by a Defendant, 63 OHIO ST. L.J. 931 (2002), 271

DeVito, Scott & Andrew Jurs, *An Overreaction to A Nonexistent Problem: Empirical Analysis of Tort Reform from the 1980s to 2000s,* 3 STAN. J. COMPLEX LITIG. 62 (2015), 103

DeVito, Scott & Andrew W. Jurs, *Doubling-Down for Defendants: The Pernicious Effects of Tort Reform*, 118 PENN ST. L. REV. 543 (2014), 1

Dilworth, Donald C., *Court Statistics Confirm No Litigation Explosion*, TRIAL (May 1996), 48

Dinerstein, Robert, Stephen Ellmann, Isabelle Gunning & Ann Shalleck, *Connection, Capacity and Morality in Lawyer-Client Relationships: Dialogues and Commentary*, 10 CLINICAL L. REV. 755 (2004), 310

Doroshow, Joanne, THE CASE FOR THE CIVIL JURY: SAFEGUARDING A PILLAR OF DEMOCRACY (1992), 47

Doroshow, Joanne, *The Secret Chamber of Commerce and its 'Tort Reform' Mission,* HUFFINGTON POST (October 28, 2009), 43

Eaton, Thomas A., *Of Frivolous Litigation and Runaway Juries: A View from the Bench*, 41 GA. L. REV. 431 (2007), 11

Eaton, Thomas & Suzette Talarico, *A Profile of Tort Litigation in Georgia and Reflections on Tort Reform*, 30 GEORGIA L. REV. 627 (1996), 19

Eggen, Jean Macchiaroli, *The Normalization of Product Preemption Doctrine*, 57 ALA. L. REV. 725 (2006), 284

Eisenberg, Theodore, *Damage Awards in Perspective: Behind the Headline-Grabbing Awards in Exxon Valdez and Engle*, 36 WAKE FOREST L. REV. 1129 (2001), 6

Eisenberg, Theodore, *Juries, Judges, and Punitive Damages: An Empirical Study*, 87 CORNELL L. REV. 743 (2002), 16

Eisenberg, Theodore, *Measuring The Deterrent Effect of Punitive Damages*, 87 GEO. L.J. 347 (1998), 277

Elkin, Peter, *The King of Pain Is Hurting,* FORTUNE, Sept. 4, 2000, 74

Finley, Lucinda M., *The Hidden Victims of Tort Reform: Women, Children, and the Elderly*, 53 EMORY L.J. 1263 (2004), 10, 117

Finley, Lucinda M., TORT LAW & PRACTICE, REV. (2nd ed. 2003, 3d ed. 2006), 117

Foley, Brian J. & Ruth Anne Robbins, *Fiction 101: A Primer for Lawyers On How To Use Fiction Writing Techniques To Write Persuasive Facts Sections,* 32 RUTGERS L.J. 459, 465–72 (2001), 122

Frankel, Alison, *Patent Litigation Weekly: Secret Details of Litigation Financing,*

THE AM LAW LITIGATION DAILY (Nov. 3, 2009), 81

Freer, Richard D., *Exodus from and Transformation of American Civil Litigation*, 65 EMORY L.J. 1491 (2016), 1

Friedman, M. and Oliver Wendell Holmes, *The Path of the Law*, 10 HARV. L. REV. 457 (1897), 5

Frost, Christopher L., *Successor Liability for Defective Products: A Redesign Ongoing,* 72 BROOK. L. REV. 1173 (2007), 114

Galanter, Marc, *Real World Torts: An Antidote to Anecdote*, 55 MD. L. REV. 993 (1996), 50

Galanter, Marc, *The Three-Legged Pig: Risk Redistribution and Antinomianism in American Legal Culture*, 22 MISS. C. L. REV. 47 (2002), 121

Galligan, Jr., Thomas C., *U.S. Supreme Court Tort Reform: Limiting State Power to Articulate and Develop Tort Law— Defamation, Preemption, and Punitive Damages*, 74 U. CINN. L. REV. 1189 (2006), 16

Galligan, Jr., Thomas C., Phoebe A. Haddon, Frank L. Maraist, Frank McClellan, Michael Rustad, Nicolas P. Terry, and Stephanie M. Wildman, TORT LAW: CASES, PROBLEMS, AND PERSPECTIVES (New York, New York: Lexis/Nexis 2007), 48

Gavin, Sandra F., *Stealth Tort Reform,* 42 VAL. U.L. REV. 431 (2008), 158, 307

Geistfeld, Mark, *Constitutional Tort Reform,* 38 LOY. L.A. L. REV. 1093 (2005), 17, 271

Gerhart, Peter M., *The Death of Strict Liability*, 56 BUFFALO L. REV. 245 (2008), 15

Gerlin, Andrea, *A Matter of Degree: How a Jury Decided That a Coffee Spill is Worth $2.9 Million.* THE WALL STREET JOURNAL, Sept. 1, 1994, 37

Gifford, Donald G., CASES AND MATERIALS ON THE LAW OF TORTS (4th ed. 2003), 112

Gifford, Donald G., LEGAL NEGOTIATION: THEORY AND APPLICATIONS (1989; 2d ed. 2007), 112

Gifford, Donald G., SUING THE TOBACCO AND LEAD PIGMENT INDUSTRIES: GOVERNMENT LITIGATION AS PUBLIC HEALTH PRESCRIPTION (forthcoming 2010), 111, 112

Gifford, Donald G., *The Challenge to the Individual Causation Requirement in Mass Products Torts,* 62 WASHINGTON & LEE L. REV. 873 (2005), 112

Gifford, Donald G., *The Peculiar Challenges Posed By Latent Diseases Resulting From Mass Products,* 64 MARYLAND L. REV. 613 (2005), 112

Gilbert, Pamela, *Class Action Legislation Will Deny Americans a Fair Day in Court*, 6 CLASS ACTION LITIG. REP. (BNA) 108 (2005), 55

Goldberg, Deborah, *et. al., The Best Defense: Why Elected Courts Should Lead Recusal Reform*, 46 WASHBURN L.J. 503 (2007), 309

Goldberg, John C.P., *The Constitutional Status of Tort Law: Due Process and the Right to a Law for the Redress of Wrongs*, 115 YALE L.J. 524 (2005), 267

Gordon, Belinda Brooks and Michael Freeman, *Trial by Jury Involving Persons Accused of Terrorism or Supporting Terrorism*, LAW AND PSYCHOLOGY (2006), 35

Green, Leon, *No-Fault: A Perspective*, 1975 BYU L. REV. 79 (1975), 10

Grose, Carolyn, *A Persistent Critique: Constructing Clients' Stories,* 12 CLINICAL L. REV. 329 (2006), 123

Gross, Richard C., *Caps on Medical Malpractice Damages Cut Doctors' Insurance Costs May 2007*, HEALTH BEHAVIOR NEWS SERVICE, May 2007, 261

Haltom, William & Michael McCann, DISTORTING THE LAW: POLITICS, MEDIA, AND THE LITIGATION CRISIS (2004), 11

Hans, Valerie, JUDGING THE JURY (1986), 35

Hans, Valerie, MEDICAL MALPRACTICE AND THE AMERICAN JURY (1995), 35

Hans, Valerie, WORLD JURY SYSTEMS (2000), 35

Hans, Valerie P. & William S. Lofquist, *Jurors' Judgments of Business Liability in Tort Cases: Implications for the Litigation Explosion Debate*, 26 LAW & SOC'Y REV. 85 (1992), 11

Harper, Fowler V. & Fleming James, Jr., THE LAW OF TORTS (Boston: Little/Brown, 1956), 50

Harris, Lee, *Tort Reform as a Carrot-and-Stick*, 46 HARV. J. LEGIS. 163 (2009), 158, 307

Harris, Lee & Jennifer Longo, *Flexible Tort Reform*, 29 HAMLINE JOURNAL OF PUBLIC LAW AND POLICY 61 (2007), 245

Harvard Medical Practice Study, PATIENTS, DOCTORS, AND LAWYERS: MEDICAL INJURY, MALPRACTICE LITIGATION, AND PATIENT COMPENSATION IN NEW YORK (1990), 9

Hazard, Jr., Geoffrey C., *The Legal and Ethical Position of the Code of Professional Ethics* (Louis W. Hodges ed. 1979), 84

Henderson & Eisenberg, *The Quiet Revolution in Products Liability: An Empirical Study of Legal Change*, 37 U.C.L.A. L. REV. 479 (1990), 99

Henderson, Jr., James A. & Aaron D. Twerski, PRODUCTS LIABILITY: PROBLEMS AND PROCESS (2d ed. 1992), 5

Hines, Laura J., *Due Process Limitations on Punitive Damages: Why State Farm Won't Be the Last Word,* 37 AKRON L. REV. 779 (2004), 276

Hines, Laura J. & William N. Hines, *Constitutional Constraints on Punitive Damages: Clarity, Consistency, and the Outlier Dilemma,* 66 HASTINGS L.J. 1257 (2015), 1

Holmes, Jr., Oliver W., THE COMMON LAW 94 (1881), 12

Howard, Philip K., *When Judges Won't Judge,* WALL ST. J., Oct. 22, 2003, 84

Hubbard, F. Patrick, *In Honor of Walter O. Weyrauch: Substantive Due Process Limits on Punitive Damages Awards: "Morals With Technique?",* 60 FLA. L. REV. 349 (2008), 271

Hubbard, F. Patrick, *The Nature and Impact of the Tort Reform Movement,* 35 HOFSTRA L. REV. 437 (2006), 13, 178

Huber, Peter, *Safety and the Second Best: The Hazards of Public Risk Management in the Courts,* 85 COLUM. L. REV. 277 (1985), 84

Hyman, David A., *Medical Malpractice and the Tort System: What Do We Know and What (If Anything) Should We Do About It?,* 80 TEX. L. REV. 1639 (2002), 9, 159

Hyman, David A. & Charles Silver, *Medical Malpractice Litigation and Tort Reform: It's the Incentives, Stupid,* 59 VAND. L. REV. 1085 (2006), 159

Jacobs, Dennis, *The Secret Life of Judges,* 75 FORDHAM L. REV. 2855 (2007), 84

Janis, Irving, GROUP THINK: PSYCHOLOGICAL STUDIES OF POLICY DECISIONS AND FIASCOES (Houghton Mifflin: 2d ed. 1983), 44

Janutis, Rachel M., *Reforming Reprehensibility: The Continued Viability of Multiple Punitive Damages After* State Farm v. Campbell, 41 SAN DIEGO L. REV. 1465 (2004), 271

Janutis, Rachel M., *The Struggle Over Tort Reform and the Overlooked Legacy of the Progressives,* 39 AKRON L. REV. 943 (2006), 12, 170

Keating, Gregory C., *Reasonableness and Rationality in Negligence Theory,* 48 STAN. L. REV. 311 (1996), 158

Kelly, Carly N. & Michelle M. Mello, *Are Medical Malpractice Damages Caps Constitutional? An Overview of State Litigation,* 33 J. L. MED. & ETHICS 515 (2005), 299

Kelner, Joshua D., *The Anatomy of an Image: Unpacking the Case for Tort Reform,* 31 U. DAYTON L. REV. 243 (2006), 102

Kidd, Jeremy and Michael Krauss, *The Collateral Source Rule: Explanation and Defense*, 48 LOUISVILLE L. REV. 1 (2009), 42

Kidd, Jeremy, Jeffrey O'Connell, and Evan Stephenson, *An Economic Model Costing "Early Offers" Medical Malpractice Reform*, 35 N.M. L. REV. 259 (2005), 42

Kielbowicz, Richard B., *The Role of News Leaks in Governance and the Law of Journalists' Confidentiality, 1795–2005*, 43 SAN DIEGO L. REV. 425 (2006), 156

King, Jr., Joseph H., *Exculpatory Agreements for Volunteers in Youth Activities—The Alternative to "Nerf (registered)" Tiddlywinks*, 53 OHIO ST. L.J. 683 (1992), 15

King, Jr., Joseph H., *The Exclusiveness Of An Employee's Workers' Compensation Remedy Against His Employer*, 55 TENN. L. REV. 405 (1987–88), 12

Kitch, Edmund W., *The Fire of Truth: A Remembrance of Law and Economics at Chicago, 1932–1970*, 26 J.L. & ECON. 163 (1983), 5

Klass, Alexandra B., *Punitive Damages and Valuing Harm*, 92 MINN. L. REV. 83 (2007), 270

Klass, Alexandra B., *Tort Experiments in the Laboratories of Democracy*, 50 WM. & MARY L. REV. 1501 (2009), 1, 267

Kluger, Richard, ASHES TO ASHES (1997), 156

Koenig, Thomas H. & Michael L. Rustad, *His and Her Tort Reform: Gender Injustice In Disguise*, 70 WASH. L. REV. 1 (1995), 45

Koenig, Thomas H. & Michael L. Rustad, IN DEFENSE OF TORT LAW (New York University Press, 2001), 45, 46, 277

Kohler, David, *Forty Years After New York Times v. Sullivan: The Good, the Bad, and the Ugly*, 83 OR. L. REV. 1203 (2004), 11

Kotler, Martin A., *The Myth of Individualism and the Appeal of Tort Reform*, 59 RUTGERS L. REV. 779 (2007), 15

Landes, William M. & Richard A. Posner, THE ECONOMIC STRUCTURE OF TORT LAW (Cambridge, Massachusetts: Harvard University Press 1987), 49

Langvardt, Arlen W., *Generic Pharmaceuticals and the "Unfortunate Hand" Dealt to Harmed Consumers: The Emerging State Court Resistance*, 17 MINN. J.L. SCI. & TECH. 565 (2016), 293

LeBlang, Theodore R., *The Medical Malpractice Crisis—Is There A Solution?*, 27 J. LEGAL MED. 1 (2006), 159

Leflar, Robert B. & Robert S. Adler, *The Preemption Pentad: Federal Preemption of Products Liability Claims after Medtronic*, 64 TENN. L. REV. 691 (1997), 225

Lens, Jill Wieber, *Punishing for the Injury: Tort Law's Influence in Defining the Constitutional Limitations on Punitive Damage Awards*, 39 HOFSTRA L. REV. 595 (2016), 2

Levinson, Daryl and Benjamin I. Sachs, *Political Entrenchment and Public Law*, 125 YALE L.J. 400 (2015), 103

Liang, Chih-Ming, S.J.D., *Rethinking the Tort Liability System and Patient Safety: From the Conventional Wisdom to Learning from Litigation*, 12 IND. HEALTH L. REV. 327 (2015), 1

Lincoln, Abraham, NOTES FOR A LAW LECTURE (1850), 74

Localio, Russell, *Relation Between Medical Malpractice Claims and Adverse Events Due to Negligence, Results of the Harvard Medical Practice Study III*, 325 NEW ENG. J. MED. 245 (1991), 9

Loeb, Basil M., *Comment Abuse of Power Certain State, Courts Are Disregarding Standing and Original Jurisdiction Principles So They Can Declare Tort Reform Unconstitutional*, 84 MARQ. L. REV. 491 (2000), 299

Lyon, Larry, Bradley J.B. Toben, James M. Underwood, William D. Underwood, James Wren, *Straight from the Horse's Mouth: Judicial Observations of Jury Behavior and the Need for Tort Reform*, 59 BAYLOR LAW REVIEW 419 (2007), 14, 199

Lytton, Timothy D., HOLDING BISHOPS ACCOUNTABLE (Harv. Univ. Press, 2008), 113

Manzer, Nancy L., *1986 Tort Reform Legislation: A Systematic Evaluation of Caps on Damages and Limitations on Joint and Several Liability*, 73 CORNELL L. REV. 628 (1988), 5, 267

Marcus, Nancy C., *Phantom Parties and Other Practical Problems with the Attempted Abolition of Joint and Several Liability*, 60 ARK. L. REV. 437 (2007), 230, 307, 309

Hatcher-Mayes, Megan, Forbes *Hypes Still-Ridiculous "Judicial Hellholes" Report* (December 19, 2013), 48

McClay, Wilfred M., *A Discipline in Denial*, THE WALL STREET JOURNAL (October 30, 2009), 50

McClellan, Frank, *The Dark Side of Tort Reform: Searching for Racial Justice*, 48 RUTGERS L. REV. 761 (1996), 45

McGarity, Thomas O., *Curbing the Abuse of Corporate Power: The Perils of Preemption*, TRIAL (Sept. 2008), 165

McQullian, Lawrence J. & Hovannes Abramyan, U.S. TORT LIABILITY INDEX: 2008 REPORT 10 (Pac. Res. Inst. 2008), 89

Mello, Michelle M., *The Medical Liability Climate and Prospects for Reform*, 312 (20) JAMA, 1

Mello, Michelle M., David M. Studdert, & Troyen A. Brennan, *The New Medical Malpractice Crisis*, 348 NEW ENG. J. MED. 2281 (2003), 159

Merritt, Deborah Jones & Kathryn Barry, *Is the Tort System in Crisis? New Empirical Evidence*, 60 OHIO ST. L.J. 315 (1999), 101

Miki, Janine Alena Brown, *Medical Malpractice Arbitration "Agreements:" the Healthcare Consumer's Hobson's Choice*, 43 W. ST. L. REV. 225 (2016), 103

Miller, Binny, *Give Them Back Their Lives: Recognizing Client Narrative in Case Theory*, 93 MICH. L. REV. 485 (1994), 123

Miller, Binny, *Telling Stories About Cases and Clients: The Ethics of Narrative,* 14 GEO. J. LEGAL ETHICS 1, 123

Miller, Kyle, *Putting the Caps on Caps: Reconciling the Goal of Medical Malpractice Reform with the Twin Objectives of Tort Law,* 59 VAND. L. REV. 1457 (2006), 12

Miller, Nelson P., *Now What? Steadying Tort Law's Pendulum*, 88 MICH. BAR J. 38 (2009), 10

Moore, Henson & Jeffery O'Connell, *Foreclosing Medical Malpractice Claims by Prompt Tender of Economic Loss*, 44 LA. L. REV. 1267 (1984), 14

Mullin, Joe, *Patent Litigation Weekly: How to win $25 million in a patent suit—and end up with a whole lot less,* THE PRIOR ART (Nov. 2, 2009), 81

Mutter, Carol A., *Moving to Comparative Negligence in an Era of Tort Reform: Decision for Tennessee,* 57 TENN. L. REV. 199 (1990), 230

Nathanson, Mitchell J., *It's the Economy (and Combined Ratio), Stupid: Examining the Medical Malpractice Litigation Crisis Myth and the Factors Critical to Reform,* 108 PENN ST. L. REV. 1077 (2004), 301

Neely, Richard, THE PRODUCTS LIABILITY MESS: HOW BUSINESS CAN BE RESCUED FROM THE POLITICS OF STATE COURTS, (1988), 86

Noah, Lars, *Reconceptualizing Federal Preemption of Tort Claims as the Government Standards Defense,* 37 WM. & MARY L. REV. 903 (1996), 16

O'Connell, Jeffrey, A RECIPE FOR *BALANCED* TORT REFORM, (2008), 65

Oakley, Ellwood F. III, *The Next Generation of Medical Malpractice Dispute*

Resolution: Alternatives to Litigation, 21 GA. ST. U.L. REV. 993 (2005), 301

Ogilvie, Dian Dickson, *Comment, Judicial Activism in Tort Reform: The Guest Statute Exemplar and a Proposal for Comparative Negligence,* 21 UCLA L. REV. 1566 (1974), 66

Olson, Walter, *The Runaway Jury Is No Myth,* WALL ST. J., July 18, 2000, 4

Owen, David G., *Defectiveness Restated: Exploding the "Strict" Products Liability Myth*, 1996 U. ILL. L. REV. 743, 15

Owen, David G., *Special Defenses in Modern Products Liability Law*, 70 MO. L. REV. 1 (2005), 16

Page, Joseph A., *Automobile-Design Liability and Compliance with Federal Standards*, 95

Page, Joseph A., BITTER WAGES: THE NADER REPORT ON DISEASE AND INJURY ON THE JOB, 95

Page, Joseph A., *Deforming Tort Reform,* 78 GEO. L.J. 649 (1990), 5

Page, Joseph A., *Deforming Tort Reform, a Book Review of Liability: The Legal Revolution and Its Consequences* (Basic Books, 1988), 95

Page, Joseph A., *Federal Regulation of Tobacco Products and Products That Treat Tobacco Dependence: Are the Playing Fields Level?,* FOOD AND DRUG LAW JOURNAL, 95

Page, Joseph A., PERÓN: A BIOGRAPHY (1999), 95

Page, Joseph A., THE BRAZILIANS, 95

Page, Joseph A., THE LAW OF PREMISES LIABILITY, 95

Page, Joseph A., THE REVOLUTION THAT NEVER WAS: NORTHEAST BRAZIL, (1955–1964), 95

Page, Joseph A. and Ralph Nader, *Liability for Unavoidably and Unreasonably Unsafe Products: Does Negligence Doctrine Have a Role to Play?,* CHICAGO-KENT L. REV., 95

Paik, Myungho, *The Receding Tide of Medical Malpractice Litigation*, 6 J. EMPIRICAL LEGAL STUD. 637 (2009), 1

Parver, Corrine Propas & Tara Hechlik Newsom, *Medical Malpractice, Insurance Crisis: An Inquiry into the Relationship Between the Crisis and Access to Health Care for Women of Color*, 3 J. HEALTH & BIOMED. L. 267 (2006), 51

Passanante, Paul J. and Dawn M. Mefford, *Anticipated Constitutional Challenges to Tort Reform*, 62 J. MO. B. 206 (2006), 155

Peck, Robert S., *In Defense of Fundamental Principles: The Unconstitutionality of Tort Reform*, 31 SETON HALL L. REV. 672 (2001), 157

Peck, Robert S., *Tort Reform 1999: A Building Without a Foundation,* 27 FLA. ST. U. L. REV. 397 (2000), 157

Phillips, Thomas R., *The Constitutional Right to a Remedy,* 78 N.Y.U. L. REV. 1309 (2003), 299

Polinsky, A. Mitchell & Steven Shavell, *Punitive Damages: An Economic Analysis,* 111 HARV. L. REV. 869 (1998), 271

Popper, Andrew F., *Unavailable and Unaccountable: A Free Ride for Foreign Manufacturers of Defective Consumer Goods,* 36 THE PRODUCT SAFETY & LIABILITY REPORTER 219 (2008), 299

Posner, Richard A., *A Theory of Negligence,* 1 J. LEGAL STUD. 29 (1972), 5

Posner, Richard A., ECONOMIC ANALYSIS OF LAW (5th ed., Aspen Publishers, Inc. 1998), 84

Posner, Richard A., ECONOMIC ANALYSIS OF LAW (6th ed., Aspen Publishers, Inc. 2003), 5

Posner, Richard A., *Utilitarianism, Economics, and Legal Theory,* 8 J. LEGAL STUD. 103 (1979), 5

Postema, Gerald J., *Moral Responsibility in Professional Ethics,* 55 N.Y.U. L. REV. 63 (1980), 310

Priest, George, *Can Absolute Manufacturer Liability Be Defended?,* 9 YALE J. ON REG. 237 (1992), 5

Priest, George, PRODUCTS LIABILITY LAW AND THE ACCIDENT RATE, IN LIABILITY: PERSPECTIVES AND POLICY (Litan & Winston eds., Brookings Inst. 1988), 69

Priest, George, *Strict Products Liability: The Original Intent,* 10 CARDOZO L. REV. 2301 (1989), 69

Priest, George, *The Constitutionality of State Tort Reform Legislation and Lochner,* 31 SETON HALL L. REV. 683 (2001), 17

Priest, George, *The Current Insurance Crisis and Modern Tort Law,* 96 YALE L.J. 1521 (1987), 69

Priest, George, *The Invention of Enterprise Liability: A Critical History of the Intellectual Foundations of Modern Tort Law,* 14 J. LEGAL STUDIES 461 (1985), 69

Prosser, Wade & Schwartz, TORTS (13th ed. 2015), 232

Prosser, William, HANDBOOK OF THE LAW OF TORTS (4th ed. 1971), 46, 111

Randall, Susan C., *Due Process Challenges to Statutes of Repose,* 40 SW. L.J. 997 (1986), 15

Rapp, Geoffrey C., *Doctors, Duties, Death and Data: A Critical Review of the Empirical Literature on Medical Malpractice and Tort Reform,* 26 N. ILL. U. L. REV. 439 (2006), 159

Rendleman, Doug, *A Cap on the Defendant's Appeal Bond?: Punitive Damages Tort Reform,* 39 AKRON L. REV. 1089 (2006), 51

Rhode, Deborah L., *Colloquium: Deborah L. Rhode's Access to Justice: Access to Justice: Again, Still,* 73 FORDHAM L. REV. 1013 (2004), 14

Rhode, Deborah L., *Too Much Law, Too Little Justice: Too Much Rhetoric, Too Little Reform,* 11 GEO. J. LEGAL ETHICS 989 (1998), 156

Richmond, Douglas R., *Rights and Responsibilities of Excess Insurers,* 78 DENV. U.L. REV. 29 (2000), 155

Robbins, Ruth Anne, *Harry Potter, Ruby Slippers and Merlin: Telling the Client's Story Using the Characters and Paradigms of the Archetypal Hero's Journey,* 29 SEATTLE U. L. REV. 767, 768–69 (2006), 122

Roederer, Christopher J., *Democracy and Tort Law in America: The Counter-Revolution,* 110 W. VA. L. REV. 647 (2008), 167

Rosenberg, D. & S. Shavell, *A Model in which Suits are Brought for their Nuisance Value,* 5 INT'L REV. L. & ECON. 3 (June 1985), 84

Rossi, Jim, *The Brave New Path of Energy Federalism,* 95 TEX. L. REV. 399 (2016), 289

Rustad, Michael L., *A Hard Day's Night: Hierarchy, History and Happiness in Law School and Legal Practice,* 58 SYRACUSE L. REV. 263 (2008), 51

Rustad, Michael L., COMPUTER CONTRACTS: NEGOTIATING, DRAFTING (Lexis/Nexis 2016), 42

Rustad, Michael L., E-BUSINESS LEGAL HANDBOOK (Aspen Law & Business, 2003), 51

Rustad, Michael L., EVERYDAY CONSUMER LAW (Paradigm Publishers, 2008), 51

Rustad, Michael L., GLOBAL INTERNET LAW (2d ed. 2016), 42

Rustad, Michael L., GLOBAL INTERNET LAW IN A NUTSHELL (3rd ed. 2016), 42

Rustad, Michael L., *In Defense of Punitive Damage Awards in Products Liability: Testing Tort Anecdotes with Empirical Data,* 78 IOWA L. REV. 1 (1992), 16

Rustad, Michael L., INFORMATION AGE LAW AND ETHICS, 42

Rustad, Michael L., INTERNET LAW IN A NUTSHELL (Westlaw 2009), 50

Rustad, Michael L., *Nationalizing Tort Law: The Republican Attack on Women, Blue Collar Workers, and Consumers,* 48 RUTGERS L. REV. 673 (1996), 43, 49

Rustad, Michael L., SOFTWARE LICENSING, CLOUD COMPUTING & INTERNET TERMS OF

USE: GLOBAL INFORMATION AGE CONTRACTS (Lexis/Nexis 2016), 42

Rustad, Michael L., *Symposium, Access to Justice: Can Business Co-Exist with the Civil Justice System: The Closing of Punitives Damages' Iron Case*, 38 LOY. L.A. L. REV. 1297 (2005), 11, 48

Rustad, Michael L., *The Closing of Punitive Damages' Iron Cage*, 38 LOY. L.A. REV. 1297 (2005), 48

Rustad, Michael L., *The Supreme Court and Me: Trapped in Time with Punitive Damages*, 17 WIDENER L. REV. 783 (2008), 51

Rustad, Michael L., *The Uncert-Worthiness of the Court's Unmaking of Punitive Damages*, 2 CHARLESTON L. REV. 459 (2008), 51

Rustad, Michael L., TORT LAW: CASES, PROBLEMS, PERSPECTIVES (Lexis/Nexis, 2008), 51

Rustad, Michael L., UNDERSTANDING SALES, LEASES, AND LICENSES IN A GLOBAL PERSPECTIVE (Carolina Academic Press 2008), 50

Rustad, Michael L., *Unraveling Punitive Damages: Current Data and Further Inquiry*, 1998 WIS. L. REV. 15, 44, 49, 277

Rustad, Michael L. & Thomas H. Koenig, *Extending Learned Hand's Negligence Formula to Information Security Breaches*, 3 I/S: J.L. & POL'Y FOR INFO. SOC'Y 237 (2007), 51

Rustad, Michael L. & Thomas H. Koenig, *'Hate Torts' to Fight Hate Crimes: Punishing the Organizational Roots of Evil*, 51 AM. BEHAV. SCI. 302 (2007), 51

Rustad, Michael L. & Thomas H. Koenig, *Reconceptualizing Punitive Damages in Medical Malpractice: Targeting Amoral Corporations, Not 'Moral Monsters,'* 47 RUTGERS L. REV. 975 (1995), 49

Rustad, Michael L. & Thomas H. Koenig, *Taming the Tort Monster: The American Civil Justice System as a Battleground of Social Theory*, 68 BROOKLYN L. REV. 1 (2002), 49

Sachs, Robert A., *Product Liability Reform and Seller Liability: A Proposal for Change*, 55 BAYLOR L. REV. 1031 (2003), 16

Saks, Michael J., *Do We Really Know Anything About the Behavior of the Tort Litigation System—And Why Not?*, 140 U. PA. L. REV. 1147 (1992), 11

Saks, Michael J., *Medical Malpractice Facing Real Problems and Finding Real Solutions*, 35 WM. & MARY L. REV. 693, 703 (1994), 48

Sales, James B. & Kenneth B. Cole, Jr., *Punitive Damages: A Relic That Has Outlived Its Origins*, 37 VAND. L. REV. 1117 (1984), 5

Scheuerman, Sheila B., *Two Worlds Collide: How the Supreme Court's Recent Punitive Damages Decisions Affect Class Actions*, 60 BAYLOR L. REV. 880 (2008), 186

Schwartz, Gary T., *Considering the Proper Federal Role in American Tort Law*, 38 ARIZ. L. REV. 917 (1996), 267

Schwartz, Victor E., *Judicial Nullification of Tort Reform: Ignoring History, Logic, and Fundamentals of Constitutional Law*, 31 SETON HALL L. REV. 688 (2001), 17

Schwartz, Victor E., PROSSER, WADE AND SCHWARTZ'S TORTS (12th Ed., 2010), 20

Schwartz, Victor E., *The Rise of "Empty Suit" Litigation. Where Should Tort Law Draw the Line?*, 80 BROOK. L. REV. 599 (2015), 26

Schwartz, Victor E. & Cary Silverman, *Category Liability: Properly Precluding Claims That Propose an Alternative Product Rather Than an Alternative Design*, 44:40 PROD. SAFETY & LIAB. REP. (Bloomberg BNA) 1 (Jan. 11, 2016), 22

Schwartz, Victor E. & Emily J. Laird, *Non-Economic Damages in Pet Litigation: The Serious Need to Preserve a Rational Rule*, 33 PEPPERDINE L. REV. 227 (2005), 223

Schwartz, Victor E. & Leah Lorber, *Judicial Nullification of Civil Justice Reform Violates the Fundamental Federal Constitutional Principle of Separation of Powers: How to Restore the Right Balance*, 32 RUTGERS L.J. 907 (2001), 86, 157, 213, 267

Schwartz, Victor E., Mark A. Behrens, Leavy Mathews, III, *Federalism and Federal Liability Reform: The United States Constitution Supports Reform*, 36 HARV. J. LEGIS. 269 (1999), 157

Scordato, Marin R., *Federal Preemption of State Tort Claims*, 35 U.C. DAVIS L. REV. 1 (2001), 284

Seaman, Scott M. & Charlene Kittredge, *Excess Liability Insurance: Law and Litigation*, 32 TORT & INS. L.J. 653 (1997), 155

Sebok, Anthony J., *Punitive Damages: From Myth to Theory*, 92 IOWA L. REV. 957 (2007), 277

Selsheimer, Thomas M. and Steven H. Stodgill, *Due Process and Punitive Damages: Providing Meaningful Guidance to the Jury*, 47 S.M.U. L. REV. 329 (1994), 19

Shalleck, Ann, *Institutions and the Development of Legal Theory: The Significance of the Feminism & Legal Theory Project*, 13 AM. U. J. GENDER SOC. POL'Y & L. 7 (2005), 122

Shapo, Marshall, *Compensation for Terrorism: What We Are Learning,* 53 DePaul L. Rev. 805 (2003), 101

Shapo, Marshall, Compensation for Victims of Terror (2005), 101

Shapo, Marshall, Experimenting with the Consumer: The Mass Testing of Risky Products on the American Public (2009), 101

Shapo, Marshall, *Responsibility for Injuries: Some Sketches,* 100 Nw. U. L. Rev. 481–500 (2006), 101

Shapo, Marshall, The Law of Products Liability, 4th edition (2001), 101

Shapo, Marshall, Tort Law and Culture (2003), 101

Shapo, Marshall and Helene Shapo, Law School Without Fear (2d Ed. 2002), 101

Shapo, Marshall and Helene Shapo, Law School Without Fear (3rd Ed. 2009), 101

Shapo, Marshall and Richard Peltz, Tort and Injury Law, 3d edition (2006), 101

Sharkey, Catherine M., *States vs. FDA,* 83 Geo. Wash. L. Rev. 1609 (2015), 293

Shepherd, Joanna M., *Tort Reforms' Winners and Losers: The Competing Effects of Care and Activity Levels,* 55 UCLA Law Review 905 (2008), 258

Spaulding, Norman W., *Reinterpreting Professional Identity,* 74 U. Colo. L. Rev. 1 (2003), 310

Stamm, Lindsay J., *The Current Medical Malpractice Crisis: The Need for Reform To Ensure a Tomorrow for Oregon's Obstetricians,* 84 Or. L. Rev. 283 (2005), 159

Stevelman Kahn, Faith, *Bombing Markets, Subverting the Rule of Law: Enron, Financial Fraud, and September 11, 2001,* 76 Tul. L. Rev. 1579 (2002), 284

Stier, Byron G., *Now It's Personal: Punishment and Mass Tort Litigation After,* 2 Charleston L. Rev. 433 (2008), 224

Studdert, David M., *Defensive Medicine Among High-Risk Specialist Physicians in a Volatile Malpractice Environment,* 293 JAMA 2609 (2005), 159

Sugarman, Stephen D., Doing Away with Personal Injury Law (1989), 55

Sugarman, Stephen D., *Doing Away with Tort Law,* 73 Cal. L. Rev. 555, 53

Sugarman, Stephen D., *Fighting Childhood Obesity Through Performance—Based Regulation of the Food Industry (with Nirit Sandman),* 56 Duke L. J. 1403 (2007), 55

Sugarman, Stephen D., *Legal Battles Over Vaccines and Autism,* 357:13 New England Journal of Medicine 1275 (September 27, 2007), 55

Sugarman, Stephen D., *Pain and Suffering: Comparative Law, Perspective,* 55 DePaul L. Rev. 399 (2005), 55

Sugarman, Stephen D., *Performance-Based Regulation: Enterprise Responsibility for Reducing Death, Injury and Disease Caused by Consumer Products,* 34 Journal of Health, Policy, Politics and Law 1035 (2009), 55

Sugarman, Stephen D., Regulating Tobacco (with Rabin 2001), 55

Sugarman, Stephen D., Smoking Policy: Law, Politics and Culture (1993), 55

Sugarman, Stephen D., *The "Necessity" Defense and the Failure of Tort Theory: The Case Against Strict Liability for Damages Caused While Exercising Self-Help in an Emergency,* 2005 Issues in Legal Scholarship 1–153 The Berkeley Electronic Press © 2005, 55

Sugarman, Stephen D., Torts Stories (2003), 55

Talmadge, Philip A. & N. Clifford Petersen, *In Search of a Proper Balance,* 22 Gonz. L. Rev. 259 (1986), 6

Taylor, Paul, *The Difference Between Filing Lawsuits and Selling Widgets: The Lost Understanding that Some Attorneys' Exercise of State Power Is Subject to Appropriate Regulation,* 4 Pierce L. Rev. 45 (2005), 83, 85

Taylor, Paul, *The Federalist Papers, the Commerce Clause, and Federal Tort Reform,* 45 Suffolk U. L. Rev. 357 (2012), 83

Taylor, Paul, *We're All in This Together: Extending Sovereign Immunity to Encourage Private Parties to Reduce Public Risk,* 75 U. Cin. L. Rev. 1595 (2007), 83

Tettenborn, Andrew, *Remedies Discussion Forum: Punitive Damages,* 41 San Diego L. Rev. 1551 (2004), 51

Thomas, Tracy A., *Proportionality and the Supreme Court's Jurisprudence of Remedies,* 59 Hastings L.J. 73 (2007), 277, 284

Thompson, Ashley L., *Note: The Unintended Consequences of Tort Reform in Michigan: An Argument for Reinstating Retailer Product Liability,* 42 U. Mich. J.L. Reform 961 (2009), 309

Tobias, Carl, *Common Sense and Other Legal Reforms,* 48 Vand. L. Rev. 699 (1995), 6

Todres, Jonathan, *Toward Healing and Restoration for All: Reframing Medical Malpractice Reform,* 39 Conn. L. Rev. 667 (2006), 309

Twerski, Aaron D., *Asbestos Litigation Gone Mad: Exposure-Based Recovery for Increased Risk, Mental Distress, and*

Medical Monitoring, 53 S.C. L. REV. 815 (2002), 95

Twerski, Aaron D., *Consumer Expectations' Last Hope: A Response to Professor Kysar*, 103 COLUM. L. REV. 1791 (2003), 95

Twerski, Aaron D., *Judge Jack B. Weinstein, Tort Litigation, and the Public Good: A Roundtable Discussion to Honor One of America's Great Trial Judges on the Occasion of his 80th Birthday*, 12 J.L. & POL'Y 149 (2003), 95

Twerski, Aaron D., PRODUCTS LIABILITY: PROBLEMS AND PROCESS (4th ed. 2000), 95

Twerski, Aaron D., TORTS: CASES AND MATERIALS (2nd ed. 2008), 95

Vairo, Georgene, *The Role of Influence in the Arc of Tort Reform*, 65 EMORY L.J. 1741 (2016), 1

Van Kirk, Robert A., *The Evolution of Useful Life Statutes in the Products Liability Reform Effort*, 1989 DUKE L.J. 1689, 15

Vandall, Frank J., *A Critique of the Proposed Restatement, Third Products Liability, Section 2(b): The Reasonable Alternative Design Requirement*, TENNESSEE L. REV. (1994), 64

Vandall, Frank J., *Constructing a Roof Before the Foundation is Prepared: The Restatement (Third) of Torts, Product Liability: Section 2(b) Design Defect*, MICHIGAN JOURNAL OF LAW REFORM (1997), 64

Vandall, Frank J., *Criminal Prosecution of Corporations for Defective Products*, INTERNATIONAL LEGAL PRACTITIONER, 64

Vandall, Frank J., *Judge Posner's Negligence-Efficiency Theory: A Critique*, EMORY LAW JOURNAL, 64

Vandall, Frank J., JUSTICE REWRITTEN: AN HISTORICAL, POLITICAL AND ECONOMIC ANALYSIS OF CIVIL JUSTICE (Oxford University Press, Spring 2011), 61, 63

Vandall, Frank J., PRODUCTS LIABILITY CASES, MATERIALS, PROBLEMS (1994, 2nd ed., 2002), 63

Vandall, Frank J., *Reallocating the Costs of Smoking: The Application of Absolute Liability to Cigarette Manufacturers*, OHIO STATE LAW JOURNAL, 64

Vandall, Frank J., *Suits by Public Hospitals to Recover Expenditures for the Treatment of Disease, Injury and Disability Caused by Tobacco and Alcohol*, FORDHAM URBAN L. REV. (1994), 64

Vandall, Frank J., *The Restatement, Third Products Liability, Section 2(b): Design Defect*, TEMPLE L. REV. (1995), 64

Vandall, Frank J., TORTS, CASES, PROBLEMS AND QUESTIONS (2nd ed., 2003), 63

Vetri, Dominick, Lawrence Levine, and Ibrahim Gassama, TORT LAW AND

PRACTICE, 5TH ED. (Carolina Academic Press 2016), 39

Vidmar, Neil & K. MacKillop, *"Judicial Hellholes," Medical Malpractice Claims, Verdicts and the "Doctor Exodus" in Illinois*, 59 VANDERBILT L. REV. 1309 (2006), 34

Vidmar, Neil & Mary R. Rose, *Punitive Damages by Juries in Florida: In Terrorem and in Reality*, 38 HARV. J. LEGIS. 487 (2001), 44

Vidmar, Neil & Mirya Holman, *The Frequency, Predictability, and Proportionality of Jury Awards of Punitive Damages in State Courts in 2005: A New Audit*, 43 SUFFOLK U. L. REV. 855 (2010), 1

Vidmar, Neil & Valerie P. Hans, AMERICAN JURIES: THE VERDICT (Prometheus Books, 2007), 34

Vidmar, Neil, K. MacKillop, and P. Lee, *Million Dollar Medical Malpractice Cases in Florida: Post-verdict and Pre-suit Settlements*, 59 VANDERBILT L. REV. 1343 (2006), 34

Vladeck, David C., *Preemption and Regulatory Failure*, 33 PEPP. L. REV. 95 (2005), 225

Vogel, Joan, Dominick Vetri, Lawrence Levine, and Ibrahim Gassama, *Cases in Context: Lake Champlain Wars, Gentrification, and Ploof v. Putnam*, 45 ST. LOUIS U. L.J. 791 (2001), 39

Vogel, Joan, Dominick Vetri, Lawrence Levine, and Ibrahim Gassama, TORT LAW AND PRACTICE (5th ed. 2016), 36

Wade, John W., *On Frivolous Litigation: A Study of Tort Liability and Procedural Sanctions*, 14 HOFSTRA L. REV. 433 (1986), 4

Wayne, Leslie, *Trial Lawyers Pour Money into Democrats' Chests*, N.Y. TIMES, Mar. 23, 2000, 156

Weiler, Paul C., MEDICAL MALPRACTICE ON TRIAL (1991), 9

Weiler, Paul C., *The Case for No-Fault Medical Liability*, 52 MD. L. REV. 908 (1993), 253

Werber, Stephen J., *Ohio Tort Reform in 1998: The War Continues*, 45 CLEV. ST. L. REV. 539 (1997), 309

Westfall, Gregory B., *The Nature of This Debate: A Look at the Texas Foreign Corporation Venue Rule and a Method for Analyzing the Premises and Promises of Tort Reform*, 26 TEX. TECH L. REV. 903, 925 (1995), 309

Wilemon, Tom, *Social Ties Bind Political Elite*, BILOXI SUN HERALD, Oct. 13, 2002, 86

Willard, Richard K., *Troubling Trends in Our Civil Justice System and the Need for*

Tort Reform, 34 FED. B. NEWS & J. 116 (1987), 4

Witt, John Fabian, *The Long History of State Constitutions and American Tort Law*, 36 RUTGERS L. REV. 1159 (2004–2005), 267

Youmans, Alice I., *Research Guide to the Litigation Explosion*, 79 LAW LIB. R. J. 707 (1987), 4

Zeiler, Kathryn, *Turning from Damage Caps to Information Disclosure: An Alternative to Tort Reform*, 5 YALE J. HEALTH POL'Y L. & ETHICS 385 (2005), 159

Zywicki, Todd J., BANKRUPTCY AND PERSONAL RESPONSIBILITY: BANKRUPTCY LAW AND POLICY IN THE TWENTY-FIRST CENTURY (Yale University Press, Forthcoming 2009), 42

Zywicki, Todd J., *Institutional Review Boards as Academic Bureaucracies: An Economic and Experiential Analysis*, 101 NORTHWESTERN L. REV. 861 (2007), 42

Zywicki, Todd J., *Spontaneous Order and the Common Law: Gordon Tullock's Critique*, 135 PUBLIC CHOICE 35–53 (2008), 42

Zywicki, Todd J., *The Law and Economics of Subprime Lending* (with Joseph Adamson), 80 UNIVERSITY OF COLORADO L. REV. 1 (2009), 42

Zywicki, Todd J., *The Market for Information and Credit Card Regulation*, 28(1) BANKING AND FINANCIAL SERVICE POLICY REPORT 13 (2009), 42

Zywicki, Todd J., *The Rule of Law, Freedom, and Prosperity*, 10 SUPREME COURT ECONOMIC REVIEW (2003), 42

Zywicki, Todd J., *Three Problematic Truths About the Consumer Financial Protection Agency Act of 2009*, 1 LOMBARD STREET, No. 12 (2009), 42

Zywicki, Todd J. & Anthony B. Sanders, *Posner, Hayek and The Economic Analysis of Law*, 93 Iowa L. Rev. 559 (2008), 42

Zywicki, Todd J. & Jeremy Kidd, PUBLIC CHOICE AND TORT REFORM (AEI Press, Forthcoming 2009), 42

Zywicki, Todd J. & Maxwell Stearns, PUBLIC CHOICE CONCEPTS AND APPLICATIONS IN LAW, (West Publishing, Forthcoming 2009), 42

MATERIALS ON TORT REFORM

Second Edition

AN INTRODUCTION TO THE TEXT AND TO TORT REFORM

■ ■ ■

While tort law has not changed dramatically in the seven years since this book was first published, the tort reform debate has shifted. In the period preceding the publication of the first edition of this text, tort reform was a battle over substantive tort law, joint and several liability, admissibility of certain types of evidence—in other words, issues pertaining to accountability and liability.[1] Typical tort reform proposals involved limitations on non-economic loss, changes in the amounts, evidentiary burdens, and standards for punitive damages,[2] changes in the definition of design defect including the quest to eliminate strict liability in tort (reflected in Section 2B of the RESTATEMENT OF TORTS, THIRD), changes in the point in time to assess "defectiveness" in failure to warn cases, changes in the standard of care applicable to plaintiffs/consumers, expanding the government standards and state of the art defense, changes in state law to include statutes of repose, changes in joint and several liability, changes in the law of evidence as it pertains to the admissibility of technical and scientific information, and more.

For the last seven years, while the above topics remain in play, focus has broadened to include fundamental procedural mechanisms that affect, enhance, or limit access to courts,[3] and particularly the availability of state courts.[4] As the essays that follow make clear, there has been an undeniable

---

[1] Georgene Vairo, *The Role of Influence in the Arc of Tort "Reform"*, 65 EMORY L.J. 1741 (2016) (on evolution of tort reform); Alexandra B. Klass, *Tort Experiments in the Laboratories of Democracy*, 50 WM. & MARY L. REV. 1501, 1510–13 (2009) (tracing trends in legislative "experiments" in tort reform); Scott DeVito & Andrew W. Jurs, *Doubling-Down" for Defendants: The Pernicious Effects of Tort Reform*, 118 PENN ST. L. REV. 543, 594–95 (2014).

[2] Neil Vidmar, Mirya Holman, *The Frequency, Predictability, and Proportionality of Jury Awards of Punitive Damages in State Courts in 2005: A New Audit*, 43 SUFFOLK U. L. REV. 855, 856 (2010); Laura J. Hines & N. William Hines, *Constitutional Constraints on Punitive Damages: Clarity, Consistency, and the Outlier Dilemma*, 66 HASTINGS L.J. 1257 (2015) (reviewing "excessiveness" cases).

[3] Richard D. Freer, *Exodus from and Transformation of American Civil Litigation*, 65 EMORY L.J. 1491 (2016).

[4] This is not to suggest that some of the most volatile components of the tort reform debate are resolved. Indeed, in some areas such as malpractice law, the fights over frequency of claims, impact of tort law, need for change, and much more is, if anything, more controversial in 2017 than it was is 2010. Chih-Ming Liang, S.J.D., *Rethinking the Tort Liability System and Patient Safety: From the Conventional Wisdom to Learning from Litigation*, 12 IND. HEALTH L. REV. 327, 344–45 (2015) (referencing several empirical studies on frequency of claims); Michelle M. Mello, et al., *The Medical Liability Climate and Prospects for Reform*, 312 (20) JAMA, 2146 (studying trends in medical malpractice claims); Myungho Paik et al., *The Receding Tide of Medical Malpractice Litigation*, 6 J. EMPIRICAL LEGAL STUD. 637 (2009) (arguing that paid and unpaid claims have been decreasing).

push to move tort cases away from state courts and into federal court raising profound federalism questions.

Those fighting for measures that limit liability or change procedures to route disputes into federal court (i.e., tort reformers) contend that the possibility of a fair hearing can best be realized in federal courts.

Those opposing tort reform assert that injured people[5] are entitled to access to justice in their own states, before judges from their own states, with basic decisions being made by a jury of their peers at a local level, i.e., federalism. This contention is consistent with a conventional formulation of what is referred to in constitutional parlance as the "police powers," meaning the obligations of the states to play a primary role in the protection of the health, safety, and welfare of their residents as a matter of constitutional imperative.

The important role of the States in this field is fully compatible with Article I, Section 8 of the Constitution. That Article makes clear that the federal government should act to protect the "general welfare." This goal is to be accomplished, *inter alia*, by formulating rules, regulations, standards, and laws that are "necessary and proper" for the well-being of the public.

Those fighting tort reform contend that Article I pertains to federal interests, matters in interstate commerce subject to federal rules and regulation. However, the core responsibility for the protection of health, safety, and welfare of individuals, to the extent it is protected by the system of tort law and civil justice, lies with the states.

In recent years, as tort reform shifted to process, various legislative initiatives have been pursued that achieve the tort reformers goal of pushing civil tort liability cases into federal court. For example, the Class Action Fairness Act Of 2005,[6] the Separation of Powers Restoration Act[7] (currently pending), and the Prevention of Fraudulent Joining Act,[8] (also pending) are good reflections of this change in the tort reform world. They are part of the tort reform universe and pertain to process, not substantive tort law.

The expanse of this field is hard to overstate. As you read this text, look at your surroundings. I will hazard a guess you are not far from food (a tort reform field), an automobile (a tort reform field), or a consumer product (take your pick—they are all tort reform topics). Whether one is involved in litigation or one has never been and hopes never to be part of a

---

[5] Jill Wieber Lens, *Punishing for the Injury: Tort Law's Influence in Defining the Constitutional Limitations on Punitive Damage Awards*, 39 HOFSTRA L. REV. 595, 603 (2016).

[6] Class Action Fairness Act of 2005, Pub. L. No. 109–2, 119 Stat. 4 (2005) (codified as amended at 28 U.S.C. §§ 1332(d), 1453, 1711–15).

[7] Separation of Powers Restoration Act of 2016, S. 2724, 114th Cong. (2016).

[8] THE FRAUDULENT JOINDER PREVENTION ACT OF 2016, H.R. REP. NO. 114–422 (2016) https://www.gpo.gov/fdsys/pkg/CRPT-114hrpt422/pdf/CRPT-114hrpt422.pdf.

lawsuit or even see the inside of a courtroom, tort reform is of consequence because it touches on fundamental forces affecting our day-to-day lives.

Are you covered by insurance? Taken an airplane? Gone to a doctor or therapist? Used or otherwise consumed a pharmaceutical product? Been a patient in a hospital or other treatment facility? Consumed diet soda, an artificial sweetener, or tap water (in certain parts of the country)? Seen a lawyer, architect, accountant, or other professional? Used an aerosol? Inhaled pollutants? Been exposed to tobacco smoke, plywood, old peeling paint, pesticides, Teflon, or old insulation? You get the idea—these are all products or services affected by issues central to the tort reform discourse.

In addition to the above areas being "flash points" in the tort reform field, the different products and services described are not just the subject of policy debate—they are undeniably central to the day-to-day lives of all of us.

Tort cases involve those aspects of life that are quite real, tactile, visible, and present, products and services fundamental to our lives.[9]

Tort law—a composite of common law, tradition, doctrine, standards, history, statutes, regulations, scholarship, and more—is the quiet force that walks with you.[10]

Tort law joins you in the operating room, surrounds you when you get into a car, purchase food, take medication, or put your children to bed for the night.

Tort law urges and channels the producers of goods and services to generate safer and more efficient products.

Tort law sanctions misconduct publicly thereby sending a potent message to others in field after field (i.e., deterrence) that there are consequences for undertaking undue risks with public safety and well-being.

Accordingly, to insure that the field is fair and vibrant is of great consequence.

Perhaps because of the omnipresence of tort reform, scholarship in this area often assumes a working knowledge of the history and goals in the field. Without casting dispersions on those who harbor this slightly myopic perspective, let's assume for a moment you are considering these issues for the first time. Rest assured, at least half of the essays in Part I and articles

---

[9] Alexandra B. Klass, *Tort Experiments in the Laboratories of Democracy*, 50 WM. & MARY L. REV. 1501, 1510–13 (2009) (tracing trends in legislative "experiments" in tort reform); Anne Bloom, *The Radiating Effects of Torts*, 62 DEPAUL L. REV. 229, 233–34 (2013) (considering the impact of tort rulings on behavior).

[10] The characterization of tort law in this and the following four paragraphs paraphrase language in my article, *On the Necessity of Preserving Access to Civil Justice: Rediscovering Federalism and Unmasking "Fraudulent" Joinder*, 45 RUTGERS L. REC. ___, (2017).

in Part II make an effort to clarify the nature and content of tort reform. By the time you finish this text, you will have the perspective of 35 or so top lawyers, academicians, and interest group representatives on the meaning and import of tort reform and, more broadly, the civil justice system.[11]

Central to most arguments regarding the necessity for—or the ill-advised nature of—tort reform are long-standing disputes[12] regarding the number of cases initiated, the processes used, the legal doctrines available to plaintiffs and defendants, the factual content of the cases themselves, and the consequences (personal, economic, and more) of personal injury claims whether litigated, settled, or otherwise resolved.

As to the merit, worth, and importance of the many and highly varied component parts of tort reform, as simple as this may sound, it depends on (a) who you ask and (b) how they understand the history of this field. As to the "who you ask" factor, the essays and articles that follow cover most of the divergent perspectives in the field. As to the history of, or even the basic reason for tort reform, there are two fundamental narratives.

The first narrative: By the late 1970s and early 1980s, politicians, lawyers, policymakers, and academicians realized that a combination of cumbersome and intrusive regulation and an "out of control" plaintiff-oriented civil justice system was exacting a terrible toll on the U.S. economy.[13] Innovation and creativity were being suppressed. Market forces that should compel improvements in the quality and cost of goods and services were constrained. Two remedies were needed: deregulation and significant changes in the civil justice or tort system that would stem burgeoning, inefficient, and unjustified civil tort claims.[14]

To proponents of tort reform, the rules governing liability leaned too heavily in favor of plaintiffs and the criteria for imposing liability were far too lax. As a result, there were too many plaintiffs filing too many suits and receiving, unjustly, too much money.[15] Tort reforms were needed to ensure that no entity or person would be dragged into court unless (a) their actions were the *actual cause* of a specific harm, and (b) their actions were genuinely wrongful. Tort reform was necessary to bring under control a

---

[11] The term "civil justice system" refers to those state and federal courts with jurisdiction over personal rights, interests, entitlements, and claims that fall within the field of tort law.

[12] By "dispute" I mean not only disagreements regarding the propriety, wisdom, or efficacy of various types of cases or proceedings, I mean disputes on the very number, nature, and impact of the entire landscape of the civil justice system.

[13] *See* Walter Olson, *The Runaway Jury Is No Myth,* WALL ST. J., July 18, 2000, at A22; Lucian A. Bebchuk, *Suing Solely to Extract a Settlement Offer,* 17 J. LEGAL STUD. 437 (1988); Kenneth S. Abraham, *Individual Action and Collective Responsibility: The Dilemma of Mass Tort Reform,* 73 VA. L. REV. 845 (1987); John W. Wade, *On Frivolous Litigation: A Study of Tort Liability and Procedural Sanctions,* 14 HOFSTRA L. REV. 433 (1986).

[14] *See* Richard K. Willard, *Troubling Trends in Our Civil Justice System and the Need for Tort Reform,* 34 FED. B. NEWS & J. 116 (1987).

[15] Alice I. Youmans, *Research Guide to the Litigation Explosion,* 79 LAW LIB. R. J. 707 (1987).

litigation epidemic that was doing violence to the best interests of businesses and consumers.[16] Accordingly, strict liability, joint and several liability, punitive damages, uncapped noneconomic damages, baseless class actions, and questionable expert testimony all had to go—and immunity had to be provided for entities that made vital products that bear unavoidable risks (*e.g.,* vaccines).[17]

The second narrative: In the late 1970s and early 1980s, as Chicago School Economics[18] moved (or bullied its way) into the legal and political arena, as "greed is good" became an acceptable economic ideology, lawyers, policymakers, and academicians became concerned that vital doctrines and legal theories needed to protect consumer interests were under fire. The challenges were orchestrated and funded by an amalgam of business interests. The consumer voice, the voices of those affected adversely by dangerous products, the voices of patients harmed by medical malpractice, were not heard. Under this narrative, tort reform meant achieving goals that were pernicious and simple: limit accountability, eliminate punitive damages, and reduce and make predictable tort liability so that costs can be passed along to consumers. Under this narrative, tort reform aided businesses of all types but provided absolutely nothing for consumers.

In this anti-tort reform narrative, state legislatures, Congress, and the courts became the setting for blistering attacks on strict liability, joint and several liability, punitive damages, retailer liability, class actions, and compensation for noneconomic losses.[19] In this narrative, the free-market rationale in the first narrative is simply false.[20] Improvement in or stabilization of health, safety, welfare, and the environment—the broad definition of consumer protection—did not occur exclusively (or in some instance at all) as a consequence of market forces. Consumers are not competitors. Consumers had to pin their hopes for improvement in the quality of goods and services on aggressive regulation (not exactly the

---

[16] *See* James A. Henderson, Jr. & Aaron D. Twerski, PRODUCTS LIABILITY: PROBLEMS AND PROCESS, 859–62 (2d ed. 1992) (describing the first round of tort reform initiatives).

[17] *See e.g.,* James B. Sales & Kenneth B. Cole, Jr., *Punitive Damages: A Relic That Has Outlived Its Origins,* 37 VAND. L. REV. 1117 (1984); George L. Priest, *Can Absolute Manufacturer Liability Be Defended?,* 9 YALE J. ON REG. 237 (1992).

[18] For some background on "Chicago School Economics" you might look at M. Friedman, Oliver Wendell Holmes, *The Path of the Law,* 10 HARV. L. REV. 457, 474 (1897); CAPITALISM AND FREEDOM (1962); Richard A. Posner, *A Theory of Negligence,* 1 J. LEGAL STUD. 29 (1972); Richard A. Posner, *Utilitarianism, Economics, and Legal Theory,* 8 J. LEGAL STUD. 103 (1979); Edmund W. Kitch, *The Fire of Truth: A Remembrance of Law and Economics at Chicago,* 1932–1970, 26 J.L. & ECON. 163 (1983) (discussing the pivotal role of Aaron Director in the evolution of Chicago School thinking); Richard A. Posner, ECONOMIC ANALYSIS OF LAW (6th ed. 2003).

[19] *See* Nancy L. Manzer, *Note, Tort Reform Legislation: A Systematic Evaluation of Caps on Damages and Limitations on Joint and Several Liability,* 73 CORNELL L. REV. 628, 633G (1988) (on the advent of legislative tort reform).

[20] *See* Joseph A. Page, *Deforming Tort Reform,* 78 GEO. L.J. 649 (1990).

mantra of the last 25 years) *and*, importantly, the presence of an effective, open, vibrant civil liability system—the tort system.[21]

Opponents of tort reform asserted that the civil justice system was an essential element of the entire U.S. legal system—and was beginning to lean in favor of defendants. Tort reform, they argued, was little more than a thinly veiled attack on the civil justice system. Tort reform wasn't reform at all—it was about nothing other than imposing gross limitations on the rights of consumer, imposing harsh and unjust standards that prevent injured consumers from securing appropriate remedies. Accordingly, strict liability, implied warranty, retailer liability, and joint and several liability had to be maintained, immunity from tort liability had to be limited, non-economic damages had to be free from arbitrary caps, punitive damages had to be maintained, and access to justice—access to the courts—had to be preserved and enhanced.[22]

Often, we hope to find common ground between competing narratives. The two narratives above have precious little, if any, common ground.[23] Disputes exist regarding every conceivable aspect of the civil justice system. Given both the emotional content and the stunning range, variety, and magnitude of the legal issues, policy disputes, and economic theories in play, the goal of this short text is not (and could not be) to complete coverage of all topics, arguments, issues, disputes, options, and theories, or anything close to it. However, there are several clear objectives:

1.   Provide diverse perspectives on tort reform. The significant variation in content, tone, and perspective of the essays in Part I reflects fairly the nature of the tort reform debate.

2.   Provide a doctrinal and theoretical foundation for appreciating the legal issues, practical and ideological challenges, and the rationale for changes in or preservation of the civil justice system.

3.   Provide a sense of the written discourse in the tort reform field.[24]

4.   Provide a few cases that demonstrate the role courts play in this field.

5.   Finally, particularly with the narratives and the essays, provide a chance to "try on" different perspectives in this field.

---

[21]   *See* Carl Tobias, *Common Sense and Other Legal Reforms*, 48 Vand. L. Rev. 699 (1995).

[22]   *See* Stephen Daniels & Joanne Martin, *Myth and Reality in Punitive Damages*, 75 Minn. L. Rev. 1 (1990); Theodore Eisenberg, *Damage Awards in Perspective: Behind the Headline-Grabbing Awards in* Exxon Valdez *and* Engle, 36 Wake Forest L. Rev. 1129 (2001).

[23]   Philip A. Talmadge & N. Clifford Petersen, *In Search of a Proper Balance*, 22 Gonz. L. Rev. 259 (1986).

[24]   To say there is abundant scholarship in the field is an understatement. I found over 250 articles, books, and public documents written by just two of the invited essayists, Victor Schwartz and Michael Rustad. The scholarship in Part II is an eclectic mix of legal theory, doctrine, politics, statistics, economics, and social policy typical in this field.

For at least the last 25 years, tort reform has been front and center on the U.S. political stage—it has been an issue in every presidential election campaign since 1980 and a plank in every major party platform since 1984. Law review articles number in the thousands and newspaper pieces on the topic in the tens of thousands. Both sides of the debate advocate their position with great passion and skill. Statistics are presented from every conceivable angle. A single appellate court decision or published study on the topic will produce press releases from every quadrant declaring victory and demonstrating how the case or study supports their position.

My hope is that you will "rise above it," see all sides, keep an open mind—and when you have formed a position, join the fray. Write, speak out, get involved—and then duck. Tort reform is not for the faint of heart.

PART I

TORT REFORM NARRATIVES AND ESSAYS

▪ ▪ ▪

A. AN INTRODUCTION TO THE NARRATIVE AND ESSAYS—AND MORE TORT REFORM ISSUES

Few people involved in the tort reform discourse take lightly the significant issues of law, economics, and policy that drive the field. While there is, generally speaking, courtesy and respect between the warring factions, there is powerful emotion and profound disagreement inherent in the discourse.[1]

On occasion, those meeting in-laws for the first time are advised to be gracious, positive, and stay away from discussions of sex, politics, and religion—change the subject if possible. Perhaps tort reform should be added to this list of topics to be avoided.

Where there are doctors and lawyers in the same family, it's a safe guess that tort reform is a topic to be avoided if one is hoping for a quiet evening. Unpleasantness at the dinner table is inevitable when the statement: "Medical malpractice cases are destroying the medical profession," receives the following response: "The reason there are so many medical malpractice cases is that there is so much malpractice." Things may deteriorate irreparably when the infamous (and usually misunderstood and misquoted) Harvard study regarding the incidence of malpractice is bandied about.[2] Tort reform, as it turns out, is theoretically and doctrinally fascinating—but quite personal.

---

[1] [Author's note: The essays in this section are a wonderful example of the professionalism that *does* exist in this field. There is profound disagreement between the essayists evident from their testimony in legislative hearings, their briefs in various legal cases, and their scholarship—yet for this text, they agreed, without exception, to devote time and thought to writing or submitting original entries to help with this project, a generosity for which I am deeply indebted. AFP]

[2] Consider glancing at the following before entering the fray on this topic: Tom Baker, *Reconsidering the Harvard Medical Practice Study Conclusions about the Validity of Medical Malpractice Claims*, 33 J.L. MED. & ETHICS 501, 502 (2005); Paul C. Weiler, MEDICAL MALPRACTICE ON TRIAL 12 (1991) (discussing the study); HARVARD MEDICAL PRACTICE STUDY, PATIENTS, DOCTORS, AND LAWYERS: MEDICAL INJURY, MALPRACTICE LITIGATION, AND PATIENT COMPENSATION IN NEW YORK (1990); Russell Localio, *et al.*, *Relation Between Medical Malpractice Claims and Adverse Events Due to Negligence, Results of the Harvard Medical Practice Study III*, 325 NEW ENG. J. MED. 245–51 (1991); David A. Hyman, *Commentary, Medical Malpractice and the Tort System: What Do We Know and What (If Anything) Should We Do About It?*, 80 TEX. L. REV. 1639, 1642 (2002).

A family devastated by a baseless lawsuit that ends up stripping them of their business, assets, retirement, or reputation is going to have a lot to say when it comes to tort reform.

A family devastated by an injury, death, or other loss (fiscal or otherwise) caused by a wrongful act that could not be addressed in court because of changes in the civil justice system is likely to be ready to pounce if the topic of tort reform surfaces.

While the differences in the opinions discussed above derive from personal experience, the vast majority of the tort reform discourse involves scholarship, advocacy, and debate by those representing various interests, clients, or groups. That said, there is an undeniable and potent zealousness that surfaces in this dispute. Advocates of the main positions in the field assert their positions with an intensity not regularly evident in other legal and policy debates. As you will see from the essays and articles, arguments about tort reform are heartfelt. Given the emotional content of the discourse, consider carefully the different ways information is presented, the apparent goals of the essayist, and the variations in methodology and style. Does the style selected or the topic chosen affect your assessment of the ideas presented?

Beyond a methodological assessment of these writings, see if you can identify any commonly accepted premises regarding (a) the origin of and (b) the reasons for tort reform. Were there significant events or trends that changed the civil justice landscape and made the tort reform movement inevitable?

It is not all that difficult to look at the civil justice system generally and tort liability specifically on a decade-by-decade basis and conclude that in some decades, plaintiffs seem to do particularly well, while in others, defendants fared better.[3] Does a "plaintiff-favoring" swing of the tort pendulum in the 1970s and early 1980s explain the tort reform movement? One can link these shifts or swings to national political trends, changes in the economy, changing ideologies within the judiciary or in Congress, evolving scientific and technical information, and numerous other phenomena. While these trends may seem like plausible explanations, they can be tracked back at least 75 years, making them an unlikely basis for the current push for tort reform.

Another possible (and common) explanation for the pressure to change the civil justice system might be a case, a series of cases, or a decisional trend that suggests the system is out-of-balance and in need of an overhaul. After all, the 1980s and 1990s were (arguably) good decades from the

---

[3]   Nelson P. Miller, *Now What? Steadying Tort Law's Pendulum*, 88 MICH. BAR J. 38 (2009); Lucinda M. Finley, *The Hidden Victims of Tort Reform: Women, Children, and the Elderly*, 53 EMORY L.J. 1263, 1269, n.21 (2004); Leon Green, *No-Fault: A Perspective*, 1975 BYU L. REV. 79 (1975).

plaintiff's side of the aisle. There were substantial judgments or settlements involving tobacco, asbestos, various chemicals, toxins, defective consumer goods, automobiles, and many other products. Do those cases explain tort reform? Were they the reason why, in every year since 1984, a tort reform bill of some type was considered by the United States Congress? Could those cases explain why tort reform legislation was—and still is—proposed in many different states year after year?[4]

What about the sheer size of jury verdicts? Is that the driving force behind those seeking modern tort reform? According to Supreme Court Justice Sandra Day O'Connor, prior to 1980 the largest punitive damage award affirmed by an appellate court was $250,000—but within ten years, awards of $10 million and more were being approved.[5] Beyond Justice O'Connor's comment, there is scant reliable data on the magnitude and frequency of large damage awards, punitive or otherwise, that are actually paid (as opposed to being awarded at trial and reversed on appeal).[6]

In David Kohler's *Forty Years After* New York Times v. Sullivan: *The Good, the Bad, and the Ugly*,[7] the author asserts that in tort cases involving defamation, "the average punitive damages award since 1980 exceed[s] $2 million. . . ." Assertions of this type are refuted as aggressively as they are asserted.[8] Often, arguments about the tort system involve not just national trends but state-by-state critiques.[9] For example, looking just to the state of Oregon, Professor Michael L. Rustad notes that, "[i]n the twenty-five year period between 1965 and 1990, Oregon juries handed down a total of two punitive damages awards in all products liability actions."[10] Looking at Georgia, Professor Thomas Eaton writes that trial judges who were surveyed find punitive damages to be "very low on average."[11]

---

[4] Stephen Daniels & Joanne Martin, *The Strange Success of Tort Reform*, 53 Emory L.J. 1225 (2004); Stephen Daniels & Joanne Martin, *The Impact That It Has Had Is Between People's Ears: Tort Reform, Mass Culture, and Plaintiffs' Lawyers*, 50 DePaul L. Rev. 453 (2000).

[5] *Browning-Ferris Industries of Vermont, Inc. v. Kelco Disposal*, 492 U.S. 257, 282 (1989) (Justice O'Connor concurring in part and dissenting in part).

[6] Michael J. Saks, *Do We Really Know Anything About the Behavior of the Tort Litigation System—And Why Not?*, 140 U. Pa. L. Rev. 1147 (1992); Valerie P. Hans & William S. Lofquist, *Jurors' Judgments of Business Liability in Tort Cases: Implications for the Litigation Explosion Debate*, 26 Law & Soc'y Rev. 85, 93–97 (1992) (public misunderstanding of the size and magnitude of judgments is the norm, not the exception).

[7] 83 Or. L. Rev. 1203, 1231 (2004).

[8] William Haltom & Michael McCann, Distorting the Law: Politics, Media, and the Litigation Crisis 61 (2004).

[9] A perfect example of this is the American Tort Reform Association's (ATRA) listing of jurisdictions that ATRA asserts have demonstrated a lack of objectivity (meaning a relentless pro-plaintiff bias) in their judicial decisionmaking when it comes to medical malpractice cases. *Judicial Hellholes® 2008* American Tort Reform Association. www.atra.org.

[10] Michael L. Rustad, *Symposium, Access to Justice: Can Business Co-Exist with the Civil Justice System: The Closing of Punitive Damages' Iron Case*, 38 Loy. L.A. L. Rev. 1297, n. 301 (2005).

[11] Thomas A. Eaton, *Of Frivolous Litigation and Runaway Juries: A View from the Bench*, 41 Ga. L. Rev. 431, 442 (2007).

With medical liability central to the current tort reform debate, you would think there is plentiful reliable data. Not so. "One of the surprising facts in the current medical malpractice debate is the lack of concrete evidence with regards to the average jury award, the average noneconomic damage award, the average punitive damage award, and, most importantly, the frequency of suits."[12]

Nevertheless, the tobacco, asbestos, and other massive cases in the 1980s and 1990s made national news and energized the tort reform movement. Were these cases, however, the driving force behind tort reform? And perhaps more fundamentally, is tort reform a creature of the last quarter-century?

Professor Rachel Janutis sees tort reform as a "struggle . . . in both the judicial and political branches throughout the *history* of the development of tort law." [emphasis added] In essence, Professor Janutis asserts that the debate on accountability, incentives, and the payment of money damages has been with us since the Industrial Revolution, since the notion of workers' rights crept into the legal discourse in the United States. From her perspective, the tort reform debate did not begin in the 1980s—it began in the 1880s with the progressive movement. She writes: "[A] more complete review reveals that with each swing of the pendulum economically interested actors were present and pushing from both sides in both the judicial and the political arenas."[13]

The view of Professor Janutis makes sense—after all, the primary venue for victims of misconduct unable to resolve their grievances has always been the civil justice—or tort system. As workers began to make use of the tort system for work-related injuries, a trade-off of historic consequence took place. In the early 20th century, in exchange for an administrative system providing workers compensation was the condition that such compensation would be an exclusive remedy.

As a general rule, an employee receiving workers compensation for injuries sustained at work was (and still is) barred from bringing a tort action against an employer. One assumption is that employers would prefer the predictability of a regulatory model (where costs are passed along to workers) rather than the risks (and accountability) the tort system presented.[14] A second view of the exclusivity of workers compensation is that the presence of an administrative remedy is adequate and a civil

---

[12]   Kyle Miller, *Note: Putting the Caps on Caps: Reconciling the Goal of Medical Malpractice Reform with the Twin Objectives of Tort Law,* 59 VAND. L. REV. 1457, n. 33 (2006).

[13]   Rachel M. Janutis, *The Struggle Over Tort Reform and the Overlooked Legacy of the Progressives,* 39 AKRON L. REV. 943, 951–52 (2006).

[14]   Joseph H. King, Jr., *The Exclusiveness Of An Employee's Workers' Compensation Remedy Against His Employer,* 55 TENN. L. REV. 405 (1987–88); *see generally* Oliver W. Holmes, Jr., THE COMMON LAW 94 (Sheldon M. Novick ed., Dover Publications 1991) (1881) (on protecting those who allegedly cause harm).

action in tort would give an injury victim two bites at the apple—all suggesting that tort reform was with us long before the current movement began.

The above timing premise is, like everything else in this field, a subject of disagreement. The scholarship in this area provides no common answer to even the most basic questions regarding the timing, origin, or driving force that initiated modern tort reform. Professor F. Patrick Hubbard writes that the

> [The] history of the 'tort reform' movement can be divided into two overlapping dimensions. The first part, which consists of ad hoc calls for reforms to address a specific liability insurance 'crisis,' began in the 1970s when reforms were sought to address a 'crisis' caused by large increases in medical malpractice liability premiums and in product liability insurance premiums. In the 1980s, a broader 'crisis' was caused by a general increase in liability insurance premiums.... [Each] of these 'crises' generated its own response in terms of proposed legal changes and in terms of support for and against these changes.[15]

One of the groups fighting against tort reform and favoring the continuation of an open and universally accessible civil justice system, the Center for Justice and Democracy (CJD), accepts Professor Hubbard's thesis—that tort reform is a creature of the last quarter-century that threatens the basic institutions of civil justice. "American consumers and citizens . . . are challenged as never before in history by a corporate-led attack against independent judges and on our precious right to trial by jury in civil cases."[16]

The CJD position on timing—that this is a movement of about the last 25 years—is shared by the American Tort Reform Association (ATRA) but beyond that, the two groups share almost nothing. ATRA supports tort reform at least as aggressively as CJD opposes it. Among other things, ATRA looks at the tort system on a state-by-state basis and makes public its findings.

For example, in describing West Virginia's civil justice or tort system, ATRA finds that the "state's highest court has a history of plaintiff-biased decisions, paying damages to those who are not injured, allowing mass trials, permitting lawsuits outside the workers compensation system, rejecting long-established legal principles, and welcoming plaintiffs' lawyers from other states to take advantage of its generous rulings."

---

[15] F. Patrick Hubbard, *The Nature and Impact of the Tort Reform Movement*, 35 HOFSTRA L. REV. 437 (2006). As may be obvious from the quotes within the quoted text (provided more fully in Part II of this text), Professor Hubbard questions the underlying economic foundation for the aforementioned crisis.

[16] From the home page of the website for the Center for Justice and Democracy, centerjd.org. More CJD materials are in Part II of this work.

Florida, ATRA finds, "maintains its reputation for legally excessive awards and plaintiff-biased rulings that make it a launching pad for class actions, dubious claims and novel legal theories creating new types of lawsuits."[17]

Five scholars, writing in the Baylor Law Review see things markedly differently from ATRA:

> [M]uch of what has been written in favor of a need for tort reform is premised upon anecdotal horror stories, surveys of public opinion or [flawed] analysis of jury verdicts. . . . [However, when you pose the question of the need for tort reform to trial judges in the "plaintiff-centered" state of Texas] more than 83% . . . had observed not a single instance of a runaway jury verdict on either actual or exemplary damages during the preceding 48 months before the survey. [L]ess than 2% of the judges reported any frequency greater than 25% of the cases involving excessively high awards of actual damages, with the percentage of judges observing excessive punitive damage awards more than a quarter of the time being somewhat higher at roughly 9% . . . . [F]ar from a tort "crisis" the vast majority of Texas district judges have observed no significant evidence of a need for tort reform. . . .[18]

Notwithstanding the views of the Texas trial court judges, it is not hard to understand why some of those affected by the civil justice system are open to change based simply on perceived inefficiency. For example, according to several scholars:

> Of all malpractice cases filed against health care providers, nearly seventy-five percent are closed without any payment to the patient. Furthermore, less than thirty percent of all money that doctors pay in liability insurance fees actually goes to patients. . . . [S]ixty cents of every dollar expended on the medical malpractice system goes to pay overhead, *i.e.,* administrative costs comprised predominantly of legal fees.[19]

Claims of inefficiency of the tort system are not limited to the medical malpractice area. They have been part of the tort reform discourse for many years.[20]

---

[17] *Judicial Hellholes® 2008* American Tort Reform Association, www.atra.org. This material is set out more fully in Part II.

[18] Larry Lyon, Bradley J.B. Toben, James M. Underwood, William D. Underwood and James Wren, *Straight from the Horse's Mouth: Judicial Observations of Jury Behavior and the Need for Tort Reform,* 59 BAYLOR L. REV. 419 (2007).

[19] James A. Comodeca, et. al., *Killing the Golden Goose by Evaluating Medical Care Through the Retroscope: Tort Reform From the Defense Perspective,* 31 DAYTON L. REV. 207 (2006).

[20] Henson Moore & Jeffery O'Connell, *Foreclosing Medical Malpractice Claims by Prompt Tender of Economic Loss,* 44 LA. L. REV. 1267, 1269–70 (1984) (the tort system is enormously inefficient); Deborah L. Rhode, *Colloquium: Deborah L. Rhode's Access to Justice: Access to Justice: Again, Still,* 73 FORDHAM L. REV. 1013, 1026 (2004), ("The tort system is inconsistent and inefficient; relatively few accident victims can afford it, and 50–60% of the payouts by defendant

Regardless of the explanation that seems most compelling regarding the timing and origins of modern tort reform, there is little question of the prominence and force of the movement. Legislative committees in Congress as well as in state legislatures have heard about tort reform, quite literally, on thousands of different occasions. There have been hundreds of judicial decisions that are easily characterized as tort reform cases. The Supreme Court has decided a number of major cases solely on the topic of the propriety and constitutionality of punitive damages.[21]

With hundreds of cases, thousands of legislative proceedings resulting in bills (some ultimately adopted in various states as well as by the Congress), and thousands of articles in law reviews, peer-reviewed journals, and other publications, you might think that the prospect of understanding tort reform would be daunting. Fear not—this is a manageable topic often distilled down to fairly basic practical and legal issues. Thus, before launching into the essays and narratives, a quick look at some of the conventional issues in tort reform might be helpful. What follows is a list of some very basic legal issues in the field and a few references:

a.   In cases involving a product, should there be liability without a showing of fault if there is a defect that renders the product unreasonably dangerous?[22]

b.   If there are multiple defendants, should they be jointly and severally liable (meaning that one defendant may end up paying more than the percentage of the harm that defendant caused)?[23]

c.   In product liability cases, should the time frame for liability be bounded only by a statute of limitations? Should there be a statute of repose that limits liability, beginning with the date the product is placed on the market, regardless of the statute of limitations?[24]

---

insurance companies end up compensating lawyers."); Joseph H. King Jr., *Exculpatory Agreements for Volunteers in Youth Activities—The Alternative to "Nerf (registered)" Tiddlywinks*, 53 OHIO ST. L.J. 683, 738 (1992) ("the tort system of compensation is notoriously inefficient. . . .").

[21]   *Exxon Shipping Co. v. Baker*, 128 S.Ct. 2605, 2624, 171 L.Ed. 2d 520 (2008); *State Farm Mut. Auto. Ins. Co. v. Campbell*, 538 U.S. 408 (2003); *BMW of N. America v. Gore*, 517 U.S. 559 (1996); *Cooper Industries. v. Leatherman Tool Group*, 532 U.S. 424 (2001); *TXO Prod. Corp. v. Alliance Res. Corp.*, 509 U.S. 443 (1993); *Browning-Ferris Indus. v. Kelco Disposal, Inc.*, 492 U.S. 257 (1989); *Pac. Mut. Life Ins. Co. v. Haslip*, 499 U.S. 1 (1991).

[22]   Peter M. Gerhart, *The Death of Strict Liability*, 56 BUFFALO L. REV. 245 (2008); David G. Owen, *Defectiveness Restated: Exploding the "Strict" Products Liability Myth*, 1996 U. ILL. L. REV. 743; Martin A. Kotler, *The Myth of Individualism and the Appeal of Tort Reform*, 59 RUTGERS L. REV. 779, 816 (2007) (discussing the strict liability experiment).

[23]   Paul Bargren, *Comment, Joint and Several Liability: Protection for Plaintiffs*, 1994 WIS. L. REV. 453.

[24]   Robert A. Van Kirk, *Note, The Evolution of Useful Life Statutes in the Products Liability Reform Effort*, 1989 DUKE L.J. 1689; Susan C. Randall, *Comment, Due Process Challenges to Statutes of Repose*, 40 SW. L.J. 997 (1986).

d. Should retailers be liable for a product that is defectively designed if they sell the product, profit from the sale of the product, even provide information about the product to the consumer—but play no role in the design of the product? Should one be liable for defective design if one is not a designer?[25]

e. Assuming a defendant engaged in reckless misconduct (short of conscious flagrant disregard for life) that leads to a plaintiff's injury, should punitive damages be imposed?[26]

f. When a product is used in a manner that is foreseeable but is contrary to the explicit instructions and clearly intended uses of the product provided by the defendant/manufacturer, what standards should apply?[27]

g. Should conformity with state or federal regulation provide a defendant a shield against tort liability? Against punitive damages?[28]

h. How does one calculate the amount a defendant should pay if the defendant's conduct is truly reprehensible—or malicious—or outrageous—or reflects a conscious disregard for life?[29]

i. Should various aspects of research, essential technologies, charitable acts (and charitable organizations), vulnerable yet vital industries (*e.g.*, vaccine producers) have limited tort liability or be immunized entirely?[30]

j. If tort law is to be "rewritten," who should undertake the task? Congress? The state legislatures? The Supreme Court? State courts? All of these institutions are caught up in the issues of tort reform—but who should be? Are the great questions of tort reform matters of public policy (ARTICLE I, SECTION 8 of the

---

[25] Robert A. Sachs, *Product Liability Reform and Seller Liability: A Proposal for Change,* 55 BAYLOR L. REV. 1031, 1035 (2003).

[26] Thomas C. Galligan, Jr., *U.S. Supreme Court Tort Reform: Limiting State Power to Articulate and Develop Tort Law—Defamation, Preemption, and Punitive Damages,* 74 U. CINN. L. REV. 1189 (2006).

[27] Martin A. Kotler, *The Myth of Individualism and the Appeal of Tort Reform,* 59 RUTGERS L. REV. 779, 823 (2007).

[28] Lars Noah, *Reconceptualizing Federal Preemption of Tort Claims as the Government Standards Defense,* 37 WM. & MARY L. REV. 903 (1996); David G. Owen, *Special Defenses in Modern Products Liability Law,* 70 MO. L. REV. 1 (2005).

[29] Michael Rustad, *In Defense of Punitive Damage Awards in Products Liability: Testing Tort Anecdotes with Empirical Data,* 78 IOWA L. REV. 1 (1992); Theodore Eisenberg et al., *Juries, Judges, and Punitive Damages: An Empirical Study,* 87 CORNELL L. REV. 743 (2002).

[30] Richard C. Ausness, *Preemption of State Tort Law by Federal Safety Statutes: Supreme Court Preemption Jurisprudence Since* CIPOLLONE, 92 KY. L. REV. 913 (2003–2004).

CONSTITUTION would give the nod to Congress) or are they state tort law questions?[31]

Much of this text looks at these and a number of other legal, economic, and political questions in the field. The essays that follow illuminate a number of these questions.

The shift from substantive tort law to process is evident in the essays and reflected in the current legislative battles referenced earlier (the legislative proposals known as the Separation of Powers Restoration Act and the Fraudulent Joinder Act). This change in focus was clear by the end of the first decade of the 21st Century. At a judicial symposium, attorney and professor Robert Peck stated succinctly the position of those opposes to the more recent change:

> Now, with the advent of tort reform, we have enhanced this undesirable trend by placing addition unreasonable obstacles and hurdles before the courthouse door that deter meritorious lawsuits or, with much the same effect, render them more expensive to pursue, make them more difficult to prove and diminish recoveries even when the plaintiffs prevail.[32]

Contrary views focus on the claim that there is a civil litigation crisis that causes critical resources to be lost along with incentives for innovation in various fields is well-represented in a number of the essays that follow. It is also apparent from the websites of some of the most prominent organizations and groups, notably the United States Chamber of Commerce and the American Tort Reform Association, who devote time and resources to put forward the point of view that is the exact opposite of those expressed above by Robert Peck. A quick look at the websites of these organizations will guide you to multiple resources making their case for continued changes in the tort system needed to stem the tide of baseless and wasteful litigation.[33]

A note on the authors: The decision to include a biography for each of the essayists was driven by the respect due the writers but also the value in learning about the backgrounds of many of the central actors in the tort reform discourse. Every essayist has played a role of consequence in this debate. Many have served as expert witnesses in congressional hearings as well as hearings at the state level. Based solely on a review of online

---

[31] *Silkwood v. Kerr-McGee Corp.*, 464 U.S. 238 (1984), holds that tort law is the province of the states. *See*, George L. Priest, *The Constitutionality of State Tort Reform Legislation and Lochner* 31 SETON HALL L. REV. 683 (2001); Victor E. Schwartz, *Judicial Nullification of Tort Reform: Ignoring History, Logic, and Fundamentals of Constitutional Law*, 31 SETON HALL L. REV. 688, 690–92 (2001); Mark Geistfeld, *Constitutional Tort Reform*, 38 LOY. L.A. L. REV. 1093 (2005).

[32] *Remarks of Robert Peck, fifth annual judicial symposium on civil justice issues; George Mason judicial education program: December 5–7, 2010, edited transcript: emerging civil justice issues*, 7 J.L. ECON AND POLICY 195, 196 (2010).

[33] The arguments and far more are noted on the websites of the Chamber of Commerce and the American Tort Reform Association, www.atra.org.

sources (firm, organization, or faculty web pages) this group has appeared in at least 250 different legislative hearings and served as counsel or filed *amicus curiae* briefs in over 100 cases. Their scholarship is extensive and in all instances includes both tort reform and other fields—but as to tort reform, there are easily 500 identifiable works. In short, these are some of the most prominent and consequential actors in the field. Learning a bit about them is a worthwhile exercise. Their career paths and commitment to this important public debate can serve as a model for those interested in the area.

B. THE ESSAYS

GROUP ONE: TORT REFORM: GREAT ISSUES, CHOICES, AND POLITICAL CHALLENGES

1.   You might think that the best way to decide whether to change the civil justice system is to look at the data. However, thus far, all attempts to quantify the virtues or distortions of the tort system have been controversial at best. Conventional legal scholarship in the field is often highly critical of the underlying statistical basis for tort reform decisions.

2.   In Janet G. Abaray's *Déjà Vu All Over Again: Ohio's 2005 Tort Reform Act Cannot Survive a Rational Basis Challenge*, 31 DAYTON L. REV. 141, 154 (2006), she attacks the statistical foundation on which the Ohio state legislature relied in adopting a tort reform law. "[T]he General Assembly cites as a basis for upsetting 200 years of common law a flawed study, which is not peer reviewed, has no indicia of reliability, omits referenced data, and reaches a conclusion that can be due to any of four different factors." This criticism is echoed throughout this text.

3.   In a 2004 Report of the Congressional Budget Office Report (CBO), *The Goal and Status of Tort Reform in the States*, the CBO focused on the effects of tort reform at the state level.[34] The report looked at the question of whether current data justified certain changes or "reforms," including limitations on punitive damages and noneconomic loss (*e.g.*, pain and suffering), abolition of joint and several liability, and changes in the collateral source rule.

In its summary, the CBO report states: "[C]aps on damage awards reduced the number of lawsuits filed, the value of awards, and insurance costs . . . [and led to] increases in insurers' profitability for both medical malpractice and general liability insurance. . . ." The qualifier in the report is blunt:

   . . . . As a whole, the studies provided little systematic evidence that any one type of reform had a significant impact on any of the

---

[34]   http://www.cbo.gov/doc.cfm?index=5549&type=0&sequence=1.

various outcome measures studied. Few of the findings—except for a reduction in the losses experienced by insurers—were independently corroborated by other studies. Some studies were unable to document any measurable effects from the tort reforms, a result that may be more reflective of the lack of data than of any failure of the reforms.

At least two issues complicate the analysis of tort reform. First, data limitations preclude separately estimating the effect of each of the many types of reform. Second, it is difficult to control for differences between states that reformed their tort system and those that have not. Controlling for such differences is critical in assessing the effect of tort reform on outcomes such as the level of insurance premiums. . . .

Despite the absence of clear data, conclusions in the CBO Report troubled those opposed to tort reform. Based on only one study, the CBO concluded: "[T]he presence of sanctions on frivolous suits or defenses, prejudgment interest, structured settlements, or any combination thereof led to a decrease in the value of both economic and noneconomic claims and in the number of lawsuits filed for automobile-related torts."[35]

The CBO Report found that in the medical malpractice area, various tort reforms could lead to "a reduction in unnecessary medical expenditures, implying both the existence of defensive medicine (excessive tests and procedures that limit doctors' malpractice liability but have minimal medical benefit) and the ability of tort reform to reduce its practice." The Report acknowledged that the studies "were conducted on a restricted sample of patients, whose treatment and behavior cannot be generalized to the population as a whole. . . ."[36]

4.   The fact is that it is next to impossible for policymakers to make crisp, irrefutable findings regarding the civil justice system, in part because the data is not reliable and in part because the civil justice system is not a singularity. It encompasses complex and multiple fields, an enormous variety of interests and parties and, as if that were not enough to make summary statements suspect, varies considerably from state to state. This problem was recognized some time ago. *See*, Thomas M. Selsheimer and Steven H. Stodgill, *Due Process and Punitive Damages: Providing Meaningful Guidance to the Jury*, 47 S.M.U. L. REV. 329 (1994); Thomas Eaton & Suzette Talarico, *A Profile of Tort Litigation in Georgia and Reflections on Tort Reform*, 30 GEORGIA L. REV. 627, 691 (1996).

---

[35] *Id.*

[36] *2004 Report of the Congressional Budget Office Report (CBO)*, "The Goal and Status of Tort Reform in the States," *Summary, Tort Reform at the State Level*, found at http://www.cbo.gov/doc.cfm?index=5549&type=0&sequence=1. A CBO report from fall 2009 produced in Part III of this text follows up on the 2004 findings.

Consequently, support for or opposition to tort reform requires more than a statistical critique. This is an area where arguments and advocacy count.

In all the essays that follow, you will get to read some of the best advocacy and arguments in the field. This first group illuminates the great issues and choices that run throughout the tort reform discourse. The first essay by Dean Victor E. Schwartz sets the stage for consideration of more recent round of tort reform initiatives. Dean Schwartz, currently a partner at a major law firm and formerly a professor and Dean at the University of Cincinnati and later at American University Washington College of Law, is considered by many to be the father of the American tort reform movement.

VICTOR E. SCHWARTZ,[37] THE DYNAMICS OF TORT LAW: ITS CAPACITY FOR CHANGE—IT CAN HELP OR HARM SOCIETY

Why Tort Law is Different from Other Courses in Law School

The first edition of "Materials on Tort Reform" was published in 2010. Through Professor Andrew Popper's exceptional efforts, it presented the entire rainbow of views on tort reform in a succinct and interesting format. In my commentary on the first edition, I stated that what is most fascinating about tort law is its organic nature; it is an area of law that is ever-changing and growing in its content. Judges have exercised their power to make changes to common law going back hundreds of years and adapt the law to modern times. While most judges try to be objective as they shape tort law, for the most part over the past two centuries, judicial modifications of tort law have strongly favored plaintiffs.

At times, there is arguably just cause to do so. For example, over the past 40 years, many courts (and state legislatures) came to believe that the traditional common law rule of contributory negligence, which barred a plaintiff from recovering for an injury caused by another if the plaintiff was even slightly at fault in bringing about his or her own harm, was an unfair rule. Change occurred through the adoption of a variety of comparative

---

[37] **Victor E. Schwartz** is Chairman of the Public Policy Group in the Washington, D.C. office of the law firm of Shook Hardy & Bacon L.L.P. He created the "Iron Triangle Defense" in litigation, which combines his team's talents in public relations, government relations, and litigation. He co-authors the most widely used torts casebook in the United States, PROSSER, WADE AND SCHWARTZ'S TORTS (12th Ed., 2010). He has served on the Advisory Committees of the American Law Institute's Restatement of the Law (Third) Torts: Products Liability, Apportionment of Liability, General Principles and Liability for Physical and Emotional Harm projects. The National Law Journal named him as one of the 100 most influential attorneys in the United States three times, and the Washingtonian magazine has twice named him one of the top government relations specialists in the nation's capital. Before going into practice, he was on the faculty at the University of Cincinnati School of Law (where he served as professor and dean) and at American University, Washington College of Law.

negligence regimes, which generally allowed a plaintiff to recover based on a comparison of the fault of all parties that caused an injury. *See* Victor E. Schwartz, *Comparative Negligence* (5th ed. 2010).

Sometimes changes in tort law favoring plaintiffs, while created by well-meaning judges applying common law, do not anticipate adverse social consequences that may flow from such changes. As I indicated in the first edition, this result is understandable to some extent because courts often consider cases in a vacuum, hearing only from the counsel for the plaintiff and the defendant. These counsel are also limited in the timing and length of arguments they are permitted to make. Thus, the full range of adverse public policy effects of a decision may never be heard by the court. By way of contrast, tort reform accomplished by legislatures is usually enacted after hearing from a wide variety of positions and stakeholders, and a consideration of the social and economic impacts of the proposed legislation.

Where judges have extended tort law in an attempt to benefit plaintiffs, but with little vision about the social and economic impacts of their decision, legislative tort reform often provides a corrective measure. Legislatures can address adverse public policy consequences of judicial decisions and even correct judicial mistakes.

That being said, most of the time judges "get it right" in their decisions from a public policy perspective. For example, my commentary in the first edition discussed the efforts of some well-meaning groups (and their lawyers) to expand the types of damages that may be obtained in cases where a pet is negligently injured or killed. In the past six years, judges of liberal, moderate, and conservative views have wisely confined such damages to actual economic losses, namely the economic value of the animal involved and certain expenditures that flow from an injury. Courts have continued to reject arguments that a pet owner should be permitted to recover noneconomic damages such as "pain and suffering" for the negligent injury or death of a pet. Numerous courts, including several state supreme courts, have appreciated the negative ripple effects on animal health and welfare if the scope of recoverable damages were expanded to include such subjective types of damages. *See, e.g., Strickland v. Medlen*, 397 S.W.3d 184 (Tex. 2013). They have understood that insurance and other cost increases would impair the work of important animal care services such as shelters and cause many pet owners (particularly low-income pet owners) to not be able to afford veterinary care, leading to more pet deaths.

I.   Tort Reform in the Courts: Changes in the Common Law of Torts Can Favor Defendants

Although judge-made changes to the common law have historically favored plaintiffs, the past six years have seen greater activity with respect to "tort reform in the courts." Tort reform in the courts occurs when a state appellate court realizes that a prior pro-plaintiff ruling, which may have made sense when it was decided, is no longer sound.

For example, the Texas Supreme Court had, for over 40 years, set forth common law rules that prevented a defendant in an auto injury case from letting the jury know that the plaintiff had not worn a seatbelt. This rule prevented a jury from considering evidence that a plaintiff's injury would have been significantly less had the plaintiff complied with laws requiring seatbelt use. Such a rule "blindfolding" the jury arose when the contributory negligence defense was the law of Texas. Under a contributory negligence regime, the rule was understandable in that it prevented a plaintiff from obtaining no recovery at all for his or her injuries on account of seatbelt non-use.

Texas, like most other states, now adopts comparative negligence. Thus, the predicate for the rule excluding seatbelt evidence no longer exists. In addition, now as compared to 40 years ago, wearing a seatbelt is standard practice for safely operating a motor vehicle. Further, public policy at both the state and federal levels encourages seatbelt use through laws requiring drivers and passengers to "buckle up." Allowing a plaintiff who fails to comply with such laws to nevertheless recover full damages undermines the safety objectives of these laws. Accordingly, when the Texas Supreme Court reexamined its common law rule precluding the introduction of evidence of seatbelt non-use in 2015, the court "got it right" and permitted a defendant, where relevant, to present this evidence to a jury. *See Nabors Well Services, Ltd. v. Romero*, 456 S.W.3d 553 (Tex. 2015).

The Texas seatbelt case is just one example of the recent trend of "tort reform in the courts." Another example is a Mississippi trial court that applied the liability-limiting doctrine of "category liability" to dismiss design defect claims against manufacturers of low-cost disposable respirators. *See Mealer v. 3M Co.*, 2015 WL 9692735 (Jones County Cir. Ct., Miss., Mar. 28, 2015), *reconsideration denied* (Nov. 10, 2015). Here, former workers who used a common type of disposable respirator mask alleged the product failed to provide the same level of protection against inhaling silica dust as higher cost, full headgear respirator products. The court rejected this argument, finding that a "plaintiff cannot demonstrate the existence of a 'safer alternative design' by pointing to a substantially different product." As the court explained, imposing liability based on such an apples-to-oranges product comparison would "eliminate whole categories of useful products from the market." *See* Victor E. Schwartz & Cary Silverman, *Category Liability: Properly Precluding Claims That Propose an Alternative Product Rather Than an Alternative Design*, 44:40 Prod. Safety & Liab. Rep. (Bloomberg BNA) 1 (Jan. 11, 2016).

Courts have invoked category liability or analogous doctrines to protect manufacturers of other products such as guns, knives, and vehicles where there is no reasonable alternative design that would eliminate an inherent known risk of a product. What is of great importance is that the defense lawyer in the Mississippi case aptly demonstrated that defense lawyers can bring about "tort reform in the courts."

A third recent example of "tort reform in the courts" occurred in the California Supreme Court. The court, which has historically been perceived as pro-plaintiff, issued a decision eliminating awards of so-called "phantom damages." These are medical costs invoiced or "billed" by a health care provider, but never actually paid by anyone due to factors such as discounted rates negotiated by health insurers. They resemble the "sticker" price for a new car which is typically not the amount one actually pays for the car. Nevertheless, in the health care world, these "phantom damages" can be substantial, and allow a claimant to recover considerably more than was actually paid for medical care expenses. The California Supreme Court recognized that such damages could provide an unjust windfall to claimants, and now allows juries to consider those amounts actually paid for medical care. *See Howell v. Hamilton Meats & Provisions, Inc.*, 257 P.3d 1130 (Cal. 2011). Over the past six years, a number of states have also adopted legislative reforms eliminating awards of "phantom damages."

Future "tort reform in the courts" can bring about rational and wise changes in tort law to help defendants, but only if defense lawyers seize upon opportunities for change. Experience suggests that, although there are some outside defense counsel with the imagination and drive to pursue positive changes in the law, change most often occurs where corporate counsel take initiative and instruct their outside counsel to advance such legal arguments.

II.   Other Recent Tort Reform Developments

1.   Innovator Liability is Rejected by Courts and Legislatures

"Innovator liability" refers to a novel theory pursued in some cases against brand name drug manufacturers to potentially subject them to liability for harms caused to a patient taking a generic version of a drug. In a nutshell, the theory posits that because a brand name drug manufacturer is the "innovator" of a drug and created its warnings, it should be responsible for any injuries caused by a generic version of that drug, even if the manufacturer of the generic drug is a direct competitor of the brand name manufacturer.

Like many novel liability theories, "innovator liability" theory is the product of imaginative plaintiff's lawyers. When the U.S. Supreme Court, in *Pliva, Inc. v. Mensing*, 564 U.S. 604 (2011), ruled that product liability claims against generic drug manufacturers were generally preempted by federal law, plaintiff's lawyers were blocked from successfully suing a group that accounts for about 80% of the drugs sold in the United States. The predicate for the Court's decision was that generic drug companies cannot change their warnings labels without permission from the Food and Drug Administration (FDA). Two years earlier, the Court, in *Wyeth v. Levine*, 555 U.S. 555 (2009), had ruled that state tort actions against branded drug companies are <u>not</u> preempted because these companies could change warnings without first obtaining FDA permission. "Innovator liability," therefore, represents an attempt by plaintiff's lawyers to shift litigation against generic drug companies that is preempted onto branded drug companies that is not preempted.

Most legal commentators have criticized "innovator liability" as unsound and contrary to one of the most basic principles of product liability that a manufacturer is only responsible for the risks associated with its own product. The overwhelming number of courts that have addressed the issue have agreed. For example, the Iowa Supreme Court recognized that the theory was based on a desire to engage in "deep-pocket jurisprudence." *See Huck v. Wyeth, Inc.*, 850 N.W.2d 353 (Iowa 2014). Courts have further appreciated that adoption of "innovator liability" would drive up the already high price of pharmaceutical products and introduce perverse incentives for drug innovators to remove their products from the marketplace if subjected to liability for harms caused to someone taking a competitor's product. *See* Victor E. Schwartz, Phil Goldberg & Cary Silverman, *Warning: Shifting Liability to Manufacturers of Brand-Name Medicines When the Harm was Allegedly Caused by Generic Drugs has Severe Side Effects*, 80 Fordham L. Rev. 1835 (2013).

Nevertheless, the Alabama Supreme Court, in *Wyeth, Inc. v. Weeks*, 159 So. 3d 649 (Ala. 2014), bought into plaintiff lawyer "innovator liability" arguments. The court, not wanting to leave an injured plaintiff without a remedy, held that a brand name drug company could be subject to liability for inadequate warnings associated with its competitor's generic product. However, here legislative tort reform came into play. In 2015, a year after the *Weeks* decision, the Alabama Legislature overruled the case. The legislature's swift action on this comparatively new tort liability issue underscored just how unsound and unprincipled many found the theory to be.

2.   Stopping Fraudulent Joinder

Fraudulent joinder arises when a plaintiff's lawyer wants to have a case heard in a "plaintiff friendly" state court (e.g. Judicial Hellhole®) and seeks to establish jurisdiction by naming a "local" plaintiff, typically a small business. In such cases, the plaintiff's lawyer has no intent of ever enforcing a judgment against the "local" business, but rather just wants a jury in that particular state forum to decide the case, which is typically against a large out-of-state corporation, instead of a federal court. Under current federal rules of civil procedure, federal courts only have jurisdiction in diversity of citizenship cases arising under state law when the plaintiff is from one state and <u>all</u> of the defendants are out-of-state. Thus, naming the "local" business ousts federal courts of their diversity jurisdiction.

Civil justice reform legislation to curb fraudulent joinder and protect small businesses against being drawn into unwarranted litigation was introduced in the House of Representatives in late 2015. The Fraudulent Joinder Prevention Act (H.R. 3624) passed the House of Representatives in 2016. While plaintiff's lawyer lobbyists blocked the bill in the Senate, the legislation will likely continue to be pressed by small businesses in the coming years.

3.   Placing Restraints on State Attorney General Hiring of Contingency Fee Counsel

In the past six years, a number of states, including Alabama, Arizona, Indiana, Iowa, Mississippi, Missouri, North Carolina, Utah and Wisconsin, have enacted laws that would place reasonable restraints and sunlight on situations where a state attorney general delegates his or her enforcement power to private contingency fee lawyers. The reason states have adopted legislation with such enthusiasm is that it is contrary to the public interest for a state attorney general to delegate law enforcement power to private individuals whose principal motivation is to maximize profit through a large damages award or settlement. Such a single-minded focus on recovery may lead to results that are not necessarily in the public's best interests.

Numerous situations have occurred in which state attorneys general have outsourced public litigation to private contingency fee lawyers who are personal friends or significant political contributors. Often these hired lawyers reap the benefits of lucrative contingency fee contracts that are paid for out the state's (i.e. taxpayers') pocket and plainly not in the public interest. For that reason, at least 15 states (at the time of this publication) have enacted laws creating reasonable restraints on state attorney general hiring of private contingency fee lawyers.

It is also important to note that under a relatively unknown Executive Order issued by President George W. Bush and continued by President Barack Obama, the U.S. Department of Justice and other federal agencies are prohibited from delegating their enforcement power to private contingency fee lawyers. The reason why? Such delegations are often not in the public interest.

4.   The Rise of "Empty Suit Litigation™"

The past six years have also shown a rise in what has been termed "Empty Suit Litigation™." This type of litigation can include two distinct types of cases.

The first group of cases involves individuals who suffer no present injury. For example, attempts have been made to subject a defendant to liability for the cost of "medical monitoring" for a plaintiff who may have been exposed to a harmful substance, but exhibits no signs of an injury. For example, the state high courts of Missouri and West Virginia have allowed such suits in the absence of an injury and without any showing that the damages recovered for medical monitoring would actually be used for that purpose as opposed to any other personal purpose. This resulted in a legislative tort reform proposal in West Virginia to require, at the very least, that any money recovered in such a lawsuit actually be used for medical monitoring purposes.

Individual "empty suit litigation™" cases have also been brought for emotional harm where there is no objective showing that a plaintiff actually suffered a severe emotional impact. Testimony alone is the jury's guide as to whether to award damages.

The second group of cases are class actions in which members of the class have not suffered any actual injury to person or property. For instance, such a class action may be premised on the notion that a product, which performs exactly as the purchaser intended and has not caused any injury, is worth less due to alleged problems experienced by other product purchasers. While some courts have favored "empty suit litigation™" most have rejected it. Nevertheless, it is still a very live part of tort law over the past six years and is likely to be into the future.

As a result of attempts to bring "empty suit litigation™," model legislation has been developed called the "Actual Harms Act." Basically, with the exception of traditional torts such as trespass, the Actual Harms Act would bar courts from allowing claims where an individual has suffered no present injury or that person is part of a class action where there is no showing that class members (other than the lead plaintiffs) have suffered an actual injury.

This topic is discussed in-depth in the law review article, *The Rise of "Empty Suit" Litigation. Where Should Tort Law Draw the Line?*, 80 Brook. L. Rev. 599 (2015).

III.   <u>The Future of Tort Reform</u>

The future of tort reform is likely to focus on situations where state supreme courts have gone beyond what is either fair or reasonable in changing existing tort law to favor plaintiffs. Some examples have been highlighted here as part of this second edition of "Materials on Tort Reform." These newer, more targeted tort reform efforts will likely co-exist with broader and simpler tort reforms of the past, such as those capping noneconomic or punitive damages.

Equally as important with respect to the future of tort reform is that reform will not simply occur in the legislature, but also in the judiciary. "Tort reform in courts," spearheaded by defense counsel, can result in judges overruling or limiting prior decisions when the reason for those decisions no longer "fits" modern times.

———————

ERWIN CHEMERINSKY,[38] THE POLITICS OF TORT REFORM

In 2003, I lost two major appellate cases that I had argued, one at the United States Supreme Court and one in the California Court of Appeal. At first glance, they have little do with one another. In *Lockyer v. Andrade*,[39] the Supreme Court in a 5–4 decision upheld a sentence of life in prison with no possibility of parole for 50 years that my client, Leandro Andrade, received under California's three strikes law for stealing $153 worth of videotapes from two K-Mart stores. The Court stressed the need for deference to the states in deciding the appropriate punishment for crimes. Prior to California's three strikes law no one in the history of the United States ever had received a life sentence for the crime of shoplifting.

In *Romo v. Ford Motors Co.*,[40] the California Court of Appeal reduced a $285 million jury verdict to $23 million for an accident that killed three members of a family and seriously injured three others. Earlier the same court had found that Ford's conduct was akin to manslaughter in rushing the Bronco to market knowing of its propensity to roll over and having neither a rollover bar nor a reinforced roof. The Court of Appeal did not question its earlier conclusion, but said that due process was violated because punitive damages may be used only to punish a defendant for harm caused to the plaintiffs in the suit.

———————

[38] **Erwin Chemerinsky** is Dean at the University of California School of Law at Irvine. He frequently argues cases before the United States Supreme Court and the United States Courts of Appeals and serves as a commentator on legal issues for national and local media. His expertise is in Constitutional law, federal practice, civil rights and civil liberties, and appellate litigation. Prior to becoming Dean, he taught at Duke Law School, Gould School of Law, University of Southern California, and DePaul College of Law, 1980–1983. He is the author of six books: EMPOWERING GOVERNMENT: FEDERALISM FOR THE 21ST CENTURY (Stanford University Press, 2008); CRIMINAL PROCEDURE (with Laurie Levenson) (Aspen Law and Business 2008); FEDERAL JURISDICTION (Aspen Law & Business 5th ed., 2007); CONSTITUTIONAL LAW: PRINCIPLES AND POLICIES (Aspen Law & Business 3d ed., 2006); CONSTITUTIONAL LAW (Aspen Law & Business 2d ed., 2005); and, INTERPRETING THE CONSTITUTION (Praeger 1987). He is the author of more than 100 law review articles in journals such as the Harvard L. Rev., Michigan L. Rev., Northwestern L. Rev., University of Pennsylvania L. Rev., Stanford L. Rev. and Yale Law Journal. He received the Criminal Courts Bar Association, President's Award in 2003, the Society for Professional Journalists, Freedom of Information Award in 2003, the Western Center on Law and Poverty, Community Service Award in 2002, and the Anti-Defamation League, Community Service Award in 2001. Before entering teaching, he served as an attorney at the United States Department of Justice and practiced with Dobrovir, Oakes & Gebhardt.

[39] 538 U.S. 63 (2003).

[40] 113 Cal.App.4th 738, 6 Cal.Rptr.3d 793 (2003).

As I reflected at the end of the year on my losses as an appellate advocate, I could not help but think that the unifying principle of these cases is that too many years in prison for shoplifting does not violate the Constitution, but too much money from a corporation for killing people does. These cases are not atypical. The Supreme Court and lower courts have consistently refused to find that criminal sentences outside of the death penalty context are unconstitutional as cruel and unusual punishment, but in a series of cases it has held that too much in punitive damages violates due process.

It is difficult to imagine the constitutional principle which explains this inconsistency. In one area, the Court is willing to give great deference to the choices of the states; in another area the Court is unwilling to give any deference to state legislatures and state common law which authorizes punitive damage awards.

What then explains this? Inescapably, it is about the ideological choices of a conservative Supreme Court, wanting to defer to long sentences for criminals, but wanting to protect businesses from large punitive damage awards. In this way, the Supreme Court's approach to tort reform—constitutional limits on punitive damages—reflect what tort reform has been all about: protecting businesses from damage judgments. Tort reform never has been about increasingly the ability of injured individuals to have their day in court or to be able to successfully sue.

The major examples of tort reform in the United States all fit this pattern. There has been a significant trend to arbitration as a way of resolving tort disputes. Not long ago, I went to a doctor for the first time and was given a sheaf of papers to fill out before being examined. Among them was a form whereby I would agree to take any complaint against the doctor to arbitration and to forego any ability to sue in court. I asked the receptionist if I needed to sign the form in order to be seen by the doctor and she replied that she did not know because she had never been asked that question before.

A few years ago, I bought a new computer and noticed that the agreement essentially said that by turning on the computer and indicating my agreement by clicking the appropriate button to use it meant that I agreed to arbitration and waived the ability to go to court if any dispute arose. I immediately wrote back a letter saying that I did not agree and that by opening my letter the company agreed that I could sue them in court. I never got a reply, though thankfully the computer did not malfunction.

In a series of decisions, the Supreme Court has strongly favored arbitration. Although arbitration has many virtues and is often highly desirable, overall business prefers it because it takes matters away from juries and puts them in the hands of professional arbiters. This is perceived as highly advantageous for defendants.

Many states have adopted tort reform in caps on damages, such as limits on pain and suffering damages, restrictions on punitive damages, and caps on the amount of contingency fees that a lawyer may recover. All of these, of course, favor business over individuals.

Such tort reform is fueled by the occasional seemingly excessive damage award, such as against McDonald's[41] for a woman who was injured by coffee that was too hot. Advocates of tort reform paint a picture of runaway juries giving huge, unjustified awards. Yet study after study has shown that the large verdict is truly the anomaly.

A serious problem in the tort system is the inability of injured individuals to find lawyers to handle their cases. Never, though, is this the focus of tort reform discussions. Tort reform has been all about protecting defendants. That is the politics and it is something too often overlooked and hidden behind the seemingly neutral label "tort reform."

Leandro Andrade remains in prison for his shoplifting. He is eligible for parole in the year 2046 when he will be 87 years old. The Romo family decided to take the $23 million rather than go through further litigation.

RONEN AVRAHAM,[42] TORT REFORM MAY REDUCE HEALTHCARE COSTS, BUT IT'S NO SILVER BULLET— SO LET'S THINK OUTSIDE OF THE BOX

When President Obama began discussing his plans for healthcare reform, he included several initiatives designed to strengthen bipartisan support. One of his stated concessions to Republicans was medical malpractice reform. "I have talked to enough doctors," said the President in his October 5, 2009 speech to Congress, "to know that defensive medicine may be contributing to unnecessary costs." He directed HHS Secretary

---

[41] *Liebeck v. McDonald's Restaurants, P.T.S. Inc.,* No. D–202 CV–93–02419, 1995 WL 360309 (Bernalillo County, N.M. Dist. Ct. August 18, 1994).

[42] **Ronen Avraham** is the Thomas Shelton Maxey Professor in Law at the University of Texas School of Law. His areas of expertise are medical malpractice, torts, tort reform, law and economics, and insurance law. Prior to joining the faculty at the University of Texas, he was the Assistant Professor of Law at Northwestern University for the academic years 2003–07. He taught a course in Torts and co-led the Law and Economics Colloquium. Prior to that Ronen served as Visiting Assistant Professor at Northwestern University for the academic year 2002–03 where he taught a course in Insurance Law and a seminar in Distributive Justice. Ronen served as the Visiting Assistant Professor at Tel Aviv and Bar Ilan Universities in the winter of 2002 where he taught Distributive Justice and Economic Analysis of Law. In the fall of 2001 Ronen visited The University of Michigan Law School as a Lecturer. He co-taught (with Jim Krier) in Behavioral Economics and served as a lecturer (with Kyle Logue) in Distributive Justice in the Law in the Winter of 2001. His primary research interests in 2009 are in economic analysis of torts and healthcare law.

Sebelius to test the waters with demonstration projects, but emphasized that these reforms are "no silver bullet."

One of my areas of research is malpractice reform, and my conclusion, as the title suggests, is that tort reform may reduce costs, but it is indeed no silver bullet. To better see why, we need to take a step back.

Both Republicans and Democrats agree that excessive treatment is a big driver of healthcare costs. There is no consensus, however, on what causes excess treatment. Democrats argue that overtreatment is primarily due to offensive medicine—doctors' tendency to provide more treatment than necessary in order to increase their income. President Obama was referring to offensive medicine when he criticized the "warped incentives" in the health care system, which he said reward quantity rather than quality. The Democrats' solutions focus on payment reforms to change these incentives. Republicans, in contrast, often assert that excess treatment is due to defensive medicine—doctors' tendency to provide more treatment than necessary in order to avoid malpractice liability. Hence, they advocate tort reform as the remedy for exploding healthcare costs. The logic behind tort reform is simple: if liability is capped, doctors need not over-treat as a means of escaping lawsuits. In other words, with tort reform there would no longer be a need to order an MRI when the patient only has a headache.

According to Democrats, the problem with malpractice reforms, *e.g.* liability caps, are that they will lead to doctors taking fewer precautions and thus more injuries. Indeed, medical errors cause tremendous pain and suffering, and by some measures up to 98,000 deaths each year. Remedial care for these errors raises our healthcare costs as well. Worse still, if doctors do not fear liability for bad decisions, they might be incentivized to perform riskier but more lucrative procedures when cheaper, safer alternatives would work just as well. Without the risk of liability why should a doctor not perform a risky, lucrative bypass on a not-terribly-sick heart patient if insurers pick up the tab and the surgeon believes the outcome is likely to be good?

Assuming interest group politics is *not* what is driving this debate (as ridiculous as that may be), who is right? Will tort reform reduce unnecessary procedures and lower costs' or will reform actually increase costs as doctors make more errors and pursue aggressive treatments?

In a series of academic studies, my co-authors and I show that tort reform decreases settlement payments, decreases insurance premiums for employer-sponsored plans, and can modestly increase health insurance coverage rates for groups that often lack access to employer plans (younger workers and the self-employed).

But, for two reasons, that does not mean that tort reform is a silver bullet. First, even though reforms enacted by the *states* have had a modest effect, there is reason to believe that the results of *federal* legislation will be more limited still. Any federal medical malpractice reform can have an impact only in states that have not adopted the reform already, and almost every state has enacted at least one type of reform. Indeed, 26 states have capped non-economic damage awards, including populous states such as California and Texas. Second, even though reforms reduce costs, they might also eliminate benefits which, as a society, we care about. Tort reforms might have adverse effects on patients' health as well as on their economic wellbeing in the event of an injury. There are no studies which demonstrate the overall welfare effects of tort reform.

Thus, tort reform at the federal level will probably not significantly lower costs. In part because savings from medical malpractice reform are likely to be modest, and in part because it has already been done.

This being said, I have proposed a system of private regulation which I believe will align all of the parties' incentives with society's to reduce both offensive and defensive medicine, as well as medical errors. The private regulators would develop and continually update medical practice guidelines which they would then compete to sell to medical providers. These firms would offer their client-providers, the organizations that bought their guidelines, safe-harbor from medical malpractice lawsuits as long as the providers follow the guidelines. Additionally, the private firms, unlike current organizations that create guidelines, would be held liable for putting forth sub-optimal guidelines. The private firms would thus be incentivized to keep care costs low so providers will buy the guidelines but to keep patient safety high so they, the firms, would not get sued for promulgating unsafe guidelines. Granting immunity to doctors who follow such guidelines would eliminate doctors' incentives to practice defensive medicine. Likewise, medical errors would be reduced because doctors would be following the optimal medical practices, through the guidelines, that the private firms developed. Lastly, imposing liability for sub-optimal guidelines, together with free market competition in the guidelines market, would go a long way towards curbing offensive medicine because either the doctors or the private firm would be liable for any complications arising from extra procedures.

Such a private regulation regime would require five essential legal components. First, firms may need some form of intellectual property protection for their guidelines to prevent hospitals and other regulators from free-riding on a firm's efforts. Second, courts must give immunity to providers who properly follow guidelines. This immunity will end the incentives to perform defensive medicine. Third, the private firms must be licensed to guarantee their financial solvency, otherwise a firm declaring bankruptcy could externalize costs onto patients. Fourth, firms must be held liable for writing sub-optimal guidelines and the liability must be judged from the ex-ante—or before the fact—perspective. That is, Firm P will be found negligent if and only if the guidelines it has written are inefficient under an analysis using evidence-based, objective research to compare the costs and benefits of medical procedures as the risks were known before the procedure took place. If there was a 5% risk of harm, the 5% risk is what determines liability in an ex-ante analysis, regardless of whether the harm actually materializes. If the firms are not held liable for bad guidelines from an objective stand-point, they will not have the proper incentives to make the guidelines safe. Fifth, to encourage the continual development of guidelines, courts must disallow the state-of-the-art defense which currently shields liability from providers whose methods compare to the rest of the industry.

Some may argue it is better to work through pre-existing entities already creating guidelines. This objection, however, ignores the bad reputation such guidelines currently have. Even if current guideline promulgators were provided enough funding, their incentives would still not be aligned with the public good. Specifically, working within the current system would do nothing to solve the problem that the pharmaceutical and medical devices industries are inseparably intertwined in medical research. The private regulators regime does not attempt to remove the industry-research connection, but instead it aligns the parties' financial interests with the society's interests.

In his congressional address President Obama solicited any reasonable ideas for health care reform. While it seems likely that, by the time this goes to print, Washington will have enacted some form of reform, legislators would still be wise to consider this private regulation regime. Unlike simple tort reform, private regulation would have a significant impact and not exacerbate other costs while attempting to cure the defensive medicine problem. Instead, the private regulation regime would align the public's interests with the health care players' incentives, creating a win-win-win for patients, doctors, and society.[43]

---

[43]   For more of Professor Avraham recent scholarship, *see Private Regulation of Medicine: A Win-Win-Win for Doctors, Patients and Public*, Huffington Post, July, 2009. http://www.huffingtonpost.com/ronen-avraham/private-regulation-of-med_b_242937.html;   [Opinion/Editorial] *Silver: Texas-Style Caps on Noneconomic Damages isn't Smart Tort Reform*, Star-Telegram, July 18, 2009 (with Charles M. Silver & David A. Hyman); *Private and Competitive Regulation of Medicine*, The Economists' Voice, August, 2009; http://www.bepress.com/cgi/viewcontent.cgi?article=1629&context=ev; *Tragedy of the Human Commons*, 29 CARDOZO L. REV. 15 (2008) (with K.A.D. Camara); http://papers.ssrn.com/sol3/papers.cfm?abstract_id=1022132 [Reprinted in 1 NORTHWESTERN INTERDISCIPLINARY L. REV. 15 (2008) (with K.A.D. Camara).]; *An Empirical Study of the Impact of Tort Reform on Medical Malpractice Settlement Payments*, 36 JOURNAL OF LEGAL STUDIES S183 (2007). http://papers.ssrn.com//sol3/papers.cfm?abstract_id=912922; *Putting a Price on Pain-and-Suffering Damages: A Critique of the Current Approaches and a Preliminary Proposal for Change*, 100 NORTHWESTERN UNIVERSITY L. REV. 87 (2006). [Reprinted in 55 DEFENSE LAW JOURNAL 711 (2006).]

NEIL VIDMAR,[44] MEDICAL MALPRACTICE TORT REFORM

Tort reform has long been a goal of the American Medical Association, the American Tort Reform Association, and other organizations. Especial emphasis has been placed on the so-called "pain and suffering" component of jury awards. Tort reform groups argue that monetary awards by juries for "pain and suffering" should be capped to as little as $250,000. The claim is that caps will reduce awards; reduce medical malpractice lawsuits; and reduce payments by insurers, thereby reducing liability insurance premiums. Moreover, with an improved litigation climate doctors can stop "defensive medicine" (*i.e.,* order unnecessary tests out of lawsuit fear). They will also migrate to states with such reforms. There are normative and empirical issues that need to be considered in these claims.

A major normative issue is why medical malpractice cases should be treated differently than other causes of action in the tort system. Should a 23-year-old person rendered a quadriplegic by medical negligence be limited to $250,000 for a lifetime of pain and suffering when another person rendered a quadriplegic by a drunk driver or the collapse of a faulty bridge has no limit on the amount that can be awarded?

Another problem is the definition of "pain and suffering." It is often used as a short hand term for damages that cannot easily be translated into dollar amounts. A better term is "general damages." Consider the 16-year-old girl whose face was horribly and permanently disfigured as a result of medical negligence. How do you put a price on her lifetime loss of happiness, marital chances, employment, etc.? Or consider a 24-year-old mother who had all four of her limbs amputated as a result of a flesh eating disease contracted in the hospital? Careful studies have produced findings indicating that the plaintiffs most likely to be affected by caps are the most severely injured persons, women, infants, and the elderly.

---

[44]   **Neil Vidmar** is Russell M. Robinson II Professor of Law at Duke Law School and holds a secondary appointment in the Psychology Department at Duke. He received his Ph.D. in social psychology from the University of Illinois in 1967. In 1973–1974 he was a Russell Sage Resident at Yale Law School and taught at Western Ontario until his appointment at Duke Law School in 1987. He has written over 100 articles, chapters and reports that include the following subjects: the jury system; small claims courts; the Ontario Business Practices Act; exemplary damages; independent paralegals; rights consciousness; dispute resolution; procedural justice; privacy; reliability of eyewitnesses; death penalty attitudes; bias in the ABA ratings of judicial candidates' and battered woman syndrome. He was co-investigator of a study of civil juries in an Arizona Superior Court (supported by the National Science Foundation and the State Justice Institute) that videotaped the actual deliberations of 50 civil juries. A continuing project is examining the parameters of medical malpractice litigation, including the outcomes of litigation and the effects (or non-effects) of tort reforms. He was lead drafter of amicus briefs in *Kumho Tire v. Carmichael* (1999), a leading Supreme Court case involving expert evidence, and *State Farm v Campbell* (2003) and *Philip Morris v. Williams* (2007), involving punitive damages as well as briefs on medical malpractice, eyewitness identification and other subjects in state courts. Recently some of his research interests have turned again to issues in criminal law. He has lectured on judging scientific evidence for judicial education programs in the United States and Canada and has testified or consulted as an expert on jury behavior for criminal and civil trials in the United States, Canada, England, Australia, New Zealand, and Hong Kong.

There is also the issue of whether "defensive medicine" is necessarily bad. If a doctor orders additional tests or takes additional measures the patient may benefit from this closer attention. Experts agree that there is both "good" and "bad" defensive medicine. Some argue that the tort system helps promote good defensive medicine, although there is meager evidence bearing on either side of this part of the tort reform controversy.

Juries are the villains in tort reform rhetoric, but consider that juries decide only 7 to 10 percent of malpractice cases, and that doctors actually win about three out of four tried cases. The rest are settled, many without any payment to the claimant. Research shows that jurors are often very skeptical of malpractice claims. This doesn't mean jurors can't be convinced of negligence, but they want solid evidence. Moreover, the bulk of jury awards and settlements is for past and future medical care and lost income.

What about the size of jury awards? That 24-year-old mother with no arms or legs will require a lifetime of medical care, not to mention possible lost income as well as care for her child (or possibly other young children). In my research on Florida malpractice cases involving million dollar payments to plaintiffs, I found approximately twice as many million dollar settlements that never became lawsuits as there were million dollar jury awards. The medical negligence in the former cases apparently was so clear that it made no sense for the health care provider to fight a losing cause in court. Moreover, the plaintiffs' past and future economic losses in these cases were enormous.

Some recent research from Texas indicates that caps may substantially reduce both jury awards and the amounts actually paid by liability insurers. However, other studies have not been able to convincingly show that liability insurance premiums are reduced as a result of tort reforms.

Furthermore, research has pretty consistently shown that the presence or absence of caps on awards bears either no relationship or at best a very modest association with the per-capita number of patient-treating physicians in a state. And in 2004 the Congressional Budget Office estimated that the costs savings of tort reforms would have only a very small impact on overall health care spending, a finding supported by a different study in 2009.

A short, peer-reviewed article summarizing my research and that of others can be found at http://link.springer.com/article/10.1007%2Fs11999-008-0608-6.pdf. Many other issues are discussed in Tom Baker, *The Medical Malpractice Myth* (University of Chicago Press, 2005).[45]

---

[45]   For more of Professor Vidmar's recent scholarship, *see* Neil Vidmar and Valerie P. Hans, AMERICAN JURIES: THE VERDICT (Prometheus Books, 2007); Vidmar, N., MacKillop, K. and Lee, P. *Million Dollar Medical Malpractice Cases in Florida: Post-verdict and Pre-suit Settlements,* 59 VANDERBILT L. REV. 1343 (2006); Vidmar, N. and MacKillop, K., *"Judicial Hellholes," Medical*

JOAN VOGEL,[46] THE TORT REFORM MOVEMENT AS A TEACHING VEHICLE

Who controls what perception law students and the general public will have about the American civil justice system? As a major political issue in the last thirty years, the regressive Tort Reform Movement has successfully controlled the political discourse about how the civil justice system works and how it needs to be changed.

This movement has been triumphant in convincing legislatures and appellate courts in all but a few states to enact limitations on the tort rights and remedies of ordinary Americans. The Tort Reform Movement has also convinced many Americans that tort remedies need to be scaled back to prevent greedy plaintiffs' attorneys and undeserving plaintiffs from wrecking the American economy. The movement has been very effective in undermining the judicial system in general. Legislatures have adopted the image of the runaway jury when enacting statutes and initiatives that limit tort damages and plaintiffs' attorneys' fees.

Tort reformers have pressed their case by electing like-minded politicians through extensive political contributions. They have been highly successful in implementing judicial processes that exclude plaintiffs' expert witnesses. The publicity campaigns of the Tort Reform Movement have resembled many of the worst political campaign tactics we have witnessed in recent years. The Tort Reform Movement has misrepresented and lied about tort cases. No mention is ever made of the corporate misbehavior in mass tort cases like the DES, the Dalkon Shield, Asbestos, Benzene and the other numerous pharmaceuticals cases where millions of consumers were seriously injured by exposure to dangerous products that

---

Malpractice Claims, Verdicts and the "Doctor Exodus" in Illinois, 59 VANDERBILT L. REV. 1309 (2006); Vidmar, *Trial by Jury Involving Persons Accused of Terrorism or Supporting Terrorism*, in Belinda Brooks Gordon and Michael Freeman, (Eds.), LAW AND PSYCHOLOGY, page 318, Vol. 9, Oxford University Press (2006); with Valerie Hans, JUDGING THE JURY (1986), author of MEDICAL MALPRACTICE AND THE AMERICAN JURY (1995); Editor/author of WORLD JURY SYSTEMS (2000).

[46]   Professor Joan Vogel specializes in employment law, anthropology of law, consumer law, medical malpractice, and tort reform at Vermont Law School and teaches Commercial Law, Employment Law, Alternative Dispute Resolution, and Torts. Professor Vogel received a BA degree from George Washington, and an MA in and a J.D. from the University of California at Los Angeles. She served as a teaching associate in UCLA's anthropology department from 1975 to 1976 and also performed research in African law. She clerked for Judge Alfred T. Goodwin of the United States Court of Appeals, Ninth Circuit, in Oregon from 1981 to 1982 and from 1982 to 1989 taught at the University of Pittsburgh School of Law, Albany Law School, and Oklahoma City University Law School before joining the faculty at Vermont Law School in 1989. She testified before the Vermont Senate Judiciary Committee on modification of the state's Human Rights Commission in 1995 and was a consultant for the drafting of Vermont's employment law bill in 1997. In 1998, she helped to write the tobacco reimbursement statute that passed the Vermont legislature. Professor Vogel has presented widely on topics of legal pluralism, new teaching methods in labor law, tort reform, and on the "Lemon Laws." She has served as chair of the Law and Anthropology and the Labor and Employment Law sections of the Association of American Law Schools.

manufacturers marketed knowing their dangers. This is a one-sided campaign aimed at an easy target. The Tort Reform Movement has mastered the basic reality about politics. What works and what lasts in the public mind matters far more than the truth of the matter at hand. After all, not many people know much about the tort system and frankly, plaintiffs' attorneys have not had the resources to respond adequately to this onslaught. Consumer groups lack the resources to respond to each false charge in a systematic way nor have they been able to publicize the benefits of the torts system in making America safer.

Even if political opponents of the Tort Reform Movement have not been able to stop this movement, it is very important that those of us who teach tort law, who believe that truth always matters and who believe that the system, even with its shortcomings, has great value, use our classes and casebooks to correct the many misconceptions that the Tort Reform Movement has helped to create. One of the best ways to do this is to remind our students how important it is for them to develop good critical-reasoning skills that all good lawyers and frankly all citizens really need to do their jobs as professionals and good citizens. We are constantly being bombarded by public relations campaigns by corporate and other political interests that want us to believe what they say about the legal system. We should take nothing at face value. We should always carefully weigh and examine the evidence and arguments before we make any decision. As we know in the legal profession, decision-making is often a complex and difficult process not amenable to thirty-second sound-bites.

One good place to start is to review some of the tort horror stories that the Tort Reform Movement have distorted for political gain. In the casebook I co-authored,[47] we used *Liebeck v. McDonald,*[48] one of the more "notorious" stories publicized by the Tort Reform Movement to highlight how the tort system veered out of control. We used the real facts of the case and two hypothetical versions of the case to demonstrate the three major branches of tort law, intentional torts, negligence, and strict liability. In our discussion of negligence, we took the opportunity to acquaint the students with the real facts of the case.

Far from being a frivolous case as claimed by the tort reformers, Stella Liebeck suffered third-degree burns after the lid slipped off the coffee cup and spilled over her groin and. thighs. McDonalds served their coffee at a much high temperature than other fast-food and coffee restaurants and the coffee at that temperature caused third-degree burns within three seconds of touching Ms. Liebeck's skin. McDonalds had received more than 700 similar claims before hers. McDonalds' own witnesses testified that the

---

[47]   Dominick Vetri, Lawrence Levine, Joan Vogel and Ibrahim Gassama, TORT LAW AND PRACTICE (5th ed. 2016).

[48]   *Liebeck v. McDonald's Restaurants, P.T.S. Inc.,* No. D–202 CV–93–02419, 1195 WL 360309 (Bernalillo County, N.M. Dist. Ct. August 18, 1994).

company had no plans to lower the temperature of the coffee despite the prior claims because the number of burns were small compared to the millions of cups of coffee they served. The jury believed McDonalds was recklessly indifferent about consumers' safety and the jury verdict for compensatory damages and punitive damages reflected its concern about McDonald's attitude. The New Mexico jury also reduced the Liebeck's compensatory damage award for her contributory negligence. Under New Mexico's state law, the jury assigns a percentage of fault to each responsible party and then apportions the fault. The jury determined that Stella Liebeck's apportionment of fault was 20% and McDonalds' was 80% responsible for the injuries that she sustained. In a system of comparative fault, the judge must then reduce Stella Liebeck's recovery by the amount attributable to the plaintiff's fault. In addition, the judge slashed the punitive damages significantly to three times the compensatory damages. Although all of these facts were mentioned in a *Wall Street Journal* article[49] on the case published several days after the verdict, these facts were conveniently excluded from the tort reform propaganda that excoriated the verdict as an example of a runaway jury.

The public tends to remember this case as an example of a frivolous coffee burn case filed by a clumsy old woman who spilled coffee on herself. The true facts are obscured by this propaganda. By using this case and showing the real facts we want students to develop a healthy skepticism of how torts cases are reported in the press. The mainstream press has been a real ally of the Tort Reform Movement in its failure to do its own reporting. If the *Liebeck* case is any indication, the press often takes the tort reform press releases and recycles these as the news. We must remind the students to critically evaluate the trial or appellate cases and not accept these reports at face value.

Why is the torts system so important in our society? We should think about the torts system as the "canary in the mine." The miners took canaries down in the mines to warn about the buildup of lethal methane gas and carbon dioxide that threatened their air supply and in the case of methane, often lead to explosions. The miners could have confidence in their air supply and that the risk of explosions was low as long as the canaries kept singing. In a functionally similar way, our torts system is the first alert system about dangerous products or practices. Like the caged canary taken into the mines, the torts system gives us an early warning to dangerous activities and products often long before governmental regulators discover them. Private attorneys who bring personal injury actions are not stymied by the political pressures and bureaucratic limitations that prevent prompt regulatory agency action. Also, injured parties can only receive adequate compensation through the torts system.

---

[49]   Andrea Gerlin, *A Matter of Degree: How a Jury Decided That a Coffee Spill is Worth $2.9 Million.* THE WALL STREET JOURNAL, Sept. 1, 1994 at A1.

Administrative agencies rarely provide for much in the way of compensation for injured parties[50]. We should also not forget all the safety innovations that may never have occurred if it had not been for tort litigation. For example, the field of medicine, sponge and instrument counts are a direct result of professional liability lawsuits. We are all much safer as the result of tort lawsuits that removed dangerously defective products from the marketplace.

If we are interested in genuine reform of the torts system, most of us who recognize its value can recommend a number of changes that we might like to see. The difference is that we would start from very different premises then the current Tort Reform Movement. Far from there being too many torts cases, the evidence suggests that far more torts occur them are ever brought. With too few cases, we do not have enough deterrence in the torts system. The empirical data also shows that many more tort cases exist than are actually brought in our courts, and of the few that are filed, the over ninety-five percent of cases that are filed are dropped or settled. It takes too long and costs too much to bring a torts case.

Our government should invest more resources in the courts system to bring down the length of time it takes to have a civil case heard in court. Our society should also increase access to court by providing more (expanding legal aid) access to lawyers especially for injured plaintiffs with smaller cases so they can recover as well. If we really want to "think outside the box," we might create a comprehensive, federal disability system that provides injured and seriously ill individuals with generous monetary support when they are rendered disabled because of an accident. Social Security disability is stingy and hard to get. At some point soon I hope, we may even get fully funded medical care for everyone in this county[51]. Both these measures would go a long way in reducing accident and injury costs that injured individuals now have to bear. We could then let plaintiffs use

---

[50]   The exceptions are of, course, workers' compensation which is an administrative system, and special government compensation claim systems like the one set up for claims after 9–11 attacks.

[51]   The Patient Protection and Affordable Care Act of 2010 (P.L no.111–148) and its companion legislation, the Health Care and Education Reconciliation Act of 2010 (P.L. no.111–152) (provisions of both legislation are spread throughout the United States Code) provided health care coverage to over 20 million Americans who did not have access to "health care insurance coverage" previously through health insurance reform, and federal subsidies for insurance premiums. *20 Million People Have Gained Health Insurance Coverage Because of the Affordable Care Act, New Estimates Show*, Health and Human Services Press Release (March 3, 2016) http://hhs.gov/about/news/2016/03/03/20-million-people-have-gained-health-insurance-coverage-because-afforable-care-act-new-estimates. In addition, more low income individuals gained access to health care through the extension of Medicaid in states that agreed to expand the program to cover more low income individuals. These changes provide a good beginning, but health care costs remain a problem in this system and not everyone is covered as they would be in a single-payer system.

the torts system to recover damages for emotional harm and other forms of non-pecuniary harm[52] that tort reformers also revile.[53]

TODD J. ZYWICKI[54] AND DR. JEREMY KIDD, [55] PUBLIC CHOICE AND TORT REFORM

Our modern system of tort law has become increasingly costly, consuming approximately two percent of U.S. GDP over the last two decades, most of which is used to run the system, rather than to compensate injured parties. In addition to these direct costs, the ever-expanding regime of liability raises the cost of such products as stepladders and vaccines. It inhibits innovation to the tune of over $360 billion in lost sales of new products each year and makes it increasingly difficult for U.S. businesses to compete internationally. It raises the cost of health care by encouraging doctors to engage in "defensive medicine," making medical judgments on the basis of avoiding malpractice suits, rather than in the best medical interests of the patient. Moreover, it is increasingly clear that these high costs do not result in the promised increased safety or services.

Reform of the tort system promises reduction in the heavy costs described above, yet tort reform efforts have met with minimal tangible

---

[52]   By the way, you should also notice that when tort reformers talk about reforming the torts system, they only mean personal injury torts like negligence and product liability that affect ordinary people. They do not mean reforming business torts, like appropriation of trade secrets, that businesses rely on to protect their own interests.

[53]   For more of Professor Vogel's recent scholarship, *see* With Dominick Vetri, Lawrence Levine, and Ibrahim Gassama, TORT LAW AND PRACTICE, 5TH ED. (Carolina Academic Press 2016); *Cases in Context: Lake Champlain Wars, Gentrification, and Ploof v. Putnam*, 45 ST. LOUIS U. L.J. 791 (2001).

[54]   **Professor Zywicki** is the University Foundation Professor of Law at George Mason University School of Law and Senior Scholar of the Mercatus Center at George Mason. He is Co-Editor of the *Supreme Court Economic Review*. He has served as Director of the Office of Policy Planning at the Federal Trade Commission. He has also taught at Vanderbilt University Law School, Georgetown University Law Center, Boston College Law School, and Mississippi College School of Law. Professor Zywicki clerked for Judge Jerry E. Smith of the U.S. Court of Appeals for the Fifth Circuit and worked as an associate at Alston & Bird in Atlanta, Georgia, where he practiced bankruptcy and commercial law. He received his J.D. from the University of Virginia, where he was the John M. Olin Scholar in Law and Economics. Professor Zywicki received his M.A. from Clemson University and A.B. from Dartmouth College. Professor Zywicki is a Senior Fellow of the James Buchanan Center, a Senior Fellow of the Goldwater Institute, and a Fellow of the International Centre for Economic Research in Turin, Italy. Professor Zywicki is the author of more than 70 articles in leading law reviews and peer-reviewed economics journals. He has testified before Congress on issues of consumer bankruptcy law and consumer credit and is a frequent commentator on legal issues in the print and broadcast media. He is a member of the Board of Trustees of Yorktown University and an Alumni Trustee of Dartmouth College.

[55]   **Dr. Jeremy Kidd** is an Associate Professor of Law at the Walter F. George School of Law at Mercer University. He received his J.D. from George Mason University where he was a Levy Fellow. He received his Ph.D. in economics from Utah State University. He has worked for the law firms of Ballard Spahr Andrews & Ingersoll in Washington, DC and Strong & Hanni in Salt Lake City, UT, and served as Legislative Assistant to former Rep. James V. Hansen (R-UT), as a law clerk for Hon. Ted Stewart in the U.S. District Court. D. Utah, and for Hon. Alice Batchelder, U.S. Court of Appeals for the Sixth Circuit.

success. Public choice theory offers insight into why those parties who stand to gain or lose from reform take the actions they do to ensure that their personal wealth is maximized, taking into consideration significant uncertainty.

Plaintiffs' attorneys push to change common law tort doctrines in favor of doctrines that increase potential liability for defendants because they stand to increase their personal wealth as their clients receive larger and larger jury awards. They also push for increasingly complex tort doctrines which increase the likelihood that any given individual will, wittingly or no, take action which will result in a tort lawsuit. Defense attorneys, while often paying lip service to tort reform, also stand to increase their wealth as they are required to defend against a larger number of increasingly complex lawsuits. Attorneys on both sides work to limit the supply of lawyers by erecting barriers to entry.

Judges have traditionally provided a barrier to the rational self-interest of lawyers, but recent decades have seen a decrease in the number of judges who see themselves as performing the modest role of maintaining the rules of an ongoing spontaneous order framework of law, society, and the market, and an increase in the number of judges who see the bench as a platform of achieving social change, much of which coincides with increased liability for manufacturers and other monied interests. In states with elected judiciaries, judges will also be subject to the pressure that arises from having wealthy plaintiffs' lawyers contributing to their campaigns; that is, if the judges are not wealthy former plaintiffs' lawyers, themselves. In many states where judges are appointed, bar associations exert a tremendous influence over those whose names are available for appointment. Judges, therefore, can no longer be relied upon to protect society from the cost of increased liability.

Other interests, such as insurers, manufacturers, and consumers may have distinct incentives to support limiting liability and lessening complexity, but those incentives are countered by high coordination costs. It is often said that insurance companies bear the cost of increased liability. However, insurance companies earn a normal return on insuring an amortized amount of risk, and as the amount of the total risk insured increases, the number and value of the policies written and the net return to the insurer also will increase. So long as liability and damages are predictable and low-variance, insurance companies will be indifferent or even favorable toward higher average liability levels and damage awards.

Manufacturers face staggering costs imposed by the tort system, but manufacturers will generally not make a very effective force in counterbalancing the incentives of lawyers and judges to expand liability, in large part because, as a group, they face a comparative disadvantage in fighting for legal reform against lawyers. Whereas a plaintiffs' lawyer collects some benefit from each case in which liability is extended, any single manufacturer has little incentive to fight for a reformed liability regime, because most of the benefits will be shared with other manufacturers. Organizing manufacturers in favor of tort reform can also be problematic because, apart from certain general limitations on liability, the various industries and sectors will have different priorities, making it difficult to decide upon a single slate of reform proposals. Only medical practitioners have been successful in organizing on behalf of reform, and those successes are likely the result of: (1) the special relationship between the public and their doctors; and (2) the strong barriers to entry into the medical profession, which allows for easier coordination of effort and punishment of those who do not participate in reform efforts.

In the end, consumers bear most of the costs of the tort system, but coordination of individuals in favor of reform is, of course, even more complicated than organizing manufacturers. In fact, consumers are generally considered to be the exemplary case of a group that is virtually impossible to organize into a coherent group to pursue collective action. Typically, the only consumer that will be heard in any case is the plaintiff, who certainly does not have any incentive to argue for limited liability. Other factors also make reform difficult, such as the fact that certain communities have realized that they can cash in on a form of litigation tourism, bringing in outside dollars via lawsuits.

With the array of forces opposing tort reform, and the obstacles to those favoring reform, it would seem improbable that tort reform would ever be successful. However, tort reform advocates have managed to achieve a certain amount of success. Reform on the federal level has been very limited, with the Class Action Reform Act as the only federal reform of the past decades. On the state level, nearly every state has enacted some form of tort reform and Texas, Missouri, Arkansas, Ohio, Mississippi, Georgia, South Carolina, Colorado, and Oklahoma have all enacted comprehensive reforms.

It appears that tort reform is likely only under certain circumstances. The deadweight costs of tort liability must be high enough to allow for reformers to claim the existence of a crisis. That crisis will open the door for a political entrepreneur, who can see and seize opportunities for reform. Such an entrepreneur will be able to achieve reforms in proportion to the scope of the crisis, with the industries most in crisis being more likely to receive relief from reform. This means that most reforms will be narrowly tailored to a specific geographical area and subject matter, such as state medical malpractice reforms. More expansive tort reform would seem to require a crisis of inefficiency generated by the current regime and/or a very capable political entrepreneur. Tort reform is still possible in the absence of a political entrepreneur, but we would anticipate that the scope and strength of the reform will be significantly lessened. Each of the states that has enacted comprehensive reform has done so only after a crisis developed, and in all but one a political entrepreneur (usually the Governor) has been the primary motivator of reform.[56]

MICHAEL RUSTAD,[57] THE ENDLESS CAMPAIGN: HOW THE TORT REFORMERS SUCCESSFULLY AND INCESSANTLY MARKET THEIR GROUPTHINK TO THE REST OF US

Americans instinctively know that between two products, one well-marketed and one well-made, the better marketed product prevails in the marketplace. The argument of consumer protection advocates and plaintiffs' attorneys that tort lawsuits serve a useful, productive, and economically efficient role in our society has never had a chance against the slick and successful marketing of the tort reform players. While the former group appeals to notions of justice and fairness, backed by empirical

---

[56] For more of Professor Zywicki's recent scholarship, see BANKRUPTCY AND PERSONAL RESPONSIBILITY: BANKRUPTCY LAW AND POLICY IN THE TWENTY-FIRST CENTURY (Yale University Press, Forthcoming 2009); PUBLIC CHOICE AND TORT REFORM (with Jeremy Kidd) (AEI Press, Forthcoming 2009); PUBLIC CHOICE CONCEPTS AND APPLICATIONS IN LAW (with Maxwell Stearns) (West Publishing, Forthcoming 2009); Editor, The Rule of Law, Freedom, and Prosperity, 10 SUPREME COURT ECONOMIC REVIEW (Chicago: University of Chicago Press, (2003); Three Problematic Truths About the Consumer Financial Protection Agency Act of 2009, 1 Lombard Street, No. 12 (2009); The Market for Information and Credit Card Regulation, 28(1) Banking and Financial Service Policy Report 13 (2009); The Law and Economics of Subprime Lending (with Joseph Adamson), 80 UNIVERSITY OF COLORADO L. REV. 1 (2009); Spontaneous Order and the Common Law: Gordon Tullock's Critique, 135 PUBLIC CHOICE 35–53 (2008); Posner, Hayek and The Economic Analysis of Law (with Anthony B. Sanders), 93 IOWA L. REV. 559 (2008), working paper; Institutional Review Boards as Academic Bureaucracies: An Economic and Experiential Analysis, 101 NORTHWESTERN L. REV. 861 (2007).

For more of Dr. Kidd's recent scholarship, see An Economic Model Costing "Early Offers" Medical Malpractice Reform, 35 N.M. L. REV. 259 (2005) (with Jeffrey O'Connell and Evan Stephenson) and The Collateral Source Rule: Explanation and Defense, 48 LOUISVILLE L. REV. 1 (2009) (with Michael Krauss).

[57] **Dr. Michael L. Rustad** is the Thomas F. Lambert Jr. Professor of Law and Co-director of the Intellectual Property Law Concentration at Suffolk University Law School in Boston, Massachusetts. He teaches international contract law, e-Business Law, and Internet Law in Suffolk's LL.M. program in U.S. and global business law. He has also taught international business law subjects and the Uniform Commercial Code in Sweden and Mexico. Professor Rustad clerked for the late Judge William E. Doyle of the 10th Circuit U.S. Court of Appeals in Denver, Colorado and served as an associate with the Boston law firm of Foley, Hoag, prior to becoming a law professor. Professor Rustad has testified before both Houses of Congress and has authored or co-authored three amicus briefs before the U.S. Supreme Court on the constitutionality of punitive damages. He is an elected member of the American Law Institute and belongs to the Member Consultative Groups of the Restatement of the Law (Third) Torts and Principles of Software Contracts. He was elected to the Executive Committee of the American Association of Law Schools Section on Torts and Compensation Systems. In 2009–10, he was elected secretary of the AALS torts section. Professor Rustad has also served as a task force leader for the ABA Business Law Section on Information Licensing. His most recent books are the five volume treatise COMPUTER CONTRACTS: NEGOTIATING, DRAFTING (Lexis/Nexis 2016) GLOBAL INTERNET LAW IN A NUTSHELL (3rd ed. 2016), and GLOBAL INTERNET LAW (HORNBOOK SERIES, (2d ed. 2016). His forthcoming books are SOFTWARE LICENSING, CLOUD COMPUTING & INTERNET TERMS OF USE: GLOBAL INFORMATION AGE CONTRACTS (Lexis/Nexis 2016) and INFORMATION AGE LAW AND ETHICS.

evidence of widespread improvements in public health and safety, tort reformers capture the public imagination with their creative and incessant use of tort horror stories. One such scary tale involves a clumsy, old woman who spilled her hot coffee on her lap and unjustly won millions of dollars in punitive damages through her frivolous lawsuit. Tort reformers are not embarrassed to cite the McDonald's hot coffee case as an example of random, "jackpot justice." The case became familiar to the public as an example of a tort world out of control. The joke was even picked up by the *Seinfeld* television show when Kramer filed suit after he burned himself when smuggling a hot latte into a movie theatre.

Each year I ask my first year tort students to fill out a brief questionnaire about their opinions about the widely-known McDonald's hot coffee case. Most of my law students view the litigation as a frivolous lawsuit and are unaware of the severity of the plaintiff's injuries or that she required skin grafts. The public never understood the dire nature of the injuries suffered by the victim nor that McDonald's own records revealed that the corporation had prior notice of more than 700 prior complaints of burns caused by coffee served between 180 and 190 degrees. The news reports about the case largely featured the tort reformers' narrative. Even lawmakers were deceived by the distorted presentations in the mass media. In a 1997 case, The Illinois Supreme Court struck down that state's 1995 tort reform statute as unconstitutional. In the majority opinion, the court observed that tort reform advocates cited the hot coffee case in misleading ways in the legislative debates that led to the enactment of the 1995 Civil Justice Reform Act. . . .

In that case, it was reported that an 81-year-old woman received a $2.9 million punitive damages verdict for injuries incurred after she spilled hot coffee in her lap. However, less widely reported was that the verdict was reduced by the court to $480,000, the elderly woman underwent numerous skin graft operations for third degree burns, and McDonald's had prior knowledge of hundreds of similar scalding incidents. Also, the excessive award was for punitive, not compensatory damages.[58]

The agenda of the tort reformers is succinctly explained by Joanne Doroshow when she challenges us to: ". . .[T]hink of their goal: to convince average Americans to give up their rights to go to court against reckless corporations and to make sure the insurance industry can keep a little more money in its pocket. That's what 'tort reform' is. And that is some PR feat."[59]

---

[58] *Best v. Taylor Mach. Works*, 179 Ill. 2d 367, 387, 689 N.E.2d 1057, 1068 (Ill. 1997) (citing Michael Rustad, *Nationalizing Tort Law: The Republican Attack on Women, Blue Collar Workers and Consumers,* 48 RUTGERS L. REV. 678, 720–21 (1996)).

[59] Joanne Doroshow, *The Secret Chamber of Commerce and its 'Tort Reform' Mission*, HUFFINGTON POST (October 28, 2009).

We need to account for the phenomenal success of the marketing campaign by the tort reformers. Irving Janis, the social psychologist, popularized the term "Groupthink" to explain the collective effort of groups to develop a single mindset rather than carefully evaluate policy alternatives individually.[60] Tort reform became one of the most successful social movements in American history by encouraging the public to adopt its' groupthink about the need for tort reform. The tort reformers have used the media to market their narrow and selfish ideology to the general public. The media obliges the tort reformer's constant and well-funded effort by its indolent failure to pursue the facts of the matter or discuss them intelligently with qualified experts. The tort reformers obviously consider the media the battleground for its views to become the dominant ones, but the media does not seem to appreciate that there is an ideological war going on.[61] The media easily slides into complacency about the need for tort reform, and adapts to and ultimately adopts the narrow, ideological tort reform groupthink. All the talking heads on MSNBC's *Morning Joe* nod that tort reform is necessary, exchanging anecdotes rather than citing objective studies. Credible scholars have presented empirical evidence questioning whether the tort system is in crisis.[62] Very little about tort law or empirical data about real world torts is in the heads of the talking heads that appear regularly on television. For instance, the vital role of "pain and suffering" awards in protecting the interests of women are ignored.[63]

Tort reformers demonize greedy plaintiffs and their even greedier attorneys as the enemies of the common good by coining slogans such as lawsuit abuse, tort tax, litigation lottery, and jackpot justice. Tort reform groupthink caricatures plaintiffs by portraying them as amoral persons who refuse to take personal responsibility for their own injuries like the careless old lady in the McDonald's case. Public relations experts use iconic tort stories that appeal to emotion rather than reason:

> These popular (and grossly distorted) law stories could be tag lines
> in a Jay Leno comedy monologue. In fact, most of them have been.
> And that's the point. Told from a certain angle, these anecdotal

---

[60]   Irving Janis, GROUP THINK: PSYCHOLOGICAL STUDIES OF POLICY DECISIONS AND FIASCOES (Houghton Mifflin: 2d ed. 1983) at 248.

[61]   Jay M. Feinman has documented how ATRA and other tort reformers have organized to convince courts and legislatures to roll back consumers' rights of recovery, therefore benefitting corporate defendants).

[62]   *See, e.g.,* U.S. Dep't of Justice, Bureau of Justice statistics, Tort Trials and Verdicts in Large Counties, 1996 (NCJ 179769) (Aug. 2000) (finding punitive awards in only three percent of cases and a median award of only $38,000); Neil Vidmar & Mary R. Rose, *Punitive Damages by Juries in Florida: In Terrorem and in Reality,* 38 HARV. J. LEGIS. 487 (2001) (finding punitive damage awards in Florida "strikingly low"); Michael L. Rustad, *Unraveling Punitive Damages: Current Data and Further Inquiry,* 1998 WIS. L. REV. 15 ("Every empirical study of punitive damages demonstrates that there is no nationwide punitive damage crisis."); and Stephen Daniels & Joanne Martin, *Myth and Reality in Punitive Damages,* 75 MINN. L. REV. 1, 64 (1990) (concluding that claims of a punitive damage crisis were "unfounded, and perhaps manufactured.").

[63]   Id.

tales are funny, and pathetic, but they pack a powerful moral punch. It's what they've been designed to do. They warn us about (1) slackers, self-professed victims, who insist on blaming others for their own faults; (2) greedy and unscrupulous lawyers who play the system for cash; and (3) hapless jurors who get hoodwinked in the process. These carefully chosen narratives reveal the plague of lawyers in our midst and the litigation explosion that they've unleashed.[64]

The proponents of tort reform have convinced the majority of Americans that their sympathies should lie with habitual corporate wrongdoers, such as the tobacco and pharmaceutical industries, rather than consumers injured by excessive preventable dangers. In reality, tort reform measures often adversely affect consumers, workers, and racial and cultural minorities.[65] The vital role of "pain and suffering" awards in protecting the interests of women is largely ignored.[66]

The first successful strategy in marketing tort reform groupthink to the rest of us was to employ the self-label of tort "reformers," a term that connotes improvements in the law. In fact, the goal is to roll back post Second World War II reforms through which legislatures and courts improved the law by eliminating harsh doctrines such as contributory negligence, the fellow servant rule, and charitable immunity, which excluded entire classes of victims of excessive risk-taking. An example of the true meaning of tort reform that evolved in the 1960s and 1970s is the patient's right to be informed of material risks of medical procedures. Hospitals developed protocols created instrument and sponge counts as a response to medical malpractice claims filed by patients who had surgical instruments, towels, and other foreign objects inadvertently sewed into their bodily cavities.

Medical malpractice liability could not have evolved without legislatures and courts repudiating charitable immunity and holding physicians to a more nationalized standard of care. Courts employed creative tort reforms to recognize nursing home neglect, bad faith insurance settlement, and premises liability to bring common sense to the common law. Prior to the 1960s, product manufacturers were shielded from

---

[64] *Litigation Public Relations: Tort Reform, New York Law School, Visual Litigation Project* (Richard K. Sherwin Founder) https://papers.ssrn.com/sol3/papers.cfm?abstract_id=1614983.

[65] See e.g., Frank McClellan, *The Dark Side of Tort Reform: Searching for Racial Justice*, 48 RUTGERS L. REV. 761 (1996); See generally, Thomas H. Koenig & Michael L. Rustad, IN DEFENSE OF TORT LAW (New York, New York: New York University Press, 2001) at 67 (documenting how tort reform negatively impacts less powerful groups in American society such as women, minorities, and workers); Martha Chamallas & Jennifer Wriggins, THE MEASURE OF JUSTICE: RACE, GENDER, AND TORT LAW (New York, New York: New York University Press, 2010) (arguing that tort reform negatively impacts women and minorities, groups that have been victimized by disparate recovery under our civil justice system).

[66] Thomas H. Koenig & Michael L. Rustad, *His and Her Tort Reform: Gender Injustice In Disguise*, 70 WASH. L. REV. 1 (1995).

liability by the harsh doctrine of privity and the notice requirement of Article 2 of the U.C.C. William Prosser wrote that the erosion of the privity rule in products liability was "the most rapid and altogether spectacular overturn of an established rule in the entire history of the law of torts."[67] Products liability could not develop in a privity of contract regime because no national manufacturer was responsible for injuries caused by placing defective products into the stream of commerce unless they had a direct contractual link with the injured consumer.

Prior to World War II, the doctrine of spousal and family immunity shielded brutal husbands that terrorized their families. Legislatures and courts throughout the country have repudiated or limited family immunities. Hotels, colleges, and shopping malls across the country have improved security after courts increasingly recognized the concept of premises liability. Progressive tort reforms after World War II recognized entire new categories of plaintiffs including, but not limited to, the victims of mass-marketed products, hospital negligence, gender discrimination, racial discrimination, and toxic exposures.[68] Today's tort reform is a regressive movement formed as a backlash to progressive reforms enacted by courts and legislatures after World War II. Tort reform is a well-financed movement, developed by some of the best legal minds that money can buy, to set the clock back on tort rights and remedies against corporate oppression, not torts employed by corporations to assert their legal rights. Tort reformers do not call for placing limitations on corporations' ability to recover punitive damages in business tort cases or to aggressively use the legal system to protect their own intellectual property rights.

Tort Limitations Backlash

Tort law has played an important role in making all Americans safer because of better designed products, improved medical protocols, and greater security. However, beginning in the 1960s and 1970s, the insurance industry launched a campaign to engineer a new consensus about America's civil justice system. Their campaign for "tort reform" focused on how lawsuit abuse by ordinary Americans was creating a tort tax on businesses, negatively affecting America's economic well-being. The insurance industry's coalition, habitual defendants in personal injury lawsuits, produced the most successful law "reform" movement in Anglo-American history. A 1970 Aetna advertisement is emblematic of the

---

[67]   William Prosser, HANDBOOK OF THE LAW OF TORTS (4th ed. 1971) 654, n.8.

[68]   In the post-War II period until the late 1960s, tort reform was largely pro-consumer. Legislatures and courts changed tort law by eliminating harsh defenses and immunities to give consumers remedies for harms or injuries caused by corporate wrongdoers. Tort reforms after World War II referred to progressive changes in medical malpractice law, products liability, premises liability, and other substantive fields to enable consumers to recover for injuries due to excessive, preventable risks. Thomas H. Koenig & Michael L. Rustad, IN DEFENSE OF TORT LAW (New York, New York, New York University Press, 2001) at 46.

insurance industry's systematic campaign to control and regiment cultural attitudes about the need for tort reform:

> Most of us know hair-raising stories of windfall awards won in court. . . . Insurers, lawyers, judges—each of us shares some blame for this mess. But it is you, the public, who can best begin to clean it up. (1970's Aetna Advertisement). The jury smiles when they made the award. They didn't know it was coming out of their own pockets. You *really* think it's the insurance company that's paying for all those large jury awards. Suicidal Impulse. . . . The system seems to be saying, 'No matter what happens, somebody must pay—preferably somebody rich!'[69]

Corporate propagandists often portray the call for tort limitations as a grass roots movement led by ordinary Americans. In reality, tort reform is an astro-turf movement by public relations professionals that represent America's most powerful corporations and insurance companies.[70] Tort reform lobbyists, accounting firms, and occasionally fellow judges have organized efforts to convince the judiciary of the need for tort reform of punitive damages.[71]

The Product Liability Coordinating Committee (PLCC), formed in 1987, coordinates the activities of eight organizations: The American Tort Reform Association (ATRA), the Product Liability Alliance, the Business Roundtable, the United States Chamber of Commerce, the National Association of Manufacturers, the Chemical Manufacturers Association, the Coalition for Uniform Product Liability Laws, and the National Federation of Independent Businesses. ATRA-sponsored state groups introduced comprehensive tort reform legislation scaling back punitive damages in several states.

ATRA released its 2015–2016 Judicial Hell Holes report listing jurisdictions that are pro-plaintiff.[72] ATRA dubbed California the "epicenter" for ridiculous class lawsuits against the food and beverage industry as well as frivolous disability access and asbestos lawsuits.[73] ATRA is funded by the pillars of America's corporate establishment. Media Matters noted "Many of ATRA's members are Fortune 500 companies, including "representatives of the tobacco, insurance, chemical, auto, and pharmaceutical companies"—all industries with a history of questionable

---

[69] Joanne Doroshow, THE CASE FOR THE CIVIL JURY: SAFEGUARDING A PILLAR OF DEMOCRACY (1992) at Appendix A.

[70] Michael Bradford, *Tort Reform Proponents See Boost From Bush Plan,* BUS. INS., February 17, 1992, at 2 ("ATRA will be heading back to 20 state legislatures in an effort to protect tort reform gains in recent years or fight bills that would expand liability.").

[71] *See e.g.,* Alliance for Justice, JUSTICE FOR SALE: SHORTCHANGING THE PUBLIC INTEREST FOR PRIVATE GAIN (1993) (describing "reeducation" programs for judges and the general public sponsored by conservative foundations and corporations).

[72] AMERICAN TORT REFORM ASSOCIATION, JUDICIAL HELLHOLES (Washington D.C. American Tort Reform Association, 2016).

[73] *Id.* at 1.

business practices."[74] The Judicial Hellhole annual reports are based upon selection distortion of anecdotal reports rather than systematic empirical data.[75] Tort scholars have long questioned whether there are tort hellholes requiring further tort reform.[76] Tort reformers reject the scientific validity of punitive damage research that does not comport with their groupthink mindset that tort law is in crisis.

Groupthink in the tort reform movement is a homogenization of viewpoints that blinds members to alternative perspectives. Groupthink leads to an unquestioned belief in the group's inherent morality. The tort reformers groupthink is that punitive damages are a remedy in crisis.[77] The stereotyped view of trial lawyers as a corrupt enemy seeking only to redistribute wealth from corporations to greedy widows and children and their still greedier attorneys is an example of groupthink promoted by tort reformers. The tort reform movement has been successful in re-orientating ordinary Americans' natural sympathy with the injured in order to advance its campaign of tort limitations. The tort reform movement, since the 1970s, has spawned special legislation reducing the recovery of injured victims of medical malpractice and products liability. More than half of the states have now adopted statutory caps on awards for pain and suffering or non-economic damages.[78] One popular misconception is that out of control juries grant primarily million-dollar-plus verdicts. Sherman Joyce, the President of the American Tort Reform Association, writes about how

---

[74] Megan Hatcher-Mayes, Forbes *Hypes Still-Ridiculous "Judicial Hellholes" Report*, MediaMatters (December 19, 2013).

[75] "[T]he report's "judicial hellhole" selection methodology is entirely subjective. The report states that hellholes are a compilation of "the most significant court rulings and legislative rulings" in jurisdictions "where judges in civil cases systematically apply laws and court procedures in an unfair and unbalanced manner." ATRA admits in the report that it "reflects feedback gathered from ATRA members," rather from statistical evidence—meaning that the very companies that underwrite the report have a hand in determining which cases are "the most significant." In the past, ATRA has admitted that previous hellhole reports "never claimed to be an empirical study." *Id.*

[76] See e.g., Neil Vidmar, Russell M. Robinson II, & Kara MacKillop, *Judicial Hellholes: Medical Malpractice Claims, Verdicts, and the "Doctor Exodus" in Illinois*, 59 VAND. L. REV. 1309 (2006); See also, Donald C. Dilworth, *Court Statistics Confirm No Litigation Explosion*, TRIAL (May 1996) at 19) (finding no evidence that the number of tort cases is increasing and that in fact tort litigation is in decline since 1996); Richard Abel, *The Real Torts Crisis—Too Few Claims*, 48 OHIO ST. L.J. 443 (1997) (contending that tort law is too restrictive and does not perform its compensatory function); Michael J. Saks, *Medical Malpractice Facing Real Problems and Finding Real Solutions*, 35 WM. & MARY L. REV. 693, 703(1994) (contending that there are too few medical malpractice reforms leaving many injured patients without a remedy); Michael L. Rustad, *The Closing of Punitive Damages' Iron Cage*, 38 LOY. L.A. L. REV. 1297 (2005).

[77] See, e.g., Michael L. Rustad, *The Closing of Punitive Damages' Iron Cage*, 38 LOY. L.A. REV. 1297, 1360 (2005).

[78] Thomas C. Galligan, Phoebe A. Haddon, Frank L. Maraist, Frank McClellan, Michael L. Rustad, Nicolas P. Terry and Stephanie M. Wildman, TORT LAW: CASES, PROBLEMS, AND PERSPECTIVES (New York, New York: Lexis/Nexis 2007) at 995.

"[h]undreds of millions in punitive damages [are] piled on top of relatively minor actual damages."[79]

Huge punitive damage awards make good headlines, but they are not typical of America's civil justice system. The tort reformers' portrayal of punitive damage awards veering out of control is rebutted by social science empirical research. All empirical studies come to the same conclusion, despite diversity of authorship and sponsorship. Punitive damages are rarely awarded and tightly controlled by trial and appellate courts.[80]

Professor William Landes and Judge Richard Posner, for example, found no evidence of skyrocketing punitive damages in either size or number.[81] The unanimous findings of academic research studies on punitive damages demonstrates that these awards are rare and tightly controlled is at odds with the tort reformers' portrayal of punitive damages as a remedy in crisis. Tort reformers insist that all scientific studies (with which they do not agree) are politically charged and evaluative, rather than neutral and methodologically valid. Their refusal to debate policy alternatives on empirical grounds also illustrates groupthink. Classical liberalism, a la John Stuart Mills, that brings all arguments to the table for a complete discussion, advances the scientific approach by facilitating creative and critical thinking.

Cultural Groupthink

Tort reformers often employ the theme of personal responsibility to marginalize plaintiffs seeking compensation for mass torts. For example, the tort reformers "attacked the plaintiff in a landmark tobacco product liability action by arguing that the plaintiff should have taken personal responsibility for the cancer caused by her smoking rather than blame the tobacco industry."[82] This groupthink about corporate victimhood "deflects attention away from the true victims: those who suffered from defective

---

[79]   Sherman Joyce, *A Message from ATRA President*, Sherman Joyce, http://www.atra.org/about/ (last visited Oct. 22, 2009).

[80]   Michael L. Rustad, *Unraveling Punitive Damages: Current Data and Further Inquiry*, 1998 WISC. L. REV. 15, 17–56 (Summarizing the result of nine empirical studies of punitive damages that confirm no punitive damages crisis despite diversity of authorship and sponsorship). "The unanimous finding of the nine punitive damage studies does not dispel the enthusiasm of tort reformers for nationalizing punitive damages. Rather, the tort reformers maintain their conclusion that social science is mere art or politics and not a science; this cynical attitude reflects their deep-seated bias against fact-based inquiry. Tort reformers' insistent that all scientific studies (with which they do not agree) are politically charged and evaluative, rather than neutral and methodological, serves only their own politics.) Michael L. Rustad, *Nationalizing Tort Law: The Republican Attack on Women, Blue Collar Workers, and Consumers*, 48 RUTGERS L. REV. 673, 703 (1996).

[81]   See e.g. William M. Landes & Richard A. Posner The Economic Structure of Tort Law (Cambridge, Massachusetts: Harvard University Press 1987) at 304–07); See also Michael L. Rustad & Thomas H. Koenig, *Reconceptualizing Punitive Damages in Medical Malpractice: Targeting Amoral Corporations, Not 'Moral Monsters,'* 47 RUTGERS L. REV. 975, 981–982 (1995) (studying punitive damages in medical liability over three decades and finding few awards).

[82]   Michael L. Rustad & Thomas H. Koenig, *Taming the Tort Monster: The American Civil Justice System as a Battleground of Social Theory*, 68 BROOKLYN L. REV. 1, 3 (2002).

products, negligent medicine, investor fraud, or unreasonably risky financial activities."[83] Similarly, neo-conservatives redefined the term "reform" to signify caps and other limitations on recovery for injured plaintiffs in an effort to improve the functioning of the American civil justice system. In the 'reformers' "common-sense" view, there are too many tort claims:

> Americans sue too readily, 'at the drop of a hat'; egged on by avaricious lawyers, they overwhelm our congested courts with mounting numbers of suits, including many frivolous claims. Irresponsible juries, biased against deep-pocketed defendants, bestow windfalls on undeserving plaintiffs, particularly arbitrary and capricious damages for pain and suffering and random outsize awards of punitive damages. Not only are the untold billions that the system costs an alarming drain on national wealth, but the system stifles enterprise and innovation, depriving society of useful products and services and undermining the international competitiveness of American businesses. To avoid these effects, we need to adopt various 'tort reform' proposals to inhibit claims (*e.g.*, loser-pays) and limit awards (*e.g.*, eliminating joint and several liability, capping damages, etc.).[84]

Tort law's remarkable ability to continually adapt by employing old causes of action to address new threats and dangers makes it an important institution of America's social order. A strong regime of tort law ensures that not even multi-billion dollar companies, such as those represented by the tort reform movement, are beyond the reach of the law. Tort law is, as it has always been, forward-looking with the ability to confront new social problems and conditions. In the words of Harper and James, "the common law of torts . . . readily accommodate[s] itself to the changing thought and action of the times."[85] The tort reformers' endless campaign of misinformation and distortion threatens to diminish the ability of our civil justice system to evolve to meet the emergent hazards of the twenty-first century. We need to expect more of our media sources and ourselves to understand the vital role of traditional American tort law. Our inspiration to recover from tort reformer Groupthink propaganda might be Aristotle's "Politics," that combined empirical observation[86] with moral and philosophical reflection.[87]

---

[83] *Id.* at 4.

[84] Marc Galanter, *Real World Torts: An Antidote to Anecdote*, 55 MD. L. REV. 993, 995 (1996).

[85] Fowler V. Harper & Fleming James, Jr., THE LAW OF TORTS xxvii (Boston: Little/Brown, 1956) (arguing that the law of torts as well as property and contract has historically proven very adaptable).

[86] *See generally* Wilfred M. McClay, *A Discipline in Denial*, THE WALL STREET JOURNAL (October 30, 2009) at W11.

[87] For more of Professor Rustad's recent scholarship, *see* INTERNET LAW IN A NUTSHELL (Westlaw 2009); UNDERSTANDING SALES, LEASES, AND LICENSES IN A GLOBAL PERSPECTIVE

GROUP TWO: TORT REFORM: WHO IS AFFECTED? WHO DECIDES?

1.   Throughout this text, there are a number of suggestions regarding desired or detested reform (limit, change, modify, enhance, *etc.*) of the civil justice system and of tort law. What then are the primary targets? A cursory glance at the literature will not help you hone in on one component or feature of tort law:

a.   Doug Rendleman, *A Cap on the Defendant's Appeal Bond?: Punitive Damages Tort Reform,* 39 AKRON L. REV. 1089, 1101 (2006) ("The discretionary procedures for setting the amount of an appeal bond are tort-reform targets.")

b.   Corrine Propas Parver & Tara Hechlik Newsom, *Medical Malpractice, Insurance Crisis: An Inquiry into the Relationship Between the Crisis and Access to Health Care for Women of Color,* 3 J. HEALTH & BIOMED. L. 267, 283 (2006) ("States can also pursue tort reform, which often targets medical malpractice claims. . . .")

c.   Andrew Tettenborn, Symposium, *Remedies Discussion Forum: Punitive Damages,* 41 SAN DIEGO L. REV. 1551, 1570 (2004) ("Punitive damages, after all, have for a long time been one of the main targets of the tort reform movement in the United States.")

d.   Michael P. Addair, Comment, *A Small Step Forward: An Analysis of West Virginia's Attempt at Joint and Several Liability,* 109 W. VA. L. REV. 831, 832 (2007) ("One of the principal targets of this tort reform movement, which is still ongoing today, has been the rule of joint and several liability. . . .")

2.   In this second group of essays, the specific targets of reform or preservation of the civil justice system shift from author to author, but the tenor of the commentary is broad and provocative. Who should be making these fundamental choices about our legal system? On what basis should such choices be made?

(Carolina Academic Press 2008); TORT LAW: CASES, PROBLEMS, PERSPECTIVES (Lexis/Nexis, 2008) (with Thomas Galligan et. al.); EVERYDAY CONSUMER LAW (Paradigm Publishers, 2008) and E-BUSINESS LEGAL HANDBOOK (Aspen Law & Business, 2003). His recent articles include: *The Uncert-Worthiness of the Court's Unmaking of Punitive Damages,* 2 CHARLESTON L. REV. 459 (2008) (Symposium Issue on Punitive Damages); *The Supreme Court and Me: Trapped in Time with Punitive Damages,* 17 WIDENER L. REV. 783 (2008) (Symposium Issue on Crimtorts); *A Hard Day's Night: Hierarchy, History and Happiness in Law School and Legal Practice,* 58 SYRACUSE L. REV. 263 (2008) (with Thomas H. Koenig); *Extending Learned Hand's Negligence Formula to Information Security Breaches,* 3 I/S: J.L. & POL'Y FOR INFO. SOC'Y 237 (2007) (with Thomas H. Koenig); *'Hate Torts' to Fight Hate Crimes: Punishing the Organizational Roots of Evil,* 51 AM. BEHAV. SCI. 302 (2007) (with Thomas H. Koenig).

STEPHEN D. SUGARMAN,[88] THE TRANSFORMATION OF TORT REFORM

Comments Regarding Changes in Tort Reform

Since the publication of the 1st edition, things have moved somewhat in the direction envisioned. While we don't have true National Health Insurance, we do now have Obamacare which means that a very large share of Americans have somewhat reasonable access to health care.

In states like California, employees now earn at least a modest number of paid sick leave days a year, and for disabilities lasting a week or more, employees are guaranteed a reasonable period of partially paid leave (up to a reasonable level of earned income). This means that those conventional California tort victims suffering relatively minor personal injuries increasingly do not need to turn to the tort system to cover their medical expenses or replace most of their lost income.

If this employee benefit package, combined with a reversal of the "collateral sources" rule with respect to these first party benefits (which a number of states have adopted), were to spread nationwide (which it seems slowly to be doing), the role of tort law for small personal injury cases could be largely eliminated, and tort law could focus its resources on serious injury cases. This, of course, puts aside claims for pain and suffering damages; and alas, tort reform with respect to those continues to focus on caps (thereby harming the most seriously injured) rather than on thresholds (apart from auto accidents in the two relatively strong auto no-fault states of New York and Michigan).

All in all, U.S. political leaders continue to seem blind to important innovations from other nations, like the threshold on pain and suffering claims adopted in Australia and the cheaper, faster, generous and comprehensive auto no-fault systems in places like Quebec and other Canadian provinces—to say nothing of the typical rule elsewhere around the world that the legal fees of successful tort claimants are paid for by their injurers (instead of out of their recovery as in the U.S.).

---

[88]   Stephen D. Sugarman is the Roger J. Traynor Professor of Law at UC Berkeley, where he has taught since 1972. He regularly teaches Torts, and occasionally teaches Sports Law, Educational Policy and Law, and other courses in the social justice curriculum. Sugarman has been a visiting professor at the London School of Economics; University College, London; the University of Paris; the European University Institute, Florence; Kobe University Faculty of Law; Kyoto University Faculty of Law; and Columbia University School of Law. Before coming to Boalt, Sugarman served as acting director of the New York State Commission on the Cost, Quality and Financing of Education. Between 1967 and 1972 he was associated with the Los Angeles office of O'Melveny & Myers. At Boalt, he served as associate dean from 1980 to 1982 and again from 2004 to 2005. He was director of the Earl Warren Legal Institute's Family Law Program from 1988 to 1999.

In the 1950s, tort law was something of a backwater. Still, UC Berkeley's Dean William Prosser, the most important figure in torts in the early post-war era, was pushing on various fronts for its liberalization in favor of victims. Many of Prosser's goals were importantly realized in the 1960s and 1970s, as common law tort doctrine became increasingly receptive to plaintiffs.

Many other reformers in the 1960s, however, concluded that tort law was inefficient and ineffective in providing needed compensation for injured people. The administrative costs of running the tort system were horrendous, with up to half the liability insurance premium dollar going to defendant expenses and with plaintiffs' attorneys typically taking as their fees one-third of the settlement or recovery. Loads of accident victims could not recover in tort because a) they were not the victim of another's fault, b) could not prove that even if it were true, c) were themselves at fault, and/or d) their tortfeasor was judgment proof. A range of alternative compensation schemes was proposed, both for specific categories of injuries (most importantly automobile "no-fault" plans) and across-the-board for all accident victims (a reform actually adopted in New Zealand in the early 1970s).

By 1985, when I published *Doing Away with Tort Law*, 73 Cal. L. Rev. 555, many of us hoped that the replacement of American personal injury law with a combination of sweeping European-style social insurance schemes plus stronger safety regulation via administrative agencies was not far in the future. But, so far, it has not played out that way.

Even in the 1960s and early 1970s, the most important torts scholars of the last third of the 20th century (Guido Calabresi and Richard Posner, both now federal judges) began to write about the safety-promoting potential of tort law, and economic models of tort law as a "deterrent" began to be taught to new generations of law students. Some friends of tort law (including both Calabresi and former Berkeley law professor and later California Supreme Court Justice Roger Traynor) envisioned that "enterprise liability" for all sorts of accidents could serve the dual functions of discouraging carelessness and providing compensation to accident victims. Yet, enterprise liability has not seriously caught on, at least not as a doctrinal matter.

Instead, through the 1970s and 1980s we found ourselves with a robust tort law based on negligence (comparative fault replaced contributory negligence as a complete bar to recovery, new doctrinal areas were opened up to plaintiffs, and lawyers representing victims became much better at their craft). This state of affairs could fairly be seen as a victory for the odd pairing of the plaintiffs' bar on the one hand and, on the other, the academic thinking of Prosser, the pragmatist, and Posner, a fan of the negligence principle and a key founder of the "law and economics" movement (even if the latter is usually seen as a conservative approach to law).

But the battle over tort law was hardly done. Since the late 1970s, business interests have objected to how much tort law costs them as a result of the liberalization of tort doctrine and the growing effectiveness of the plaintiffs' bar in convincing juries to award huge sums in many celebrated cases. Yet, the defense side could hardly object to the imposition of tort liability on real wrong-doers, and those critics of tort law were unlikely to favor social insurance-like replacements. Instead, they have waged a campaign before state legislatures (with substantial success), Congress (with no real success so far), and in state Supreme Court elections (with some success) to roll back victims' legal rights. Most of the effort has been focused, not on tort doctrine, but on tort damages law and the procedures governing tort law. This effort has yielded reforms in some states like caps on pain and suffering, a reversal of the "collateral sources" rule so that tort law becomes secondary to other forms of compensation, restrictions on joint and several liability (so that deep pocket defendants are less likely to have to bear the risk that more-at-fault defendants are insolvent), and so on. Common law judges, at least in some states, also seem to have been influenced by this well-coordinated political campaign, scaling back on some earlier pro-victim decisions. In the 21st century, some think we have reached a détente between the defense community and the well-healed and populist-talking "trial lawyers."

Yet, federal legislation now in the offing could still change things dramatically. Most importantly, of course, we may finally be joining the other rich nations of the world by having something of a comprehensive national health insurance program. In addition, legislation is now moving through Congress that would guarantee workers paid sick leave for very short term disabilities and paid temporary non-occupational disability income benefits that would last for up to a year. Suppose these measures are enacted, and suppose further the adoption of changes in the law of tort damages that would a) require liable defendants to pay their victims' reasonable legal fees and expenses, b) reverse the collateral source rule for these new federal health and income schemes, and c) impose a threshold requirement for pain and suffering (requiring, say, as is the law in New South Wales Australia, that the injured party be at least 15% disabled before any pain and suffering damages may be awarded).

Under such a scenario, most of the small injury tort claims that are made today would disappear, and tort law for bodily injury would be left to focus primarily on a much fewer number of serious injuries. In such a sharply changed world, those of us favoring focused no-fault schemes for serious harm (especially from auto accidents) and/or more comprehensive New Zealand-like reforms might, once more, gain a hearing (especially with Ralph Nader, the plaintiffs' bar's greatest ally, having somewhat tarnished his reputation as Mr. Consumer with his Quixotic runs at the Presidency).[89]

PAMELA GILBERT,[90] THE HUMAN FACE OF TORT REFORM

Kathy and Scott Olsen's son Steven is blind and brain-damaged after an HMO refused to give him an $800 CAT scan when he was two years old. While walking in the woods, Steven had fallen on a stick that penetrated into his eye socket. His eye was fixed in the emergency room, but the doctors never bothered to check whether there had been brain damage. Steven was sent home and his condition worsened. By the time the brain damage was discovered, it was too late. A jury awarded Steven $7.1 million in non-economic compensation for his life of darkness, loneliness, pain, physical retardation and around-the-clock supervision. However, the judge was forced to reduce the amount to $250,000 because of a law capping non-economic damages in California, where the Olsens lived.

Janey Fair's high school daughter Shannon and 26 other people were killed in a bus accident in Carrollton, Kentucky while on a church outing. The accident was caused by an uninsured drunk

---

[89] For more of Professor Sugarman's recent scholarship, see DOING AWAY WITH PERSONAL INJURY LAW (1989), SMOKING POLICY: LAW, POLITICS AND CULTURE (with Rabin) (1993), PAY AT THE PUMP AUTO INSURANCE (1993), REGULATING TOBACCO (with Rabin 2001), and TORTS STORIES (with Rabin) (2003). Some of his recent articles include: *Performance-Based Regulation: Enterprise Responsibility for Reducing Death, Injury and Disease Caused by Consumer Products,* 34 JOURNAL OF HEALTH, POLICY, POLITICS AND LAW 1035 (2009); *Fighting Childhood Obesity Through Performance—Based Regulation of the Food Industry (with Nirit Sandman),* 56 DUKE L. J. 1403–1490 (2007); *Cases in Vaccine Court—Legal Battles Over Vaccines and Autism,* 357:13 NEW ENGLAND JOURNAL OF MEDICINE 1275 (September 27, 2007); *The "Necessity" Defense and the Failure of Tort Theory: The Case Against Strict Liability for Damages Caused While Exercising Self-Help in an Emergency,* 2005 ISSUES IN LEGAL SCHOLARSHIP 1–153 The Berkeley Electronic Press © 2005; *Pain and Suffering: Comparative Law Perspective,* 55 DEPAUL L. REV., 399 (2005).

[90] Pamela Gilbert is a partner in the law firm of Cuneo Gilbert & LaDuca, LLP, based in Washington, DC. Cuneo Gilbert & LaDuca fights for consumers, businesses, workers and governments using the tools of litigation, lobbying and public advocacy. She heads up the lobbying practice at the firm and is the former Executive Director of the U.S. Consumer Product Safety Commission (CPSC). She has over 20 years of experience in consumer advocacy in Washington, D.C. She has testified before the U.S. Congress over 50 times and made dozens of appearances in the national print and electronic media. She is a graduate from Tufts University and received her law degree from New York University in 1984. Gilbert served as Consumer Program Director at the U.S. Public Interest Research Group from 1984–1989 where she specialized in civil justice and consumer protection issues. She worked for Public Citizen's Congress Watch, one of Washington's largest consumer advocacy organizations, first as Legislative Director and then as Executive Director from 1989–1994. She served as Executive Director of the CPSC from 1995–2001, that agency's senior staff position. After she left the government, Gilbert served as Chief Operating Officer of M & R Strategic Services, a national firm that lobbies and conducts grassroots and media campaigns around public policy issues. Gilbert joined the Cuneo Law Group in 2002 and became a named partner in 2003. Her recent scholarship includes, *Class Action Legislation Will Deny Americans a Fair Day in Court,* 6 CLASS ACTION LITIG. REP. (BNA) 108 (2005).

driver who hit the bus in a head-on collision. But the crash didn't kill anyone. The bus passengers died because the bus had a defective fuel tank that ruptured and engulfed the vehicle in flames.

Charles Prestwood is an Enron retiree who lost his retirement savings—$1.3 million, all in Enron stock—in Enron's death spiral. He never had a choice: when the company he worked for was bought by Enron his stock was automatically converted over. But Prestwood wasn't concerned. Ken Lay and Jeff Skilling and the rest of the Enron management told their employees and their investors that Enron was the safest investment imaginable and that the company was going to have a fantastic future. Prestwood believed all of those lies until he was locked out of his accounts and was unable to sell his shares as the stock tanked and the company went bankrupt. His retirement savings of over a million dollars was reduced to $8000.

These courageous individuals, and hundreds of thousands like them, are the flip side of the "tort reform" movement. They are the human beings who are personally and devastatingly affected by the nefarious proposals that carry such legalistic and non-threatening names as caps on noneconomic damages, abrogation of joint and several liability, and elimination of aiding and abetting liability. I have had the good fortune to get to know Kathy Olsen, Janey Fair and Charles Prestwood in my work defending access to the civil justice system for victims of negligent, reckless or criminal conduct. Each of them traveled to Washington, DC to tell their stories and to educate policymakers about what happens to real people when their legal rights are taken away.

I met Kathy Olsen when she came to lobby Congress against adopting the California law that places a limit of $250,000 on the amount of damages a person injured by medical malpractice can recover for "pain and suffering." "Pain and suffering," or "non-economic" damages, are awarded to compensate for losses that are not easily quantifiable. Economic damages are generally comprised of lost wages and medical expenses. Non-economic damages compensate people for losses that are not monetary, but are nonetheless very real, including pain, suffering, loss of quality of life, discomfort, embarrassment, anguish, and shame.

Proponents of capping pain and suffering damages claim that injured persons are still "made whole" because there is no limit on compensation for their out-of-pocket expenses. But try explaining that to a woman who loses her ability to ever bear children, a child whose childhood is stolen away because of prolonged illness or injury, or parents who lose their children, all due to medical negligence. In fact, caps on pain and suffering affect only the most unfortunate victims—those who are permanently or catastrophically injured—because only the most seriously injured individuals ever receive over $250,000 in pain and suffering awards. Moreover, placing limits on pain and suffering damages has discriminatory results because it targets a very specific population—low-wage, or non-wage, earners. In other words, those most affected by caps on pain and suffering are women, children, and the elderly.

Like Kathy Olsen, Janey Fair's life was forever altered the day of the devastating bus crash that killed her daughter and so many other members of her church. Days after the crash, lawyers representing the Ford Motor Company, the manufacturer of the bus chassis, converged on Carrollton, Kentucky to offer cash settlements to the victims. Janey and her husband wouldn't settle. They wanted to learn what had happened in the crash and why so many people had died. Ford tried to blame the tragedy on the drunk driver who caused the accident. And it was true that, but for the drunk driver, the accident would never have occurred. But the litigation also uncovered another truth—that the school bus carrying Shannon Fair and the other parishioners had a deadly defect. The drunk driver caused the accident, but the deaths were caused by the defective gas tank and the ensuing fire.

Janey Fair came to Washington to lobby Congress against limitations on joint and several liability in product liability lawsuits. This legalistic term was at the heart of the Fairs' successful suit against Ford. Under joint and several liability, if more than one person or entity is responsible for an injury, they may each be held liable for all the damages. Joint and several liability is critical in cases, like the Kentucky bus crash, in which there is an insolvent defendant. In this case, that defendant was the drunk driver who had no insurance. Without joint and several liability, Ford would try to put as much blame as possible on the driver, and then only be responsible for the portion of the damages that the jury deemed to be Ford's fault. The victims of the crash would receive only a portion of their losses, and Ford would escape most of its responsibility. Under joint and several, on the other hand, Ford is responsible for all the damage caused by its negligence. It can't escape accountability just because there happened to be another party that was also negligent.

Compared to the Olsen and Fair families, Charles Prestwood seems to have gotten off pretty easily. He lost only money, albeit his life savings. All told, it is estimated that investors in Enron collectively lost about $40 billion due to the fraud perpetrated by Enron's executives and their accomplices. That doesn't include the incalculable damage that was done to the public's trust in the financial markets by the greed-induced lies and manipulations carried out by these presumably upstanding members of the business and Wall Street communities.

Charlie Prestwood traveled from his home in Houston, Texas to lobby the Bush Administration to support his side in the shareholders' lawsuit against the Wall Street banks that orchestrated the Enron fraud. Because Enron went bankrupt, its accounting firm collapsed and its lawyers had limited assets and insurance, legal action against the investment banks that helped to mastermind the fraudulent schemes was the only recourse for victims to recover any significant portion of their Enron losses. Internal Enron documents and testimony of bank employees detailed how the banks engineered shame transactions to keep billions of dollars of debt off Enron's balance sheets and create the illusion of increasing earnings and operating cash flow. It seemed only fair that those banks should be held accountable to the defrauded investors who had nowhere else to turn to for redress.

The shareholders managed to reach settlements of over $7 billion with a number of Enron's banks, and were working on preparing for trial against the remaining banks who assisted Enron's fraud, when they were stopped in their tracks by a ruling in the Fifth Circuit Court of Appeals. In a 2–1 decision, the court ruled that, while the banks' conduct was "hardly praiseworthy," because the banks did not themselves make any false statements to the market about their conduct, they could not be held liable to the victims even if they knowingly participated in the scheme to defraud Enron's shareholders. The shareholders appealed the case to the Supreme Court, which brought Mr. Prestwood out to the east coast.

Charlie Prestwood, along with a number of his fellow Enron victims, came to Washington to urge the Bush Administration to side with the defrauded shareholders and against Enron's banks in the Supreme Court case. They held press conferences and even had a meeting with Christopher Cox, then Chairman of the Securities and Exchange Commission. The victims did manage to convince Cox of the merit of their position, and Cox subsequently recommended that the Bush Justice Department support holding the banks accountable for the Enron fraud. Unfortunately, the Justice Department took a different view and filed a brief in the Supreme Court urging that aiders and abettors of securities fraud, such as Enron's Wall Street banks, should not be held responsible under the securities laws. The Supreme Court ultimately adopted the Bush Administration's view, and the remaining Enron banks were dismissed from the suit. While the $7 billion Enron settlement is still today the largest securities fraud settlement in history, it returned less than 20 cents on the dollar back to the defrauded investors.

Kathy Olsen, Janey Fair and Charlie Prestwood represent millions of Americans who suffer unspeakable harms because of someone else's negligent, reckless, or criminal conduct. We owe them, and hundreds like them, a great debt of gratitude for being willing to take time from their busy lives to speak out in favor of a strong and accessible civil justice system. They are the human faces of "tort reform," and policymakers and opinion leaders should never forget them when they consider whether to limit access to justice in America.

Mark Behrens,[91] Who Should Decide Tort Law? A Fundamental Issue in the Public Debate Over Civil Justice Reform

One of the most frequently raised questions in the public dialogue about civil justice reform is whether courts or legislatures should make tort law. Tort law affects people's lives every day. It can discourage misconduct and help remove truly defective products from the marketplace. On the other hand, unchecked and unbalanced liability can discourage innovation, limit the availability of affordable health care, slow economic growth, result in loss of jobs, and unduly raise costs for consumers. It is, thus, very appropriate to ask, who should decide tort law—courts or legislatures? It is also appropriate to ask whether changes, if they are to occur, should be made at the federal or state level. This brief essay discusses these two fundamental questions and seeks to give students some perspectives that may generate interesting classroom debate.

Courts or Legislatures?

The vast majority of tort law has been, and should continue to be, decided by state courts. I often point out when talking to students that they will notice that the popular law school text co-authored by my law firm partner Victor Schwartz is called *Prosser, Wade and Schwartz's Torts: Cases and Materials,* not *Torts: Cases and Statutes.* Also, the text is popularly referred to as a "casebook." These titles reflect the reality that most tort law in this country is judge-made, even in states that have enacted comprehensive civil justice reforms.

State legislatures, however, have an important, overlapping role in the development of tort law. As a matter of history and sound public policy, neither branch of government should have a tort law "monopoly." If that were true—if only "one voice" could be heard to the exclusion of the other—the public would lose out in the long run. The balanced development of tort law would suffer, and so would the public's perception of the judiciary.

---

[91]   Mark A. Behrens co-chairs the Washington, DC-based Public Policy Group of Shook, Hardy & Bacon L.L.P., an international law firm that primarily represents corporate defendants in complex civil litigation. In October 2015, Mark received the U.S. Chamber Institute for Legal Reform's Individual Achievement Award. A member of the American Law Institute, Mark taught Advanced Torts as a Distinguished Visiting Practitioner in Residence at Pepperdine University School of Law in 2010. Earlier, he served on the adjunct faculty of The American University's Washington College of Law. Mark received his J.D. from Vanderbilt University Law School in 1990 and his B.A. in Economics from the University of Wisconsin-Madison in 1987.

Legislatures are uniquely well equipped to reach fully informed decisions about the need for broad public policy changes in the law. Through the hearing process, the legislature is the best body equipped to hold a full discussion of the competing principles and controversial issues of tort liability, because it has access to broad information, including the ability to receive comments from persons representing a multiplicity of perspectives and to use the legislative process to obtain new information. This process allows legislatures to engage in broad policy deliberations and to formulate policy carefully. Ultimately, legislators make a judgment. If the people who elected the legislators do not like the solution, the voters have a remedy through the ballot and the processes of democratic government. Furthermore, legislative development of tort law gives the public advance notice of significant changes affecting rights and duties, and the time to comport behavior accordingly.

Courts, on the other hand, are uniquely and best suited to adjudicate individual disputes concerning discrete issues and parties. This is an essential part of the tripartite structure of our system of government. The Founding Fathers recognized this when they drafted the United States Constitution to give the judiciary jurisdiction to decide "cases and controversies." This advantage also has its limitations: the focus on individual cases does not provide comprehensive access to broad scale information, and judicial changes in tort law may not provide prospective "fair notice" to everyone potentially affected.

A well-functioning government requires mutual cooperation between the branches. If a state legislature makes a broad policy decision with respect to tort law, that action should be respected by the courts unless the law is not rationally related to any legitimate governmental objective. These changes may not always favor defendants. Furthermore, a reform may be pro-consumer in the aggregate even if it negatively impacts the distinct minority of the population that may be involved in a tort case. Students should keep an open mind as to all of these perspectives as they debate what role the courts and legislatures should have in the development of sound tort policy rules.

State or Federal?

Students also may wish to consider whether changes to tort law rules, if any, should be made at the state or federal levels. This particular debate is interesting because the responses may not fall neatly along traditional lines, namely, plaintiffs and their political allies lined up on one side and defendants and their political allies lined up on the other. For example, some highly conservative Members of Congress that frequently vote to support business interests have been known to express reservations about federal initiatives that, in their opinion, may go too far in displacing the rights of states to decide their own tort law rules. It is also interesting to hear Members of Congress that frequently support broad expansion of the federal government suddenly become concerned about "states' rights" in the debate over a federal tort reform initiative. Whether these positions are based on ideology or political expediency, the point is that there is often a healthy debate about the role of the federal government when civil justice reforms are considered on Capitol Hill.

Just as the question as to who should decide tort law rules—courts or legislatures—does not require granting either branch a monopoly, the same type of calculus may apply with respect to the federal-state issue. Legislative changes to tort law rules need not be made exclusively at the state or federal level. There may be times, for instance, when the involvement of interstate commerce provides an appropriate "hook" to bring about federal action. Students may come to their own conclusions as to the proper federal-state balance.

FRANK J. VANDALL,[92] TORT REFORM, A POWER PLAY

Let's be clear. The goal of tort reform, in the area of product liability, is to take from the consumers and give to the corporations. This is not based on morality or philosophy. It is based on power.[93]

The theme of my recent scholarship[94] is to manifest the expansion of civil liability from 1466 to 1980, and the cessation of that growth in 1980 when corporations realized they could affect the content of the law. My work examines the creation of tort causes of action during the period of 1400–1980 and then explores the reconceptualization and limitations of those developments from 1980 to the present. A keystone case to this work is *MacPherson v. Buick Motor Co.* (1916)[95] because it rejects the transparent and unmanageable legal fictions and adopts negligence as a foundational cause of action. During the period from 1916 to 1944, the courts used numerous causes of action, such as express and implied warranty and fraud, as well as negligence, to accomplish justice and provide a means for injured consumers to recover.

---

[92] Frank J. Vandall teaches first-year torts and advanced courses in products liability and torts at Emory Law School. A member of the Emory faculty since 1970, he has served as scholar-in-residence at the Institute of Advanced Legal Studies at the London School of Economics, was the Roger Traynor Research Professor at the University of California, Hastings College of Law during 1993, and testified before the Senate Judiciary Committee in 2006. Professor Vandall was President of the Emory University Senate in 2001.

[93] This argument is the core of my forthcoming book; JUSTICE REWRITTEN: AN HISTORICAL, POLITICAL AND ECONOMIC ANALYSIS OF CIVIL JUSTICE, (Oxford University Press, Spring 2011).

[94] Id.

[95] 111 N.E. 1050, 217 N.Y. 382 (1916).

The policies supporting the more than 500 year expansion in tort liability[96] were forcefully presented by Judge Roger Traynor in a products case, *Escola v. Coca Cola Bottling Co.* (1944):[97]

> . . . I believe the manufacturer's negligence should no longer be singled out as the basis for a plaintiff's right to recover in cases like the present one. In my opinion it should now be recognized that a manufacturer incurs an absolute liability when an article that he has placed on the market, knowing that it is to be used without inspection, proves to have a defect that causes injury to human beings . . . . Even if there is no negligence, however public policy demands that responsibility be fixed wherever it will most effectively reduce the hazards to life and health inherent in defective products that reach the market. It is evident that the manufacturer can anticipate some hazards and guard against the recurrence of others, as the public cannot.

> Those who suffer injury from defective products are unprepared to meet its consequences. The cost of an injury and the loss of time or health may be an overwhelming misfortune to the person injured, and a needless one for the risk of injury can be insured by the manufacturer and distributed among the public as a cost of doing business. It is to the public interest to discourage the marketing of products having defects that are a menace to the public. If such products nevertheless find their way into the market, it is to the public interest to place the responsibility for whatever injury they may cause upon the manufacturer, who, even if he is not negligent in the manufacture of the product, is responsible for its reaching the market . . . .

> . . . It is needlessly circuitous to make negligence the basis of recovery and impose what is in reality liability without negligence. If public policy demands that a manufacturer of goods be responsible for their quality regardless of negligence there is no reason not to fix that responsibility openly. . . .

> . . . As handicrafts have been replaced by mass production with its great markets and transportation facilities, the close relationship between the producer and consumer of a product has been altered. Manufacturing processes, frequently valuable secrets, are ordinarily either inaccessible to or beyond the ken of the general public. The consumer no longer has means or skill enough to investigate for himself the soundness of a product, even when it is not contained in a sealed package, and his erstwhile vigilance has been lulled by the steady efforts of manufacturers to

---

[96]   Id. My scholarship uses products cases and policies for much of its argument.

[97]   24 Cal.2d 453, 150 P.2d 436 (1944).

build up confidence by advertising and marketing devices such as trade-marks. . . .

. . . Consumers no longer approach products warily but accept them on faith, relying on the reputation of the manufacturer or the trade mark. . . .

These policies can be summarized as a shift from a balanced playing field, negligence, to one that favored injured consumers. The strict liability foreshadowed by Traynor, was not adopted until 1962, when Traynor wrote the majority opinion in *Greenman v. Yuba Power Products*.[98] For the doctrine, he relied on the policies earlier stated in *Escola*. The American Law Institute quickly followed Traynor's lead and adopted strict liability in Section 402A, the Restatement Second of Torts, in 1964. From 1964 to 1980 almost all states adopted the strict liability cause of action for defective products. This wave of adoption was the most rapid and dramatic expansion in consumer protection in over 500 years. Corporate America was bloodied, but not knocked out by these expansions in liability.

The wake-up call for product consumers was the adoption in 1980 and proliferation of statutes of repose. This was followed by numerous "reforms" in tort theory and civil procedure that had the effect of reducing the plaintiffs' chance to win and reducing the eventual size of the settlement or verdict.

In my upcoming work, first I argue that civil justice no longer rests on historic foundations, such as, fairness and impartiality, but has shifted to power and influence. Reform in the law, both legislative and judicial, is today driven by financial interests, not precedent and not a neutral desire for fairness or to "make it better." Second, I examine the role of persuasive agencies, such as the American Law Institute, in reforming and shaping civil justice. Never has it been less true that we live under the rule of law. Congress, the courts, and agencies make the law, but they are driven by those who have a large financial stake in the game.

The medium for the story presented[99] will be reality-in-fact—actual cases, agency decisions, and enacted legislation, not theory and not philosophy. This work prompts me to conclude that political science should be taught as a required law school course. Since law is driven by financial incentives, rather than precedent, it is appropriate to teach political science more so than history and philosophy, which are vague and rarely on point.[100]

---

[98]   59 Cal.2d 57, 27 Cal.Rptr. 697, 377 P.2d 897 (1963).

[99]   JUSTICE REWRITTEN: AN HISTORICAL, POLITICAL AND ECONOMIC ANALYSIS OF CIVIL JUSTICE, (forthcoming, Oxford University Press, Spring 2011).

[100]   Professor Vandall is the author of a first-year casebook (TORTS, CASES, PROBLEMS AND QUESTIONS) published in early 1997 (2nd ed., 2003); a products liability casebook, PRODUCTS LIABILITY CASES, MATERIALS, PROBLEMS (1994, 2nd ed., 2002); *Our Product Liability System: An Efficient Solution to a Complex Problem*, DENVER L. REV.; a theoretical tort book for lawyers and

JEFFREY O'CONNEL[101] AND CHRISTOPHER ROBINETTE,[102] TORT LAW'S FLAWS

Some areas of tort law, as applied to personal injury, especially but not necessarily limited to medical malpractice and product liability, have a central defect: the huge uncertainty involved in both applying the fault principle and calculating payment for pain and suffering. This defect leads ineluctably to two others: huge delay and forbidding transaction costs. Uncertainty breeds delay because the parties dispute their entitlements; in turn, high transaction costs follow as the parties are forced to pay highly trained, expensive specialists to attempt to resolve their complex, adversarial disputes.

This means that the present system of tort liability for personal injury also achieves the anomalous and tragic result of protecting everyone but those who need it most—namely, seriously injured parties whose medical expenses and wage losses exceed their own insurance coverage, public or private. The present legal system tenders to that tragic cohort of people a

---

business people, STRICT LIABILITY: LEGAL AND ECONOMIC ANALYSIS; AND POLICE TRAINING FOR TOUGH CALLS: DISCRETIONARY SITUATIONS. His articles include *Suits by Public Hospitals to Recover Expenditures for the Treatment of Disease, Injury and Disability Caused by Tobacco and Alcohol*, FORDHAM URBAN L. REV. (1994); *Reallocating the Costs of Smoking: The Application of Absolute Liability to Cigarette Manufacturers*, OHIO STATE LAW JOURNAL; *Criminal Prosecution of Corporations for Defective Products*, INTERNATIONAL LEGAL PRACTITIONER; *Judge Posner's Negligence-Efficiency Theory: A Critique*, EMORY LAW JOURNAL; *A Critique of the Proposed Restatement, Third Products Liability, Section 2(b): The Reasonable Alternative Design Requirement*, TENNESSEE L. REV. (1994); *The Restatement, Third Products Liability, Section 2(b): Design Defect*, TEMPLE L. REV. (1995); and *Constructing a Roof Before the Foundation is Prepared: The Restatement (Third) of Torts, Product Liability: Section 2(b) Design Defect*, MICHIGAN JOURNAL OF LAW REFORM (1997).

[101] Jeffrey O'Connell, who passed away prior to the publication of this edition of this text, was THE SAMUEL H. McCOY, II PROFESSOR OF LAW at the University of Virginia, specializing in accident and insurance law. He was the co-author of the principal work which proposed no-fault auto insurance. Prior to teaching at Virginia, he taught law at the University of Illinois, University of Iowa, and visited at Northwestern, Michigan, Southern Methodist University, University of Texas, Oxford, and the University of Washington. He graduated from Dartmouth College and Harvard Law School. He received two Guggenheim Fellowships and served as the Thomas Jefferson Visiting Fellow at Downing College, Cambridge University, U.K. He received a Convocation Medal for his work on medical malpractice law from the American College of Cardiology. He served as the John Marshall Harlan Visiting Distinguished Professor at New York Law School and was the recipient of the Robert B. McKay Award of the American Bar Association for outstanding scholarly contributions to tort and insurance law. Prior to teaching law, he practiced at Hale & Dorr. He was a Presidential appointee to the National Highway Safety Advisory Committee, a member of the Board of Directors of Consumers Union, and served on the Educational Advisory Board of the John Simon Guggenheim Memorial Foundation.

[102] Christopher Robinette is Associate Professor of Law at Widener University School of Law. He is a graduate of the College of William & Mary and the University of Virginia School of Law. He served as an Honorable Abraham L. Freedman Fellow and Lecturer in Law at Temple University School of Law from 2003 through 2005, and received an LL.M. in Legal Education from Temple in 2005. He practiced law at Tremblay & Smith, L.L.P. in Charlottesville, Virginia, before going into teaching. He teaches Torts, Evidence, and Professional Responsibility. In 2009, he won the Douglas E. Ray Excellence in Faculty Scholarship Award at Widener.

deal whereby they *may* be paid something years from now, but only after paying from any recovery lawyers' fees and expenses of thirty to fifty percent or more. Note too that plaintiffs' lawyers should be the last people to deny the formidable complexity of the present criterion of payment. How else could they justify charging clients a third or more of any payment to help get it?

Now turn from the seriously injured and uninsured or underinsured victims to everyone else. First, those same plaintiffs' lawyers probably will not take a case unless they are confident it is likely to lead to at least some substantial payment. And even if the risk of nonpayment for a given claim is high, the lawyer or his firm minimize this risk by taking multiple cases to assure portfolio diversification, a form of protection denied the seriously injured victim with normally only one such claim in a lifetime. Second, defense lawyers are paid win or lose. Third, insureds are (at least financially) protected by the very fact of their liability insurance coverage. Fourth, insurers are protected, of course, by their risk-spreading, undergirded by actuarial calculations. Finally, the less seriously injured are protected by the very fact of their lesser losses which, in turn, are more likely covered by health insurance or sick leave. So what is one to make of tort law's boasts of justice when everyone is substantially protected except those who need protection most?

As a solution I propose an "early offers" statute, whereby a defendant would have the option of offering an injured claimant periodic payments of his/her net economic losses within 180 days after a claim is filed. The early offer statute would guarantee coverage of medical expenses, including rehabilitation and lost wages. An additional amount is payable for the claimant's reasonable attorney's fee. The early offer plan does not provide coverage for pain and suffering.

If a claimant declined an early offer in favor of litigation, the statute would raise the standard of misconduct, allowing tort payment only if gross, and not just ordinary, negligence, were proven. It would also raise the standard of proof itself, requiring the patient to prove such misconduct beyond a reasonable doubt. Although injury victims who accepted an early offer would lose their recourse to full-scale tort rights, they would be assured of prompt payment of their essential losses—especially valuable to the seriously injured. See O'Connell & Robinette,[103] A RECIPE FOR

---

[103] Professor Robinette recently co-authored, with Jeffrey O'Connell, A RECIPE FOR BALANCED TORT REFORM (2008). He has authored or co-authored articles in the University of Illinois Law Review, George Mason Law Review, Connecticut Law Review, Northern Illinois University Law Review, and Brandeis Law Journal. He has also written for symposia published in the Charleston Law Review and Widener Law Journal. Additionally, Robinette serves as an editor of *TortsProf Blog*.

BALANCED TORT REFORM: EARLY OFFERS WITH SWIFT SETTLEMENTS (2008).[104]

CARL T. BOGUS,[105] INTRODUCTION: GENUINE TORT REFORM[106]

I am not sure who coined the term "tort reform," but as far as I know it was first used in 1974 in a student article published by the UCLA Law Review. That article was very much a Sixties piece. The author praised Justice Roger Traynor and the California Supreme Court for their leadership in "placing tort liability on the party who is best able to spread the risk of loss." She continued:

Though judicial activism is generally regarded by traditional legal process scholars as undesirable, in tort law, it appears to be an appropriate fulfillment of the historical function of the common law-to meld the precedents of the past and needs and concerns of the present. [Dian Dickson Ogilvie, *Comment, Judicial Activism in Tort Reform: The Guest Statute Exemplar and a Proposal for Comparative Negligence*, 21 UCLA L. REV. 1566 (1974)]

For nearly a decade thereafter, "tort reform" was still occasionally used to refer to efforts to make the tort system more dynamic by making it easier for victims to hold accountable wrongdoers and those who were in a position to prevent harm. Times, however, were changing. The modern conservative movement was gaining force. That movement was repelled by what it considered judicial activism. The movement's original target was the Warren Court and its constitutional innovations in civil rights, voting rights, and criminal procedure. In 1968, Richard M. Nixon campaigned for the presidency on a promise to appoint "law and order" judges, by which he

---

[104]   Jeffrey O'Connell is the author or co-author of fourteen books mostly dealing with accident law; his latest one from Carolina Academic Press, co-authored with Christopher Robinette, is entitled "A Recipe for Balanced Tort Reform: Early Offers with Swift Settlements" (2008). O'Connell has also written extensively for numerous popular, legal, and insurance journals including The New York Times, The Wall Street Journal, and The Harvard L. Rev.

[105]   Carl T. Bogus, is a professor of law at Roger Williams University, where he teaches Advanced Torts, Products Liability, Antitrust, Administrative Law, and Evidence. Prior to coming to Roger Williams, he visited at Rutgers University School of Law in Camden, New Jersey. Before going into teaching, he was a partner at two law firms, MESIROV GELMAN JAFFE CRAMER & JAMIESON, and STEINBERG, GREENSTEIN, GORELICK & PRICE, where he specialized in complex litigation. He is the author of WHY LAWSUITS ARE GOOD FOR AMERICA: DISCIPLINED DEMOCRACY, BIG BUSINESS AND THE COMMON LAW (NYU, 2001) and edited THE SECOND AMENDMENT IN LAW AND HISTORY (New Press). His articles include, *Rescuing Burke*, 72 MO. L. REV. 387 (2007); *Fear-Mongering Torts and the Exaggerated Death of Diving*, 28 HARV. J.L. & PUB. POL'Y 17 (2004); and *The Hidden History of the Second Amendment*, 31 U.C. DAVIS L. REV. 309 (1998).

[106]   This excerpt can—and probably should—be read in full at 13 ROGER WILLIAMS UNIVERSITY L. REV. 1 (2008). It is the first piece on a symposium in tort reform that you might find highly illuminating.

meant judges who would stop enlarging protections for criminal defendants. Conservatives felt that an era of permissiveness had frayed the social fabric. Stability was breaking down.

Before long conservatives began seeing tort reforms—especially the advent of strict liability for defective and unreasonably dangerous products—as part and parcel of the same phenomenon. That is, they increasingly saw courts as anti-order, anti-establishment, anti-free enterprise. In 1971, Lewis F. Powell, Jr., who was then a corporate lawyer, wrote a memorandum for the U.S. Chamber of Commerce in which he famously said "the American free enterprise system is under broad attack." Powell lumped together "Communists, New Leftists, and other revolutionaries" with the American Civil Liberties Union and Ralph Nader, whom Powell called "perhaps the single most effective antagonist of American business." Powell urged that the Chamber of Commerce lead a political and social counterassault. He wanted the counterassault launched in the venues where public opinion is molded: college campuses, graduate schools, secondary schools, textbooks, television and radio, scholarly journals, newspapers and popular magazines as well as in all branches of government. Powell wanted the Chamber and its allies to focus particularly on the courts. Powell was not arguing against an activist judiciary; he was arguing for a pro-business activist judiciary. "Under our constitutional system," he wrote, "especially with an activist-minded Supreme Court, the judiciary may be the most important instrument for social, economic, and political change." Powell continued: "This is a vast area of opportunity for the Chamber, if it is willing to undertake the role of spokesman for American business and if, in turn, business is willing to provide the funds." [*Memorandum from Lewis Powell to Eugene B. Snyder, Jr., Chairman, Education Committee, U.S. Chamber of Commerce, Attack On American Free Enterprise System: Confidential Memorandum, 10* (1971), available at http://www2.bc.edu/=plater/Newpublicsite05/02.5.pdf]

Powell saw his vision realized more quickly and effectively than he could have imagined. The Chamber led the assault that Powell envisioned, helping to develop a powerful infrastructure of trade association and advocacy groups. The Business Roundtable was founded in 1972, the Heritage Institute in 1973, the Cato Institute in 1977, the Washington Legal Foundation in 1978, the Manhattan Institute in 1980, and the American Tort Reform Association (ATRA) in 1986, to name only the most prominent groups dedicated to protecting business from governmental regulation generally and from the civil justice system specifically. Moreover, only two months after Powell wrote his famous memorandum, President Nixon nominated him to a seat on the United States Supreme Court. Powell's elevation to the Court was the beginning of a long conversion of the Court from protector of citizen rights to hold big business accountable to protector of business from citizen lawsuits.

Today "tort reform" means the opposite of what it meant a quarter of a century ago. Notwithstanding the progressive sound of the word reform, the phrase tort reform now stands for a collection of regressive proposals designed to shield big business and medicine from citizen lawsuits. It has been enormously successful. ATRA is able to boast that "85 percent of Americans believe too many frivolous lawsuits clog our courts," and "more than 45 states have enacted portions of ATRA's legislative agenda." Those two facts are directly related. Powell's strategy of simultaneously waging a two-front war, one in the branches of government and the other in the media, on the newsstands, and in universities and think tanks, worked. ATRA achieved successes in legislatures and the courts because it and its allies worked at shaping public opinion. Meanwhile, for too long the principal defender of the civil justice system, the American Association of Justice, directed its efforts principally at lobbying the political branches of government and litigating in the courts and largely neglected the public relations war. As a result, AAJ was like the boy with its thumb in the dike. It was able to succeed for a while but with the waters of adverse public opinion rising constantly, its position became increasingly untenable.

The public today believes that citizen litigation is expanding and that the courts are filled with frivolous lawsuits notwithstanding that the data prove otherwise. The conventional wisdom, however, affects not only voters, but legislators, judges, and juries. Champions of civil justice are increasingly defeated in all forums. At least twenty-five states have capped non-economic damages. Thirty-four states have capped punitive damages. The United States Supreme Court has also effectively imposed a constitutional cap on punitive damages by declaring that punitive awards are constitutionally suspect if they are more than four times compensatory damages and that "few awards exceeding a single-digit ratio between punitive and compensatory damages . . . will satisfy due process." Taking advantage of hysteria over rising medical malpractice premiums, in the first half of 2005 alone the health care industries persuaded thirty-one state legislatures to enact some form of medical malpractice tort reform. A majority of states have also enacted tort reform measures regarding joint and several liability and the collateral source rule. At the federal level, Congress has enacted a panoply of statutes designed to protect particular industries including gun manufacturers and an industry of special importance to national welfare, namely, the cruise ship industry from lawsuits.

The success of the tort reform movement is unfortunate. The common law plays an important role in protecting public health and safety. Lawsuits shine light into dark corners, exposing corporate wrongdoing or shortcuts that have placed citizens at risk. Indeed, it may be the exposure function that matters most, even more than the money judgments. But of course money matters too, providing incentives for business and health care providers to find ways to reduce injuries. Examples abound. Evidence shows that products liability has played a significant role in reducing the automobile fatality rate by 79 percent since the adoption of strict liability and the crashworthiness doctrine. Escalating medical malpractice premiums provided the incentive that caused the health care and insurance industries to team up, analyze why there were so many anesthesia-related fatalities, and find ways to make anesthesia safer indeed, making a twenty-fold improvement in the anesthesia mortality rate. Moreover, contrary to popular opinion, the tort system is cost effective: the best evidence is that the "tort tax," how much of the retail price we pay for products, covers litigation costs is on average 0.21 percent and the "malpractice tax" is between one and two percent of health care expenses. Although more research must be undertaken to provide conclusive evidence, the best data available now suggest that there is an inverse relationship between malpractice risk and injuries due to medical negligence, that is, the stronger the medical malpractice litigation system the safer the health care system. . . .

GEORGE PRIEST,[107] THE ECONOMIC CASE FOR TORT REFORM

Since the 1960s, courts in the United States have vastly expanded modern tort law. The expansion began with the adoption of the standard of strict liability for product defects by the California Supreme Court, but has extended to all states and across the full range of tort subjects, beyond the standard of strict products liability. The expansion is reflected both in the liberalization of standards of tort liability and in the restriction of earlier tort law defenses. A casual sample of tort cases thought worthy of litigation in the 1950s compared to tort cases litigated today will demonstrate the enormous legal changes that have occurred.

The chief economic effect of these changes is to introduce a wide range of insurance into tort judgments and settlements. Whenever a party is held liable for damage where the party could not have prevented the harm cost-effectively, the economic effect is to provide a form of insurance in the

---

[107] George Priest is a Professor of Law and Economics at Yale Law School. Before coming to Yale, he taught at the University of Chicago, SUNY/Buffalo, and UCLA. His subject areas are antitrust; capitalism or democracy; products liability; regulated industries; insurance and public policy; constitutional law; federalism; state and local government law; and civil procedure. Professor Priest has a B.A. from Yale and a J.D. from the University of Chicago. He has written widely on the history of the development of tort liability and on the economic effects of tort law, among other subjects. His scholarship includes Priest, The *Invention of Enterprise Liability: A Critical History of the Intellectual Foundations of Modern Tort Law*, 14 J. LEGAL STUDIES 461 (1985); *The Current Insurance Crisis and Modern Tort Law*, 96 YALE L.J. 1521 (1987); PRODUCTS LIABILITY LAW AND THE ACCIDENT RATE, IN LIABILITY: PERSPECTIVES AND POLICY at 184 (Litan & Winston eds., Brookings Inst. 1988); *Strict Products Liability: The Original Intent*, 10 CARDOZO L. REV. 2301 (1989).

damage award. Although courts will routinely state that they have no intent to make tortfeasors insurers, judgments (or settlements anticipating judgments) where the defendant could not have effectively prevented the harm inescapably introduce an insurance effect. As a consequence, modern tort law incorporates broad insurance features.

Despite these developments, it is widely accepted that tort law is a highly ineffective means of providing insurance in comparison to first-party insurance. The benefits provided through the third-party mechanism of tort law are substantially different—greater—than benefits provided in first-party insurance programs. There are clear conceptual reasons for these differences: Third-party tort law damages are designed to internalize all injury costs to the liable party to deter harm-causing behavior. In contrast, first-party insurance benefits are designed to best equalize income over periods where losses are suffered and where not. The highly competitive market for first-party insurance demonstrates that consumers for good economic reasons prefer insurance benefits limited in various ways to control moral hazard and adverse selection by insured parties in order to reduce premiums. Moral hazard and adverse selection by victims are not phenomena thought necessary to control in the definition of third-party tort law damages.

Third-party tort law damages and first-party insurance benefits differ in many respects. For example, first-party medical benefits uniformly incorporate deductibles and co-insurance, again to optimize premiums by controlling moral hazard. First-party disability and loss of employment benefits typically incorporate even greater deductibles and co-insurance. There is no first-party coverage of pain and suffering losses whatsoever because such losses do not typically affect income, the equalization of which over time is the function of insurance. Quite to the contrary, third-party tort law damages incorporate full medical and disability losses and full lost income—no deductibles or coinsurance—as well as substantial amounts for pain and suffering. As a consequence, insurance provided through the tort system provides benefits many multiples greater than optimal first-party insurance benefits and, of course, provides those benefits at administrative costs far greater than those of first-party insurance systems. The only economic explanation for the withdrawal of useful products and services with the expansion of tort liability is that tort law is providing insurance benefits in the price of products or services whose value to consumers is not worth the additional costs.

The principal economic role of tort reform is to rationalize the insurance system established by modern tort law. The most effective tort reform in this respect is to roll back standards of liability to only make liable those parties who could have cost-effectively prevented harms. Tort reform efforts of this nature, however, have been widely attacked chiefly by the tort bar and by consumer advocates who do not understand that modern tort law makes consumers pay prices for insurance far greater than their net benefit. Nevertheless, there have been some successes in this regard—successes ultimately for consumers—for example, the adoption of the negligence standard for medical malpractice in California during the 1980s and the federal statute limiting liability for general aircraft manufacturers which resuscitated an industry earlier driven out of business by expanded tort liability.

Other tort reform proposals seek to make modern tort law more resemble first-party insurance systems. Caps on pain and suffering damages approach this end partially; only partially, because first-party insurance provides <u>no</u> coverage of pain and suffering. Caps on punitive damages are similar; no consumer is willing to pay premiums sufficient to generate benefits equal to punitive damages. Restrictions on the doctrine of joint and several liability can be easily justified where tort law is providing a form of insurance; first-party insurance policies eliminate duplicative insurance requirements by incorporating what is called the "other insurance" clause, making only one insurer, not the insurers of many co-defendants, obligated to provide coverage. Similarly, restrictions on the collateral source rule serve to rationalize the insurance offering of modern tort law.

The economic effects of these various limitations on modern tort law damages judgments are complicated, however, because modern tort law continues to serve two purposes. The first purpose is to deter accident-causing behavior. In order to achieve this end, full third-party tort law damages should be awarded to achieve the optimal deterrent. The second purpose is to provide a form of compensation insurance, where full third-party damages are inappropriate and force consumers to pay for insurance in the prices of products and services at costs far higher than benefits. If courts continue to expand tort liability, the insurance function of tort law will expand and tort reform will become even more necessary to reduce costs for consumers. If courts begin to restrict tort liability or if tort reform efforts restricting liability become more successful, the need to adopt limitations on damages or collateral liability will decline.

GROUP THREE: TORT REFORM: A PERSONAL, PUBLIC, AND INSTITUTIONAL DISCOURSE

1.   Could it be that from the perspective of those seeking tort reform, everything about the tort system is broken—everything is in need of change—nothing works properly? By the same token, could it be that from the perspective of those opposed to tort reform, everything about the tort system is in good order—nothing should be changed—everything works just as it should?

While these two positions sound (and are) absurd, come to Washington and spend some time listening to testimony on tort reform. Nuanced positions, give and take on virtually any aspect of the civil justice system, or common ground does not appear to exist. While one commentator takes a stab at "common ground," it remains *terra incognita*.[108]

2.   As the essays in this section will demonstrate, there are irreconcilable disputes about the amount of jury verdicts, the effect of tort reform legislation at the state level, the ease with which cases can be brought, and the long-term future of the civil justice system—and disputes are appropriate. Data exists to support virtually any point of view regarding the size and frequency of judgments.[109] However, as will also be clear, the quality of the arguments, on both sides, is remarkably compelling. As you read through the next seven essays, try to stay objective. Of the powerful arguments put forward, which do you find most convincing?

---

[108] See Peter P. Budetti, *Tort Reform and the Patient Safety Movement: Seeking Common Ground*, 293 J. Am. Med. Assn. (No. 21) 2660 (2005).

[109] (Mark Twain wrote: "There are three kinds of lies: lies, damned lies, and statistics." Mark Twain's Autobiography (edited by Albert Bigelow Paine) Vol. 1, (1924), though there are many, including Benjamin Disraeli, credited with that particular insight.

LISA A. RICKARD,[110] MATTHEW D. WEBB,[111] AND MARY H. TERZINO,[112] AMERICAN TORT AND CIVIL LITIGATION— STILL AT A CROSSROADS?[113]

Introduction

When this essay was first published in 2010, it posited that American tort and civil litigation jurisprudence was at a crossroads. As the shape and scope of U.S. civil litigation continue to develop, the crossroads image remains apt. Consider for a moment the following statements, and how these divergent views—some of them spoken or written long ago –may still relate to the current American practice of law:

- [W]hat I call the "magic jurisdiction," . . . [is] where the judiciary is elected with verdict money. The trial lawyers have established relationships with the judges that are elected; they're State Court judges; they're popul[ists]. They've got large populations of voters who are in on the deal, they're getting their [piece] in many cases. And so, it's a political force in their jurisdiction, and it's almost impossible to get a fair trial if you're a defendant in some of these places. The plaintiff lawyer walks in there and writes the number on the blackboard, and the first juror meets the last one coming out the door with that amount of money . . . . The cases are not won in the courtroom. They're won on the back roads long before the case goes to trial. Any lawyer fresh out of law

---

[110] As president of the U.S. Chamber Institute for Legal Reform (ILR), Lisa A. Rickard provides strategic leadership to ILR's comprehensive program aimed at improving the nation's legal culture. Rickard has led multiple comprehensive legal reform campaigns at the state, federal and international level. Prior to joining ILR, Rickard served as vice president of federal and state government affairs for The Dow Chemical Company, senior vice president of federal and state government relations for Ryder System, Inc., and was a partner in the Washington, D.C., law firm of Akin, Gump, Strauss, Hauer & Feld. Rickard graduated from Lafayette College in Easton, Pennsylvania, and received her JD from the American University Washington College of Law, where she was executive editor of the L. Rev. She is a member of the District of Columbia Bar.

[111] As Senior Vice President for Legal Reform Policy at the U.S. Chamber Institute for Legal Reform, Matt Webb oversees the development and advocacy of the ILR's position and policy on key federal legal reform issues. Prior to joining the ILR, he was research director for Safe Streets, a not-for-profit foundation focusing on criminal justice reform. He is a member of the bar of the State of Maryland and graduated magna cum laude from American University's Washington College of Law where he was an Articles Editor on the L. Rev. He also holds a B.A. degree in Political Science from the University of Colorado and volunteers his free-time as a firefighter and paramedic in Northern Virginia.

[112] Mary H. Terzino is an attorney practicing in Michigan. Her work focuses on litigation and legal policy both within and outside the United States. She retired in 2010 as Assistant General Counsel and Director, Corporate Legal Issues at The Dow Chemical Company. Since 2010 Mary has advised several companies and organizations, including the U.S. Chamber Institute for Legal Reform. She obtained an A.B. from Marquette University and a J.D. with honors from the University of Wisconsin Law School, where she received the Dean's Academic Achievement Award and was elected to Order of the Coif.

[113] Portions of this essay are drawn from various prior publications and web postings of the U.S. Chamber Institute for Legal Reform.

school can walk in there and win the case, so it doesn't matter what the evidence or the law is.[114]

- I have the greatest practice of law in the world, I have no clients.[115]

- Litigation is the basic legal right which guarantees every corporation its decade in court.[116]

- Courts were not set up to be regulatory enterprises. They can serve that purpose, but compared to administrative bodies they're expensive and cumbersome. The explosion in litigation ... has been accompanied by a sense, held by lawyers, many judges, and law professors, too, that litigation is the best means to solve everybody's problems.[117]

- Discourage litigation. Persuade your neighbors to compromise whenever you can. Point out to them how the nominal winner is often a real loser—in fees, expenses, and waste of time. As a peacemaker the lawyer has a superior opportunity of being a good man. There will still be business enough.[118]

These statements raise important questions. Ultimately, is the modern practice of law solely a business concerned with maximizing the profits of the lawyers who engage in it? Who should control decisions made in litigation, such as whether to settle the case—the lawyers who handle the litigation or the clients? Do concepts like "justice" or "truth" still have a place in the current legal system or have they been effectively driven from it due to gamesmanship and the costs associated with modern litigation? Does our current system breed corruption? Does litigation as used today over-punish wrongdoers, especially when coupled with regulatory penalties? What sort of legal system should we strive towards and are we actually heading in that direction?

---

[114] Richard 'Dickie' Scruggs, Asbestos for Lunch, Panel Discussion at the Prudential Securities Financial Research and Regulatory Conference (May 9, 2002), in Industry Commentary (Prudential Securities, Inc., N.Y., New York), June 11, 2002, at 5. Dickie Scruggs was considered one of the leading members of the plaintiffs' trial bar handling asbestos and tobacco litigation. He served six years in federal prison after pleading guilty to attempting to bribe two Mississippi state court judges in separate cases. He was released in 2014.

[115] Peter Elkin, *The King of Pain Is Hurting,* FORTUNE, Sept. 4, 2000, at 190 (quoting William Lerach). William Lerach was one of the most prolific and successful securities class action plaintiffs' attorneys. He (along with several of his former law partners) served a federal prison sentence for illegal payments to lead plaintiffs in a number of his securities cases.

[116] Quotation attributed variously to David Porter, Microsoft Corporate Vice President of Retail Sales, and David Porter, British Member of Parliament (1988–1997).

[117] James M. Beck ("Bexis"), *Litigation—Has The Process Become The Purpose?*, published at https://www.druganddevicelawblog.com/2010/03/litigation-has-process-become-purpose.html.

[118] Abraham Lincoln, NOTES FOR A LAW LECTURE (1850), *reprinted in* THE COLLECTED WORKS OF ABRAHAM LINCOLN, at 81 (Roy P. Basler ed., Rutgers Univ. Press 1953).

These questions drive straight to the core of our legal system and its actors. Unfortunately, to answer them fully would require far more space than what is allotted for this brief essay. There are a few key areas, however, that we would like to touch upon that thematically highlight several of the crucial and interrelated issues facing today's American tort and civil litigation system.

The Distorting Effect of Large Scale Litigation

In the not-too-distant past, the evolution of tort law was largely driven by individualized disputes with relatively finite damages at stake. However, that perspective is rapidly giving way to a system identified with high stakes, high dollar cases largely initiated and controlled by the lawyers who bring them. These types of cases are frequently too expensive and risky for most defendants to seriously contemplate fully litigating even if they have done nothing wrong. This is due to the possibility of astronomical damage awards coupled with the extraordinarily expensive process of discovery in civil litigation. Furthermore, because of their size, these types of cases have a disproportionate impact on the overall legal system due to their ability to take up a disproportionate amount of judicial resources and attention. They also possess the very real potential of fostering significant corruption. Take, for example, asbestos-related litigation—the "granddaddy" of mass torts that has been the catalyst and ultimate funding source for many other types of mass tort lawsuits.

As a result of the widespread use of asbestos in manufacturing prior to the 1970s, tens of thousands of Americans were subject to occupational exposure to asbestos. This exposure placed them at particular risk for developing asbestos-related diseases, including asbestosis, lung cancer, and mesothelioma, an incurable cancer linked to asbestos. Personal injury litigation related to asbestos exposure "has continued for over 40 years in the United States with hundreds of thousands of claims filed and billions of dollars in compensation paid."[119] Thousands of companies have been named as defendants in asbestos cases, making this type of litigation the most expensive in U.S. history. To date, approximately 100 companies have filed for bankruptcy due to asbestos litigation liability,[120] affecting the American economy to the tune of $1.4 to $3 billion and costing as many as 60,000 Americans their jobs.[121] Experts at the RAND Institute for Civil

LOL

---

[119] Lloyd Dixon, et al., *Asbestos Bankruptcy Trusts: An Overview of Trust Structure and Activity with Detailed Reports on the Largest Trusts*, Rand Institute For Civil Justice, 2010, at xi.

[120] *Where are They Now, Part Six: An Update on Developments in Asbestos-Related Bankruptcy Cases*, Mealey's Asbestos Bankr. Rep., Vol. 11, No. 7 (February 2012).

[121] Joseph E. Stiglitz et al., *The Impact of Asbestos Liabilities on Workers in Bankrupt Firms*, Sebago Associates, 2002, at 27–29, 42).

Justice have projected that total corporate asbestos liability to U.S. plaintiffs could reach or exceed $260 billion.[122]

The bankruptcies of major asbestos companies gave rise to trust funds intended to compensate future asbestos victims. Today, these trusts control assets with an estimated value of more than $18 billion.[123] But the existence of the asbestos trusts has not slowed the wave of lawsuits against American businesses. In fact, one prominent plaintiffs' lawyer described asbestos litigation as an "endless search for a solvent bystander."[124]

The asbestos trusts operate in parallel with the traditional tort system and produce only rudimentary reports on the claims they receive and pay. As a result, plaintiffs' lawyers are sometimes able to mask the fact that a single individual is, or will be, making multiple claims against multiple trusts and solvent companies in which they cite contradictory information about the products to which they were exposed. The structure of the bankruptcy trust system, which gives control of the trusts (including payment criteria) to asbestos plaintiffs' lawyers, has exacerbated abuses. Asbestos claims "double dipping" occurs both between the tort and trust systems, and among trusts within the bankruptcy system. It exposes innocent businesses to abusive lawsuits, and by reducing the pool of available funds in the trusts, deprives legitimate victims of compensation from those assets.

In 2014, fraud in the tort system was demonstrated during the bankruptcy proceedings of Garlock Sealing Technologies, Inc., a manufacturer of asbestos-containing gaskets. The court required existing Garlock claimants to respond to personal information questionnaires and to provide information they had previously filed with other asbestos bankruptcy trusts. The court held that these disclosures revealed that some law firms had engaged in "suppression of evidence" when their clients were "unable to identify exposure in the tort case, but then later (and in some cases previously) were able to identify it in [t]rust claims."[125]

Problems have also been found in claims made to multiple trusts. A report published this year by the U.S. Chamber Institute for Legal Reform[126] examined a subset of 100 claims from the *Garlock* database and

---

[122] Stephen J. Carroll, et al., *Asbestos Litigation Costs and Compensation: An Interim Report*, Rand Institute For Civil Justice, 2002, at vii.

[123] Marc C. Scarcella & Peter R. Kelso, *Asbestos Bankruptcy Trusts: A 2013 Overview of Trust Assets, Compensation & Governance*, Mealey's Asbestos Bankruptcy Report 12, no. 11 (2013), Exhibit 2.

[124] Richard Scruggs & Victor Schwartz, *Medical Monitoring and Asbestos Litigation—A Discussion with Richard Scruggs and Victor Schwartz*, 1–7:21 Mealey's Asbestos Bankr. Rep. 5 (Feb. 2002) (quoting Scruggs).

[125] *In re Garlock Sealing Technologies*, 504 B.R. 71, 73 (W.D.N.C. 2014).

[126] James L. Stengel and C. Anne Malik, "Insights and Inconsistencies: Lessons from the Garlock Trust Claims," U.S. Chamber Institute for Legal Reform, February 2016. *See also* other documented cases discussed at http://www.wsj.com/articles/SB10001424127887323864304578318611662911912.

analyzed the dates, places, products, and descriptions of exposure provided by each claimant to each trust to determine what effect, if any, the trust system's flawed design might have in practice.

This review identified three widespread inconsistencies in the information provided to different trusts by claimants. Sixty-nine percent of claimants did not list with every trust every place of employment at which they alleged exposure. Fifteen percent of claimants did not list specific products or brands to which they alleged exposure. Over half of the claimants (55%) had date discrepancies across claim forms. Furthermore, 21 percent of the claims displayed even more worrisome inconsistencies, such as incompatible dates for jobs (where the dates for different jobs overlapped), inconsistent job descriptions, and implausible exposure allegations.[127]

unless these were required is it rlly an inconsistency?

ppl work multiple — jobs dude.

The *Garlock* story demonstrates that a lack of coordination between the tort and trust systems is creating abuse, and that asbestos bankruptcy trusts, by design, do not adequately compare the allegations made across trusts. This pattern underscores the problem that without external oversight and federal-level reform of the current trust system, fraudulent and inconsistent claims will continue.

Outsourcing of State Police Power and Over-Enforcement

A second troubling trend in American tort litigation is the outsourcing of state police power by government officials. This trend began with and then accelerated after the tobacco lawsuits of the 1990s generated significant state revenue and huge profits for certain plaintiffs' lawyers. This style of litigation now regularly occurs in a myriad of other areas. In this situation, officials such as state attorneys general hire outside members of the plaintiffs' trial bar to represent the state on a contingency fee basis. Unfortunately, this too results in an extreme level of distortion in the overall legal system.

Traditionally, government litigators, including state attorneys general, are charged with doing "justice" rather than solely focusing on the generation of a maximized monetary recovery (or legal fee) for the state (or its litigators). State attorneys general now, however, operate in a highly competitive and politically charged environment, where "activism" is the norm and generating media headlines is an ever-present goal. Accordingly, there is now enormous pressure to find new lawsuit targets and novel legal approaches as a way to generate positive press and revenue. However, "justice" is frequently lost when the personal profit motive associated with contingency fee litigation is inserted into the picture. By way of analogy, this situation is akin to police officers receiving a portion of their pay based on the dollar value of the traffic tickets they write and successfully win

---

[127] Stengel, *supra*, at 8–10.

enforcement of in court. Obviously, as in the asbestos context discussed above, this creates a situation ripe for overreaching, corruption and abuse.

Some plaintiffs' attorneys hired by attorneys general have been found to be major contributors to the campaigns of the government officials responsible for making the determination to hire a particular law firm or outsource a case in the first place. As plaintiffs' lawyers make huge personal profits from successful lawsuits, money effectively goes back into those government officials' election campaigns. Furthermore, a number of settlements in these types of cases are specifically designed to politically advantage the incumbent office holder and operate as a way to circumvent important separation of powers safeguards. These alliances raise significant concerns about conflicts of interest, favoritism, use of a public entity for personal gain, separation of powers, and fairness in government-sponsored litigation.

Fortunately, 21 states—Alabama[128], Arizona[129], Arkansas[130], Colorado[131], Florida[132], Indiana[133], Iowa[134], Kansas[135], Louisiana[136], Minnesota[137], Mississippi[138], Missouri[139], Nevada[140], North Carolina[141], North Dakota[142], Ohio[143], Texas[144], Utah[145], Virginia[146], West Virginia[147] and Wisconsin[148]—have passed "sunshine" legislation to create an open process of hiring outside contingency fee counsel. These measures vary, but more recent laws require state attorneys general to disclose their contingency fee contracts, ensure that they maintain control of the litigation and impose reasonable limitations on fee awards to private attorneys. Other attorneys general have adopted office policies that

---

[128] H.B. 227 (2013) codified at Ala Code § 41–16–72.

[129] H.B. 2423 (2011), as amended by S.B. 1132 (2012) codified at Ariz. Rev. Stat. § 41–4801 et seq.

[130] S.B. 204, (2015), codified at Ark. Code Ann. § 25–16–714.

[131] Colo. Rev. Stat. § 13–17–301 et seq.

[132] S.B. 712 (2010) codified at Fla. Stat. Ann. § 16.0155.

[133] S.B. 214 (2011) codified at Ind. Code Ann. § 4–6–3–2.5.

[134] H.F. 563 (2012) codified at Iowa Code §§ 13.7, 23B.1 et seq.

[135] Kan. Stat. Ann. § 75–37,135.

[136] La. Act No. 796 (2014) amending La. Rev. Stat. §§ 42:262, 49:259.

[137] Minn. Stat. § 8.065.

[138] H.B. 211 (2012) codified at Miss. Code Ann. §§ 7–5–5, 7–5–8, 7–5–21, 7–5–39.

[139] S.B. 59 (2011) codified at Mo. Rev. Stat. §§ 34.376, 34.378 and 34.380.

[140] S.B. 244 (2015), codified in Nev. Rev. Stat. ch. 228.

[141] S.B. 648 (2014) codified at N.C. Gen. Stat. § 114–9.2 et seq.

[142] N.D. Cent. Code § 54–12–08.1.

[143] S.B. 38 (2015), codified at Ohio Rev. Code Ann. § 9.49 et seq.

[144] Tex. Govt. Code § 2254.101 et seq.

[145] S.B. 233 (2015) amending Utah Code § 63G–6a–106.

[146] Va. Code Ann. § 2.2–510.1.

[147] H.B. 4007 (2016) amending W.Va. Code §§ 5–3–3, 5–3–4.

[148] A.B. 27 (2013) codified at Wis. Stat. §§ 14.11, 20.9305

implement many of these reforms. However, other government officials, including at the local level, have adopted the practice of hiring contingency fee counsel. This form of outsourcing is not likely to go away as long as the plaintiffs' bar continues to pitch government officials to obtain this business, and officials continue to ignore concerns about conflicts of interest and favoritism.

Outsourcing focuses on who prosecutes claims for the government. Recent events have shown that government enforcement actions also increasingly overstep other reasonable bounds related to the type, number and duplication of actions. Over-enforcement occurs when individual government agencies exercise unfettered discretion to rely on novel or expansive interpretations of laws to coerce settlements. Targeted companies cannot be certain that the courts will set aside these actions, given the often vague and broad statutory language that confers authority on these agencies.

Over-enforcement also occurs when the prosecution of wrongdoing is carried out by multiple regulators conducting duplicative investigations and legal actions, either simultaneously or in succession, which are directed at the very same conduct. Faced with these "pile on" multiple assaults, companies often have little choice but to agree to whatever *are they ???* settlements those various government officials demand, even if the *the victims...* company has meritorious arguments against the underlying charges.

An example of this type of over-enforcement arises in the context of drug manufacturers' promotion of off-label uses for its pharmaceutical products. Increasingly, state attorneys general are requiring companies to abide by expansive conditions of settlement which exceed those imposed by the federal laws and regulations of the Food and Drug Administration to *Is it rlly over-* which these companies are already subject. Where a comprehensive, *reach or just* sophisticated regulatory scheme already exists, it makes little sense for *trying to* states to transform the attorney general's office into a "mini FDA." These *protect their* requirements not only encroach on the federal regulatory power; they *citizens!* impose a patchwork of obligations which force companies to adhere to the most restrictive requirements to avoid further conflict. But such adherence is not necessarily in the best interests of society: It can reduce needed research on existing products; raise drug prices; and slow development of new beneficial products. *Not like that already happens... the HORROR :o*

Awww sad, so shouldn't have done it in the 1st place then. Another consequence of both coercive and "pile-on" over-enforcement is large and duplicative fines and penalties that too often are disproportionate to the alleged wrongdoing. It is irrational to punish a wrongdoer multiple times for the same malfeasance and for state and federal agencies to compete to wield the biggest stick, wasting public resources on duplicative efforts. A national conversation is needed about these practices to reform the practice of multiple, duplicative government agency involvement and to promote the goal of fostering compliance by providing more certainty to companies about the consequences of their actions.

Control over Litigation

A third problematic trend is the extent to which clients are no longer in control of their litigation. In the original Anglo-American jurisprudential model, clients were ultimately in charge of their cases. They sought out and hired the lawyer, had the final say (within key ethical boundaries) over how the case was to be handled as well as the ultimate authority to accept or reject settlement agreements. This model no longer holds true in much of America's large-scale litigation.

Today, lawyers routinely seek out clients rather than wait for the client to come to them. Lawyer advertising has expanded exponentially, with expenditures increasing by 68% over the past eight years to an estimated $892 million in 2015.[149] Ads targeting prescription drugs and medical devices are the most popular, with about 360,000 of them airing at a cost of $123 million in 2015. In the first half of 2016, about 217,000 such ads have aired.[150] One risk posed by such advertising is that through it, lawyers will control not only litigation, but also medical care. Lawyer's ads about drugs and medical devices often include extensive descriptions of serious adverse reactions, with little context about how common these side effects are.

For example, advertising involving the drug Xarelto™ is at the top of plaintiff lawyer ad buys. Millions of people take this drug each year. According to a recent medical report,[151] at least 30 people suffered serious medical problems—such as strokes, heart attacks and pulmonary embolisms—because they stopped taking the drug without their doctors' approval after seeing the commercial. Two of those patients died, including a 45-year-old man being treated for blood clots. Two others were paralyzed.

Lawyer control is also evident in the government litigation context, where state officials are frequently solicited to hire particular outside law firms who developed a new legal theory and possible targets for the state official to pursue. All the official has to do is sign the contingency fee agreement and the litigation is off and running—the legal equivalent of a fire-and-forget missile.

The problem is also present in the context of class action litigation. Admittedly, the legal rules surrounding class action litigation provide a patina of client-based control due to the requirement that there be a class

---

[149] http://www.forbes.com/sites/danielfisher/2015/10/27/lawyers-bump-advertising-spending -to-890-million-in-quest-for-clients/#236b6b6b35cf.

[150] http://legalnewsline.com/stories/510964259-ama-lawyer-ads-alarming-prescription-drug- users-jeopardizing-health-care.

[151] http://www.heartrhythmcasereports.com/article/S2214-0271(16)00014-2/fulltext.

representative as the "named" party as well as judicial oversight in the proceeding. The problem, however, is that in far too many circumstances the class representative and the judge hearing the case are unable or unwilling to truly exercise the level of oversight needed in this type of litigation. Furthermore, in some circumstances, lawyers have been known to effectively keep a stable of potential class representatives so the lawyer can have a "captive" client that will not question anything the lawyer does.

Perhaps even more troubling is the emerging trend of third-party funding of litigation (TPLF). This occurs when an outside financier "invests" in a lawsuit for profit, paying case costs and fees in exchange for a portion of the settlement or judgment, plus a repayment of its investment. If the claimant does not receive a recovery, the funder is paid nothing. Unlike the lawyer, the funder owes no fiduciary duty to the plaintiff.

While funders claim they do not control the litigation, they set budgets, decide when to pay, have input into which firm will represent the client, and exchange referrals with law firms. All of these are control mechanisms in practice if not in name. Increasingly, funders are investing in law firm litigation portfolios, thereby making the lawyer even more beholden to the views of the funder. Difficult issues arise when the interests of funder and client diverge; for example, whether to accept a settlement that would be satisfactory to the claimant, but does not match the funder's projection of the profits it seeks.[152]

The practice of litigation financing is virtually unregulated. There are no requirements to report the presence of financing in cases. This matters because litigation funding can have a material impact on the outcome of a case. Does the presence of a funder rule out non-monetary resolutions to the dispute? Would a judge's decisions be different knowing the presence of deep-pocketed financiers? And when there are true victims in a case, should they now take a third seat behind the lawyer and the funder in getting compensation?

Solutions and Conclusion

Ultimately, what should be done about the problematic trends discussed above? In our view, the first significant step is to limit the incentives for corruption associated with large scale litigation. In the asbestos context, the Furthering Asbestos Claim Transparency (FACT)

---

[152] *See, e.g.*, Altitude Nines, LLC v. Deep Nines, Inc., No. 603268–2008E (N.Y. Sup. Ct.) Deep Nines had an agreement with a funder which provided $8 million to finance patent litigation. The lawsuit settled for $25 million. The funder took $10.1 million (the return of its investment, plus 10% annual interest, plus a $700,000 fee). After this payment, attorneys' fees and court costs, Deep Nines kept $800,000. The funder, however, sued Deep Nines for an additional profit on its investment. The parties settled this lawsuit on confidential terms. *See also* Alison Frankel, *Patent Litigation Weekly: Secret Details of Litigation Financing*, THE AM LAW LITIGATION DAILY (Nov. 3, 2009); Joe Mullin, *Patent Litigation Weekly: How to win $25 million in a patent suit—and end up with a whole lot less*, THE PRIOR ART (Nov. 2, 2009).

Act[153] is federal legislation that would require asbestos personal injury settlement trusts to disclose information on their claims on a quarterly basis. This would allow trusts and businesses to identify and contest questionable claims. In addition, several states have proposed legislation or changes to court rules that would mandate greater transparency for trust claims. In 2012, Ohio[154] became the first state in the nation to enact a law that requires plaintiffs to file and disclose trust claims before proceeding to trial. Arizona[155], Oklahoma[156], Tennessee[157], Texas[158], Utah[159], West Virginia[160], and Wisconsin[161] have enacted similar laws. Other states should follow their lead.

In all civil matters, the costs associated with modern litigation need to be controlled (particularly discovery costs) so that all parties in a particular lawsuit can afford to let the system work rather than have external cost factors drive all of the significant decision-making in a case—particularly whether or not to settle. In addition, the loopholes that currently allow so much gamesmanship in modern litigation need to be closed—venue reform chief among them. In short, there should be no more "Scruggsian magic jurisdictions."

Government practices that foster a profit-making litigation mind-set need to be reined in. Outsourcing of government litigation should be closely controlled with clear disclosures of the contingency fee contracts in those types of cases. Only a single government entity should be permitted to take action with respect to a particular course of corporate conduct, and to the extent state authorities are involved, they should be prohibited from entering into settlement agreements that effectively regulate conduct in other states.

Finally, legal rules that make clear that it is the client who ultimately controls the litigation need to be clarified, expanded and where already in existence, actively enforced. TPLF agreements should be transparent in litigation, disclosed to the court and parties, and the industry should be subject to government oversight.

For those who are just beginning their journey into the law, this is an interesting time. The civil justice system is still at a crossroads—in part because the system keeps evolving at a rapid pace. Those active in the system—especially plaintiffs' lawyers and government lawyers—continue

---

[153] H.R. 1927 and S. 357 (114th Congress, 2015–2016).
[154] H.B. 380 (2012) codified at Ohio Rev. Code §§ 2307.951 to 2307.954.
[155] H.B. 2603 (2015) codified at Ariz. Rev. Stat. § 12–782.
[156] S.B. 404 (2013) codified at Okla. Stat. tit. 76, §§ 81 to 89.
[157] S.B. 2062 (2016) codified at Tenn. Code § 29–34–601 et. seq.
[158] H.B. 1492 (2015) codified at Tex. Civ. Prac. & Rem. Code § 90.051 et seq.
[159] H.B. 403 (2016) codified at Utah Code § 78B–6–2001 et. seq.
[160] S.B. 411 (2015) codified at W. Va. Code § 55–7E–1 et seq.
[161] A.B. 19 (2014) codified at Wis. Stat. § 802.025.

to develop new theories of liability and new ways to enhance their recoveries. Perhaps never before has the overall American tort and civil litigation system been in such a continuous state of transformation. No matter one's particular philosophical leanings, it is fair to say that the outcomes of those changes will have profound implications for generations to come—not just for the lawyers who work in these areas on a daily basis, but for American society as a whole.

PAUL TAYLOR,[162] STRENGTHENING DEMOCRACY THROUGH TORT REFORM

When I think of tort reform, I think "Power to the People!" That may seem odd, especially when many opponents of tort reform present themselves as the people's saviors. But our constitutional republic envisions "the People" as being their own masters, and I hope in this short essay to present a picture of tort reform as I understand it: as a predominantly pro-democracy movement.

To see how tort reform is pro-democracy, consider the anti-democratic aspects of tort law. The Constitution defines a judge's role as deciding "cases and controversies" between specific individuals. But tort law today, with its emphasis on cost-benefit analysis, makes judges into policymakers who can impose policies that bankrupt national companies, enjoin productive activity, and set national product standards. Those decisions can trump policies enacted by the elected branches of government. Federal judges are unelected and serve for life, and state judges are often appointed, and when they do run for election they often run unopposed and have lengthy terms. Consider further that judges don't have to worry about being sued for handing down decisions that do harm because the long-established doctrine of judicial immunity shields them from claims that their own actions or inactions made things worse.[163] And given that

---

[162] Paul Taylor is a graduate of Yale College, summa cum laude (1991), and of the Harvard Law School, cum laude (1994). He is Chief Counsel to the House Subcommittee on the Constitution and Civil Justice. The conclusions and opinions expressed in this article are exclusively those of the author, and do not represent any official or unofficial position of the House Committee on the Judiciary, any of its subcommittees, or any of its members. The gist of this essay derives from three of the author's longer articles: *The Difference Between Filing Lawsuits and Selling Widgets: The Lost Understanding that Some Attorneys' Exercise of State Power Is Subject to Appropriate Regulation*, 4 PIERCE L. REV. 45, 51 (2005); *We're All in This Together: Extending Sovereign Immunity to Encourage Private Parties to Reduce Public Risk*, 75 U. CIN. L. REV. 1595 (2007); and *The Federalist Papers, the Commerce Clause, and Federal Tort Reform*, 45 SUFFOLK U. L. REV. 357 (2012).

[163] The Supreme Court has held that absolute judicial immunity applies to protect judges even when they are accused of acting maliciously or corruptly. *See* Pierson v. Ray, 386 U.S. 547, 554 (1967) ("This immunity applies even when the judge is accused of acting maliciously and corruptly"). This is so even though, as Peter Huber has written, "The legal system has no special competence to assess and compare public risks, and the legal process is not designed or equipped to conduct the broad-ranging, aggregative inquiries on which sensible public-risk choices are

freedom, judges are too often eager to accede to lawyers' demands that the power of the judiciary be expanded, at the expense of other branches of government, and democracy generally.[164]

Now let's consider the anti-democratic aspects of lawyers who sue in tort. They exercise state power, just as judges do.[165] Lawyers who sue in tort have become in large part state actors[166] who exercise state power for their own financial gain.[167] They can file complaints after paying nominal filing fees, at their unfettered discretion, and immediately subject defendants to the threat of a default judgment against them (enforced by the state) if they fail to respond, thereby requiring those defendants to spend money and other resources toward their own defense, no matter how frivolous the claims against them.[168] Plaintiffs' lawyers can exert the leverage they enjoy in virtue of this state-enforced economic bargaining advantage to extort monetary settlements from defendants that fall just short of the costs of defense that would be necessary for defendants to litigate the case to a costly "victory," since the current American legal

---

built." Peter Huber, *Safety and the Second Best: The Hazards of Public Risk Management in the Courts*, 85 COLUM. L. REV. 277, 310–11, 329 (1985).

[164] *See* Dennis Jacobs, *The Secret Life of Judges*, 75 FORDHAM L. REV. 2855, 2857–58 (2007) ("Public interest cases afford a judge sway over public policy, enhance the judicial role, make the judge more conspicuous, and keep the law clerks happy. Whether fee-paid or pro bono publico, when lawyers present big issues to the courts, the judges receive the big issues with grateful hands; the bar patrols against inroads on jurisdiction and independence and praises the expansion of legal authority; and together we smugly congratulate ourselves on expanding what we are pleased to call the rule of law. Among the results are the displacement of legislative and executive power, the subordination of other disciplines and professions, and the reduction of whole enterprises and industries to damages . . . . [O]ur highly ramified litigation system imposes vast costs on other fields of endeavor, on our democratic freedoms, and on the unrepresented and the non-litigious.").

[165] Juries, too, exercise government power, and just like any other entity that exercises government power, they should be subject to reasonable checks. But while jury decisions can be checked by courts to some extent (for example, courts can issue a judgment notwithstanding the verdict), judges often fail to fulfill their role as legal gatekeepers, and allow reckless claims to proceed. *See* Philip K. Howard, *When Judges Won't Judge*, WALL ST. J., Oct. 22, 2003 ("Judges today consider civil justice as a private dispute, rather than a use of state power. They can't imagine on what basis they should have the authority to limit claims. Just let the two litigants slug it out in front of the jury. As one judge suggested to me, 'Who am I to judge?' ").

[166] As leading legal ethics scholar Geoffrey Hazard has written, "The function of lawyer is closely related to the exercise of government power. We wish to control the exercise of government power through constitutions and laws. So also we wish to use constitutions and laws to control the exercise of the quasi-governmental power that is exercised through our profession." Geoffrey C. Hazard, Jr., *The Legal and Ethical Position of the Code of Professional Ethics* 7 *in* 5 SOCIAL RESPONSIBILITY: JOURNALISM, LAW, MEDICINE (Louis W. Hodges ed. 1979).

[167] Richard A. Posner, ECONOMIC ANALYSIS OF LAW 565 (5th ed., Aspen Publishers, Inc. 1998) ("[T]he legal process relies for its administration primarily on private individuals motivated by economic self-interest rather than on altruists or officials.").

[168] *See* D. Rosenberg & S. Shavell, *A Model in which Suits are Brought for their Nuisance Value*, 5 INT'L REV. L. & ECON. 3, 4 (June 1985) ("Suppose, for instance, that the plaintiff files a claim and demands $180 in settlement. The defendant will then reason as follows. If he settles, his costs will be $180. If he rejects the demand and does not defend himself, he will lose $1000 by default judgment. If he rejects the demand and defends himself, the plaintiff will withdraw, but he will have spent $200 to accomplish this. Hence, the defendant's costs are minimized if he accepts the plaintiff's demand for $180; and the same logic shows that he would have accepted any demand up to $200. It follows that the plaintiff will find it profitable to file his nuisance claim; indeed, this will be so whenever the cost of filing is less than the defendant's cost of defense.").

regime generally does not require lawyers filing frivolous lawsuits to pay the defendant's costs of defending themselves, or impose other significant penalties that would deter meritless lawsuits.[169] Members of no other profession enjoy the same coercive power to extort money from innocent people and businesses by merely filing a piece of paper. Consequently, lawyers have become more politically influential, and governments and (largely elected) state court judges have created means for satisfying a greater and greater demand for their services[170] while providing greater and greater protections for lawyers from lawsuits directed against them, at the expense of other professions. In the field of malpractice, for example, judges (almost all former lawyers) have crafted rules that make it much more difficult to sue a lawyer for malpractice than to sue a doctor for malpractice.[171]

So the judiciary can tend toward oligarchy, and tort lawyers can tend toward piracy. These tendencies can scare private citizens into inaction. For example, a company might produce a beneficial product and sell lots of them. A full 99% of those products may yield tremendous benefits to consumers, but if just 1% or less come to be associated with some harm—for whatever reason, including user error—lawsuits may follow claiming the companies are financially responsible for the associated harm, whether or not the company is to blame in any larger moral sense. The foreseen, potentially infinite liability to which those few lawsuits can expose a company may tend to deter it from selling any of the products in the first place, which, if sold, would have yielded vastly greater social benefits. Because the common law imposes neither a duty on private entities to act

---

[169] Sanctions for the filing of frivolous lawsuits are not mandatory in the large majority of states and the District of Columbia.

[170] *See* Paul Taylor, *The Difference Between Filing Lawsuits and Selling Widgets: The Lost Understanding that Some Attorneys' Exercise of State Power Is Subject to Appropriate Regulation*, 4 PIERCE L. REV. 45, 51 (2005) (elaborating on history of attorney regulations) ("Attorneys' fees were heavily regulated in the American Colonial Era and in the Post-Revolutionary Period. Then, in the mid-nineteenth century, New York's influential Field Code of Civil Procedure rejected any regulation of attorneys' fees but conceded that a 'loser-pays' rule was justified by the costs attorneys could impose on innocent victims simply by virtue of filing a lawsuit. In the years that followed, however, fee-shifting provisions materialized in this country in a manner that benefited plaintiffs only, and not defendants. The result has been an abdication of any significant limits on the power of attorneys to file lawsuits, the encouragement of the filing of lawsuits through fee-shifting rules that benefit plaintiffs alone, and—with the rise of the numbers and influence of attorneys in America—the triumph of rules that only create additional demand for attorneys.").

[171] *See* Benjamin H. Barton, THE LAWYER-JUDGE BIAS IN THE AMERICAN LEGAL SYSTEM 162, 187 (Cambridge Univ. Press: 2011) ("It is much harder to prove legal malpractice than medical malpractice. This is because lawyers have enjoyed several unique advantages as defendants in malpractice actions. . . . Courts have justified many of these differences on the now-familiar ground that lawyers are special and need special treatment. . . . When other types of litigants argue that the threat of a lawsuit disrupts their place of business and their ability to do a job, courts are generally unsympathetic. . . . When this reasoning is used against lawyers or courts, however, there is an overriding public policy interest in avoiding lawsuits. Between these rules and the relative lack of judicial or disciplinary authority oversight, what is keeping us safe from incompetent or malicious lawyering?").

for another's benefit nor liability for failing to act,[172] in most instances, if a private entity decides not to provide a good or service, that private entity cannot be sued for a failure to act. On the other hand, in most instances, when a private entity voluntarily acts, it opens itself up to costly lawsuits claiming the private entity's actions fell short in some way. And because manufacturers have no practical way of keeping their products out of certain states, personal injury lawyers generally get to choose the forum (and consequently the law) of their choice.[173] As a result, the jurisdictions most friendly to personal injury lawyers can unfairly impose the costs of their rules on consumers nationwide and redistribute income from out-of-state parties to in-state parties.[174]

If costly tort lawsuits are preventing private entities from voluntarily producing goods and services that would benefit the American public if sold, the public may spur their legislatures to enact tort reform that removes barriers that discourage private entities from taking actions that increase public benefits or reduce public risk. In this way, tort reform can provide the sort of "check and balance" that helps ensure the "separation of powers" the Framers of the Constitution insisted upon—namely a mode of government designed to limit state power in ways that allow "the People themselves" to have the ultimate say in the policies that govern them. Yet at the state level, duly-elected representatives in state legislatures that enact statutes that aim to do just that often see those same state statutes overturned by the very judges whose failures the state legislatures sought to address.[175]

---

[172] *See* RESTATEMENT (SECOND) OF TORTS § 314 (1965) (stating that, absent a special relationship, an actor is under no duty to aid or protect a third party).

[173] Richard "Dickie" Scruggs, one the nation's wealthiest personal injury attorneys, *see* Tom Wilemon, *Social Ties Bind Political Elite*, BILOXI SUN HERALD, Oct. 13, 2002, at 10, described so-called state "magic jurisdictions" as follows: "[W]hat I call the 'magic jurisdiction' . . . [is] where the judiciary is elected with verdict money. The trial lawyers have established relationships with the judges that are elected. . . . They've got large populations of voters who are in on the deal. . . . And so, it's a political force in their jurisdiction, and it's almost impossible to get a fair trial if you're a defendant in some of these places. . . . Any lawyer fresh out of law school can walk in there and win the case, so it doesn't matter what the evidence or the law is." Jim Copland, *The Tort Tax*, WALL ST. J., June 11, 2003, at A16 (quoting Dickie Scruggs).

[174] *See* Richard Neely, THE PRODUCTS LIABILITY MESS: HOW BUSINESS CAN BE RESCUED FROM THE POLITICS OF STATE COURTS 4 (1988) (in which former West Virginia Supreme Court Justice Neely stated "As long as I am allowed to redistribute wealth from out-of-state companies to injured in-state plaintiffs, I shall continue to do so. Not only is my sleep enhanced when I give someone else's money away, but so is my job security, because the in-state plaintiffs, their families and their friends will reelect me.").

[175] *See* Victor E. Schwartz & Leah Lorber, *Judicial Nullification of Civil Justice Reform Violates the Fundamental Constitutional Principle of Separation of Powers: How to Restore the Right Balance*, 32 RUTGERS L.J. 907, 919–20 (2001) ("[S]tate constitutions are usually lengthy, prolix, and filled with open-ended provisions. These provisions are malleable and provide an opportunity for a judge who perceives the judiciary to be the dominant branch of government to easily forget the appropriate powers of its co-equal branch, the legislature. For example, a number of state constitutions have so-called 'open courts' provisions. As a practical matter, they are intended to provide citizens of a state with justice and reasonable access to the courts. Open court provisions, however, can be stretched to suggest that *any* time a legislature in *any* way limits any person's rights to sue, it is violative of the 'open courts' provision. There is no state constitutional

In the modern era, Congress has enacted many federal tort reform statutes that supersede contrary state laws, and judicial precedents leave little doubt as to their constitutionality.[176] Even President Ronald Reagan, known for his deference to the states, established a special task force to study the need for tort reform that concluded the federal government should address the modern tort liability crisis in a variety of ways, including by placing federal limits on lawsuits.[177]

The principal architects and advocates of the federal Constitution— James Madison and Alexander Hamilton—made clear in the *Federalist Papers* that Congress has the constitutional authority to enact legislation that breaks down the types of barriers to trade and free enterprise caused by abusive state tort laws.

James Madison called the *Federalist Papers* "the most authentic exposition of the text of the federal Constitution, as understood by the Body which prepared & the Authority which accepted it."[178] And what did Hamilton and Madison have to say about the Constitution's Commerce Clause—which grants Congress the power "to regulate Commerce among the several States"—in the *Federalist Papers*? The Commerce Clause was necessary to allow Congress the ability to provide for the free flow of labor, goods, and services nationwide so America could become a dominant economic power. As Hamilton wrote in Federalist No. 11, "An unrestrained intercourse between the States themselves will advance the trade of each by an interchange of their respective productions, not only for the supply of reciprocal wants at home, but for exportation to foreign markets. The veins of commerce in every part will be replenished, and will acquire additional motion and vigor from a free circulation of the commodities of every part. Commercial enterprise will have much greater scope, from the diversity in the productions of different States. When the staple of one fails from a bad harvest or unproductive crop, it can call to its aid the staple of another. . . ."

Further, the Commerce Clause was necessary to allow Congress to counter not only the sorts of state-imposed trade barriers that increased

---

history that suggests this extreme result. Respect for fundamental principles of separation of powers abhors such an interpretation. Nevertheless, in the area of civil justice reform and judicial nullification of legislative efforts to improve our system of justice, such interpretations have grown like weeds in some jurisdictions.").

[176] The Congressional Research Service "concludes that enactment of tort reform legislation generally would appear to be within Congress's power to regulate commerce, and would not appear to violate principles of due process or federalism . . . In concluding that Congress has the authority to enact tort reform 'generally,' we refer to reforms that have been widely implemented at the state level, such as caps on damages and limitations on joint and several liability and on the collateral source rule." Henry Cohen, CRS REPORT TO CONGRESS: FEDERAL TORT REFORM LEGISLATION: CONSTITUTIONALITY AND SUMMARIES OF SELECTED STATUTES 1 (2003).

[177] U.S. Dep't of Justice, Report of the Tort Policy Working Group on the Causes, Extent and Policy Implications of the Current Crisis in Insurance Availability and Affordability 80 (1986).

[178] Letter from Madison to Thomas Jefferson (Montpellier, Feb. 8, 1825).

prices in existence at the time, but also future trade barriers the nature of which would change with time. As Madison wrote in Federalist No. 42, "We may be assured by past experience, that such a practice would be introduced by future contrivances" if Congress did not have the authority to break down barriers to trade imposed by the states.

How does all this relate to modern tort law? In Federalist No. 42, Madison wrote the Commerce Clause is necessary to allow Congress to counter "future contrivances" in the states that limit the free flow of goods and services nationwide. One such "future contrivance" is the vast expansion of tort liability in the states, and the adverse economic effects of such an expansion, that has occurred since 1789. As legal historian Lawrence Friedman has describes the current situation, "The dramatic extension of the tort system in the twentieth century is unquestionably real. People brought lawsuits which would have been unthinkable in the nineteenth century, or even in the earlier part of the twentieth."[179]

While some may argue that federal action to address overly expansive state tort liability is unnecessary because businesses can simply avoid states that have oppressive tort laws, Madison rejected that argument against Congressional action. As Madison argued, Congress should have the power to enact rules that allow products and services to enter into a state jurisdiction without having to worry that doing so would dramatically increase the price of their products and services elsewhere.[180] Madison described the purpose of the Commerce Clause as providing for "the relief of the States which import and export through other States, from the improper contributions levied on them by the latter [that] load the articles of import and export, during the passage through their jurisdiction, with duties which would fall on the makers of the latter and the consumers of the former."[181] He foresaw the problem in which products or services would be made to cost more to consumers in one state because other states those products and services passed through would levy costly duties on them. Just like the levied duties Madison complained of, state tort law has dramatic negative effects on the interstate movement of labor, goods, and services.

The arguments made in the *Federalist Papers* support federal products liability reforms that prevent some states from disadvantaging nationally

---

[179]   Lawrence Friedman, American Law in the 20th Century 372 (2002).

[180]   Federalist No. 42 (Madison). Madison, in his own notes on the debates over the Commerce Clause at the Constitutional Convention, described himself (in the third person) as saying the following about the Commerce Clause: "Whether the States are now restrained from laying tonnage duties [under the Commerce Clause] depends on the extent of the power 'to regulate commerce.' These terms are vague, but seem to exclude this power of the States . . . He was more & more convinced that the regulation of Commerce was in its nature indivisible and ought to be under one [federal] authority." Notes of Debates in the Federal Convention of 1787, Reported by James Madison 644–45 (W.W. Norton & Co. 1987).

[181]   Federalist No. 22 (Madison)

sold and distributed products through state tort laws that stifle national commerce.[182] A modern manifestation of the problem Madison and Hamilton foresaw is that, today, some states' tort laws allow virtually unlimited lawsuits that increase the costs of selling products or services that cross into their jurisdictions. The modern term applied to that phenomenon is the "tort tax,"[183] and when it is applied to national industries, it is passed on to consumers everywhere. The result is higher prices, and lost jobs, across multiple states, or nationwide. When that happens, Congress can, and often should, enact federal tort reform to preserve federalism principles. Tort reforms, of course, can be enacted at the state level. In the absence of state action, however, the *Federalist Papers'* understanding of the Commerce Clause allows ample room for federal action, on behalf of the people, through their duly-elected representatives.[184]

---

[182] Federalist No. 22 (Hamilton) ("[Y]et we may reasonably expect, from the gradual conflicts of State regulations, that the citizens of each would at length come to be considered and treated by the others in no better light than that of foreigners and aliens.").

[183] *See, e.g.*, Lawrence J. McQullian & Hovannes Abramyan, U.S. TORT LIABILITY INDEX: 2008 REPORT 10 (Pac. Res. Inst. 2008) (concluding that excessive tort liability imposes "an annual 'excess tort tax' of $7,848 on a family of four").

[184] Of course, the Constitutional Convention was convened to create a more powerful, but still limited, federal government, and a system of enumerated Congressional powers that contained an enumerated power without limit would have thwarted that core purpose. And so the Commerce Clause was understood by Madison and Hamilton as being confined to limited purposes. One can discern at least two limiting principles governing *The Federalist Papers'* understanding of the limits on Congress' Commerce Clause power. First, only those Congressional regulations that facilitate voluntary commerce, and not those that interfere with it, fulfill the purpose of the Commerce Clause as described in *The Federalist Papers*. Second, as Madison wrote, the states' interference with the free flow of goods and services nationwide must be significant enough to become a danger to "the great and aggregate interests" that are the proper domain of the federal government. *See* Federalist No. 10 (Madison) ("The federal Constitution forms a happy combination in this respect; the great and *aggregate* interests being referred to the national, the local and particular to the State legislatures.") (emphasis added); *see also* Federalist No. 46 (Madison) ("Every one knows that a great proportion of the errors committed by the State legislatures proceeds from the disposition of the members to sacrifice the comprehensive and permanent interest of the State, to the particular and separate views of the counties or districts in which they reside. And if they do not sufficiently enlarge their policy to embrace the collective welfare of their particular State, how can it be imagined that they will make the *aggregate* prosperity of the Union, and the dignity and respectability of its government, the objects of their affections and consultations?") (emphasis added) (arguing for greater federal control over states). Hamilton later made the same argument at the New York Convention to ratify the Constitution, saying that under the Constitution "The powers of the new government are general, and calculated to embrace the *aggregate* interests of the Union, and the general interest of each state, so far as it stands in relation to the whole. The object of the state governments is to provide for their internal interests, as unconnected with the United States, and as composed of minute parts or districts . . ." Hamilton, Speech in the New York Ratifying Convention on Interests and Corruption (June 21, 1788) *in* HAMILTON: WRITINGS 498–99 (Libr. of Am. 2001) (emphasis added).

SUE STEINMAN,[185] TORT REFORM:
A PERSONAL REFLECTION

I have a confession to make. I hated civil procedure in law school. And if you told me that my job at the American Association for Justice would morph from fighting limits on damages to more pernicious, more manipulative, but harder to quantify threats to civil procedure, I would not have been interested. And yet, the job of protecting Americans' access to the courts has shifted dramatically in the course of just a few years.

First, caps on damages fell out of favor. It's not just that the Senate has failed to pass medical malpractice damage caps on numerous occasions. The rise of medical errors was making patients and their families uneasy. A study published in May, 2016 in the British Medical Journal by Dr. Marty Makary[186] found that medical errors are the third leading cause of death in the United States. That's about 700 deaths a day—around five 737 jetliners crashing every day. People, and that includes members of Congress, know patients who have been harmed by medical errors. The problem that actually needs to be solved is a reduction of medical errors, not the passage of damage caps which would only hurt patients with the most serious injuries.

Second, Congress—and more specifically, the House Judiciary Committee—has come up with some unnecessary changes to civil procedure that would make it much more difficult for tort victims to recover in court. One bill, the Lawsuit Abuse Reduction Act (LARA), would make Rule 11 sanctions mandatory instead of discretionary. Rule 11 sanctions were mandatory for a period of time between 1983 and 1993 during which time there an explosion of satellite litigation causing delays and wasted judicial resources. Incidentally, the changes from discretionary to mandatory and then back to discretionary were made by the Judicial Conference, the policy-making arm of the federal courts, which views mandatory Rule 11 sanctions as a failed experiment.[187]

Another piece of legislation, the Fairness in Class Action Litigation Act, would make it virtually impossible for federal courts to certify class actions. The bill requires that the named plaintiff or plaintiffs suffer the same type and scope of injury as the other class members. This is almost impossible to prove. For example, in a wage and hour class action, the class members generally suffer vastly different economic loss based on the specifics of their job, how many hours each employee works per week, how

---

185 Sue Steinman is Director of Policy for the American Association for Justice (formerly the Association of Trial Lawyers of America) where she oversees the development of AAJ policy positions, and specializes in health care and medical liability, preemption, and civil procedure issues. In addition, she lobbies against so-called "tort reform" and for protection of consumer remedies. Ms. Steinman holds a J.D. from George Washington University National Law Center and a B.A. in political science from Tufts University.

186 http://www.bmj.com/content/353/bmj.i2139.

187 http://www.afj.org/wp-content/uploads/2015/04/Judicial-Conference-Letter.pdf.

long the employee has held the position, and many other factors, but these factors certainly do not affect or even diminish a claim for wage discrimination or for failure to pay overtime.

The Fraudulent Joinder Prevention Act (FJPA) is another bill in search of a problem. The bill is really about fraudulent removal, and if I try to explain it to you, it will make your head hurt, but I will try. If a plaintiff brings a case against an in-state defendant and out-of-state defendant in state court, that case should stay in state court because there is incomplete diversity and no basis for federal court jurisdiction. Under FJPA, the diverse defendant removes the case to federal court and then argues that the nondiverse defendant does not belong in the case. The bill changes the rules so that remanding the case back to state court where it properly belongs becomes more difficult. Currently, the test for improper joinder is a straight-forward one part test—no possibility of a claim against a nondiverse defendant. The bill, as passed by the House, is a novel four-part test.[188] For example, if a plaintiff brought a claim against a local insurance agent (nondiverse defendant) and a national insurance company (diverse defendant) for alleging bad faith for failing to pay insurance claims, and the national insurance company removed the case to federal court, the FJPA would make it much more difficult for plaintiff to remand the state-based insurance claims to state court. There is no reason to remove these cases to federal court. There is nothing inherently federal about them, and with an increasing number of district courts in judicial crisis due to judicial vacancies, flooding those dockets with state claims makes no sense from a case management perspective.

Taken together the three bills provide unnecessary obstacles to plaintiffs seeking access to justice. The drafters of the legislation originally offered the bills to deal with a specific case or particular genre of cases, but sometimes other cases receive media attention. The proponents of the Fairness in Class Action Litigation Act argued that the bill was necessary because courts were certifying class actions in which class members did not suffer actual injury. Using the examples of front loading washing machines that grew mold, proponents argued that not all consumers should receive compensation because the threat of mold is not the same thing as actual mold. Whirlpool even developed a product, Affresh Cleaner, consumers can purchase to alleviate mold and mildew. Still, the consumer didn't get the benefit of the bargain. The washing machine doesn't actually work like it should, and requiring the consumer to spend more money to get it to work

---

[188] The test is 1) whether there is a "plausible" claim for relief against each nondiverse defendant; 2) whether there is "objective evidence" that clearly demonstrates no good faith intention to prosecute the action against each defendant or intention to seek a joint judgment; 3) federal or state law that bars claims against the nondiverse defendants; or 4) there is actual fraud in the pleading of jurisdictional facts.

properly while the manufacturer earns additional profits from a cleaning product is actually pretty outrageous.

While Congress was debating the injuries involved with moldy washing machines, Volkswagen happened. When consumers realized that their cars were polluting machines worth a fraction of what they paid for them with no resale value whatsoever, it was not hard to fight back against the idea that every class member has the exact same injury.

As an aside, I actually own one of these front-loading washing machines manufactured by a different company, and it does get a funky smell if the door isn't left open. It's a good thing that the washing machine is located in my basement and not in a corridor or a closet where the door would have to be closed some of the time. I leave a dehumidifier running in the summertime so the machine actually dries out, and every few weeks, I have to run a cycle with no clothes and bleach to keep the machine fresh smelling. All of this is annoying, and I did not get what I bargained for.

Third and finally, unsatisfied that these bills have not gone anywhere in the Senate, proponents have looked to another venue—the courts—to try to accomplish their goals. The Judicial Conference is the policy-making arm of the federal courts and under the Rules Enabling Act has the authority to amend the Federal Rules of Civil Procedure and the Federal Rules of Evidence. Frustrated by lack of action by Congress, the U.S. Chamber of Commerce and the Lawyers for Civil Justice have submitted proposals to change the rules of civil procedure, including Rule 23 (class actions), in an effort to address issues that Congress has not addressed.

I think everyone who works in and around Washington, DC should spend part of each year away speaking to other people because it provides such a different perspective on government, its purpose, and how it can best serve the public. No one outside of DC and federal court litigators believes that changing the federal rules of civil procedure would affect their lives whatsoever. It's clear that Congress could and should spend its time on legislation that would have a more meaningful impact on its constituents.

AARON D. TWERSKI,[189] MUSINGS OF A SO-CALLED TORT REFORMER

What constitutes tort reform? Who is a tort reformer? If it is defined as anyone who disagrees with the full agenda of the American Trial

---

[189] Professor Aaron D. Twerski is the Irwin and Jill Cohen Professor of Law at Brooklyn Law School. Professor Twerski is a preeminent authority in the areas of products liability and tort law. The American Bar Association's Tort Trial & Insurance Practice Section has honored him with the Robert B. McKay Law Professor Award, which recognizes law professors who are committed to the advancement of justice, scholarship and the legal profession in the fields of tort and insurance law.

Lawyers Association, then I would say that a large number of academics, myself included, are tort reformers. However, if those who advocate sensible moderate views designed to strengthen the litigation system are not swept into the all-encompassing term "tort reformers," then I do not view myself and like-minded colleagues as tort reformers.

Consider the following examples:

(1)   Reasonable Alternative Design as the Test of Design Defect.

As co-reporters for the Products Liability Restatement Professor Henderson and I took the position that for most cases alleging a design defect, a plaintiff must establish a reasonable alternative design. In some instances such proof is unnecessary. For example, when a product fails in its essential function and a plaintiff can draw a *res ipsa*-like inference that the product was defective, it is not necessary to suggest a reasonable alternative design. Our view was opposed by many (not all) in the plaintiff's bar who advocated for a "consumer expectations" test as the governing rule for design defect.

In 1998 when the PRODUCTS LIABILITY RESTATEMENT was approved, Professor Henderson and I wrote an article in the Cornell Law Review proclaiming that the reasonable alternative design test was the consensus view in the country. We were roundly criticized. A decade later we did a state-by-state analysis of the law on design defect and we found an overwhelming majority of states committed to risk-utility balancing and reasonable alternative design as the appropriate test for design defect. See 74 Brooklyn Law Rev. 1061 (2009). The consumer expectation test has fallen into dispute because it is vague, open-ended, and often unfair to plaintiffs. In several cases of note, courts have negated liability because a product met consumer expectations even though plaintiff's counsel suggested a reasonable alternative design that would have reduced or avoided the injury.

My point here is that one does not turn into a tort reformer merely because of a disagreement with a position taken by the plaintiff's bar. Those familiar with the Products Liability Restatement know that it takes positions that are anathema to defense bar interests. It is a balanced and

He was co-reporter for the American Law Institute's Restatement of the Law (Third) Torts: Products Liability, and for his distinguished performance, the ALI named him the R. Ammi Cutter Reporter.

Professor Twerski's expertise has been widely called upon by state and federal legislative bodies considering product liability and mass tort legislation, and he is a frequent lecturer to the practicing bar. He serves as special counsel to the law firm of Herzfeld and Rubin, and he was appointed as a special master in the federal 9/11 cases dealing with the injuries claimed by those involved in the clean-up of the World Trade Center site. Professor Twerski has also taught at Duquesne University School of Law and was a visiting professor at Cornell, Boston University, and the University of Michigan law schools. More recently he served as dean of the Hofstra Law School before returning to teach at Brooklyn Law School in 2007. His background also includes a teaching fellowship at Harvard Law School, and work as a trial attorney with the U.S. Department of Justice in its Civil Rights Division.

thoughtful Restatement that espouses sensible solution to difficult problems. Its acceptance has grown with time and it is not a piece of work off the desk of a hard-hat tort reformer.

(2) Tobacco Litigation

Though I have not written much on this subject, my views might well be associated with tort reformers. The current spate of litigation against the tobacco companies based primarily on claims of fraudulent concealment of the danger of smoking is, in my opinion, a bad joke. I hold no brief for the tobacco companies. I loathe smoking. However, several decades from now, with hindsight, this litigation will be viewed as a blot on the American judiciary. For anyone post-1980 to argue that they smoked because they were not aware of the dangers of smoking is ludicrous. Perhaps one did not know the difference between addiction and a very bad habit that was hard to break. But to sustain an argument for causation, one would have to posit that had they but known the additional information, they would not have smoked. This contention is not sustainable.

Regulation by Congress and the FDA to reduce smoking makes good sense. Litigating individual cases of little merit solely because the defendant has been a bad actor debases our judicial system. It permits hysteria and prejudice to take center stage. If that makes me a tort reformer, then I wear the title proudly.

(3) Medical Malpractice

I am aware of the controversy in the literature as to whether the malpractice crisis is real or something cooked-up by the insurance companies. I sit as a member of the Board of Trustees of a hospital in metropolitan New York. In the past year our finest high-risk obstetrical specialist has decided that he will do only gynecology and will not take on any more obstetrical cases. Insurance premiums for obstetrics have driven him out of business. Our hospital delivers over 7000 babies per year (the most of any hospital in the state). This year we are losing $2000 per delivery of every baby. These losses are solely the result of malpractice premiums. The hospital has undertaken exhaustive steps to monitor deliveries and to reduce malpractice to an absolute minimum. But, one bad result (whether negligent or not) can lead to settlements from 10–20 million dollars. No one argues that there should not be recovery for economic loss. But unlimited recovery for non-economic loss is unsustainable. No other country in the civilized world permits such unbounded damages. Does this area of the law require a careful look? I believe so. But, it is taboo from the viewpoint of the plaintiff's bar. Everyone who seeks to deal with the problem is dubbed a "tort reformer."

Thus, if the willingness to question some of the positions of the plaintiff's bar and seek possible alternatives that will strengthen our litigation system constitutes law reform, I plead guilty. But, the failure to do so will ultimately result in draconian restrictions on the tort system. There are no free lunches. If voices of moderation are not heard then hotter heads will prevail. The results will not be pretty.[190]

JOSEPH A. PAGE,[191] AN EXCERPT FROM: *DEFORMING TORT REFORM, A BOOK REVIEW OF LIABILITY*: THE LEGAL REVOLUTION AND ITS CONSEQUENCES (BASIC BOOKS, 1988)[192]

THE MANY MEANINGS OF "TORT REFORM"

The storms buffeting the tort system over the past two decades have come in three distinct waves. In the late 1960s, steep increases in the insurance costs incurred by health care providers protecting against negligence claims by patients triggered what came to be known as the "medical malpractice crisis." In the mid-1970s, manufacturers whose liability insurance premiums suddenly soared raised obstreperous complaints that called public attention to the existence of a "product liability crisis." Finally, other groups whose activities created risks exposing them to lawsuits found that their liability insurance rates had also risen precipitously. A full-blown "torts crisis" was at hand.

. . . . As a consequence, those adversely affected by rising insurance costs demanded, and often achieved, what they called "tort reform."

---

[190] Professor Twerski's recent scholarship includes: TORTS: CASES AND MATERIALS (2nd ed. 2008) (with J. Henderson); TORTS: CASES AND MATERIALS (2003) (co-author: J.A. Henderson); PRODUCTS LIABILITY: PROBLEMS AND PROCESS (4th ed. 2000) (co-author: J. A. Henderson); *Consumer Expectations' Last Hope: A Response to Professor Kysar*, 103 COLUM. L. REV. 1791 (2003) (co-author: J.A. Henderson); *Judge Jack B. Weinstein, Tort Litigation, and the Public Good: A Roundtable Discussion to Honor One of America's Great Trial Judges on the Occasion of his 80th Birthday*, 12 J.L. & POL'Y 149 (2003); *Asbestos Litigation Gone Mad: Exposure-Based Recovery for Increased Risk, Mental Distress, and Medical Monitoring*, 53 S.C. L. REV. 815 (2002) (co-author: J.A. Henderson).

[191] Joseph A. Page is a Professor of Law and Director of the Center for the Advancement of the Rule of Law in the Americas at Georgetown University Law Center. Professor Page's academic interests lie in the fields of torts, products liability, and food and drug regulation. His most recent scholarly projects include articles entitled *Automobile-Design Liability and Compliance with Federal Standards*, co-authored with Ralph Nader and published in the GEORGE WASHINGTON UNIVERSITY L. REV., *Liability for Unavoidably and Unreasonably Unsafe Products: Does Negligence Doctrine Have a Role to Play?*, published in the CHICAGO-KENT L. REV., and *Federal Regulation of Tobacco Products and Products That Treat Tobacco Dependence: Are the Playing Fields Level?* in the FOOD AND DRUG LAW JOURNAL. He also writes about Latin America. His latest book THE BRAZILIANS explains what makes Brazilians Brazilian. His other books include THE REVOLUTION THAT NEVER WAS: NORTHEAST BRAZIL, 1955–1964; BITTER WAGES: THE NADER REPORT ON DISEASE AND INJURY ON THE JOB (co-author); THE LAW OF PREMISES LIABILITY (two editions); and PERÓN: A BIOGRAPHY (A second updated edition of the Spanish-language edition of Perón was published in Argentina in 1999). He has also written a lengthy introduction to Eva Perón, *In My Own Words*. Professor Page is a Director of Public Citizen, Inc., and of the American Museum of Tort Law, a member of the Associated Faculty of the Latin American Studies Program at Georgetown University, and a member of the Biography Group of Washington.

[192] 78 GEORGETOWN LAW JOURNAL 649 (1990).

Responding to pressure, states enacted pro-defendant legislative adjustments to common law rules of medical malpractice, products liability, and general tort law. By equating tort reform with unidirectional statutory modification of the common law, its advocates succeeded in investing the term with a politically useful, if skewed, meaning.

Until the dawn of the present age of tort-related "crises," the notion of tort reform was likely to evoke images of a movement to change pro-defendant common law rules so that injured plaintiffs could more easily win judgments or recover full damages. Indeed, through the first half of the twentieth century, the tort system tended to protect the interests of defendants in general as well as particular categories of defendants. What might be called the "old tort reform" was partly an effort to rectify these imbalances.

. . . . In addition to legislative enactments, the far more usual method for reforming tort law in the pre-crises period was through the courts. Appellate judges exercising the creative powers at the core of the common law system rewrote a good deal of the law of torts. Although the stirrings of the old tort reform can be traced through judicial decisions during the first half of this century, the pace did not quicken until the 1950s and 1960s. With an extraordinary outburst of energy, the courts recognized their new duties, abolished immunities, and adopted expansive rules for measuring damages. Perhaps the most dramatic development was the judicial adoption of a rule of strict tort for harm caused by defective, unreasonably dangerous products.

Assigning any single cause to this judicial activism would be an oversimplification. The courts were responding to arguments that existing rules were illogical, unfair to plaintiffs, or inconsistent with tort law's goals of deterrence and compensation. . . .

As history suggests, the old tort reform constituted but one swing of a pendulum that later began to reverse itself in the wake of the crises of the 1970s and 1980s. Thus, construed most favorably, the "new tort reform" has become an effort to eliminate alleged excesses perpetrated by the old tort reform and to restore equilibrium to the system.

Despite their apparent similarities, there is an important difference between the old and the new tort reform. The former derived inspiration and major impetus from the ideas of scholars and had its primary influence on the courts. The latter is fueled by the economic self-interest of those who perceive themselves as adversely affected by the tort system. In essence, the new tort reform is a political attack on tort law in the legislative arena.

This has important implications. Politicians tend by nature to be much more pragmatic than theoretical. To convince them of the real need for legislation, contemporary tort reformers stress the most dramatic argument for their case—skyrocketing liability insurance rates. Yet there is no guarantee that making tort rules more favorable to defendants will decrease premiums. Moreover, the political process inevitably involves the sort of compromise that can blunt the efforts of the new tort reformers and open the door to legislative counterattacks. . . .

What [Peter Huber, author of *Liability* and proponent of comprehensive tort reform] proposes is a giant leap backward. He would roll back a significant number of pro-plaintiff common law doctrines adopted not only during the great revolution but also earlier in the century. . . . He fails to explain why the political and economic realities that previously left workers, consumers, and others at the mercy of those with whom they did business will somehow produce more just and humane relationships under the sort of libertarian regime he espouses, rather than replicate the conditions that initially gave rise to the old tort reform. . . .

Those who argue that the tort system cries out for drastic overhaul bear the responsibility to show that what they propose to set up in its place will not only work but will work better. *Liability*, with its "slash-and-burn" approach . . . vastly overstates the case against tort law. . . .

CORRINE PARVER,[193] HEALTH COURTS: A MODERN-DAY SOLUTION FOR MEDICAL MALPRACTICE LITIGATION[194]

Traditional tort reforms seek to reduce the overall costs of medical malpractice primarily by reducing the number of lawsuits through increased restrictions on and barriers to plaintiffs bringing suits, and by reducing the risks of medical liability for defendants. Different states have adopted different types of reforms, and there are wide variations among reforms of a similar type between states. But tort reforms at the federal

---

[193] Corrine Parver is a Practitioner-in-Residence and Executive Director, Health Law Project, Program on Law and Government at American University, Washington College of Law. She designed and implemented the law school's health law specialization as part of the LL.M. Program on Law and Government's Administrative and Regulatory Law concentration. She is the Faculty Advisor to the Health Law and Justice Initiative, a student organization, and the WCL Health Law and Policy publication. Prior to joining WCL, she was a Partner in the Washington, DC, office of Dickstein Shapiro Morin & Oshinsky LLP (now: Dickstein Shapiro), where she headed the firm's Health Law Services Practice, focusing on: fraud and abuse prevention and counseling; health care compliance; reimbursement, coding and coverage of services and devices; privacy; mediation and litigation strategy; legislative and regulatory advocacy; and general health law. Previously, Ms. Parver was the President of Parver & Associates, a legal and consulting firm, and the President & CEO, National Association for Medical Equipment Services (now American Association for Homecare). She received her Juris Doctor cum laude, December 1982, from American University Washington College of Law, where she was an Assistant Editor of The American University L. Rev., and her Bachelor of Physical Therapy degree and P.T. Diploma from McGill University.

[194] Information included in this paper is adapted from a proposal to establish Health Courts by the organization "Common Good," as presented to WCL students by its former employee, Paul Barringer, Esq.

and state levels have thus far failed to deter future injuries and leave many victims uncompensated.

If one believes that there is a medical malpractice insurance crisis and the current system of medical malpractice litigation is broken, what would provide the best solution to help end the crisis? Many specialty courts already exist in the United States: tax, immigration, admiralty, patent, probate, domestic violence, and family law, to name a few. So, how about establishing Health Courts to handle all medical malpractice litigation?

The proposal to create Health Courts envisions a system of administrative compensation for medical injuries. Core components include: trained judges who are both attorneys and health care practitioners; neutral experts; a compensation standard of "avoidability;" evidence-based, expedited proceedings; written opinions that create precedent; and fully compensated economic damages and "scheduled" non-economic damages.

Health Courts could prove to be an effective mechanism of controlling costs, as litigation would not be as lengthy and outside experts would not have to be hired. Medical injury claims would be decided and compensated more quickly as a result of using decisional aids and compensation schedules that result from a body of science-based common law that would emerge from the Health Courts. More injured patients would be eligible for compensation because of the more inclusive avoidability standard of compensation that would allow a plaintiff to recover if she can prove that the medical injury was avoidable, regardless of whether it was negligence.

Further, Health Courts could offer a way to restore the connection between medical liability and patient safety. Published opinions based on scientific evidence presented by neutral experts would help develop a body of common law that could be a guide to physicians in understanding the risks of liability associated with various medical treatments they provide and, it is hoped, help them practice safer medicine.

While Health Courts may not provide the perfect solution to fixing a broken medical malpractice litigation system, they do present a solid proposal to compensate victims of medical malpractice and deter doctors from making bad decisions about medical treatment.

What follows is Professor Shapo's testimony on one of the most sweeping federal tort reform bills of the last decade of the 20th Century.[195]

---

[195] Ultimately, the bill was not adopted.

MARSHALL SHAPO,[196] THE PRODUCT LIABILITY REFORM ACT, STATEMENT OF MARSHALL S. SHAPO, BEFORE THE SENATE COMMITTEE ON THE JUDICIARY ON S.1400, JULY 31, 1990

All during the decade of the eighties, proposals for general products liability legislation continually surfaced in various Congressional committees. Much of the argument on those proposals has been politically centered. Relatively little has focused on the intrinsic legal merits of the bills. An appearance before the Judiciary Committee thus presents a special opportunity to discuss these lawyers' issues.

Thus, I now offer some views on the subject that grow out of my own scholarship, which includes a dozen books on tort and injury law, about half of which focus on the law of products liability. I would like to make five basic points.

First: The proponents of this legislation have sadly misconstrued the history of judicial decisionmaking in products cases over the last generation. They have neglected the sensitive efforts of state and federal judges to get to the practical root of the problems of hazard, conduct and injury that have brought thousands of these cases to court. That history, now going on three decades, is an extraordinary one. For during that time, the courts have probed ever more deeply for justice, both the justice of individual cases and the justice of more general rules. Those who have read those decisions have seen the New Jersey Supreme Court redraw the frontier of its products liability law to pull back from a much criticized position. They have witnessed the developments now statistically reported by Henderson and Eisenberg as a significant pro-defendant trend in products liability decisions.[197] Moreover, they have observed that a substantial amount of the much decried increases in the number of products cases primarily are attributable to asbestos and Dalkon Shield litigation—cases where many courts have judged thousands of horrendous injuries to have occurred because of seriously culpable conduct.

---

[196] Marshall S. Shapo, the Frederic P. Vose Professor at Northwestern University School of Law, is a nationally recognized authority on torts and products liability law. He received an AB, summa cum laude, and LLB, magna cum laude, from the University of Miami, where he was first in his class and editor-in-chief of the University of Miami L. Rev. His graduate degrees are an AM in history and an SJD, both from Harvard. Before his appointment to the Northwestern faculty in 1978, he was Joseph M. Hartfield Professor of Law at the University of Virginia and a member of the faculty of the University of Texas School of Law. Professor Shapo has been a visiting fellow at Wolfson College, Oxford University (1975), and twice at Wolfson College, Cambridge University (1992 and 2001). He also served as a visiting professor at the Juristiches Seminar, University of Gottingen. In 2005 he was the principal speaker, delivering five lectures on various aspects of tort and injury law, at a seminar attended by leading European torts scholars at the University of Girona. He also has given lectures in Barcelona and in Italy, Portugal, Japan, Germany, and Brazil.

[197] Henderson & Eisenberg, *The Quiet Revolution in Products Liability: An Empirical Study of Legal Change*, 37 U.C.L.A. L. REV. 479 (1990).

This leads me to my <u>second</u> point: It seems strange that in an America that has pulled back from federal involvement in many lines of activity, the representatives of many American enterprises should seek to nationalize a body of law that has grown basically from the clash of proofs in local courts and federal courts applying local law. We do not need the ghost of Brandeis to remind us of the importance of state experimentation with a variety of legal regimes. We need look no further than the creative efforts of our courts in shaping this body of law, now stretching it and now limiting it in the service of the realities of justice and practical economics. If ever there were a proposal whose natural consequence would be to stultify local intellectual initiative, it would be a statute that nationalizes tort doctrine.

In this regard, I want to emphasize that I am not being sentimental about a federalism whose virtues have long gone; I am suggesting that one place where federalism is alive and well is in our system of resolving injury disputes.

A <u>third</u> point is that much of the firepower directed at the substantive rules of products law is misdirected. My analysis of the tort system for the A.B.A.'s Special Committee led to the conclusion that most of society's problems with tort law are more systemic than substantive. They have to do with such things as the need for social data, the necessity for more experimentation with methods of dispute resolution, and a variety of problems related to case management.

My <u>fourth</u> point confronts what appears to be the fact that most proponents of federal legislation in this area simply want defendants to win more cases. I have a few brief responses on this from both empirical and philosophical points of view. One response is that defendants are, in fact, winning more cases, and they are doing so under a state-based legal regime. My second observation is to repeat an empirical judgment that has been widely reported: the G.A.O.'s conclusion that "most" proposed federal products liability reforms "would potentially have affected only a minority" of cases studied in that office's five-state analysis.[198]

A more policy-oriented response is to amplify what I said earlier: with the statistics on wins and losses in the process of evolution, the desire to shift the vector of who wins tort cases is not a good enough reason to nationalize tort law. Moreover, it seems fair to ask: Which cases would the proponents of this bill want defendants to begin to win? With the history that has emerged on asbestos, would they have preferred that the Fifth Circuit had never handed down the <u>Borel</u> decision? Would they have wanted courts to have rung up a no-hitter for the defenders of the Dalkon Shield?

---

[198]   United States General Accounting Office, Product Liability: Verdicts and Case Resolution in Five States 62 (GAO/HRD–89–99, 1989).

In this regard, it is interesting that some members of Congress who advocate federal legislation limiting products liability law are also fervent in their calls for increased regulatory response to one sort of product hazard or another. Here I want to emphasize a strongly held belief that has emerged from my scholarship: *One of the great strengths of tort law has been its ability to respond to patterns of injury where regulation has proved ineffective and compensation law has been inadequate.*

Fifth, I wish to re-express a concern that I mentioned some years ago to this body, a concern that seems especially important for the Judiciary Committee. This is that a proposal of this sort, besides seriously dampening the creativity of state courts, would actually complicate the law, viewed as a system, rather than simplify it. For many years, people have been complaining about the workload of the Supreme Court, and complaints about the burdens of the federal courts generally have escalated over the last decade or so. It would seem that legislation of this sort can only deposit more reams of litigation on the desks of federal, as well as state, judges. Why would this Committee want to involve our nation's courts in a new set of wrangles about the meaning, let alone the constitutionality, of a federal statute that attempts to change a quite serviceable body of state law?

This testimony has not dealt with the lack of data on the need for change, nor the question of how the current bill would relate to insurance. Nor has it explored the adverse deterrence consequences that might well be associated with this sort of legislation. Rather, I have tried to focus on lawyers' concerns. And I conclude that from a legal point of view, broad federal legislation like S.1400 is unjustified and that it would harm the public interest.[199]

GROUP FOUR: TORT REFORM: JUSTICE DELAYED, DENIED, OR ENHANCED?

1.   There has always been a dispute about the extent of the "crisis" fueling tort reform. Deborah Jones Merritt & Kathryn Barry, *Is the Tort System in Crisis? New Empirical Evidence*, 60 OHIO ST. L.J. 315 (1999). There is no dispute about the nature and tone of the discourse. It is pointed and direct. As anyone who has ever been involved in this field will attest,

---

[199] Professor Shapo's publications include TORT AND INJURY LAW, 3D EDITION (with Richard Peltz) (2006); COMPENSATION FOR VICTIMS OF TERROR (2005); TORT LAW AND CULTURE (2003); THE LAW OF PRODUCTS LIABILITY, 4TH EDITION (2001), with Supplements 2002–2006 (two volumes); LAW SCHOOL WITHOUT FEAR, 2D ED. (2002) (with Helene Shapo). Some of his most recent Publications include: EXPERIMENTING WITH THE CONSUMER: THE MASS TESTING OF RISKY PRODUCTS ON THE AMERICAN PUBLIC (2009); LAW SCHOOL WITHOUT FEAR: STRATEGIES FOR SUCCESS, 2009; *Responsibility for Injuries: Some Sketches*, 100 NW. U. L. REV. 481–500 (2006); *Compensation for Terrorism: What We Are Learning*, 53 DEPAUL L. REV. 805–820 (2003).

legislative and congressional hearings in this area involve a good deal of argument or advocacy but are often short on concrete and reliable data. Until there is a reliable, accurate, and comprehensible study that portrays accurately the current health of the civil justice system, rhetoric, anecdote, and passionate advocacy will remain the norm.

2.   In Joshua D. Kelner's, *The Anatomy of an Image: Unpacking the Case for Tort Reform*,[200] the author asserts that academicians have failed to provide the public a working understanding of the tort system ("the public remains woefully undereducated about the purposes and operations of the civil justice system"). After painstakingly reviewing the practical and legal consequences of tort reform, Kelner writes that the "discourse taking place is a political one. As such, while logical arguments are important, they are perhaps of lesser value than effective use of symbols, imagery, and rhetoric. . . ." Assuming that is true, is it really all that different than other significant controversies? Consider if school desegregation, abortion/right to life, the death penalty, climate change, or the regulation (or deregulation) of major sectors of the U.S. economy were ever non-political and purely "legal" matters.

3.   The essays in this section (and for that matter, in each of the four sections) are, of their very nature, political. It is the nature of this discourse. They are also carefully written and thoughtful presentations of important arguments. One cautionary note: the idea that one can pin down facts that serve as a foundation to untangle the tort reform puzzle is not just optimistic—it is impossible. One Comment sized up the veracity of the pro-tort reform argument as follows: "Based in many little lies, in which cases are exaggerated, and the amount of and the effect of frivolous lawsuits, the impact of regulations on property rights, as well as the impact of liberal adjudication on the sanctity of contract are all overstated. When combined, they feed into the big lie that the common law has been hijacked by greedy plaintiffs and lawyers, as well as by liberal activist judges." Roland Christensen, *Comment: Behind the Curtain of Tort Reform*, 16 B.Y.U.L. REV. 261, 275 (2016).

As you go through the final group of essays, notice the way in which the authors approach the field. In some cases, they "unpack" the civil justice system, looking at discrete sub-issues and fields. Other essayists write (and argue) more broadly. Which style is most compelling? Which style is most likely to change the mind of a policymaker or judge?

4.   Last set of essays demonstrates, *inter alia*, pointed disagreements between experts in the field regarding the impact or consequences of various tort reform initiatives. Sherman Joyce and Joanne Doroshow, on opposing sides, set forth that disagreement quite clearly. Having come this far in your study, do you believe that the potential for an injured litigant

---

[200]   31 DAYTON L. REV. 243, 305 (2006).

to succeed has been enhanced by changes/reforms that have taken place or stifled by those same reforms.

5.   How does the Class Action Fairness Act[201] affect individual claimants? As is the case with much of this field, it is extremely difficult to marshal credible empirical evidence on this question.[202] There are many reasons why empirical study of class actions has not been successful, including imperfect information on the number of cases settled (and the results of the settlement sealed), dropped, resolved through arbitration with no public record,[203] or never initiated because of actual or perceived obstacles to litigation.

SHERMAN JOYCE,[204] NEW ISSUES IN "TORT REFORM"

What is "tort reform"? As is the case with many policy issues, defining the issue often is a major part of the broader policy debate. From the standpoint of the American Tort Reform Association (ATRA), it is a broad set of issues, and I will describe some of them briefly below.

1.   Who should make law? This might sound like a philosophical or academic issue, but it is not. For well over a decade, the role of state legislatures in enacting tort reform legislation has been challenged in court by opponents after statutes have been enacted. This trial bar's aggressive and coordinated effort has resulted in about 530 challenges to "tort reform" legislation in state courts since 1983. Most of the time these laws are upheld, but not always. ATRA has identified approximately 390 state court cases since 1983 in which state civil justice reform legislation was upheld; we also have identified almost 140 state court cases overturning civil justice reform statutes in whole or in part since 1983. In some instances, including decisions by the Supreme Courts of Illinois in *Best v. Taylor Machine Works, Inc.*, 689 N.E.2d 1057 (Ill. 1997), and Ohio in *State ex rel.*

---

[201]   Class Action Fairness Act of 2005, Pub. L. No. 109–2, 119 Stat. 4 (2005) (codified as amended at 28 U.S.C.§§ 1332(d), 1453, 1711–15).

[202]   Daryl Levinson, Benjamin I. Sachs, *Political Entrenchment and Public Law*, 125 YALE L.J. 400, 438–41 (2015) (drawing a link between campaign financing and tort reform legislations); Stephen Daniels & Joanne Martin, *Where Have All the Cases Gone? The Strange Success of Tort Reform Revisited*, 65 EMORY L.J. 1445, 1445–46 (2016) (updating the 2004 edition); Scott DeVito & Andrew Jurs, An *Overreaction to A Nonexistent Problem: Empirical Analysis of Tort Reform from the 1980s to 2000s* 3 STAN. J. COMPLEX LITIG. 62 (2015) (arguing that capping noneconomic damages creates a "doubling down" effect by decreasing filings not only in the state where the cap was adopted).

[203]   Janine Alena Brown Miki, *Medical Malpractice Arbitration "Agreements:" the Healthcare Consumer's Hobson's Choice*, 43 W. ST. L. REV. 225 (2016).

[204]   Sherman "Tiger" Joyce is the President of the American Tort Reform Association (ATRA). A graduate of Princeton University and Catholic University Law School, he served as Legislative Assistant to U.S. Senator John C. Danforth until 1984. In 1987, he became minority counsel to the U.S. Senate Committee on Commerce, Science, and Transportation, where he worked on product liability legislation. Mr. Joyce assumed his current position at ATRA in August 1994.

Ohio Academy of Trial Lawyers v. Sheward, 715 N.E.2d 1062 (Ohio 1999), one could conclude that those courts precluded the legislature from playing ANY role in reforming the civil justice system. The courts essentially declared tort law to be the exclusive province of the judiciary. More recently, the Supreme Court of Wisconsin overturned a key medical liability reform statute in *Ferdon v. Wisconsin Patients Compensation Fund*, 701 N.W.2d 440 (Wis. 2005), stating that there was no "rational" basis for the legislature's decision to enact such reform. Our view is, regardless of whether a reform proposal advances a position we embrace or not, as a general matter, the authority to "reform" the system is a shared one. Neither the courts nor the legislatures should consider tort law to be their exclusive domain.

2.   "Private" lawyers bringing lawsuits for the "public." The Master Settlement Agreement between state attorneys general and the tobacco industry over a decade ago established several important precedents, but two, in particular, are noteworthy. First, the payouts went to governmental entities—the states for the costs incurred in treating smoking related illnesses—rather than individuals (or the heirs of those who died) who experienced physical injuries or death as a result of the products' use. The notion that injured persons should be compensated was not an issue in these cases; the purpose was to allow states to "recover" THEIR losses. The other precedent pertained to the counsel representing the states in these cases. Virtually every state was represented by personal injury lawyers working on a contingency fee basis. In some cases, the hiring practices used to engage these lawyers failed to meet the most basic standards of transparency and "good government." Perhaps the worst case was in Texas, where the former attorney general's conduct resulted in a lengthy prison sentence for corruption in retaining counsel. ATRA's view is that if a state attorney general, or any governmental entity, plans to use outside counsel, it should be done through a process that is open to the public so all qualified attorneys can compete to provide the service. ATRA also believes that outside counsel should not be working under a contingent fee arrangement for a governmental entity. The state's interests and outside lawyer's interests should be in complete alignment, and decisions on whether to bring such cases and how to do so should reflect the public's interest, not the desire of a lawyer to earn a fee. Governmental functions should not be outsourced and delegated to lawyers with a profit motive.

3.   The advent of state consumer fraud statutes. It is highly unlikely that the U.S. Congress could have envisioned the highly publicized $54 million "pantsuit" case in Washington, D.C., when Congress decided in 1914 not to allow private citizens to enforce section 5 of the Federal Trade Commission Act. That law prohibits "unfair or deceptive acts or practices affecting interstate commerce." The local D.C. version of this law, however, was the basis for the "crazy case," which attracted substantial attention

and was the subject of derision on late night comedy shows. Laws intended to empower regulators to protect the public interest broadly should not be allowed to be used to allow outrageous cases, such as the D.C. pantsuit case, to be brought. Such state laws, given their breadth and lack of clarity, are an area of major concern for civil justice reform advocates.

4.   Health care liability. The health care policy debate is front and center on the national stage, and medical liability reform is an important part of that dialogue. Reasonable people can disagree about some of the medical liability reforms enacted around the country, such as limits on noneconomic damages, but there can be little dispute that the medical liability system has a substantial impact on access to affordable health care, particularly with regard to high risk specialties, such as obstetric care or neurosurgery. Moreover, in addition to the direct costs of the system, "defensive medicine" imposes an enormous financial burden on the system that does not treat a single patient or help to cover any individual lacking coverage. It is, as economists say, "dead weight social loss." It should be noted, as T.R. Reid, author of a recent book on health care systems in other developed countries, stated in a recent interview on C-SPAN, the United States is alone in providing the "full" tort system's remedies to those who may have been injured due to negligence. As Congress considers changes to the basic structure of our health care system, ATRA believes that reforms enacted in the states, as well as new ideas that are being developed, should be on the table.

5.   Trespass. Law students typically study real property and torts in year one, and "trespass" is a term that all must learn. What we typically remember is that trespassers have no rights when they come on someone else's land. That is pretty easy to remember, and it makes sense. This, however, may be changing soon. The American Law Institute recently established a new kind of trespasser duty. Apart from a new category called "flagrant trespassers," all who enter upon the land of others would now be owed a duty of reasonable care. In addition to causing casebook authors to rewrite basic tort law, this new duty rule would create new headaches for landowners (particularly those who may not occupy their property for long stretches of time) and business owners.

6.   Venue. In 2010, the American Tort Reform Foundation released their comprehensive Eighth Judicial Hellholes® report that identified what we believe are the most unfair jurisdictions for civil defendants in the country. As the report states, "Equal justice under law" is not available to defendants in Hellholes. Frequently, the question is asked, "What one 'thing' could be done to change a hellhole from its current status to a jurisdiction that is more balanced?" The reply frequently, but not in every case, is "fix the state's venue rule." Too often hellholes are characterized as "dumping grounds" for cases that did not arise there, are not where the plaintiff(s) reside, or where the defendant(s) reside (or principal place of

business). When judges stretch venue rules, as they did for many years in Madison County, Illinois, or Hampton County, South Carolina, no one wins. Defendants in these hellholes often are forced to settle and equally important, when such cases fill up the courts' dockets, the local citizens whose taxes pay for the court house get pushed to the back of the line when they bring their cases. The bottom line here is to make sure that cases only be brought in jurisdictions where there is an appropriate nexus between the parties, the claim, and the jurisdiction. The scope of the challenges that reform advocates face every day continues to grow. Among the biggest challenges we face is ensuring that we continue to address the challenges that confront us right now, while recognizing that new issues will continue to arise all the time.

————————

JOANNE DOROSHOW,[205] ACCESS TO JUSTICE

The right of injured people to sue and collect compensation from the perpetrators of their harm is one of the great achievements of American democracy. In our system, the poorest and most vulnerable, including those who are in need of medical care or the disrupted families of sick and injured children, can challenge the largest corporation or government agency and hold them accountable for causing their injury.

This right has become even more precious since the 1980s, when regulatory oversight of corporate practices virtually ground to a halt. Corporate lobbyists, using their gross imbalance of advocacy resources, have made tremendous strides in weakening safety laws and safety standards for prevention of harm and protection against new technological hazards. Often times, corporations which may have otherwise blocked regulatory oversight, have been forced to change their practices because of lawsuits brought by average Americans, and by subsequent jury verdicts.

With corporate wealth and power already dominating our two other branches of government, America's civil jury system is perhaps the only place left in America where individual citizens can successfully confront raw corporate power, force changes in corporate behavior, and in some

---

[205] Joanne Doroshow is Executive Director the Center for Justice & Democracy (CJ & D), based in New York City. CJ & D is the first national consumer organization dedicated exclusively to educating the public about the importance of the civil justice system and stopping "tort reform." Joanne is also co-founder, along with Consumer Federation of America Director of Insurance J. Robert Hunter, of Americans for Insurance Reform (AIR). AIR is a coalition of 100 consumer groups from around the country working to strengthen oversight of insurance industry practices. Under Joanne's direction, CJ & D also founded the Civil Justice Resource Group, a group of over twenty scholars from law and graduate schools around the country formed to respond to the widespread disinformation campaign by critics of the civil justice system. Joanne is an attorney who has worked on civil justice issues since 1986, when she first directed a project for Ralph Nader on liability and the insurance industry. In that capacity, she developed some of the first educational materials used to fight tort reform around the country.

cases, challenge a corporation's existence. As a result, the power and authority of civil jurors, who cannot be wined, dined and bought-off by corporate lobbyists, represents a tremendous threat to the corporate power structure in this country.

Most states have now enacted some form of "tort reform", weakening the civil justice system's ability to hold corporate wrongdoers accountable. Add to that the "echo effect" of tort reform in the jury box, with jurors becoming increasingly anti-plaintiff due to their repeated exposure to anti-lawsuit public relations campaigns, and the increasing reluctance of individuals to pursue civil remedies in court, and it becomes clear that the tort reform movement is changing the entire landscape of the civil justice system to the benefit of corporate wrongdoers.

Corporate America has sunk hundreds of millions of dollars into numerous conservative, industry-sponsored organizations, "think-tanks," public relations, polling, and lobbying firms.

These organizations are part of a much larger movement to enhance corporate power, which has grown exponentially since the late 1970s. In the civil justice arena, these organizations are setting legislative agendas, devising strategies, and purchasing expensive media to persuade public officials that the tort system is out of control. The intensity of their efforts leaves no doubt that a weakened civil justice system is only their first goal. Control of the entire judicial process and elimination of trial by jury in personal injury cases are their plain objectives.

There is a shocking lack of public education and understanding of who is hurt and who benefits from tort reform. Most people think of tort reform as hurting only two groups: trial lawyers and people with "frivolous" lawsuits. In reality, however, this movement is having devastating consequences for many vulnerable children and families. These laws can result in untold suffering, economic devastation, and for some, the destruction of family life. In many cases, "tort reform" completely shuts the court house door to many in need who, as a result of being seriously or permanently injured, are unable to provide for their families.

It is also weakening the ability of the civil justice system to protect us all from injury and disease, whether or not we ever go to court. This is because the prospect of civil liability deters manufacturers, builders, chemical companies, hospitals, and other potential wrongdoers from repeating their negligent behavior and provides them with an economic incentive to make their practices safer.

Unfortunately, the media have become the movement's unwitting agents. There is a natural tendency for the media to publicize large jury awards without reporting the full facts and later actions by judges and appellate courts, and to bash the lawyers responsible.

It is important that we become better educated about the value and importance of this nation's civil justice system. We should all be concerned about the media's reporting on civil justice issues. We must involve and educate academics and students in the movement to protect and expand the civil justice system.

Our goals must include preserving and improving consumers' access to the civil justice system, not weakening it. We should increase corporate, professional, and governmental accountability through the tort system, and support the civil jury system. Exposing the damage "tort reform" is causing this country and at expanding civil justice protections for all individuals, is a worthy goal for us all.[206]

MARTHA CHAMALLAS,[207] CIVIL RIGHTS AND CIVIL WRONGS

"Tort reform" has become a code word for initiatives that seek to limit liability for defendants and reduce the amount or type of damages plaintiffs receive. It is a one-way street that promises few benefits for injured parties or consumers. It's important to recognize that tort reform has not always had this meaning. Prior to the 1980s, it was more frequently linked to measures, such as comparative negligence, that sought to soften the effect of restrictive doctrines and ease recovery for seriously injured parties. At that time, tort reform was more reciprocal in structure. For example, the reform of no-fault compensation for automobile accidents, or the earlier reform of workers compensation, brought something for everyone—under the *quid pro quo* enacted by these statutory regimes, plaintiffs were no

---

[206] Joanne Doroshow has written or co-authored numerous CJ & D studies and White Papers on civil justice issues including *Premium Deceit: The Failure of "Tort Reform" to Cut Insurance Prices, The CALA Files: The Secret Campaign by Big Tobacco and Other Major Industries to Take Away Your Rights, The Bitterest Pill,* and *The Racial Implications of Tort Reform.* She also edited *Lifesavers: CJ & D's Guide to Lawsuits that Protect Us All, The Secret Chamber, Workers Compensation—A Cautionary Tale, How the Civil Justice System Protects Environmental Health* and many other CJ & D publications. She is regularly quoted in newspapers nationwide, including the Wall Street Journal, New York Times, Washington Post, Chicago Tribune, Miami Herald and Los Angeles Times.

[207] Martha Chamallas holds the Robert J. Lynn Chair in Law, Moritz College of Law at The Ohio State University where she teaches Torts, Employment Discrimination and Gender and the Law. Prior to joining the Ohio State faculty, she was on the faculty at LSU, Pittsburgh and the University of Iowa and has held distinguished visiting Chairs at Washington University, University of Richmond and Suffolk University. In anti-discrimination law, she has published numerous articles on sexual harassment, pay equity, unconscious bias, and constructive discharge law. In torts, she has written articles on race and gender bias in intentional torts, emotional distress cases and the calculation of damages. Her treatise—INTRODUCTION TO FEMINIST LEGAL THEORY (2d ed. 2003) explains major trends and themes in legal feminism. Her forthcoming book THE MEASURE OF INJURY: RACE, GENDER AND TORT LAW (N.Y.U. Press 2010) (with Jennifer B. Wriggins) explores how tort law is affected by cultural views on gender and race. In 2007, she was named University Distinguished Lecturer at Ohio State. She is a member of the Litigation Committee for the AAUP and the American Law Institute.

longer required to prove negligence, while defendants were relieved of paying for pain and suffering and became liable only for economic losses.

In my view, the most influential tort reformers were the mid-20th century legal realists who sought to reshape legal doctrine and connect it to real-world experience. Their biggest enemy was legal formalism, the kind of abstract thinking that organized tort doctrine into strict conceptual categories, such as duty, breach, and proximate cause, regardless of the factual context and divorced from the social experience of the parties. Although it is often said that "we are all legal realists now," the realist reform project is not over. The unfinished work has to do with linking tort law to our developing understanding of civil and human rights and with bringing social equality to torts, the law's premier system for compensating injuries.

Students rarely see the connection between "ordinary" civil litigation and civil rights. If we look solely at the surface of tort claims, issues of social justice are generally visible only in certain kinds of intentional tort claims. One of the more interesting developments of the last few decades is how older causes of action—most prominently battery, false imprisonment, and the tort of intentional infliction of emotional distress—have been used by sexual and racial harassment victims and victims of domestic violence to challenge longstanding patterns of oppression and exploitation. On this front, however, tort law has functioned mainly as a modest supplement to other remedies in some jurisdictions. Most states, for example, still refuse to regard discrimination as an actionable tort.

Beyond these intentional tort cases, it is even harder for attorneys, judges, and experts to see a civil rights issue in what looks like an ordinary tort claim. Because civil rights attorneys tend to be a separate and distinct group from personal injury litigators, even plaintiffs' attorneys often fail to detect the ways in which their clients' injuries are devalued or infected by racial and gender bias. They also may not realize that the particular tort claims and types of damages least protected under the law are often the most vital for marginalized groups in society. For example, claims for emotional harm and negligent interference with relationships are low in the hierarchy of compensable harms in tort law, but are of disproportionate importance to women because they afford recovery for important and recurring injuries in women's lives, such as emotional distress resulting from stillbirths and miscarriages caused by physician negligence, shock at seeing one's children killed or injured, and injuries caused by sexual exploitation and abuse. Additionally, empirical scholarship has documented that legislative caps on non-economic damages are particularly harsh on women, the elderly, and children, the groups who are not likely to recover large sums for wage replacement or other economic loss.

Hidden race and gender bias in tort awards is also present in the standards used to calculate economic harm, particularly the methods used to determine an accident victim's loss of future earning capacity. Many states still allow experts and juries to calculate a victim's lost earning potential on the basis of gender-based and race-based tables that have the effect of dramatically lowering awards for women and minority men. Race and gender-based tables are in effect race-specific and gender-specific assessments, comparing women only to other women, blacks only to other blacks. This saddles plaintiffs with generalizations about their group, the very kind of stereotyping that anti-discrimination laws were meant to prevent. In the recent Staten Island ferry crash case, Judge Jack Weinstein held for the first time that using race-based tables to calculate tort damages was an unconstitutional practice in violation of equal protection and due process. (*McMillan v. City of New York*, 253 F.R.D. 247 (E.D.N.Y. 2008)). His ruling went a step further than Kenneth Feinberg who had earlier relied on "public policy" grounds to reject use of female-only tables to calculate damages under the September 11 Victim Compensation Fund.

These progressive tort reforms have only just scratched the surface and have not yet woven gender and race equality into the basic fabric of tort law. Such an alternative tort reform would, for example, push for a change in the concept of "outrageousness" to ensure that it covered discriminatory harassment and abuse and replaced outmoded views of what is regarded as an actionable affront to dignity. In negligent infliction cases, tort reformers should press courts to impose a duty of due care in any case which implicates a plaintiff's interest in sexual integrity or reproduction, affording such claims the high priority they are given in constitutional law as fundamental rights. And courts should follow the lead of the Israeli Supreme Court which recently rejected the use of gender and ethnic-based statistics to calculate damages in a personal injury case, making the significant determination that an award of tort damages should not simply return the victim to the status quo ante, but to a "just and fair" status that does not reproduce past inequalities among social groups (*Migdal Ins. v. Rim Abu Hanna*, 2006). Although this kind of tort reform rarely gets discussed in Congress or state legislatures, it is nonetheless pressing and long overdue (and a lot more fascinating than abolishing joint and several liability).

———————

DONALD G. GIFFORD,[208] TORT REFORM AS A TWO-WAY STREET

As a law professor and a former plaintiff's attorney, I frequently have testified in state legislatures and lobbied against tort reform. I have argued that legislatures should not alter fundamental principles of tort law. I have suggested that they respect basic principles of separation of powers.

It may surprise you then that most of my legislative efforts have been sponsored by either an industry trade association or one of the largest chemical companies in the world. You see, it is not just business interests that have urged legislatures to change the rules governing tort litigation in their favor. Plaintiffs' attorneys are among the most powerful "special interests" lobbying state legislatures, and they often pursue legislative changes tilting the common law in their favor, just as business interests do. For example, during the states' tort litigation against the tobacco manufacturers in the late 1990s, a number of states changed the fundamental rules governing such litigation to make it possible for the states to recover. More recently, plaintiffs' lawyers and public interest groups in my own state of Maryland annually have pursued legislation that would eliminate the requirement that the plaintiff must prove that the defendant caused plaintiff's harm in order to establish liability—a requirement that William Prosser described as "the simplest and most obvious"[209] aspect of determining tort liability—in cases brought against lead pigment manufacturers.

The operating premise that lies behind the common law as a precedent-based system is that a certain degree of fairness is assured when a court, at least in the absence of an articulated, compelling contrary justification, applies the same rules governing causation to actions against any defendant, regardless of the nature of its business or products. But during the past decade, plaintiffs' attorneys pursued special rules that disadvantaged *specific* industries disfavored by legislators—such as cigarette manufacturers and lead pigment producers. Most often these changes in rules favoring plaintiffs who sued a particular industry were passed when it was the state itself that was acting as plaintiff. At a very fundamental level of fairness, one must ask "since when does one player in litigation get to be the umpire that can change the rules in its own favor?"

---

[208] Don G. Gifford is a Professor of Law at the University of Maryland, School of Law where he specializes in torts and mass products torts. During the past decade, Professor Gifford has testified in numerous state legislative proceedings on issues relating to the prevention of childhood lead poisoning and the potential liability of producers of lead pigment or paint. In this role, his testimony has been sponsored by either the National Paint and Coatings Association (later renamed the American Coatings Association) or E.I. du Pont de Nemours & Co. Earlier, Gifford served as Chair of the Maryland Lead Poisoning Prevention Commission. For more on the respective functions of the judicial and legislative branches in solving product-caused public health problems, *see* Donald G. Gifford, SUING THE TOBACCO AND LEAD PIGMENT INDUSTRIES (forthcoming, University of Michigan Press, 2010).

[209] William Prosser, HANDBOOK OF THE LAW OF TORTS § 41, at 337 (4th ed. 1971).

When legislatures change the rules of the game so that their states can sue manufacturers of products that cause public health problems, such as cigarettes or lead pigment, they turn the traditional, constitutionally-based allocation of powers between the legislative and judicial branches on its head. Preventing tobacco-related diseases and finding ways (and funds) to remediate the lead-based paint hazards in older, deteriorated housing that often cause childhood lead poisoning are precisely the kinds of activities in which legislatures ought to engage. But often during the last decade, legislators have forgotten both the powers and the limitations of their own role. They invited courts to fill the void they created when they defaulted on their own responsibilities to address product-caused public health problems. For example, effective prevention of childhood lead poisoning requires the legislature to enact stronger regulation prohibiting the deteriorated housing conditions that cause most cases of lead poisoning, to require greater expenditures by business owners (landlords), and to spend additional government funds—all admittedly politically courageous steps given the current political climate. Legislators who are unlikely to appear in any updated version of *Profiles in Courage* pass the buck to the judicial system and rig the contest so that the courts are not bound by otherwise universally accepted principles of tort law. Never mind that our constitutions expect that state legislatures will regulate, tax, and spend to solve public health problems. Or that solving massive, multi-faceted public health problems is beyond both the institutional capacities and the appropriate constitutional role of courts.

That is why I—a once-upon-a-time plaintiff's personal injury lawyer and the former chair of the Maryland Lead Poisoning Prevention Commission (whose recommendations led to the enactment of one of the nation's most effective lead poisoning prevention laws)—have lobbied on behalf of industry. Demands for unwise tort reform do not always originate with insurance companies and business interests. Let us leave what is better left to the legislature to the legislature, and what is better left to the courts to the courts.[210]

---

[210] Donald Gifford's recent publications include: SUING THE TOBACCO AND LEAD PIGMENT INDUSTRIES: GOVERNMENT LITIGATION AS PUBLIC HEALTH PRESCRIPTION (forthcoming 2010); LEGAL NEGOTIATION: THEORY AND APPLICATIONS (1989; 2d ed. 2007); CASES AND MATERIALS ON THE LAW OF TORTS (4th ed. 2003) (with Oscar S. Gray); *The Peculiar Challenges Posed By Latent Diseases Resulting From Mass Products*, 64 MARYLAND L. REV. 613 (2005); *The Challenge to the Individual Causation Requirement in Mass Products Torts*, 62 WASHINGTON & LEE L. REV. 873 (2005).

RICHARD L. CUPP, JR.,[211] TORT REFORM OR TORT RESTRICTION: RHETORIC AS SCOREKEEPER

Tort reform's name is interesting. The phrase "tort reform" brings to mind conscientious lawmakers thoughtfully studying tort issues to craft legislative alterations that enhance justice. One might think that this would include contractions of tort law where it is overly expansive, and expansion of tort law where it is overly restrictive.

But if one were to think this, of course one would be wrong. If tort reform is about correcting injustice, it is only about correcting the injustice of overly expansive tort rules. The injustice caused by overly restrictive tort rules is generally ignored. When a legislature is asked to pass a bill described as "tort reform," it is almost always a one-way street toward contracting rather than expanding the common law.

Thus, the name "tort reform" is not very descriptive of what is actually taking place with this kind of legislation. "Tort restriction" would be a much more accurate term. However, use of this more accurate term would likely make the process less appealing to voters. The harsh word "restriction" sounds much less desirable than "reform." If these legislative efforts had been talked about from the outset in the language of "tort restriction" rather than "tort reform," I would venture to guess that fewer of the statutes would have been passed into law.

Professor Timothy D. Lytton has written persuasively about the significance of "framing" in public policy debates involving tort issues.[212] Participants in public policy debates compete to frame the issues for the public and news media in ways favorable to their positions. The party whose framing of the issues becomes dominant in public perception typically prevails in the policy struggle. Despite being less accurate than other possible descriptions, the business community has been successful in framing the issue as whether "tort reform" is needed to restrict lawsuits. The business community's success in framing the issue reflects its success, on the whole, in legislative tort restriction battles.

---

[211] Richard L. Cupp, Jr. serves as John W. Wade Professor of Law at Pepperdine Law School. Professor Cupp has authored more than 20 significant scholarly articles and numerous shorter articles. He is an elected member of the American Law Institute, and he has served as chair of the Association of American Law Schools Section on Torts and Compensation Systems. In addition to his work in torts and products liability, Professor Cupp writes and speaks extensively about the legal and moral status of animals. He has advised many organizations on these subjects, including the National Academy of Sciences Committee on Science, Technology and Law, the National Academy of Sciences Committee on Neuroscience, the American Veterinary Medical Association, the Animal Health Institute, and the American Animal Hospital Association. He has also been awarded research grants from the National Association of Biomedical Research. Professor Cupp served as an associate dean at Pepperdine Law School and coordinated Pepperdine Law School's successful application for membership in Order of the Coif, which was granted in 2008. As a law student Professor Cupp served as editor-in-chief of the UC Davis L. Rev. He teaches torts, products liability, remedies, and animal law.

[212] Timothy D. Lytton, HOLDING BISHOPS ACCOUNTABLE 82–107 (Harv. Univ. Press, 2008).

I like some but not all of the tort reform legislation that has been enacted. What I like most about legislative tort reform in general is that it relies on the will of citizens, and the majority of citizens have obviously been persuaded over the past 30 years that tort law should be restricted. However, it is interesting to note that in an earlier era, when tort law was perceived by many as too restrictive in the wake of the industrial revolution, legislative tort reform to expand liability was not in the forefront.

For example, prior to *MacPherson v. Buick Motor Co.*[213] in the early part of the twentieth century, people harmed by products generally could not sue manufacturers unless they were in direct privity of contract. With the rise of broad distribution systems increasingly involving wholesalers and retailers rather than direct manufacturer-to-consumer sales, the direct privity requirement severely impeded plaintiffs' ability to attain justice when they were injured due to product manufacturers' negligence. Remedying this injustice was left to the courts, rather than being resolved through legislative tort reform to expand liability. One is left to wonder why legislative tort reform has been so successful in restricting liability, but more or less absent in compelling situations in which justice demanded expanding tort liability.

I suspect that resources and organization play a significant role in legislative tort reform's propensity to restrict rather than to expand. By the late 1970's, when tort law had gone through unprecedented and rapid common law expansion, the business community had ample funds and expertise to inform citizens of their concerns and to channel their concerns into the legislative process. Organization and funding to gain passage of significant pro-victim tort reform apparently did not exist when *MacPherson* was decided, and it apparently still does not exist today. Rather, the phrase "tort reform" has been and remains merely a framing rhetoric for legislatively restricting litigation and damages awards. Some of these restrictions have been needed in the wake of tort law's explosion in the 1960s and 1970s, but true tort reform that in appropriate situations favors defendants and in appropriate situations favors plaintiffs would be better yet.[214]

---

[213] 111 N.E. 1050 (N.Y. Ct. of App., 1916).

[214] Professor Cupp's recent scholarship includes, *Moving Beyond Animal Rights: A Legal/Contractualist Critique*, 46 SAN DIEGO L. REV. 27 (2009); *Paint by Numbers*, L.A. DAILY JOURNAL, July 14, 2008, at 6A.; *Emotional Distress and Loss of a Pet*, PHILADELPHIA INQUIRER, Apr. 27, 2007; *A Dubious Grail: Seeking Tort Law Expansion and Limited Personhood as Stepping Stones Toward Abolishing Animals' Property Status*, 60 SMU L. REV. 3 (2007); Christopher L. Frost, *Successor Liability for Defective Products: A Redesign Ongoing*, 72 BROOK. L. REV. 1173 (2007); *Believing in Products Liability: Reflections on Daubert, Doctrinal Evolution, and David Owen's* PRODUCTS LIABILITY LAW, 40 U.C. DAVIS L. REV. 511 (2006).

PAUL FIGLEY,[215] CALLS FOR JUSTICE & "JOINT AND SEVERAL LIABILITY"

My first trial was before United States District Judge Vincent P. Biunno of the District of New Jersey. During a debate on a small, procedural motion, one of the attorneys argued that "Justice" required a certain result. Judge Biunno's response was simple but profound. He said, "That which is Justice for the early bird is not Justice for the worm." We all understood his point: when an advocate says, "Give me Justice," what the advocate means is, "Let my side win." We also understood that Judge Biunno wanted specific, reasoned arguments, not abstract hyperbole. A similar approach might guide our consideration of various proposals to reform our tort system, including those pertaining to "joint and several liability."

Under the joint and several liability rule, liability "may be apportioned either among two or more parties or to only one or a few select members of the group, at the adversary's discretion. Thus, each liable party is individually responsible for the entire obligation . . . ." *Black's Law Dictionary* (8th ed. 2004). This means that when multiple defendants are found liable, each defendant is liable for the entire amount, and the plaintiff can choose to recover all its damages from any one defendant regardless of that defendant's proportionate share of fault. That defendant is left to seek some recompense from the other tortfeasors if they can be located and are not judgment proof. The issue in the tort reform debate is whether this rule should continue where each party's proportionate share of fault is determined by the judge or jury.

Joint and several liability became established doctrine during the period when the law applied harsh rules to both tort plaintiffs and defendants who were found to be at fault. If the plaintiff was contributorily negligent its suit was barred. If a defendant was jointly liable to plaintiff with other defendants, it was responsible for the entire judgment and could be called on by plaintiff to pay it all. Thus, the risk of non-paying defendants fell on defendants, not plaintiffs.

The contributory negligence rule barred any recovery whatsoever by a plaintiff who was even marginally at fault. As Prosser explained, the rule "places upon one party the entire burden of a loss for which two are, by

---

[215] Paul Figley is the Associate Director of the Legal Rhetoric Program, at the American University Washington College of Law. Prior to joining the Washington College of Law community, he was a career litigator for the U.S. Department of Justice, representing the United States and its agencies in appellate and district court litigation involving torts, national security, and information law. His expertise is in motions practice. He is a graduate of Southern Methodist University School of Law, where he was leading articles editor for the Journal of Air Law & Commerce. Since coming to the Washington College of Law, he has given writing workshops to national organizations and government agencies and has written for national legal writing publications and scholarly journals. In addition to Legal Rhetoric, he teaches first year Torts and upper level Advanced Lawyering Skills: Tort Litigation.

hypothesis, responsible." William A. Prosser, *Torts* (4th ed. 1971) § 67, 433. A harsh defense, contributory negligence was always disfavored by the courts. Early on, an exception was made where the defendant had the "last clear chance" to avoid an accident. Other exceptions were created where defendants' actions could be characterized as "reckless" or "wanton," or plaintiffs' as "remote." Courts reduced defendants' likelihood of success with contributory negligence arguments by putting the burdens of pleading and proof on defendants, and by letting sympathetic juries decide the issue. Increasingly, the doctrine was seen as severe or "unjust." The Supreme Court of California summarized this viewpoint in its opinion which rejected contributory negligence, stating, "The basic objection to the doctrine—grounded in the primal concept that in a system in which liability is based on fault, the extent of fault should govern the extent of liability—remains irresistible to reason and all intelligent notions of fairness." *Li v. Yellow Cab Co.*, 13 Cal.3d 804, 811 (Cal. 1975) (adopting comparative negligence).

Ultimately, most jurisdictions abandoned contributory negligence altogether and replaced it with some version of comparative negligence. Comparative negligence allows recovery by a plaintiff whose negligence contributed to the injury, but reduces that recovery by the percentage of her fault in "pure" comparative negligence jurisdictions, or by the percentage of her fault if it is less than fifty (or forty-nine) percent in "modified" comparative negligence jurisdictions. Under a comparative negligence regime, the parties' comparative fault is determined at trial.

Which brings us to the question whether the joint and several liability rule should continue in jurisdictions that have adopted comparative negligence. The joint and several liability rule grants the plaintiff complete freedom to choose which defendant will be required to pay a judgment. For example, if the plaintiff had no fault in causing his own injury, a defendant whose negligence was a one percent cause of the accident could have to pay all of plaintiff's damages. In another example, if the plaintiff is found to be forty-eight percent at fault, a defendant who is one percent at fault could be required to pay fifty-two percent of plaintiff's damages, even though that defendant is forty-eight times less culpable than the plaintiff. Such a result is inconsistent with the logic that undermined the contributory negligence doctrine; it "fail[ed] to distribute responsibility in proportion to fault." *Id.* at 810. Nonetheless, many jurisdictions have adopted comparative negligence and retained joint and several liability in one form or another, leaving a defendant to pay a greater percentage of damages than its proportionate share of responsibility.

The better approach is that taken by the Supreme Court of Tennessee which addressed joint and several liability in *McIntyre v. Balentine*, 833 S.W.2d 52, 58 (Tenn. 1992), the decision in which it abandoned contributory negligence and adopted comparative negligence:

[T]oday's holding renders the doctrine of joint and several liability obsolete. Our adoption of comparative fault is due largely to considerations of fairness: the contributory negligence doctrine unjustly allowed the entire loss to be borne by a negligent plaintiff, notwithstanding that the plaintiff's fault was minor in comparison to defendant's. Having thus adopted a rule more closely linking liability and fault, it would be inconsistent to simultaneously retain a rule, joint and several liability, which may fortuitously impose a degree of liability that is out of all proportion to fault.

In my view (colored perhaps by a career defending Americans' tax dollars in tort suits brought against the United States), this is the correct result. Our tort system is not comprised entirely of deep pocket defendants and unsophisticated plaintiffs. Its purpose is not income redistribution. No sound policy requires one defendant to pay for injuries caused by someone else, particularly where our ingrained system has increased how we calculate "damages" so they will both make plaintiffs whole and cover contingency fees. Rules that apply to one should apply to all. When a plaintiff's recovery is reduced only in proportion to its fault in causing the damage, a defendant's liability should likewise be in proportion to its fault in causing that damage. Logic calls for an end to joint and several liability. I know better than to suggest what Justice requires.

LUCINDA M. FINLEY,[216] WHAT IS TORT REFORM REALLY ABOUT?

I have followed the tort reform debates as a torts professor interested in the perceptions and impact of the civil justice system, as a scholar who

---

[216] Lucinda M. Finley is the Vice Provost for Faculty Affairs, and the Frank Raichle Professor of Law at the State University of New York at Buffalo School of Law. Her research and teaching areas include tort law, women and the law, reproductive rights, employment discrimination, and first amendment and equal protection law. She has also served as the Director of the law school's Concentration in Civil Litigation, Moot Court Faculty Advisor, advisor to the Buffalo Women's Law Journal, and Director of the Gender, Law and Social Policy Program of the Baldy Center for Law and Social Policy. She is the co-author of a leading Torts casebook, TORT LAW & PRACTICE, REV. 2nd ed. 2003, 3d ed. 2006) (with Vetri, Levine & Vogel). Her recent research includes *The Hidden Victims of Tort Reform: Women, Children and the Elderly*, 53 EMORY L. J. 1263 (2004). She is active as a litigator and appellate advocate in the federal courts, and also brings her scholarship to bear on public policy issues with frequent testimony before the U.S. Congress and state legislative committees on issues ranging from tort reform and its impact on women to violence targeted at reproductive health clinics. After law school she served as law clerk to Judge Arlin Adams on the U.S. Court of Appeals for the Third Circuit, and then practiced law with the Washington D.C. law firm of Shea and Gardner before becoming a law professor. Prior to joining the Buffalo law faculty, she was on the Yale Law School faculty, and she has also been a visiting professor at the University of Sydney law school in Australia. In 1999, she was the Distinguished Visiting Professor at DePaul University Law School in Chicago. She has been awarded a Bunting Fellowship at the Bunting/Radcliffe Institute of Harvard University and a MacArthur Foundation

has studied the effect of non-economic damage caps, and as a participant in the legislative and litigation process. As a result of my research on the disparate impact of tort reform damage caps on women, children, and the elderly, I have frequently been invited to address legislative committees, and to serve as an expert witness in cases challenging the constitutionality of damage cap laws. I have accepted several of these invitations, because I believe that the legislative process should be informed by impartial empirical research. I have experienced how disinterested, and often downright hostile the legislative forum is to empirical reality, I still retain some faith in the courts as more receptive to empirical research and less influenced by the raw political power of special interests.

My experiences lead me to ponder several important questions. Why do certain interest groups continue to push for tort reform, especially medical malpractice changes, when the empirical research continually demonstrates that the problems in insurance and health care markets are substantially disconnected from trends in tort and medical malpractice cases? Why do these interest groups—insurance companies, doctors and medical societies, pharmaceutical and medical device manufacturers and other business interests—continually push for legal changes that will do so little to alleviate their concerns while doing so much to disadvantage the already most disadvantaged amongst the injured? Why are non-economic damages the favorite target of tort reformers?

Taking up the latter question first, I have come to conclude that non-economic damages are under attack because what they compensate for and the role they play in fair and equitable compensation are poorly understood. Because this type of damages is not calculated based on seemingly objective quantitative measures such as medical costs or wages, they can too easily be perceived as subjective and arbitrary. Thus, they get demonized as a "windfall," or as non-compensatory because they do not "make whole." But no one who has to endure a serious injury in order to obtain any form of damages receives a "windfall." And no monetary damages, whether economic or non-economic, "make whole." Damages for lost wages do not restore the ability to perform a job and to gain all that goes with it. Damages for medical costs do not restore the broken body part or the ability to live an ambulatory or pain free life. Monetary compensation, whether economic damages or non-economic, simply "compensates," as in "makes up for."

Tort reformers and the legislators that support tort reform damage caps do not sufficiently appreciate that the non-pecuniary aspects of injury are no less real, no less devastating, and no less deserving of recognition and valuation through the device of damages than the aspects of injury that are more easily monetizable such as wage loss or medical bills. The

Women's Health Policy Fellowship at the University of Illinois at Chicago Center for Research on Women and Gender.

non-pecuniary aspects of injury that get recognized and compensated through non-economic damages include the ability to interact with and enjoy one's family and intimate partner, the ability to perform and enjoy so many of the non-job activities that make one's life meaningful and often worth living, the ability to have and raise children, the ability to be a whole and fully functioning person whose life is not reduced to a compressed and depressing world of debilitating pain. Indeed, the aspects of life that are the most priceless are those that are recognized by non-economic damages. Damage caps present the danger that the priceless will be rendered worthless. If an injury cannot be compensated through the tort system, this sends a societal policy message that it is not important, or not as deserving of recognition and protection as those aspects of injury that can be redressed. It also sends a message that people who earn less, who are past their working years, or who have not yet started theirs, or people whose injuries are to sexual or reproductive functioning, are not as important and deserving of recognition and protection through the civil justice system.

When I have pointed out the priceless aspects of life that are recognized by non-economic damages, and the disparate impact that caps have on women, children, the elderly, and the poor, to their credit many legislators have paid attention and re-thought their position. But the reaction from representatives of the powerful interest groups pushing for tort reform has largely been hostility, because they recognize the powerful potential of these points to retard their momentum.

This brings me to the second and third questions I posed above. Why, then, are these tort reform advocates so intent on getting caps on non-economic damages, despite their inequitable impact and despite many empirical studies showing that caps will not fix the principal insurance market problems that underlie the calls for changes in the tort system?

Actual impartial empirical data about the tort system, about medical malpractice, and about the effects of various legislative changes on either is of so little concern to the groups pushing for tort reform because they are not really interested in reducing medical error or in devising a fair way to efficiently compensate the injured. The motivation for tort reform is much less high minded, no matter what protagonists might say for public consumption.

Insurance companies know that medical malpractice reform, particularly damage caps and anything else that makes it less likely that negligently injured people will be able to pursue claims, increases their profitability, plain and simple. They know that tort reform measures are very unlikely to be coupled with any meaningful insurance regulation or scrutiny of their rate and reserve and investment practices. Thus, they know that tort reform will produce fewer claims with lower payouts, but that they will not be forced to lower premiums or increase coverage to any significant extent. They also know that when a first round of reforms does not in fact produce the promised large reductions in premiums or a reduction in the cyclical fluctuations in the insurance market, and does not in fact augment the supply of doctors in a particular area or specialty, that most legislators will not take a hard look at the lack of fit between the reform measures and these professed goals. They know that instead they will be able to use their lobbying might and campaign contributions and phony grass roots public relations scare campaigns to convince legislators to give them even more draconian measures further reducing the ability of injured people to find legal representation to pursue claims. And then they will be even more profitable.

Organizations that represent doctors know that tort reform will reduce the incidences of doctors being sued. Quite understandably, being sued for allegedly delivering substandard care to a patient is a traumatic event for a health care provider, one that arouses gripping fear of financial and professional ruin, no matter how unjustified the claim. It also arouses resentment that people who do not understand the inevitable risks and have unreasonable expectations of perfect outcomes will second guess them and question their professional capability and compassion. Consequently, doctors' groups embrace any change that will make it less likely that doctors will get sued. Thus, research that shows that damage cap laws render several types of malpractice claims, such as claims for sexual or reproductive injuries, or claims by certain types of people, nonviable, is good news to many health care provider groups. Doctors and groups that advocate for them have traditionally shown little stomach for taking the hard steps to reform their professional practices and institutions to reduce medical error or to root out the handful of repetitively negligent doctors who are responsible for the great majority of malpractice claims and drive up premium rates for the good along with the bad. Tort reform, cutting back on the rights of injured people, and cutting down on the profitability of malpractice lawyers, seems like an easier, less internalized way of alleviating the specter of devastating lawsuits.

Large companies, including insurance companies, pharmaceutical and medical device manufacturers, as well as producers of products that allegedly injure vast numbers of people, have also enthusiastically embraced tort reform for reasons that go beyond their interest in profitability and insurance cost reduction. These reasons, in my view, strike at the heart of the civil justice system's role in our democracy. The civil justice system embodies participatory democracy in a fundamental sense. An individual, or group of individuals, people with limited resources, and otherwise limited access to information about companies and the impact of their products, or without meaningful access to the halls of legislative power, can meet some of society's largest and most powerful institutions on a relatively level playing field in the civil justice system.

They can obtain intelligent and skilled representation without a large initial outlay of resources—representatives with relatively equal knowledge and expertise and often resources as the legal representatives of the large and powerful interests. They can force companies to reveal a great deal of information they would rather not reveal—information that can then be used by other injured people, by consumer advocacy groups, and by regulators or legislators. They can demand that the powerful interests explain and attempt to justify their actions to decision makers— community members in the case of a jury, or a judge—who cannot be captured or influenced in the ways that too many legislators or regulators can be. They can try to gain some individual recompense from the large and powerful interests. Indeed, the civil justice system may well be the only forum in U.S. society where the so-called "little guys" or "ordinary people" can engage with large and powerful institutions in such a relatively equal or at least less unequal way, with some meaningful opportunity to extract things of value from the large and powerful interest or to expose suspect behavior or decision making or to bring about changes in behavior that might benefit the public.

I am not being overly dewy eyed or romanticized about the civil justice system. I am not claiming that it functions perfectly or even efficiently as an institution of participatory democracy. I am simply saying that it can function in such a way, albeit imperfectly, and that its ability to function in this way has a lot to do with the antipathy towards it by interests that otherwise would be able to play exclusively in forums where they are more in control of the game. And, it is precisely because the civil justice system can serve as a significant institution of participatory democracy with a more level playing field that unfettered and uncapped access to it is worth preserving.

One final note: Changing or defending the civil justice system is no small task. Some extraordinarily talented lawyers and other interest groups representatives on both sides have devoted large portions of their professional lives to the topic. The essays and writings above reflect that commitment and passion. This seems a noble and important calling, on both sides.[217]

---

[217] There is a personal critique of both those defending the civil justice system and those seeking tort reform. Professor Marc Galanter notes that this field creates "opportunities for professional aggrandizement and careerism. Business people concerned about liability are surrounded by retainers and entrepreneurs . . . [a] host of professionals, consultants, and publicists [who] thrive by magnifying the sense of crisis and touting their ability to exorcize the menace of enhanced liability. . . . Politicians and organizational entrepreneurs, in turn, echo the jaundiced view in order to cultivate financial support and garner votes. Marc Galanter, *The Three-Legged Pig: Risk Redistribution and Antinomianism in American Legal Culture*, 22 MISS. C. L. REV. 47, 50 (2002). Does that strike you as a fair criticism? Careers are made on both sides of this question. [Author's note: For what it's worth, while you should know the critique, it is not consistent with my approach to tort reform issues or to the actors in the field. AFP].

Consider both the arguments and the backgrounds of the essayists. Did you have the sense that these were arguments carefully structured for a client interest—or that the positions asserted were the personal positions of the authors? How does one's personal experience affect one's perceptions about tort reform? This question, among others, is central to the narratives that follow.

C. THE NARRATIVES

The narratives that follow are designed to give you a somewhat different perspective on the issues raised in the preceding essays and personalize your understanding of the field, providing a firsthand look at the lives of those affected by the civil justice system.[218] Two important caveats: (1) these are entirely fictional accounts and (2) these are *not* advocacy pieces. They are two storylines that illuminate client perspectives. They are presented with the hope that you can relate to the challenges that people face when they become enmeshed in the civil justice system.

You may decide to skip the narratives after completing the essays and move on to the articles, position papers, and cases. The narratives are, after all, caricatures. However, both Miranda Daine (the plaintiff) and Devon Armstrong (the defendant) offer a view of tort reform and a perspective different from the essayists and other authors, a storyline most easily captured in a narrative.[219]

In classes, both in law schools and in many other areas of study, tort reform is a topic of consequence. Cases are read, questions posed, readings assigned and discussed—but all too often little or nothing is known of the parties in the cases. In legal studies, plaintiffs and defendants can be reduced to the symbols π and Δ. It is not unusual in a first-year torts class for a student to discuss a case using symbols instead of names. ("In this case π was a patient of Δ" or "π was injured when Δ's washing machine exploded.") There is, of course, far more to the cases, to the people involved, than the Greek letters π and Δ suggest.

---

[218] For those interested in the use of narrative in legal education and beyond, you might look at: Anthony J. Bocchino & Samuel H. Solomon, *What Juries Want to Hear: Methods for Developing Persuasive Case Theory*, 67 TENN. L. REV. 543, 543 (2000); David F. Chavkin, *Fuzzy Thinking: A Borrowed Paradigm for Crisper Lawyering*, 4 CLINICAL L. REV. 163 (1997); Brian J. Foley & Ruth Anne Robbins, *Fiction 101: A Primer for Lawyers On How To Use Fiction Writing Techniques To Write Persuasive Facts Sections*, 32 RUTGERS L.J. 459, 465–72 (2001); Ruth Anne Robbins, *Harry Potter, Ruby Slippers and Merlin: Telling the Client's Story Using the Characters and Paradigms of the Archetypal Hero's Journey*, 29 SEATTLE U. L. REV. 767, 768–69 (2006); Ann Shalleck, *Institutions and the Development of Legal Theory: The Significance of the Feminism & Legal Theory Project*, 13 AM. U. J. GENDER SOC. POL'Y & L. 7 (2005).

[219] Peter Brook & Paul Gewirtz, Eds., LAW'S STORIES: NARRATIVE AND RHETORIC IN THE LAW (1996); Kathryn Abrams, *Hearing the Call of Stories*, 79 CAL. L. REV. 971 (1991).

At a minimum, the narratives will help you answer these two questions:[220]

1.   What is it like to be the parent of a profoundly injured child, to know the person or entity that caused the injury and be unable to pursue successfully that entity in a court of law?

2.   What is it like to have all that you have worked for, all that is of consequence to you, taken from you in a lawsuit—or series of lawsuits— where you are certain you have done nothing wrong?

Narrative 1: The Restaurant, the Accident, Miranda and Simon Daine[221]

Every table is full by noon but when Simon's teacher calls a few hours later, dishwashing is underway, the tables are clean, and Alex is going over the dinner menu.

"I have to take this," I say.

"Do we order more soft shells for tonight?" Alex asks.

"Honestly, Alex, give me a minute." My last few discussions with Mrs. Rommigen have been brief. No, I don't have time to handle the wrapping paper drive this year. Yes, I will come in and talk to the class about running one's own business. If those are the topics, this will be a short call.

I start: "Mrs. Rommigen, this is Miranda Daine."

"There's been an accident, Ms. Daine. Simon was in the locker room after gym class."

I wait for her to continue but there is nothing. "And?" I ask. "What happened? Is he hurt?"

I hear her inhale. "Gym class was over and he was changing back into his school clothes. He was sitting on a bench . . . the bank of lockers in front of him fell forward."

"*On* him?"

"Yes, I'm afraid so. The gym teachers pulled the lockers off him and called the rescue squad. He's on the way to Children's Hospital."

------

[220]   Carolyn Grose, *A Persistent Critique: Constructing Clients' Stories*, 12 CLINICAL L. REV. 329 (2006); Binny Miller, *Give Them Back Their Lives: Recognizing Client Narrative in Case Theory*, 93 MICH. L. REV. 485, 487 (1994); Binny Miller, *Telling Stories About Cases and Clients: The Ethics of Narrative*, 14 GEO. J. LEGAL ETHICS 1.

[221] Television or movie performance rights for the narratives that follow are the property of the author.

"Oh—my Simon!" Something about my voice quiets the background noise in the restaurant—my restaurant. The lunch crowd has thinned. I slump against the wall next to the phone. "Children's . . . on Michigan Avenue?"

"Yes," says Mrs. Rommigen. "Just off North Capitol Street." After a pause: "He was breathing—they said his heart rate was strong . . . but some part of the lockers caught him in the head, just over his left ear. They stopped the bleeding. . . ."

"How could this have happened?" I ask.

"I am not entirely sure, Ms. Daine—Michael Kearney. . . ."

"Michael is Simon's friend," I say.

"Yes. I know. He was there. He told me that some boys—he won't say whom—threw his pants—Michael's pants—on top of the lockers. The older boys tease Michael. . . . In any case, Michael began to climb up to get his pants, pulling himself on the locker door, when the lockers started to lean forward. Michael let go and managed to jump out of the way, but Simon. . . . Poor Simon was just sitting on the bench, still wearing his gym shorts—he had no time to get out of the way."

"I need to get to the hospital," I say.

Alex, the chef, runs with me to the car and offers to help. I tell him to stay at the restaurant, take care of things. I assure him that I'll be back as soon as I can and will call when I know more. It's mid-afternoon on Capitol Hill. Traffic is light and I am across East Capitol Street, Maryland Avenue, and on North Capitol in a matter of minutes. I am at the hospital as the ambulance arrives at the emergency entrance. In seconds I see Simon. He is intubated, on a respirator, his head covered in bandages.

I am with Simon when a doctor appears. "I'm Dr. Starling." He waits for a moment. "I am chief of pediatric neurosurgery."

"Miranda Daine," I say. "This is Simon."

Dr. Starling opens Simon's eye and lets it close, peels back the bandage, talks to the paramedics, and turns to me. "He is going to need surgery and time is precious. The accident happened less than an hour ago—that's important—but there's no time to waste. I need to clean out the wound and see if I can put him back together."

"Surgery?"

———————

I follow the gurney into the hospital, down a corridor, into an elevator, and up several floors. We stop at the double doors to the operating room. "Miranda, Simon and I have work to do," Dr. Starling says. A medical entourage accompanies him into the operating room—and I am shown the waiting room.

An orderly helps me to an orange plastic chair and asks for my insurance card. I sign a form attached to a clipboard, the orderly departs, and I am alone. In a matter of minutes, a man sits next to me. "Ms. Daine, my name is Tom Burlington. I am the hospital chaplain."

"Why are you here . . . Oh God . . . he's not. . . ."

"No, but when I get a call, it is because the injuries are serious." He pauses. "Dr. Starling is a fine neurosurgeon. Your son is in good hands."

"Oh, my beautiful little boy."

"Do you want to pray with me?" Burlington asks.

"I'm not a religious person. . . ."

"I don't think that's of much consequence." He smiles. "Shall we?" I close my eyes as he speaks. "Almighty, please care for and protect Simon Daine. . . ." I pray hard and cry harder.

My eyes are closed when the chaplain says, "It's a good sign we haven't heard anything yet." I cannot speak. As chaplain, he probably knows I am well into a negotiation with a supreme being with whom I almost never speak. As the chaplain talks, I pledge in silence to give anything, do anything, trade all for raw survival. Disabilities, deficits; paralysis, are all perfectly acceptable. I promise, in prayer, that this deal will not be forgotten if Simon survives.

Narrative 2: Simon Daine

Hours pass before I see Dr. Starling. "Your son is stabilized but extremely weak. The injury he sustained is severe. He has a massive subdural hematoma and there are skull fragments. . . ."

The chaplain intercedes. "You know I don't follow that kind of language, Bernie."

I appreciate the chaplain's lie which produces an explanation for my benefit. "There is a leathery covering on the brain called the dura mater. It surrounds the brain. A hematoma is a swelling, an accumulation of fluids. A subdural hematoma is a swelling below the dura mater. It puts pressure on the brain. We have relieved the pressure." Starling pauses. "The head trauma has activated modest seizure-like activity. It will be hours before we have better information."

I turn to my new friend of unspecified faith. "How could this happen?"

The chaplain shakes his head and has the good judgment to spare me the 'God works in mysterious ways' lecture and holds my hand.

Four hours later, Dr. Starling emerges from the operating room. "Simon has made it through surgery and is on his way to post-op. You can see him in the ICU within an hour." He sits down next to me. "We think that there has been damage to the cranial nerves . . . it's pervasive. The first symptom we observed is problematic swallowing. Simon's cricopharyngeus is in spasm." He pauses. "Swallowing mechanisms are complicated. A series of things must happen in the right sequence for a person to swallow. Right now it would appear that a section of his throat is, for lack of a better term, paralyzed. If dysphagia persists, meaning he cannot swallow, he will be fed through a nasal gastric tube—a tube inserted through his nose down into his stomach—because he will not be able to eat food and then swallow it. If the situation continues, a tube is inserted into his abdomen." He stops. "You understand this means he won't be able to process his own saliva."

———————

A second elevator ride takes me to the ICU. I navigate to the far end of the room, passing physicians and nurses administering to tiny patients. I pass bloodied bike riders, hairless cancer patients, and countless carts with monitors that track every manner of bodily function. I am surrounded by softly buzzing timers and blinking lights and then, finally, staring at my son.

Dr. Starling is speaking with a technician a few feet away. "Doctor. . . ." A nurse sitting next to Simon notices movement. He spins around and walks to the head of the bed.

"Do you know where you are?" Dr. Starling stares into Simon's eyes.

There is a silence and then, in a squeaky and hyper-nasal tone, Simon speaks. "I'm right here."

He shakes his head. "Nothing wrong with that answer."

I lean back. The voice is unfamiliar. Could this be my son? The shaved head, the blue and black face. Yellow markings running down from his ear to his neck. I look down at the body of my son. It is as if he has been deflated. His arms look tiny, his face misshapen.

Simon turns and says to me. "Don't leave."

Starling backs away and turns to me. "This is a strong first response."

———————

I have been at Simon's bedside for six hours when I hear a loud beeping and see a flashing light. As I would learn in the months that followed, this is the Code Blue alert that sounds when a patient stops breathing. Doctors, technicians, and nurses fly out of the wings of the ICU and surround the sides of my son's bed.

First a crash cart, then chest paddles, a countdown, and: "Clear!" Everyone takes a step away from the bedside, Simon's body jolts, and Dr. Starling says: "We have a heartbeat." The revival process is efficient, practiced, and successful.

"His heart stopped. It took time . . . I'm sorry. That was a bad one."

Over the next 36 hours, Simon lights the Code Blue alarm three more times. I am told there is significant brain damage. There will be no return of the sentences he used immediately after surgery.

When not at Simon's side, I am on the phone. My mother, now a Floridian, says she will drive to D.C. to help. I tell her: "There's nothing to do. Wait until Simon and I are home." I have a fleeting thought about Simon's father, a charming waiter who ran off the moment he heard I was pregnant. Despite efforts to locate him, I haven't seen him in 12 years.

After grandparents, aunts, uncles, a few neighbors, and dear Alex, my chef (who has been a complete mess since the accident), are notified, I call Simon's godfather—and my lawyer—Richard Monroe.

Narrative 3: Richard and Simon, Through Miranda's Eyes

Richard Monroe and I attended the same undergraduate university, pursued the same major (political science), and, for a brief time, were romantically involved. We planned to go to law school together, but when my father passed away my senior year, I came home to Washington to run the family restaurant and Richard went on to the world of Socratic method, law reviews, and the bar exam. He graduated, married, and moved to Houston. I stayed home, in D.C., on Capitol Hill, buying blue crabs off the dock on Maine Avenue. In time, my mother retired to Florida and I became the sole owner and proprietor of Daine's Seafood Grill. My interest in politics and government did not abate, however, and I harbored the fantasy of returning to the field in the future.

"Richard, it's Simon. He's had an accident. He's in the ICU." I can say no more.

I am asleep sitting upright in the waiting room of the ICU when Richard arrives. He still holds his suitcase.

I stand up and hug my friend. "Simon is in the ICU."

Richard nods. "I got a report at the desk."

Richard and I slip on green hospital gowns and enter the ICU, stopping first at the wash basin to scrub. We walk through the room, passing flashing monitors attached to other small patients and arrive at Simon's bedside.

"Oh. . . ." Richard places his hand over his mouth.

"I know," I say, "it's as if he's shrunk by half."

Richard studies Simon. His shaved head is bandaged on the left side, the site of the impact of the locker. His face is dark yellow and green.

Richard eases into a chair next to Simon's bed and studies his godson. We sit quietly for more than an hour, speaking softly as Simon sleeps. By the time we are done talking, Richard has a clear sense of the accident. Finally, he turns to me. "Miranda, I would guess that the last thing on your mind is the legal ramifications."

"You're wrong, Richard. My insurance is limited. This is costing a huge amount of money—I realize that much—and I'm not sure how I'm going to pay for what comes next." My voice catches briefly. "It wasn't his fault, Richard. He was just sitting there and it fell on him."

Richard places his hand on my forearm. "I'm going to take care of Simon. Never forget that. There are things I need to do, as his godfather and lawyer. You are about to be in a battle, Miranda. You must become Simon's advocate in this hospital and thereafter—and he will need you. I will handle his legal claim." I nod and Richard continues. "I want the lockers secured immediately—before there is a chance to alter them in any way. I also will have to get reports from the police, ambulance driver, and the school into safe hands."

"What if there was nothing wrong with the lockers, Richard? What if this was a freak accident? How am I going to pay for all this?"

Richard puts his hand on my shoulder. "Lockers are not supposed to fall over on little children." He reaches down for his briefcase and pulls out a few sheets of paper. "I have a consent form, some medical releases, a representation agreement. I'm asking you if you will let me protect my godson's interests."

————

Simon stays in Children's Hospital for eleven weeks. I learn how to insert and remove a nasal gastric tube so that Simon can be fed at home. They put off inserting the tube abdominally. There is hope the swallowing will return, and more surgery, at this point, is terribly risky. Further, whether the tube is in his nose or his stomach does not matter. He cannot swallow. He drools constantly. His mental capacity is greatly impaired. He is Simon, loving and loved, and yet so very different.

Narrative 4: *Daine v. Armstrong Industries*

Alex agrees to run the restaurant but still makes daily visits to the hospital. "Are you sure you should use a lawyer from Texas," he asks one afternoon. "Wouldn't you be better off with a local. . . ."

"Richard is the best lawyer I know, Alex," I say, cutting him off, "and he understands me—and this case. I trust him. He's already filed suit against the locker manufacturer—Armstrong Industries."

"Is Richard a member of the bar in this area?"

"He hired a D.C. lawyer who is helping with local rules and getting him admitted *pro hac vice* for this case," I say. "And there's more—Richard is an expert on tort reform."

"He's a politician?" Alex asks.

"No—but he's a fighter. Do you know what this is about?" I don't wait for an answer. "The idea is to cut costs, get rid of frivolous cases. . . ."

"Sounds right to me," Alex says.

"No, Alex, it's anything but right. The reforms they're talking about will limit the ability—the right—of injured people to hold accountable those who cause harm," I say. "Richard is fighting against those limitations."

Alex shakes his head. "Do you remember what happened to us a couple of years ago? We were sued when someone claimed they got sick after eating dinner at the restaurant—and it was settled for $5000? You were furious."

"This is different," I say.

"Tell me," Alex says.

"I understand that businesses, large and small, need to limit excessive claims. I understand that lawsuits can exact a terrible toll. But there has to be a balance, Alex. Simon is entitled to his day in court. He is entitled to a system that is not tilted in favor of those who caused him such harm. Richard fights for that—and now, that is my fight as well."

"I won't argue with you, Miranda," Alex says. "Of course you are right about protecting Simon, but what you're talking about is about more than your son. When we went through that lawsuit you said that trial lawyers were vipers."

"That was different," I say. "And I said some were. . . ."

"Richard Monroe?"

"Shut up, Alex," I say.

————————

I am learning more from Richard about tort reform than I ever wanted to know. I know about debates on the Hill, formal hearings, year after year, focused only on civil tort liability.

One afternoon, I stand with Richard at the front entrance of Children's Hospital. From our vantage point we can see the nation's Capitol.

Richard points. "Those buildings, just behind the Capitol, are where public policy and political currency are traded," he says. "The Hart Office Building . . . the Rayburn Office Building—Miranda, in the week that changed Simon forever, the topic of tort reform was front and center before congressional committees in those two buildings. Those fighting for and against limiting the tort system have spent countless millions on this debate."

Richard tells me that the investment in the tort reform fight—on both sides—is far more than has been invested by the federal government in finding a cure for the kind of subdural mayhem underway in the cranial cavity of my son.

Richard tells me about consumer advocates, legislators, lawyers, lobbyists, law professors, economists, and business owners arguing over the fate of the civil justice system.

Richard tells me it is a well-fought battle—but I assume these experts have little stomach for the awful reality of children like Simon.

I assume theirs is a more distanced discourse of consumer rights, corrective justice, redistributive goals, free enterprise, market forces, and regulatory balance.

I assume talk of a little boy who is brain injured and bruised beyond recognition is simply distracting.

————————

I secured for myself and my employees at the restaurant modest medical insurance. Like many restaurateurs, I struggled to balance salary and benefits to a staff that turns over, sometimes, on a weekly basis. Most of my workers are young, and health insurance is low on their list. The policy I bought reflected those interests, and thus, I am not surprised to learn that within several months of the accident, the massive costs of continuous care obligations cause the limits on my health insurance policy to be exceeded.

The insurance payments dwindle down to nothing.

The cost of continuous care rises.

Monthly bills from physical therapy, swallow therapy, and tutoring alone greatly exceed my monthly income.

I borrow from my mother, take a second mortgage on my home, but it is clear: I am going broke.

Nine months after the accident, I place Daine's Seafood Grill on the market. On the day of the sale, I am bankrupt.

My mother has been flying back and forth from her retirement home in Florida, trying to help, but like me, has run out of funds. Also like me, my mother finds it impossible to deal with the changes in Simon.

Before the accident, Simon was a typical, manageable kid. Since his return from the hospital, he is difficult to handle. He is given to temper tantrums and, on occasion, will strike at anything near him, much like a two-year-old. The difference is that Simon is almost a teenager and his physical strength has returned.

Psychologists tell me the injury to Simon's brain affected his capacity to assess social situations and govern behavior accordingly. One therapist tells me the rate of "acting out" behavior in brain-injured children is five times that of children who do not suffer such injuries. The statement is confirming but hardly reassuring.

"Too much spit everywhere," Simon screams. There is no comfort in explaining the mechanics of dysphasia. My son wears a bib.

On good days Simon pretends to swallow; on bad days, he is saturated with his own saliva and in a constant rage.

Six months after we leave Children's Hospital, Dr. Starling returns my call. "There is a surgical procedure," Dr. Starling says, "that will allow Simon to swallow—somewhat. It is risky."

"He cannot live this way," I say. "When can you see us?"

After a one-hour discussion with Dr. Starling, I decide to go forward with the procedure he has outlined, a cricopharyngeal myotomy. Dr. Starling explains that a minute portion of the musculature associated with the swallow cycle and pharynx will be severed, rendering it "incompetent." This will relieve the spasm in Simon's throat and should allow him to process fluids.

"The injuries Simon sustained are, for lack of a better term, diffuse. Impact to the parietal region affected brain and the cranial nerves. Miranda, this surgery does not always produce optimal results when the underlying cause for the dysphasia is not identifiable. In other words, we don't know exactly why Simon cannot swallow—accordingly, I cannot promise that the surgery will produce a better response. Swallow training and other remedies will be needed."

"We have been down that road, Doctor, and we need to try something else," I say.

The surgical team Dr. Starling assembles for the cricopharyngeal myotomy spends five hours on a tiny portion of the interior of Simon's cricopharyngeal region. I wait with Alex and Richard.

I can tell by Dr. Starling's expression as he emerges from the operating room—the news is not good.

"Things did not go well, Miranda. I can't say with certainty, but I am not optimistic."

A week after the surgery, two things are clear; Simon's swallowing is barely improved—some fluids now get down his throat. However, Simon's speech was affected drastically by the surgery. He emits an audible hiss every time he tries to speak. I can understand almost nothing he says. This is not among the side effects Dr. Starling described before the surgery.

We visit the Swallow Center at Johns Hopkins Hospital in Baltimore, and they review Simon's case. They undertake a videofluoroscopic swallow study and an electromagnetic midsagittal articulography, both of which permit sophisticated imaging of the swallow mechanism—neither of which were undertaken by Dr. Starling's team. These tests, we are told, are not always done.

The conclusions of the doctors at the Swallow Center are staggering.

Surgery was not indicated, their report states. The surgery itself was "unlikely" to resolve Simon's problems.

In short order, Richard files a complaint against Dr. Bernard Starling, the physician who saved my son's life.

A medical board is convened to review the case.

In the interim, Richard sends Dr. Starling a "notice of intent" to initiate a malpractice claim.

Unlike every other legal proceeding in which I have been involved regarding Simon's case, the medical malpractice claim is resolved with stunning speed.

Dr. Starling's insurance carrier proposes a settlement that provides us $100,000. With our primary lawsuit still off in the distance, and no funds to speak of, we take the money.

The funds from the malpractice settlement are enough to make the initial payments required to take care of Simon for several years.

One evening, a few weeks after we settle the malpractice case, Richard calls.

"I received a call from Dr. Starling's wife earlier today," Richard says. "She was quite upset. She asked me to tell you something. This is not going to be easy, Miranda, but I thought you should know."

"What could she possibly want me to know?" I ask.

"Dr. Starling has been relieved of all responsibilities at Children's Hospital. His malpractice premiums were tripled—almost overnight—as a result of the settlement of this claim. He is, for all practical purposes, no longer able to practice medicine."

"How can that be? This was just one case and the settlement was appropriate. The surgery was a mistake—but he is otherwise a fine doctor," I say.

"That is not how this works, Miranda. In the world of medical malpractice, doctors often bear the brunt of these cases, either in terms of their reputation or finances—and often both. I'm sorry. I know this is not welcome news," Richard says. "Try not to think about this. There is really nothing that you can do."

"I will do what I have been doing since the day this all started—I will protect my son. I am sorry about Dr. Starling but I cannot worry about him. He is a skilled physician and I am sure that over time he will find a way to return to the medical profession. Simon, from all I can tell, has no chance of a recovery. He is, forever, profoundly injured," I say.

I consider writing Dr. Starling, telling him that I wish he had been able to stay on at Children's Hospital.

I write no such note.

My focus is Simon.

It is nearly a year since the accident—and the first time Richard begins a call by saying, "I have good news."

"Is Armstrong going to settle?" I ask. Our suit against the locker manufacturer has been pending for months.

"No—not that. Miranda, we got an encouraging report about the mechanics of the fall. Our expert is sure—there were signs of premature metal fatigue before the lockers fell."

"What does that mean—premature metal fatigue? What are you trying to tell me?" I ask.

There is a long pause and then: "Let me read you the summary statement of our expert:

> *The lockers at Lincoln Elementary are manufactured by Armstrong Industries. They are attached to the floor with stainless steel screws. The feet of the locker banks, through which the screws are placed, are made of the same material as the lockers, a less expensive and more vulnerable metal than stainless steel. Industrial cleaners—corrosives—used to clean the slime that accumulates on the locker room floor mixed with a daily dosing of water generated by showering students. This caused rust and deterioration around the sockets through which the screws are placed. When Michael Kearney climbed up the lockers, he caused the entire bank to rock. The rusted sockets expanded under the pressure. As Kearney reached the dust covered top of the lockers, the bank pulled loose from the screws on the floor.*

I do not respond to the information and instead address my only concern. "I have maxed out my credit cards, borrowed from every relative I can find, and still it is not enough. I can't wait for a trial. Settle this, please, Richard, settle it now."

"Settle? Miranda, did you hear the expert's summary? We've got a design case—and while they are difficult, I think we can show the presence of a reasonable alternative design. We'll have to deal with the other factors that led to the accident: the school's use of cleaners and the actions of his friend, Michael Kearny and the other children involved. I'm also trying to find out if any manufacturer uses a different method to secure banks of lockers—thus far no luck—but we're just getting going."

"Richard, I need the money."

"You mean take the fifty thousand dollars?" We received an offer some weeks earlier.

"Take it. I mean it," I say.

"Miranda, this isn't a real offer. For God's sake, this is a tiny fraction of what you already owe and much less than what you will need. You cannot sell out Simon's interests at this point. All I need to do is get in front of a jury; once they see what you've been through, they're going to make Armstrong Industries pay."

"There will be nothing left of me by the time this goes to trial, Richard. Simon is impossible to handle, I can't pay the bills. . . ."

Richard waits a few moments. "All they had to do to keep this from happening was use a different type of footplate for their lockers. A couple of dollars, Miranda, a couple of dollars is all it would have taken. Giving this case up for fifty thousand dollars lets them get away with murder. Please don't make me do that."

I am silent as Richard continues. "Before doing anything, why don't we wait to hear what happens to the defendant's motion to dismiss. Once I get that tossed out, they may come up with a more generous settlement offer, and at that point we can make a judgment about going forward."

"Push, Richard. I can't hang on much longer."

_____

Our case has been removed to federal court in Northern Virginia (Simon and I live in Alexandria, Virginia) based on diversity of citizenship because the locker manufacturer is a North Carolina company. It is unfortunate, Richard tells me, but there is nothing to do but go forward. "The trial court—the U.S. District Court—is a fine venue for us, but if this is appealed we head to the Fourth Circuit in Richmond."

"And?" I ask. "What's with the Fourth Circuit?"

"Let's hope that doesn't happen. They seem—how to put this—a bit hostile to injured plaintiffs."

"An entire appellate court is hostile?"

Richard sighs. "I shouldn't have said that—try not to worry."

_____

Narrative 5: *Daine v. Armstrong* Ends

Eighteen months after Simon's accident, Richard appears in federal court to respond to the manufacturer's motion to dismiss. He expects the judge to take the matter under advisement at the end of the argument. Instead, he finds himself at the receiving end of a most unusual colloquy from the bench.

_____

"Mr. Monroe, please approach." Counsel for Armstrong stands but the judge motions her to sit back. "We're off the record." The judge leans over the front of the bench and speaks to Richard. I strain to listen.

"The law is changing in Virginia and North Carolina—throughout this country—Mr. Monroe. I hope you understand that. My clerk tells me that by the time this case goes to trial, the state legislature will have adopted a new product liability law. It's written to be applied retroactively. If that holds up, it will make things quite difficult for your client. Even if it does not hold up, the existing common law reflects—right now—many of the features of this legislative proposal." The judge pauses, looking out at the courtroom and then continues. "You're from out of state. Take a walk around the statehouse in Richmond. Find out what's going on, and after you do, perhaps you and opposing counsel would like to consider whether this is the kind of case you should try."

The judge turns to the court reporter. "We're back on the record now. Defendant's motion to dismiss is denied. As is the custom in this court, I strongly urge counsel to discuss this situation and report back to this court in 90 days. There are many ways of resolving disputes of this nature without putting the plaintiffs and the defendants through the expensive and difficult process of civil litigation. Am I making myself clear?" Richard and opposing counsel both say, "Yes, Your Honor."

"Good. This court is adjourned."

Richard turns to me the moment we're in the hallway outside the courtroom. "I guess you heard," he says.

"Is he right?" I ask.

"Quite," Richard answers. "It's not just Virginia and North Carolina. It's every state. Even Texas. If there's a good offer here, it may be in Simon's interest to accept it."

"How can the law be against us? This was a dangerous product that devastated my son. You told me that with one simple change, a few dollars, this accident never would have happened. How can we lose?"

"The problem is that neither we, nor anyone else, have data suggesting that other companies use a different foot-plate. Not one. The manufacturer's records do not show a history of metal fatigue with any other lockers. That means Armstrong had no notice. In fact, they are a great company—they test everything they sell, they spend a fortune on research." He pauses. "I need to show this was a foreseeable risk—it will be a challenge. This defect was apparent only after Simon's accident . . . at least that is what Armstrong will contend. Moreover, they're going to argue that the cause-in-fact of this accident was twofold: that poor boy, Michael, who climbed up on the locker—and the school's use of cleaning products that caused the metal to deteriorate. Unfortunately, the school used kinds of products in use at all schools and, as far as I can tell, are the "right" products to use."

"Poor Michael," I say. "His mother told me that he has not been the same since the accident." I pause. "Richard, I need you to be honest—completely honest. Are they going to win? You know what's happening to me—financially."

Richard takes hold of me with both hands. "I'll do everything I can," he says.

―――――――――

At Richard's urging, I rejected a $250,000 settlement offer, the last we would receive, and the case goes to trial eighteen months later. It is a decent trial in which Simon's horrendous journey is described vividly. Richard presents Simon accurately: a disabled little boy, unable to swallow, living a life that no one would choose.

The jury awards Simon $2 million.

The judgment is appealed and in less than a year, reversed. The United States Court for the Fourth Circuit finds error in almost everything done at the District Court level. Applying Virginia law, the Court refuses to apply strict liability in tort, finds the accident unforeseeable, finds the risk of this event "unknowable" in advance, and even finds that lockers are not consumer goods and that if there is any claim at all it should involve the school system, not the manufacturer. "Consumer expectations," they write, "is not a proper standard in this case. We understand this was an unexpected event—but it was as unexpected by the defendant as it was by the plaintiff. While we are saddened by Simon Daine's injury, we cannot let emotion cloud our judgment."

Richard advises me that the school system will fight hard. Like Armstrong, they had no notice of this risk. Their report blames the children in the locker room. They claim that Michael and others "rocked the locker bank to and fro, repeatedly, trying to retrieve Michael's pants. The students were properly supervised. This tragic event happened in a matter of seconds. Quite simply, the school system is not at fault."

I read the opinion of the court and get the sense that the judges see me as a profiteer seeking an undeserved windfall.

Richard files a petition with the United States Supreme Court seeking review, but, as is almost always the case, review is denied. Unbelievable as it seems, it is over.

―――――――――

Narrative 6: Devon Armstrong, CEO, Armstrong Industries and the Birmingham Case Through the Eyes of Miranda Daine

This much I know about the owner of the company that manufactured the lockers that nearly killed Simon:

Devon Armstrong was a sophomore in high school when he began working alongside his father in a large tool and die shop in the industrial flats of Cleveland. By the time he left for college, he was an expert machinist and welder. He spent his college vacations working full-time in the shop and by the time he graduated could have returned in a management role—but he wanted more.

At 28, Armstrong had a doctorate in engineering and was a nationally recognized star in his field. One year later he moved from Ohio to Buffalo and opened his own tool and die shop.

In time, Armstrong's business went public. His initial public offering raised nearly ten million dollars—and Armstrong Industries was on its way. The company specialized in recreational and athletic equipment—playground equipment, goal posts, tackle and blocking sleds, machines that propelled tennis balls as well as baseballs (pitching machines), and similar equipment. Their signature item, however, was lockers—Armstrong lockers were high quality, long lasting, perfectly machined, and, until Simon's accident, rock-solid.

Armstrong married his college girlfriend and had three children, all of whom worked at Armstrong Industries. He sponsored athletic teams—an Armstrong sponsored Little League team made it once to the semi-finals of the Little League World Series. He was a leader in his community, his church and was asked on more than one occasion to run for public office. Devon Armstrong was an American success story.

He was in his early 60s, at the pinnacle of his career, when the lockers at Lincoln Elementary toppled over onto Simon.

A few months after Simon's case came to an end, Richard receives a call from a lawyer in Birmingham, Alabama, who represents the family of a child killed in a batting cage accident. The defendant in that case, once again, is Armstrong Industries. "I know them well," Richard says to the Birmingham attorney. "I am pleased to help."

While client confidentiality guarantees that I will learn almost nothing about the Armstrong pitching machine case from Richard, in the years that follow, Devon Armstrong tells and retells the tale. I have heard his story in congressional hearings more than once, and I know the facts by heart.

The batting cage was similar to those found throughout the United States, a wire-mesh enclosed area where batters attempt to hit a baseball propelled by a pitching machine made by Armstrong Industries.

The case began when a baseball rolled down the chute of the Armstrong pitching machine and picked up a small metallic fragment. The fragment lodged in the ball as it continued down the chute. The mechanical arm of the machine hurled the ball toward the batter, a fourteen-year-old boy.

The metal chunk caused the ball to curve wildly, striking the boy in the temple, just below the protective batting helmet. It was a freak accident and a freak injury. Sections of skull shattered, piercing the dura mater, but unlike Simon, the boy died.

At the time Simon's case began, Richard knew Armstrong Industries and Armstrong products. When it ended, he knew about pitching machines as well.

The machine responsible for the death in Birmingham had been properly installed and was well-maintained. Devon Armstrong was personally involved in the design development of all products sold by his company, including the model in question. Before the pitching machine was placed on the market, a prototype had been subjected to the most extreme testing used for products of that type.

Up until the injury, Armstrong pitching machines had not been the cause of a single accident, much less the centerpiece of any litigation. When the accident occurred, Devon Armstrong was among the first to arrive at the sports park and participate in the investigation. He was deeply troubled by the loss of life and determined to learn how something like this could occur. When he saw the baseball bearing the metal fragment, he was stunned. His equipment was designed to prevent the release of a ball that did not meet precise shape and weight requirements; a baseball with a metal fragment of this size should not have been propelled. Something had gone terribly wrong.

As it turned out, despite extensive inquiry, despite all of Richard's efforts, despite all the testing by both those hired by Richard and Devon Armstrong, as the trial approached, there was no coherent theory to explain why a baseball carrying the lethal metal fragment was propelled forward.

Several weeks before the scheduled trial, Devon Armstrong met with his lawyers. They urged him to settle the case but Armstrong was adamant.

"I have done nothing wrong," Armstrong told his lawyers. "I have done everything humanly possible to make these machines safe. There is nothing wrong with our machine. An alternative design sensitive enough to pick up every weight anomaly would cost a fortune. It would not be practicable. Our machine defines the state of the art. I've invested my whole life in this business. I have three children; all of them work at Armstrong Industries. I am not going to give in because this hot-shot trial lawyer from Houston has appeared on the scene."

It was not irrational for Armstrong to believe he would prevail. He believed in his products, believed in his company, and, as every lawyer in the room knew well, had spent a fortune defending his company in Simon's case and in the Birmingham case. The company profit margin was narrow, the cash reserves low, and by the end of the proceeding, legal fees were paid from Armstrong's personal checking account.

Narrative 7: Devon Armstrong and the Consequences of the Birmingham Trial

By the time Richard finished his closing argument, Devon Armstrong knew he was in trouble. A number of the jurors were in tears. One became physically sick listening to Richard recount the final moments of life of the plaintiff. The trial was a masterpiece for Richard despite the lack of any evidence of negligence.

Richard stressed that this was a product the public could not test, could not examine, and therefore the duty of the manufacturer was to make sure events like this did not take place and the manufacturer had failed. Years later, Devon Armstrong could still repeat the last few sentences of Richard's closing argument.

"And there sits Mr. Armstrong. Look at him. You can see his concern. He knows you, the jury, must make a decision. It is your sacred task. He knows you are people of conscience, he knows you will follow the instructions of the judge, and he knows you will impose on him a penalty. He is concerned because his company produced a time bomb, a machine he admits malfunctioned in a manner he does not understand, a machine designed to be experienced and enjoyed by children. Now the bomb has gone off. Mr. Armstrong asks you to ignore the explosion. Don't do it. You must remember the life that once was. You must see in your own mind the family that once was. It will hurt. It will hurt you badly, but bring them to your mind, remember them, hear this accident one last time, do that for this child."

The jury did just that and found against Armstrong Industries, holding them liable for actual damages of $5 million and punitive damages of $20 million.

As was the case with Simon, appeals were taken and, although the judgment was ultimately reduced to $7.5 million, it held.

By any measure, Devon Armstrong was underinsured. Notwithstanding the advice of his insurance agent and lawyers, his liability coverage had a $3 million policy limit—and excess liability coverage was non-existent.

As with Simon, a petition for review was filed in the United States Supreme Court, this time by the defendants, but the Court chose to spend its time in other ways and denied review.

The Birmingham case stunned Devon Armstrong.

How could there possibly be punitive damages? What had his company done that was so reckless, or as his lawyer said, reflected "conscious flagrant disregard" of life? Of course, more testing might have revealed the problem—but no one tested more than Armstrong Industries.

Armstrong also could not understand the compensatory damages. The boy was dead—it was awful and final—but how did that entitle his parents to such wealth? Why would they get "non-economic" damages? It made no sense to Armstrong, and, he later argued, to the economy at large.

What is gained from punishing a company that does everything properly?

What incentives does this provide to other companies?

Isn't there a reward for being a decent and competent company?

He would pay the judgment—and it would take everything he had. He had already cleaned out the standing reserves of Armstrong Industries and both he and the company were broke.

Once the judgment was paid, Armstrong turned inward. He refused to speak with the family of the child who had died. He knew what they would say: your machine killed our son. Our son did all the right things. He trusted your machine, a product that has to be made very carefully, a product that should be tested and retested, a product that killed our child. Armstrong understood their plight. They were innocent victims.

It was thus that Devon Armstrong found himself involved in the tort reform debate. His company was first in fiscal free-fall—and then crashed.

Armstrong was financially ruined and personally humiliated. The consequences of the case were mind boggling.

Armstrong—and his three children—were unemployed.

Overnight, an inventory worth millions lost all value. There is no market for lockers that harm small children or pitching machines with an undiagnosed and apparently, undiagnosable design flaw. The taint on the good name of Armstrong Industries was permanent.

All four Armstrong production plants closed.

Two hundred faithful employees were jobless and desperate to secure unemployment compensation.

Thousands of investors who believed in the present and future of Armstrong Industries were wiped out as Wall Street responded to another tort system casualty.

And it didn't stop there.

Overcome with anger over the verdict and guilt and sadness for the inexplicable loss of an innocent life, for a time, Devon Armstrong came undone. When he lost his house, he began to drink.

He and his wife of forty years were living in the basement of his oldest son when he hit bottom. His wife found him unconscious on the bathroom floor and, with the help of his son, got him to a hospital. Painful recovery followed.

Devon Armstrong lost two years of his life, but in time, he was back, determined to rebuild his business, determined to change a legal system that had nearly taken his life, his reputation, his family, and, at a fundamental level, his identity.

Narrative 8: Senator Horace Voltman, Through the Eyes of Miranda Daine

Some months after Simon's verdict is reversed, I make a concerted effort to re-start my life. With the restaurant gone, Alex and I start a catering business and it is a success. Alex and I discuss menus, not tort reform. After all that has happened, he still thinks I am blinded by Simon's case and that the civil justice system favors plaintiffs unfairly. He's lucky he's such a darn good chef—I now define friends by their view of the tort system and Alex is no longer my friend. He is my partner in business—and that's it.

Between Simon and the business, I have no time for much of anything for several years, but finally, things begin to open up. I volunteer at the Legal Center for the Rights of Injured Children. I speak to groups of parents of brain-injured children and am invited to testify on legislation to provide funding for cutting-edge medical research. In the course of these activities, I meet a senior aide to Senator Horace Voltman who asks for my resume and, within a few weeks, introduces me to the Senator.

In our first meeting, Senator Voltman asks about my university experience and learns of my love of government and politics. He asks about Simon (he has been well-briefed) and learns of my feelings regarding tort reform. In later discussions with Senator Voltman it becomes clear that my instinctive response to issues I had not considered before match those of the Senator.

At the conclusion of the interviews, after an endless background check, I am hired as a legislative aide to Senator Voltman. With Simon in good hands (he lives in a rehabilitation center in Silver Spring, Maryland and all of his costs not covered by the Starling malpractice case are paid by Richard), it is time to get on with my life.

Working with Senator Voltman gives me the chance to observe the politics of tort reform firsthand. I know the issues and central actors in the debate—one of whom is Senator Voltman. At age 61, Horace Voltman is one of the few remaining populists in the Senate. His political career began as an elected member of the local school board. He developed decent political ties and, after two unsuccessful attempts, won a seat in the state senate. A dozen years later, he was elected to the House of Representatives and ten years after that to his current position in the United States Senate. Voltman has opposed changing the tort system and votes against tort reform bills.

His constituency is not with him on this issue. He is facing a rough election next year. His advisers tell him that most of his major contributors, with the exception of plaintiff's lawyers, will support his opponent unless he softens on tort reform.

This morning, the Senator and I discuss the challenges he faces in the upcoming election and, mid-stream in our discussion, the topic shifts to the importance of tort reform and this morning's hearing which is focused on a federal tort reform bill. I know the bill well—as does Richard Monroe, who will be testifying against it.

When Richard enters the hearing room in the Hart Senate Office Building, he sees me and smiles. He will testify on what has been dubbed the White-Lawson Bill. It is identical to earlier bills, except that it now has a dozen more sponsors. As a matter of federal law, the bill is designed to eliminate punitive damages, abolish joint and several liability, abolish strict liability for those who produce dangerous products, force plaintiffs to prove negligence, and otherwise undo the system of tort law.

The goal is to make it difficult, if not impossible, to sue manufacturers like Devon Armstrong, businesses that while not negligent, have nonetheless produced dangerous products.

As far as I am concerned, the proposal is little more than a transparent relief act to assist the insurance and manufacturing community. Before the hearing begins, I whisper to the Senator: "Remember, Mr. Monroe is my lawyer—from Simon's case—make sure the others on the committee don't rough him up."

"Your Mr. Monroe can take care of himself, Miranda," the Senator says.

"He's not "mine," Senator. He is here testifying on behalf of the Texas Association for Brain Damaged Children. I spoke with him several times this week. You'll like his approach. The other witnesses. . . ."

Senator Voltman interrupts me. "We're going to disagree on this one, Miranda. These tort suits are out of control. This is a chance for me to do something that will help the little guy and I intend to support it."

His comment comes as a shock. To support this legislation is unthinkable.

Narrative 9: A Tort Reform Hearing Through the Eyes of Miranda Daine

"What do you mean, Senator? You're going to vote for this bill?"

"I just *might*, Miranda," Senator Voltman says and turns away. The hearing starts and in a monotone voice, the committee chair reads his opening statement.

"Ladies and gentlemen, we are here to consider the National Product Liability Act, referred to as the White-Lawson Bill, a proposal sponsored by 24 members of the United States Senate, four of whom are on this committee. This legislation will provide relief to the small businesses in the United States who for too long have been subjected to the uncertainty and unfairness of the tort system in the United States. Insurance rates are skyrocketing, jury verdicts are out of control, and it is time for the Senate to take formal action."

The chair of the committee then invites a representative from the Justice Department to explain the White House position. It is a dry statement supporting the bill, explaining that the President has some concerns about health care issues for women and children but in the grand scheme of things feels that this is a matter meriting congressional attention.

Following the Justice Department, three individuals testify in favor of the bill. They are from a national group representing manufacturing interests, a trade association representing the insurance industry, and, finally, the committee hears from Devon Armstrong.

Armstrong is a fairly typical witness in product liability hearings. He is willing and able to tell Congress about a system that stole his livelihood, destroyed jobs, shattered reputations, and rewarded generously and without logic or reason persons who have no entitlement to those funds.

The committee listens with interest to the tale of Devon Armstrong. He details the money his company expended to test lockers and pitching machines. He describes, holding up various government studies as well as industry reports, how his products were superior to others in the American market.

At the conclusion of the panel supporting the legislation, Richard's panel is called. Like the first panel, witnesses are informed that they have five minutes to make their statements. Richard is first to testify:

"There is no tort crisis. Every meaningful peer-reviewed study that has looked at the American civil justice system over the last 20 years has come to the conclusion that this is a crisis manufactured in the media, created by those who would like to be relieved of responsibility when the products they produce or the services they provide fail. "Over the last decade, the average punitive damage award in the United States has been somewhere around $80,000, not millions of dollars. Perhaps more telling, there have only been a few hundred punitive damage cases in recent years. Tell me Senators," Monroe looks up at the committee and continues. "How is that a crisis that requires federal intervention?

"Those who support this legislation want only one thing: certainty. It is a compelling argument. It is understandable that a business would want to know the risks it faces. However, if you pass this bill, a business will be able to calculate in advance its exposure if it produces a defective product.

"It will then insert that cost into the price of its goods and services.

"It will pass that cost along to the consumer, and having done that, there is no longer any sanction for misconduct or incentive for innovation and product improvement. It has all been paid for in advance.

"Our legal system is premised, in part, on the proposition that those who injure others must be held accountable. The fear that a sanction could be substantial forces businesses to be more efficient, forces companies to make safer products. If you pass this legislation, you eliminate that incentive. This bill legislates against accountability. This bill legislates irresponsibility.

"You must not abdicate. You have a responsibility to your constituencies, no matter how much money is in play. . . ."

Senator Voltman interrupts Richard Monroe. "Mr. Monroe, are you implying that those who support this legislation have been co-opted, bought out by business interests? Is that what you are trying to say?"

"Senator, I don't know what goes on in the Senate. I don't know what prompts a Senator to take a particular position. I only know that this legislation is opposed by every consumer organization in the United States. It is opposed by those who fight on behalf of children, on behalf of women's health issues, on behalf of those who are poor, on behalf of those who are vulnerable. I know that this legislation is supported by business and financial interests that have far more power and resources than do consumer groups."

"With all due respect, Mr. Monroe," Voltman continued, "I believe you are avoiding my question. Are you implying that members of this Congress have been bought?"

"I don't know that members of this Congress have been bought."

"That is what you are implying."

"That would be one interpretation of my comments, Senator."

"Well, frankly, sir, you are out of line. What you are talking about is a federal crime. Neither I nor my colleagues take such accusations lightly."

I move closer to Senator Voltman and write furiously on a yellow pad: "Let him finish his statement. You gave him five minutes to talk and he has only spoken for two or three. I need to understand what position our office is taking."

The Senator turns to me. "Your Mr. Monroe may be a good lawyer, but his political judgment stinks." He turns back to Richard, listens for a few moments, picks up the papers in front of him, and leaves the hearing room. Normally, I would follow the Senator out of the hearing room but I have no interest in speaking with him at the moment. I am likely to say something I will regret. Instead, I decide to listen to the remainder of Richard's statement and to hear the questions that follow.

"I have more, Senators, but I sense your questions are more important than my prepared remarks. I ask that my entire statement be made part of the record."

Senator Lawson, acting committee chair with Senator Voltman out of the room, responds: "Without objection, so ordered. Now, Mr. Monroe, are you aware how many companies have been driven out of business by costs stemming from our current civil justice system?"

"Companies that make safe products have nothing. . . ."

Senator Lawson cuts off Richard. "In other words, no. You have no idea. If I were to tell you that conservative estimates place the number at over 25,000, would you be surprised?"

"I don't have any information. . . ."

"Well, I do. How about jobs lost?"

"Come on," Richard says. "There is no way accurately to count. . . ."

"I disagree, Mr. Monroe. I think the number is over a million—at least. What do you have that refutes that?"

"I can do some research on the topic," Richard says.

"Not necessary, Mr. Monroe. Next time, come here with your data. Now, are you aware that the potential for tort liability has caused pharmaceutical companies in the United States to restrict research and move away from important new technologies, denying us essential medical products?"

"I believe that the data would show precisely the opposite, Senator. . . ."

"Oh, but it doesn't," Senator Lawson says. "You plaintiffs' lawyers have done quite a number on pharmaceutical companies. I wouldn't be all that proud of that, Mr. Monroe."

"Companies that make products that kill innocent users. . . ."

"Careful, Mr. Monroe. Unless you have data that backs up such statements, they hardly belong in testimony made under oath. Now, Mr. Monroe," Senator Lawson continues, "are you aware that burglars have brought successful million dollar lawsuits against home owners after the burglars were injured while attempting to enter the homes of their own victims?"

"That is a myth, Senator. The data does not. . . ."

Senator White takes over. "Mr. Monroe, you have become wealthy representing people in personal injury cases, correct?"

"I represent people who have been injured by defective products. I would hardly call myself wealthy. Last year my. . . ."

"I understand you belong to an organization of trial lawyers and that members of your organization have participated in insurance fraud, bringing lawsuits against insurance companies solely designed to get money when there hasn't even been an accident. Is that correct?"

"I know of no such person who has done that, Senator. . . ."

"Mr. Monroe, are you aware that various charitable organizations involved in scouting, sports, religion, and other valuable activities have lost volunteers and have been devastated by massive lawsuits?"

"Senator, your statements are not only wrong but they are destructive. . . ."

A buzzer sounds. "Mr. Chairman," Senator White turns to Senator Lawson, "there is a roll call vote."

"So there is," Senator Lawson says. "We are adjourned for now. I instruct the witnesses to remain close by. We will resume shortly."

Richard knows that after the votes, one or two senators will be present. This hearing, for all practical purposes, is over.

"I was sandbagged," Richard says to me later in the day.

"I'm sorry," I say. "I certainly did not see it coming."

Richard smiles. "I'll get over it."

Narrative 10: Marty Correll, Through the Eyes of Miranda Daine

Marty Correll is a lobbyist hired to pursue changes in the tort system. He sees his task as pure and noble. He tells me that he is sure of the legitimacy and objectives of his clients. He tells me he knows Devon Armstrong personally—and I tell him I know him as well—and then I tell him why. He tells me that words cannot express his sorrow. I tell him to give it a try.

When it comes to cutting back on damages for pain and suffering or capping damages of any kind, Marty is a space devoid of gray areas.

In the majestic structures on the Hill, Marty Correll carries forward the message of his clients with a clarity and simplicity that had become his trademark. He is the type of lobbyist who never works a room but rather greets and embraces individuals. Any cause he represents is assured of being displayed and explained in the best light humanly possible.

For some lobbyists, the essential task is communication, with a continuous undercurrent of transparent flattery designed to elevate the person courted. Marty Correll's style is different.

He believes in his clients or he does not represent them. He is honest to a fault. In my view, he is also wrong.

The power of Marty Correll's inner belief is impressive. On those rare occasions when members of Congress disagree with the position he espouses, you can almost see disappointment in their eyes. Those who stray from the path he defines are rejecting legitimacy. To deviate from Marty Correll's position is to run the risk of ignoring the obvious.

The motives of those who hire Marty could not be more simple: make the tort system predictable. This is a prize of incalculable value and Marty Correll is the perfect treasure hunter to secure victory.

―――――――

Not long after I started working with Senator Voltman, Marty Correll spent thirty minutes with the Senator and me. I remember the discussion:

"It's a crazy quilt out there, Senator," Marty says. "Many businesses, particularly the smaller ones and the doctors, the sole practitioners, just can't afford it anymore."

"You keep an eye on Marty, Miranda," the Senator says to me. "He'll snatch your soul when you're not looking." He turns to Correll. "Marty, this type of legislation is something that should be left to the individual states." I can tell the Senator likes Marty Correll, though I am quite sure he disagrees with his position.

Marty moves forward: "Even if all the states were to act to limit liability, there is nothing to insure any uniformity. Given nationwide and international market competition, the only answer is federal legislation. More importantly, we need to give small business a fair shake, allow them to have some certainty with their risk. You can do that by supporting this legislation."

Correll pauses. "You know the way I work. I look at the issue, try to learn what I can, research it thoroughly. This is what I see: businesses are leaving the United States. Research isn't getting done. Good products are being taken off the market. Every day I hear about another jury, unguided by any uniform standards, using sympathy instead of logic in some personal injury case. It's an enormous drain on the economy, costing us billions. The legislation proposed is pretty simple. Uniform standards, reasonable limits on damages, that kind of thing."

"What do you want, Marty?" the Senator asks.

"I didn't come over here to change your mind, Senator. I've spent a long time studying this. I know that this means a different system, a different way of looking at what we do in the economy, but I'm positive that this is a step forward. The world has changed. Our economy is strong and competition protects consumers. Competition for the quality of goods creates better goods. The rest of the world, unburdened by the tort system, is going to pass us by. Think about this, please, Senator."

Marty Correll reaches for the doorknob. Senator Voltman clears his throat. "Marty, if you have any information that supports your point of view, something in summary fashion that tells me about how insurance rates have skyrocketed or how some of these verdicts are out of control, give it to Miranda."

Correll opens his briefcase and takes out a large manila folder with a tie-down flap. On the front of it is typed in large letters: "Senator Horace Voltman, United States Senate," and below that "Strictly Confidential." He hands it to me.

"I appreciate your willingness to look at this." Again Correll moves toward the door and again Voltman stops him.

"How about a cup of coffee before you go, Marty," Voltman says.

"I'd love one."

Narrative 11: Marty Correll's Discussion with Senator Horace Voltman

On the evening after the Commerce Committee hearing in which Richard testifies (after a fashion) on the White-Lawson Bill, the Senator calls me into his office. I have ignored him most of the afternoon because I am angry about the way he treated Richard earlier today. I enter his office and see Marty Correll on the couch.

"Miranda," Senator Voltman says. "You probably want to know why I've changed my mind."

"Have you?" I ask.

"I am not sure," he says.

"Do you want me to leave?" Marty asks.

"No." Senator Voltman picks up a copy of the White-Lawson Bill. "In the end, this seems like a simple way to address so many issues and yet. . . ."

"What are you talking about?" I say. "Marty, Senator Voltman doesn't favor White-Lawson. I don't know what was going on earlier today but. . . ."

"Stop, Miranda," the Senator says. "I have an open mind on this. I want to hear what Marty has to say. You have a closed mind—a good mind—but closed." He pauses. "I mean it, Miranda—you refuse to listen to anyone except those with whom you agree. You may think you are objective—but you are anything but. My job requires me to hear all sides—and on this one, you are no help. You have concluded somehow that the vast, vast majority of American are wrong or stupid when it comes to tort reform. Think about it—that assumption can't be correct."

"I feel like I don't know you, Senator."

"For once, Miranda, just listen."

"You're treating me like a child, Senator. You'll have my resignation in the morning," I say.

"I won't accept it. For God's sake, can you get off your high horse, detach your son from this debate, and give me a chance to hear out Marty? Is that asking too much?"

"Yes, Senator, it is. This is personal and you know it."

"Please, Miranda. Just listen—or leave. Marty?"

"Thank you, Senator." Marty says. "Let me give this a try. I represent a very wide array of interests as you know. It may come as a surprise to you, but we don't have a problem with paying damages. Bad apples need to be sanctioned. All we need is a way to pay for those damages, a reliable way to calculate liability in advance. That, Senator, is what every business on the face of God's good earth needs to do. The current system does not allow us to do that. That's why we're trying to change it."

"I can't believe you're listening to this," I say.

"Good God, Miranda, there's no arrogance like the arrogance of the left."

"Somehow, for someone who claims to be a progressive, you have a remarkable ability to insult, infantilize, and marginalize people— particularly women—and particularly me. I can't work with you anymore," I say.

"Miranda," Marty says, "give me a few minutes. I know you'll never agree with me—and that's fine. I think you actually may not understand that my position has legitimacy. You've told me about Simon. . . ."

"Don't you even mention his name!"

"I am sorry. I did not mean any offense."

I look at Senator Voltman. "Five minutes, Marty, that's it. Miranda, please—it can't hurt," he says.

"This will be quick," Marty says. "Senator, imagine you're in a house— a small one . . . one room—and from where you sit you can see windows on two walls. You get a different view from each window. Now imagine that what is outside the house is the tort landscape. Let me tell you what's outside the window on my side of the house—what's in the briefing papers I've given you over the years."

"Don't patronize me, Marty," Voltman says.

"I would never do that," Marty says. "This is a situation where there are multiple conflicting realities, Senator. Contrary to what we think are immutable laws of physics, this is a field in which opposites occupy the same space. What industry representatives have been telling you, year after year, is true. Oddly enough, what consumer groups have maintained—and what Mr. Monroe tried to say today, under oath—that is true as well."

"Multiple conflicting realities?" Voltman says. "Most of us in the Senate, and I would say most politicians, understand precisely what you have just said. An overwhelming majority of those who testify before the Senate and House committees, who write position papers trying to influence legislation, are telling the truth. It is their truth, how they experienced a particular problem or crisis or, in some instances, a benefit."

"Right!" Marty says. "Exactly. You'll understand then what I am about to say. When we look out our window, we see hundreds of small town newspapers, in some ways the core of American free speech, out of business. We see physicians, specialists in the disciplines of gynecology and obstetrics, surgeons, leaving their practices because of absurd malpractice premiums. We see the tired remains of what was once a fine small aircraft industry, again because of large tort judgments and, thereafter, unmanageable insurance rates. We see pharmaceutical companies who have shied away from new ventures, new possible cures, because the risk is too high. In one field after the next, across the whole of the American economy, we see frightened risk managers advising against anything that poses the risk of liability. What we see, in short, is the suppression of innovation and, ultimately, the diminution of our society. It is a painful picture.

"We want to change the view. We need a different economic reality. American companies should be motivated by opportunity and growth, not by the nervous concerns of risk assessment teams."

"And out the other window?" the Senator asks.

"It's an equally troubling view—perhaps more so." He pauses. "The view out the other window—looking out from the same house—is crowded. Certainly, one would see a collection of hundreds of thousands—no, millions of people who have suffered, lost loved ones due to the effects of tobacco. Vast numbers of women who have been harmed or rendered infertile because of defective birth control devices. An endless parade of children who have been injured by dangerous products, choked by dangerous toys, killed or maimed in cars that could have been safer. You would see hundreds of thousands of families mourning for people killed in automobile accidents that could have been far less dangerous had certain safety devices been employed. You would see victims of asbestotic cancer, families devastated by illness and death caused by contaminated ground water . . . you get the picture."

"And when I look to the future—the future you ask me to embrace," says Voltman, "are the victims you described likely to be helped by the system you seek to create?"

"They will need good evidence and a solid, fault-based legal theory. Some may find it more difficult to prevail," Marty says. "Just claims against genuine wrongdoers will be heard—and the wrongdoers will have to pay for the harms they caused.

"And just how is this supposed to change my mind?" Senator Voltman asks.

Marty smiles. "It's not. No one can change your mind—except you, Senator. Earlier today it seemed to me you were open—genuinely open—to the notion that placing reasonable limits on civil liability was an idea worth considering. I also got the sense, and I could be wrong, that you have come to understand that those seeking tort reform. . . ."

"*Reform*? What are you reforming?" I say.

Marty stops and looks at me. "I apologize if my use of the term *reform* offends you. I won't use it." He looks back to Senator Voltman. "Anyway, I got the sense that you understand that those seeking to make changes in the civil justice system, to make it more predictable—and predictability is the bottom line—are not the living embodiments of evil, not inhumane or uncaring."

"I never thought that," Voltman says.

"I think that," Miranda says.

"And why wouldn't you?" Marty says to me. "Who wouldn't, under your circumstances?" He pauses. "I very well might. This may come as a shock but I have a family—a life beyond Capitol Hill. I love my family, Miranda."

"And you are putting them in harm's way, Marty. Every day, you are putting them at risk," I say.

"If I believed that, I could not do what I do," Marty says.

"There is a right and wrong, Marty. You know that," I say.

Marty leans forward, closes and rubs his eyes, and speaks quietly. "Miranda, I am no more wrong than you are right."

Senator Voltman, who had been thumbing through the White-Lawson Bill, turns and looks at Marty. "Well said," he says.

Marty does not look at the Senator. He is staring at me. "There is a deadlock on tort reform—excuse me—on limiting the civil justice system—precisely because we are both right. Don't you think I know that injured people need access to the courts?" Marty says. "Companies that create and profit from undue risks, companies that harm innocent consumers, must be held accountable. Everyone with a conscience—or a soul, take your pick—understands that. Look closely at what we are proposing, Miranda. What I've just said is consistent with tort reform. It's simply a matter of degree."

"Like hell it is," I say. "Your clients have a scorched-earth mentality. They won't be content till nothing remains of civil tort liability."

"That is simply not so," Marty says. "A typical federal tort reform bill—or those in the states—improves the civil justice system—makes it more efficient, effective, and fair. Give us some credit."

"Credit? You attack witnesses who dare disagree with you and you spare no expense to win over. . . ."

"That's enough!" Senator Voltman says. "Quite enough." He walks across his office, opens the door, and looks at Marty and then at me. "I appreciate the depth of your beliefs—both of you." He nods toward the door. "But I have to make decisions based on more than emotion and deeply held beliefs. There is a civil justice system in place. It works—and it is flawed. It can be made better—and it can be destroyed. It is both hardy—able to provide a civil forum for the most complex and bitter disputes one can imagine, and also fragile. Make things too easy for either side and the entire system collapses. Do I have it right?" When neither of us responds, he says: "Good. Now. The door is open. Have a nice day."

Narrative 12: Lunch with Marty Correll

"This place used to belong to my family," I say as we are shown our table.

"Why did you pick this restaurant?" Marty asks. "The last thing I want to do is make you even more angry with me—and it has to be tough to be here."

"I am not really angry," I say. "You have a job to do."

"It's more than that," Marty says. "I believe in what I am doing."

"I realize that," I say. "It's the reason I thought we should talk. Earlier today, you implied that you know what I've been through with Simon."

"I am sorry. I told you that. It was presumptuous. . . ."

"I don't want to scold you, Marty. No more apologies. I wanted to tell you something personal. You're right—you can't know—and shouldn't pretend to know—what I went through. I don't expect that."

Marty nods but does not respond and I continue. "I know Devon Armstrong. I know what happened to him. I know how it colors his feelings about tort reform—and yes, I am capable of saying those words. He lost his business, his wealth, everything he had worked for his entire adult life . . . but not his health. He can rebuild—I understand the newly reconstituted

Armstrong Industries has shown a profit in the last three quarters. Marty, what I lost, what Simon lost . . . that never comes back. It's not the same."

A waiter takes our order, drinks arrive, and the discussion wanders. I do not want to discuss tort reform any further and neither does Marty. When the check arrives, there is no dispute—we'll split the tab.

We walk a few blocks before Marty says: "I think Voltman is going to support White-Lawson."

"That's bad news," I say.

———————

I confront Senator Voltman after my lunch with Marty and ask him point blank about White-Lawson. "It's a bad bill," I say.

"Perhaps," Senator Voltman says, "but it's a good fight. It's endemic to the civil justice system." He pauses. "You and Marty are supposed to disagree—ultimately, the tension is healthy. You represent two strong positions, both reflecting fundamental notions of justice—from two different perspectives, of course. It would be a shame for either side to throw in the towel." He pauses. "Take a moment, Miranda—try to see the dignity, wisdom, and nobility underlying both positions, both sides. You'll feel better about all of this."

———————

In the end, I am glad Horace Voltman refused my resignation. I realize that it is a privilege to work on Capitol Hill. It is likewise a privilege and a great opportunity to play a role in rethinking our system of civil justice.

NOTES, QUESTIONS AND A SIMULATION

1) You can assume Miranda would have challenged the retroactive application of the tort reform statutes if Simon's injury occurred before the final changes in state law were enacted. Could such statutes still affect the claim made on his behalf? *See* Paul J. Passanante and Dawn M. Mefford, *Anticipated Constitutional Challenges to Tort Reform*, 62 J. Mo. B. 206 (2006).

2) For a good overview of excess liability coverage, *see* Douglas R. Richmond, *Rights and Responsibilities of Excess Insurers*, 78 Denv. U.L. Rev. 29 (2000); Scott M. Seaman & Charlene Kittredge, *Excess Liability Insurance: Law and Litigation*, 32 Tort & Ins. L.J. 653 (1997).

3) Marty Correll's job is complex. Like many lobbyists, he must be politically astute, informed of developments in his field, and aware of the policy preferences of any member of Congress who might affect the legislation on which he works. It is easy to condemn "special interest groups" and to take pot shots at lobbyists, yet without lobbyists like Marty Correll, essential information would not flow to members of Congress. Further, while the

narrative did not provide a consumer advocate counterpart for Correll, be assured that there are talented, powerful, and effective lobbyists on all sides of the tort reform debate.

4) There have been lobbyists in Washington for as long as there has been a Congress. A series of incidents in the latter part of the 19th century (notably the Credit Mobilier scandal) generated a few principles to guide "factions" and were directed to the press more than to lobbyists.[222] In 1946, the FEDERAL REGULATION OF LOBBYING ACT was adopted,[223] followed in 1978 by the ETHICS IN GOVERNMENT ACT,[224] and in 2007 by the HONEST LEADERSHIP AND OPEN GOVERNMENT ACT.[225] Taken as a whole, this legislation boils down to an obligation to disclose lobbying efforts and to identify lobbyists, without imposing significant other constraints.

Task:

Consider each of the steps taken by Marty Correll as well as his approach and dialogue with Senator Voltman. Does any of this strike you as unethical? What are the ethical norms in play?

5) Before the hearing in the above narrative, Senator Voltman told Miranda that they would not be in agreement when it came to tort reform. He was concerned about his constituency—he has been advised that those who support his electoral efforts also support tort reform. Is there anything unethical about Senator Voltman changing his mind on this issue so that he can act in a manner consistent with his primary campaign contributors? What ethical norms apply to Senator Horace Voltman?

When it comes right down to it, tort reform struggles are fought between very substantial financial interests; lawyers who make their livelihood representing injured plaintiffs have invested in campaigns of those who will preserve the current civil justice system, while entities from business, insurance, and health care support candidates advocating for tort reform.[226] In the absence of significant changes in campaign finance law, it is quite possible to direct funds, in one form or another, to different candidates in public office. Should it be? Is disclosure of contributions alone enough to satisfy those who feel that Washington is governed by special interests?[227]

---

[222] *See, e.g.*, H.R. Rep. No. 42–77 (3d Sess. 1873), H.R. Rep. No. 43–268 (2d Sess. 1875), H.R. Rep. No. 43–262 (2d Sess. 1875), and H.R. Rep. No. 44–799 (1st Sess. 1876) referenced in Richard B. Kielbowicz, *The Role of News Leaks in Governance and the Law of Journalists' Confidentiality, 1795–2005*, 43 SAN DIEGO L. REV. 425 (2006).

[223] 60 Stat. 839, 2 U. S. C. §§ 261 *et seq.; See generally* Steven A. Browne, *The Constitutionality of Lobby Reform: Implicating Associational Privacy and the Right To Petition the Government*, 4 WM. & MARY BILL RTS. J. 717 (1995).

[224] 28 U.S.C. §§ 591–599, the 1995 LOBBYING DISCLOSURE ACT, § 3, 2 U.S.C. § 1602(10) (2008).

[225] § 201, 2 U.S.C. § 1603(a)(3) (amending LOBBYING DISCLOSURE ACT OF 1995).

[226] Deborah L. Rhode, *Too Much Law, Too Little Justice: Too Much Rhetoric, Too Little Reform*, 11 GEO. J. LEGAL ETHICS 989, 1004 (1998), citing Peter A. Bell & Jeffrey O'Connell, ACCIDENTAL JUSTICE: THE DILEMMAS OF TORT LAW 58 (1997).

[227] See Leslie Wayne, *Trial Lawyers Pour Money into Democrats' Chests*, N.Y. TIMES, Mar. 23, 2000, at A1; Richard Kluger, ASHES TO ASHES (1997) (describing in detail the contributions

6)   When it comes right down to it, what is the point of having well-known partisans testify before congressional committees? Certainly, members of Congress are not bound by a "record" the way judges are in ARTICLE III tribunals—so what is the purpose of maintaining a record? In the above narrative, Richard Monroe asks to have his complete statement made part of the record and it is entered "without objection." Why the formality? Here's one answer: Many of the essayists in Part I and the authors in Part II have appeared as expert witnesses in congressional hearings, some on numerous occasions. Each time a witness testifies, there is a precious opportunity by the force of argument to influence the very content of federal statutes or state statutes. There is also public scrutiny—media attention—given to such hearings. Without public hearings, those opportunities would be lost.

7)   Thinking primarily about the essays, what arguments for limiting the tort system did you find most compelling? What arguments opposing limitations on the civil justice system did you find most convincing? Think about the essays in the aggregate. Can you identify an area, issue, or topic for which there was "common ground"?

8)   Task:

The essayists in Part I were asked to send in a short statement to give students insight into tort reform. Writing a short statement on a topic as expansive as tort reform is a challenging but worthwhile task. The essayists were given the option of commenting on their personal experiences or on any topic or issue on tort reform they deemed appropriate. You are extended the same invitation. Try to keep your essay to two pages or less.

9)   There are two constitutional arguments expressly or impliedly raised in the essays. On the one hand, those supporting tort reform claim that excessive damage awards, particularly punitive damages, violate substantive due process. In recent years, the Supreme Court has agreed with that position. Those opposing tort reform assert that state or federal laws that strip plaintiffs of sums awarded by a jury, cap verdicts arbitrarily, limit the nature and substance of common law claims, and limit access to the courts are unconstitutional. Looking through the essays above, does it strike you that tort reform ought to be assessed in constitutional terms?[228]

---

tobacco companies made to thwart liability); and Richard L. Abel, *Questioning the Counter—Majoritarian Thesis: The Case of Torts*, 49 DEPAUL L. REV. 533 (1999) (suggesting that state legislatures are more affected by lobbying resources—money—than are the courts).

[228] Robert S. Peck, *In Defense of Fundamental Principles: The Unconstitutionality of Tort Reform*, 31 SETON HALL L. REV. 672 (2001); Robert S. Peck *et al., Tort Reform 1999: A Building Without a Foundation*, 27 FLA. ST. U. L. REV. 397, 416–20 (2000) (on the constitutional challenges tort reform presents); Andy D. Bennett, *State Constitutional Issues Arising from Tort Reform*, 40 TENN. B.J. 27 (2004); Victor E. Schwartz, Mark A. Behrens, Leavy Mathews III, *Federalism and Federal Liability Reform: The United States Constitution Supports Reform*, 36 HARV. J. LEGIS. 269 (1999); Perry H. Apelbaum & Samara T. Ryder, *The Third Wave of Federal Tort Reform: Protecting the Public or Pushing the Constitutional Envelope*, 8 CORNELL J. L. & PUB. POL'Y 591 (1999). Victor E. Schwartz & Leah Lorber, *Judicial Nullification of Civil Justice Reform Violates the Fundamental Constitutional Principle of Separation of Powers*, 12 RUTGERS L.J. 907 (2001).

10) One of the many questions raised in the essays involves the liability of retailers. Should retailers who profit from the sale of a product bear responsibility for the harms caused when that product turns out to be defective or dangerous *if* they neither designed nor manufactured the product?[229]

11) For other perspectives on many of the fundamental issues discussed in the essays, see Peter M. Gerhart, *The Death of Strict Liability*, 56 BUFFALO L. REV. 245 (2008); David G. Owen, *Defectiveness Restated: Exploding the "Strict" Products Liability Myth*, 1996 U. ILL. L. REV. 743; and, Gregory C. Keating, *Reasonableness and Rationality in Negligence Theory*, 48 STAN. L. REV. 311 (1996), and *compare* with Sandra F. Gavin, *Stealth Tort Reform,* 42 VAL. U.L. REV. 431 (2008); Lee Harris, *Tort Reform as a Carrot-and-Stick*, 46 HARV. J. LEGIS. 163 (2009); Conference, Center for Democratic Culture at UNLV, *The Law and Politics of Tort Reform,* 4 NEV. L.J. 377 (2003).

12) Dr. Starling. In a short section of the narrative, not central to the tale of Miranda Daine, is a brief dialogue between Miranda and Richard regarding the seemingly botched cricopharangeal surgery that cost Dr. Starling his career.

     a.   The catastrophic effect of one medical malpractice case on the life of a talented pediatric neurosurgeon is disproportional and grossly unfair—but could such a thing actually happen? Could one medical malpractice case have such devastating consequences? Assume this was the only medical malpractice case in which Dr. Starling was a named defendant—do you believe an insurance company would have settled the claim so easily?

     b.   Take another look at the essay section and reread Ronen Avraham's essay, *Tort Reform May Reduce Healthcare Costs, but It's No Silver Bullet. So Let's Think Outside of the Box*, Neil Vidmar's *Medical Malpractice Tort Reform*, Corrine Parver's *Health Courts: A Modern-Day Solution for Medical Malpractice Litigation*—and then take a sneak peak at a few of the articles and interest group pieces in Part II, Section 4 (James A. Comodeca, *et al. Killing the Golden Goose by Evaluating Medical Care Through the Retroscope: Tort Reform from the Defense Perspective*, the Center for Justice & Democracy piece on *Health Courts*, and the Congressional Budget Office [CBO] *Report of October 9, 2009* found in a *Letter on Tort Reform Focused on Medical Malpractice*). The CBO letter states that the malpractice system exacts a $50 billion cost on the health care industry.

     c.   The Center for Justice & Democracy disputes all the findings of the CBO report.[230] A number of CJD pieces are in Part II of this text. CJD characterizes recent proposals regarding medical malpractice thusly:

The medical malpractice and drug industry liability protections contained in the proposed House health care "Substitute Offered by Mr. Boehner of Ohio"

---

[229] Robert A. Sachs, *Product Liability Reform and Seller Liability: A Proposal for Change,* 55 BAYLOR L. REV. 1031, 1035 (2003) (liability without fault should not be imposed on one in the chain of distribution who "did not create the defect. . . .").

[230] *See* www.centerjd.org and check out the hot-links on medical malpractice.

. . . contemplate severely reducing the rights of those injured by unsafe medical care or drugs. It is so outrageously broad that it would limit liability not only of malpracticing doctors, hospitals, HMOs, and nursing homes, but also the pharmaceutical industry! And it would overturn countless state laws. . . .[231]

d.   For contrast, take a look at the American Tort Reform Association's website (http://www.atra.org/) and check out the links on medical malpractice. A number of ATRA documents are in Part II of this text. The ATRA position is as clear as the CJ & D position—it's simply the opposite position:

In state civil justice systems that lack reasonable limits on liability, multi-million dollar jury awards and settlements in medical liability cases have forced many insurance companies to either leave the market or substantially raise costs. Increasingly, physicians in these states are choosing to stop practicing medicine, abandon high-risk parts of their practices, or move their practices to other states. . . . To help bring a degree of predictability and fairness to the civil justice system that is critical to solving the growing medical access and affordability crisis, ATRA recommends a medical liability reform packages that includes: (1) a $250,000 limit on noneconomic damages; (2) a sliding scale for attorney's contingent fees; (3) periodic payment of future damages; and (4) abolition of the collateral source.[232]

e.   Dr. Starling's story is, like the rest of the narratives, a caricature. Yet for many involved in the tort reform dialogue in the last decade, the problems associated with the consequences of a malpractice claim are the most important part of the debate.[233] As you might guess, scholars with a health policy perspective have a different view of malpractice and the need for reform than traditional legal scholars.[234]

f.   The national debate on health care in 2009 was influenced directly by the tort reform debate. Take a look in Part II of this text at the *Remarks* by President Barack Obama on June 2009 before the American Medical Association. Later in the fall, Obama addressed a Joint Session of Congress on health care and again brought up tort reform in the medical malpractice field, stating: "I don't believe malpractice reform is a silver bullet, but I've talked to

---

[231]   www.centerjd.org

[232]   www.atra.org

[233]   See David M. Studdert, et al., *Defensive Medicine Among High-Risk Specialist Physicians in a Volatile Malpractice Environment*, 293 JAMA 2609 (2005); David A. Hyman & Charles Silver, *Medical Malpractice Litigation and Tort Reform: It's the Incentives, Stupid*, 59 VAND. L. REV. 1085 (2006); David A. Hyman, *Medical Malpractice and the Tort System: What Do We Know and What (If Anything) Should We Do About It?*, 80 TEX. L. REV. 1639 (2002); Kathryn Zeiler, *Turning from Damage Caps to Information Disclosure: An Alternative to Tort Reform*, 5 YALE J. HEALTH POL'Y L. & ETHICS 385 (2005); Geoffrey C. Rapp, *Doctors, Duties, Death and Data: A Critical Review of the Empirical Literature on Medical Malpractice and Tort Reform*, 26 N. ILL. U. L. REV. 439 (2006).

[234]   Richard E. Anderson, *Effective Legal Reform and the Malpractice Insurance Crisis*, 5 YALE J. HEALTH POL'Y L. & ETHICS 343 (2005); Michelle M. Mello, David M. Studdert & Troyen A. Brennan, *The New Medical Malpractice Crisis*, 348 NEW ENG. J. MED. 2281 (2003); and Lindsay J. Stamm, *Comment, The Current Medical Malpractice Crisis: The Need for Reform To Ensure a Tomorrow for Oregon's Obstetricians*, 84 OR. L. REV. 283 (2005); Theodore R. LeBlang, *The Medical Malpractice Crisis—Is There A Solution?*, 27 J. LEGAL MED. 1 (2006).

enough doctors to know that defensive medicine may be contributing to unnecessary costs."[235]

———————

Author's Note: As with all of the material in this text, there is no intention to advocate for one view or the other on tort reform issues. The hope is that you see the challenges this field presents, have a grasp of the major conflicting points of view, and have a sense of what is at stake. A.F.P.

———————

Simulation

While Miranda Daine, Richard Monroe, Devon Armstrong, Horace Voltman, and Marty Correll may seem like caricatures, people not unlike these five individuals have been involved in the tort reform debate for years. Assume Congress is considering legislation that would:

i.   Limit attorney's fees in class actions.

ii.   Cap punitive damages.

iii.   Mandate pretrial mediation or arbitration in all personal injury cases.

iv.   Cap noneconomic loss at $750,000.

v.   Establish a ten-year statute of repose for all product liability actions filed after the effective date of the bill, whether such legislation is in state or federal court.

vi.   Declare as a matter of federal law that conformity with applicable federal statutes, in any area, serves as an effective bar to punitive damage claims.

vii.   In the event a defendant offers settlement in advance of trial to a plaintiff and the plaintiff turns down that award, and at the conclusion of the trial the plaintiff loses—or prevails but is awarded less than the settlement offer proffered pretrial—the plaintiff will be required to pay the defendant's legal fees.

Prepare for and conduct a congressional hearing focused on the above proposal.

Draft testimony supporting your point of view as well as a short statement to be used in presenting your oral testimony. In most congressional hearings, oral presentations are limited to five minutes. A five-minute statement covers two to three double-spaced pages and is more difficult to write, in many instances, than a longer well-documented testimony (really, a position paper) setting forth a particular point of view.

———————

[235] Ceci Connolly, *Obama to Speed Up Tort Reform Tests, but Doctors Want More*, WASHINGTON POST [ON-LINE], September 18, 2009. http://www.washingtonpost.com/wp-dyn/content/article/2009/09/17/AR2009091704676.html

Five teams: For this exercise, consider forming five teams, each identified by one of the five main characters in the narrative (Miranda Daine, Devon Armstrong, Richard Monroe, Horace Voltman, and Marty Correll). Each team should have a witness as well as legal teams.

Hearing: Conduct a Senate hearing. The hearing can be convened by Senator Voltman (with the help of his staff). Roles can be assigned to Senators White and Lawson (or more—in a typical hearing in the product liability field, seven or eight members of Congress might be present at the outset of the hearing). Stick closely to the five-minute rule for statements and allow each senator five minutes for questioning.

Each team, as well as the staff of Horace Voltman, should draft a one-page press release following the hearing.

PART II

SELECT ARTICLES, STATEMENTS, AND RELATED MATERIALS FROM ACADEMICIANS, INTEREST GROUPS, AND OTHERS

■ ■ ■

The articles and statements that follow are representative of some of the scholarship and advocacy literature in the tort reform field. In most of the articles, substantial blocks of information have been eliminated. Footnotes, with only a few exceptions, have been deleted. Enough remains to allow one to gain some insight into the legal doctrine and theory supporting the different points of view expressed in these articles. However, it would be a mistake to believe that these edited-down versions are comprehensive and thorough representations of the scholarly efforts of the authors. They have been reduced for use in this text. You are urged to read the full text for each of the pieces that follow.

As noted earlier in this text, there are, quite literally, thousands of carefully researched and well-written articles in the tort reform area. For those interested in pursuing the field further, track the name of any of the authors included in the work that follows or any of the essayists in Part I and an entire universe of tort reform literature will be at your disposal.

As you read the excerpts that follow, consider the following questions:

1)   What is the fundamental position of the author in terms of tort reform?

2)   From an advocacy standpoint, were you persuaded by the excerpt you read? What made the piece persuasive—or what more would you need to find the argument compelling?

3)   Many of the writings that follow make use of legal doctrine, theory, economic reasoning, and statistics. For each article, how were these different disciplines used?

Task: Maintain a research log for the material that follows. For each article or advocacy piece, draft no more than a paragraph or two that summarizes the article. Research logs can be valuable tools for subsequent scholarship and advocacy. If the log entries are well done, they can save an enormous amount of time down the road. Much like the skill of briefing cases, a well-prepared research log can bring back the fundamental point or points of an article or advocacy piece.

The Articles

A. A BRIEF LOOK AT THE BACKGROUND AND GENERAL GOALS OF TORT REFORM

NOTES AND QUESTIONS

1.   The goal of any reform is obvious: to improve or make things better. For what it's worth, the term "reform" derives from the Latin *reformare*—"to form again," though it is not clear if *reformare* meant "to change" in a positive manner or simply to rebuild or recreate. A similar (though not interchangeable) Latin term was *res novae*, which suggested significant change, something new, different, unfamiliar, and (particularly in Roman culture) not something necessarily desirable.

In current jargon, *res novae* might be seen as a sea-change, a curious phrase as well, deriving from Ariel's haunting chant in Shakespeare's *The Tempest* ("But doth suffer a sea-change—Into something rich and strange. . . ."). This digression may strike you as off-point—but after being pounded for 200 pages on nothing but tort reform, there is no harm in a bit of *The Tempest*.

2.   Consider the possibility that the term "reform" in this debate genuinely means different things to different participants. Importantly, to know what would be an improvement or make better the civil justice system, we would have to agree on the current state of that system. As the essays in the first part of this text demonstrate, there is no agreement on the current state of the civil justice system.

     a.   Quickly scan the essays by Victor Schwartz, Mark Behrens, Sherman Joyce, Lisa Rickard, Donald Gifford, Paul Taylor, and Aaron Twerski—each eloquent, each forceful—and each detailing the need, in the name of fairness and justice, to reform the civil justice system.

     b.   Now quickly scan the essays by Erwin Chemerinsky, Neil Vidmar, Michael Rustad, Sue Steinman, Pamela Gilbert, Joan Vogel, and Joanne Doroshow—each eloquent, each forceful—and each detailing the need, in the name of fairness and justice, to retain the civil justice system and stop the engine of tort reform in its tracks.

3.   President William J. Clinton vetoed a major tort reform bill noting, *inter alia*, that it failed to "provide adequate protection to consumers."[1] In contrast, President George W. Bush saw the civil justice system as deeply problematic, plagued with "vexatious litigation," and ripe for reform.[2] On September 10, 2009, President Obama stated that he had "talked to enough doctors" (one wonders how many that would be) to know that there was a problem with defensive medicine that related, presumably, to the current civil justice system.[3] Assuming that these statements represent some meaningful quantum and cross-section of public opinion, what should be "fixed" and what should be left alone?

4.   Could it be that negative publicity regarding the trial bar is the driving force behind public opinion regarding the need for tort reform? If so, does that strike you as a legitimate basis to take action that changes fundamental rights? If that notion sounds compelling, take a look at David C. Johnson's *The Attack on Trial Lawyers and Tort Law*, Commonweal Inst. Rep. (2003).

5.   In the excerpted articles that follow, see if you can determine the perspective of the author on the need for tort reform, the current health of the civil justice movement, and the dominant issue or topic on which reform activity should focus—or leave unchanged.

————————

JAMES A. COMODECA, MARGARET M. MAGGIO, PHILIP J. TRUAX, AND JOSHUA M. BILZ, KILLING THE GOLDEN GOOSE BY EVALUATING MEDICAL CARE THROUGH THE RETROSCOPE: TORT REFORM FROM THE DEFENSE PERSPECTIVE[4]

A.   The History of the American Medical Malpractice Tort Reform Movement

Medical liability tort reform did not come to the American legal forefront until the 1970s. Before that time, medical malpractice claims were not a significant part of the tort litigation system. During the 1970s and 1980s, the United States experienced separate medical malpractice insurance crises that resulted in sharply increased premiums and even non-availability of malpractice insurance, due in part to the withdrawal of insurance companies from the business of medical malpractice coverage. While Plaintiffs' attorneys blamed insurance financial mismanagement as

---

[1]   June 26, 1996 letter from President Clinton, on file with author. The letter notes that the bill would be unfair to sellers and manufacturers, though it does not explain the source of the unfairness.

[2]   Thomas O. McGarity, *Curbing the Abuse of Corporate Power: The Perils of Preemption*, TRIAL, 20, 21 (Sept. 2008).

[3]   An excerpt of those remarks follows in this text.

[4]   31 DAYTON L. REV. 207 (2006).

the sole cause of these crises, the Government Accounting Office ("GAO") concluded that losses on medical malpractice claims were, and continue to be, the primary driver of medical malpractice premium rate increases. In response, state legislatures enacted tort reform laws to address fears that the number of medical malpractice claims would leave patients without necessary medical services. Physicians also attempted to stem the tide of the crisis by creating "physician-sponsored malpractice insurers."

In 1975, a mountain of malpractice litigation in California sent insurance premiums to record levels, causing most insurers in the state to determine that medicine was not an insurable risk and to refuse coverage to health care providers. California doctors went on strike and took their case to Sacramento. The state legislature responded with the Medical Injury Compensation Reform Act ("MICRA") and never looked back. Between 1976 and 2002, malpractice premiums in California rose 235 percent, while premiums in the rest of the country rose more than 750 percent. Before the MICRA was adopted, California's percentage of loss payments was significantly higher than its proportion of physicians as compared to the rest of the country. Since then, medical malpractice costs have fallen substantially as a percentage of the U.S. total, while physician residency in the state has held steady at approximately fifteen percent of the U.S. total.

Under California's MICRA law, noneconomic damages are capped at $250,000 (while actual damages remain unchecked), defendants can introduce evidence of collateral sources of compensation for injury, the statute of limitations period to bring a claim is shortened, and damage payments may be periodic, allowing awards to be paid over the time frame they are intended to cover. Additionally, MICRA contains attorney's contingency fees with a sliding scale. For example, a California patient-plaintiff keeps $778,333 of a $1 million jury award under MICRA; but, in states without contingency fee reforms, that same patient's portion of the same $1 million judgment amount would only be $600,000 because the personal injury lawyer typically takes a forty percent contingent fee. Thus, not only does MICRA's contingency fee provision directly benefit the injured patient, it also makes it more difficult for attorneys to finance large numbers of non-meritorious cases with the few that they win.

MICRA's features not only aim to control malpractice litigation, but they also limit jury awards and keep insurance rates in check. According to the Insurance Information Institute, awards greater than $1 million are three times more frequent in New York than in California—a state almost twice as large as New York. Additionally, despite Los Angeles' high cost of living, its malpractice insurance premiums are less than half of the rates in Cleveland, Ohio and as low as one-sixth of the rates in Miami, Florida. The California experience indicates that properly implemented medical malpractice tort reform can reduce the cost of medical malpractice insurance.

While medical malpractice insurance was more readily available in the 1980s, the cost of premiums for physicians became an epic and widespread problem. In 1986, state legislatures, following California's lead, began enacting legislation that capped the noneconomic and punitive damages a jury could award tort victims in medical liability cases. Caps varied in range, from $250,000 to $875,000. By 2004, medical malpractice premiums were 17.1 percent lower in those states that capped court awards.

Proponents of tort reform often asserted that damages were "out of control," pointing to large jury verdicts in support of their position. Opponents of tort reform on the other hand, persistently attacked the constitutionality of the measures. Opponents argued, in some cases successfully, that caps represented "a violation of a plaintiff's equal protection guarantees, in that they discriminated against tort victims whose damages exceeded the amount they could recover." In the following years, some state courts struck down these caps as unconstitutional, marking a defeat for tort reform advocates. Nonetheless, proponents of reform were able to introduce medical liability reform ideology into the mainstream, thus paving the way for modern tort reform legislation.

CHRISTOPHER J. ROEDERER, DEMOCRACY AND TORT LAW IN AMERICA: THE COUNTER-REVOLUTION[5]

. . . .

V. THE TORT REVOLUTION AND COUNTER-REVOLUTION

A. Tort reform in general

1. Progressive democratic Tort Reform

The earliest sign of democracy reinforcing tort reform began in the early 1900s, when workmen's compensation schemes started to spread. The schemes attempted to find collective justice for workers who were severely disadvantaged by the extant rules of the tort system. However, other than workmen's compensation and Cardozo's opinion in *MacPherson v. Buick Motor Co.*, little reform occurred, until the "Democratic Expansionary Era" after the Second World War.

During the Democratic Expansionary Era, the courts moved from a view of the tort system as providing case-by-case corrective justice, to a view of the system as a mechanism for collective justice, or providing justice across classes of cases. This transition, in part, contributed to courts using

---

[5]   110 W. VA. L. REV. 647 (2008).

tort law, not only for restorative justice (putting plaintiffs back to where they were before the tort) but also for other social goals, namely deterring wrongs and providing incentives for manufacturers to make their products safer for society. Courts stopped merely accepting the status quo distributions of power and wealth and began tailoring corrective justice to collective and distributive justice concerns.

. . . .

2.   Regressive Tort Reform

The Tort Policy Working Group from the Ronald Reagan-Edwin Meese Justice Department, one of the main catalysts of the counter-revolution in torts, came to life, in part, because of the liability insurance crisis of the 1980s. The Group identified a number of "causes" of the so-called "crisis" and a set of recommendations or strategies for attacking the "crisis." They summarily excluded all other explanations besides the civil justice system, and thus, unsurprisingly, their recommendations or strategies focused only on attacking that system by: 1) making it harder for injury victims to get into court; 2) making it more difficult to win once plaintiffs are in court; and 3) restricting damage recoveries for plaintiffs who do win. This, in perhaps oversimplified terms, has provided the core agenda for the tort reform movement ever since. Recently, the movement has also adopted the strategy of preempting state tort law through the promulgation of federal administrative rules.

a.   *Keeping plaintiffs out of court*

There are a whole range of mechanisms or tactics that help reduce the number of claims made by potential plaintiffs (other than reducing negligence and making products safer). One mechanism for keeping plaintiffs out of court has been to make it less attractive for lawyers to take cases, by putting limits on contingency fees and creating "early offer" mechanisms (which include attorney fee limits) for economic damages, which would preclude, or make it very difficult to receive non-economic damages, such as pain and suffering. Another tactic is to make it difficult for states to hire attorneys for complex litigation (*e.g.*, tobacco and gun cases). And finally, one can make it harder for people to join together in class actions.

This last tactic is embodied in the Class Action Fairness Act of 2005, which transfers many class actions from state courts to federal courts. The federalization of class actions may act to deny or impede plaintiffs' access to justice for a number of reasons, including the relative difficulty of certifying classes in federal courts, and delays that result from further burdening the already overcrowded federal courts. Further, to the extent that conservatives have managed to take over the federal judiciary and/or to secure anti-litigation justices on the federal bench, one would expect more bias against plaintiffs, in general, and against class actions, in particular. As shown below, access to courts can also be limited through the enforcement of arbitration agreements, which often preclude class actions and by definition limit access to the courts, both in the first instance and as a matter of review.

b.   *Making it harder for plaintiffs to win cases*

The more direct route to reducing the number and amount of claims is to change the liability rules to make it harder for plaintiffs to win when they get to court. This occurs by making liability less strict in products liability cases, setting up procedural obstacles in medical malpractice cases, and providing immunity from suit for certain industries. This has been the case with gun manufacturers, as well as with biomaterials manufacturers. This also makes it less likely that plaintiffs and their lawyers will sue in the first place.

c.   *Capping damages and making punitive damages harder to get*

Finally, one of the most active areas of tort reform has centered around limiting damages, which has occurred by placing limits on joint and several liability, limiting the collateral source rule, and capping non-economic damages, including both punitive damages and pain and suffering damages. In addition to placing caps on punitive damages, tort reform has also included legislation that increases the plaintiff's burden of proof in order to receive punitive damages. As Michael L. Rustad explains:

> Forty-five out of the fifty-one jurisdictions either do not recognize punitive damages or have enacted one or more restrictions on the remedy since 1979. These reforms include capping punitive damages, bifurcating the amount of punitive damages from the rest of the trial, raising the burden of proof, allocating a share of punitive damages to the state, and restricting use of evidence of corporate wealth. The handful of jurisdictions that have yet to enact tort reforms are mostly punitive damages cold spots rather than tort hellholes.

All of these mechanisms undermine achievements from the 1960s and 1970s, which made it easier for relatively weak and unorganized victims to organize and to access justice to vindicate their rights. They undermine the deterrent effects of tort law, designed to keep consumers safe and hold those who profit from placing dangerous products into the stream of commerce responsible for those products. These changes benefit the few, at the expense of the majority of Americans.

RACHEL M. JANUTIS, THE STRUGGLE OVER TORT REFORM AND THE OVERLOOKED LEGACY OF THE PROGRESSIVES[6]

. . . .

III. The Overlooked Progressive Era

. . . . As Professor Page [see Professor Page's essay in Part I of this text] ultimately concedes, the tort expansion of the 1950s and 1960s was "but one swing of a pendulum" and the current tort retraction may be a return swing seeking to "restore equilibrium." However, the pendulum began swinging much earlier than the 1950s and 1960s. Indeed, the pendulum began swinging as early as the 1890s. A more complete review of this evolution, including its early history, reveals that the struggle over tort reform has taken place in both the judicial and political branches throughout the history of the development of tort law. Moreover, a more complete review reveals that with each swing of the pendulum economically interested actors were present and pushing from both sides in both the judicial and the political arenas.

A. The Political Successes of the Progressive Era Tort Expansionists

1. The Legislative Front

As discussed above, the scholarly account of tort reform paints tort expansion as primarily a judicial process. However, a more complete review of the evolution of tort law demonstrates that tort expansion has been a political as well as judicial process. As early as the 1890s, the Progressive movement gained prominence in American politics and society. The Progressive movement sought greater government regulation of America's emerging industrial economy to protect workers and promote social welfare. That government regulation included, in part, expansion of tort rights. Progressive Era tort expansionists did not resort solely to the courts in their battles for tort expansion and against tort retraction. Instead, they also sought tort expansion through the political branches. In fact, Progressive Era reformers succeeded in winning significant legislative expansion of tort rights. . . .

Progressive Era efforts to provide better compensation to injured workers culminated in the replacement of the tort system with an administrative compensation scheme. As a result of Progressive lobbying and campaigning, almost all states enacted workers' compensation legislations. Indeed, 42 of the then 48 states adopted workers compensation laws by 1920. These workers compensation statutes substituted the injured employee's judicially enforced tort rights for an administrative remedy funded by the employer. Employers were held strictly liable under the administrative scheme. Thus, the administrative system afforded the worker a more guaranteed recovery with lower transaction costs than the

---

[6]   39 AKRON LAW REVIEW 943 (2006).

tort system. However, the administrative remedy awarded lesser compensation than was theoretically available through the tort system and the costs of the system were spread across all employers. Thus, the system was less costly to employers. . . .

2.   The Progressive Era Constitutional Conventions

Progressive Era reformers did not confine their political efforts to the state and federal legislatures. Instead, Progressive Era reformers used state constitutions to expand tort rights. Progressive Era reformers sought and won constitutional amendments aimed at limiting the legislature's ability to curb common law torts and remedies. Eighteen states convened constitutional conventions between 1870 and 1915. During these conventions, Progressive Era reformers sought constitutional provisions aimed at expanding tort rights outright and at limiting the legislature's control over common law tort actions. For example, South Carolina amended its constitution in 1895 to constitutionally ban the fellow-servant rule. In several other states, reformers proposed and won measures prohibiting the legislature from adopting special statutes of limitations aimed at shortening statutes of limitations in lawsuits against railroads and corporations. Likewise, in many states, reformers sought measures prohibiting the legislature from limiting damages in personal injury and wrongful death actions.

Illustratively, in 1873 Pennsylvania delegates proposed and adopted a constitutional amendment prohibiting the legislature from limiting damages in personal injury and wrongful death actions and from shortening the statute of limitations in lawsuits against corporations. As amended, Article III, Section 21 provided:

[No act of] the general assembly [shall] limit the amount to be recovered for injuries resulting in death, or for injuries to persons or property; and, in case of death from injuries, the right of action shall survive, and the general assembly shall prescribe for whose benefit such actions shall be prosecuted. No act shall prescribe any limitations of time within which suits may be brought against the corporations for injuries to persons or property, or for other causes different from those fixed by general laws regulating actions against natural persons, and such acts now existing are void.

Progressive Era reformers sought these constitutional provisions expressly because they feared corporate interests' influence in state legislatures. For example, in 1891, Kentucky amended its constitution, in part, to prohibit the legislature from limiting the amount to be recovered for injuries resulting in death, or for injuries to a person or property and to provide that "[w]henever the death of a person shall result from an injury inflicted by negligence or wrongful act, then, in every such case, damages may be recovered for such death, from the corporations and persons so causing the same." The provisions apparently were enacted because delegates feared that the legislature had granted privileges and immunities to railroads and other corporate interests because of their political power.

Ohio's experience follows similar lines. Ohio convened a constitutional convention in 1912. Delegates to the convention ultimately adopted Proposal 240 prohibiting the legislature from imposing statutory limits on the amount of damages recoverable in wrongful death actions. As originally submitted, Proposal 240 also would have expressly prohibited the legislature from abrogating the right of action in wrongful death cases. Comments of the delegates reveal that at least some of the delegates supported Proposal 240 specifically because the Ohio General Assembly had passed legislation that reduced mining companies' liability in wrongful death actions. In opposing an amendment to Proposal 240 which eliminated the prohibition on abrogating the right of action, Delegate James Tallman a lawyer from Bellaire stated:

I do regard this one thing of importance, and that is the power of the legislature to take away from the next of kin the right of action in case of the death of a child or unmarried man. You take the law as it now exists with reference to a man who works in a mine, and he may be under age or he may be an adult and in neither case does his next of kin, father, mother, brothers or sisters, have a right of action, and the amendment of the gentleman from Erie leaves to the legislature the power to pass a law of that kind.

B.   The Motivations of the Progressive Era Tort Expansionists

Likewise, by focusing on the tort expansion of the 1950s and 1960s, the scholarly account of tort reform is able to credit a legal academy unmotivated by self-interest for driving the expansion. Contrary to this account, the history surrounding the struggle for legislative tort expansion demonstrates the political nature of Progressive (and Populist) tort expansion. For example, in her book, "Roots of Reform: Farmers, Workers, and the American State 1877–1917," Professor Sanders chronicles this struggle and describes a coalition of multiple interests that ultimately brought about federal legislative reform. She identifies three groups responsible for legislative tort expansion. First, she identifies a group of middle class reformers or "urban social intelligentsia." This group most closely resembles the detached legal academy that the current scholarly account credits with the tort expansion of the 1950s and 1960s in that these middle class reformers appear unmotivated by any economic self-interest. However, she also identifies a group of labor interests and a group of "periphery agrarian" interests composed of farmers in the southern, plains and western states. She describes how legislative expansion of tort rights was a product of a consensus of these groups. For instance, she notes that agrarian states were the first to legislatively abrogate common law defenses in workplace accident cases.

In contrast, Progressive Era reformers sought but were unable to obtain federal workers compensation legislation for railroad employees because this coalition fell part. Initially, a coalition of labor unions, middle class reformers and railroad interests along with rural interests supported a bill that would have abrogated an employee's private cause of action for railroad workplace injuries and replaced it with an administrative compensation scheme. Reported estimates predicted that the administrative system would increase the amounts paid by railroads for workplace injuries by 25% and eliminate litigation transaction costs bore by injured workers. After labor unions began to withdraw their support for the bill on the grounds that it was too beneficial to railroads, several Democratic congressmen from these periphery agrarian states withdrew their support for the legislation. These congressmen ultimately were able to block adoption of the bill. Professor Sanders notes that these congressmen objected to the bill on the grounds that compensation was too low and that it precluded any judicial remedy. These congressmen offered amendments to the bill that would have allowed injured workers to opt out of the administrative scheme and seek a common law remedy and would have preserved state court jurisdiction over such tort suits. Professor Sanders also observes that many of these congressmen were plaintiffs' attorneys who represented railroad workers in lawsuits against railroads as a "significant part of their practices."

At the Ohio convention at least some of the strongest proponents for tort expansion were economically motivated actors. For instance, one of the most forceful advocates for Proposal 240 to prohibit caps on wrongful death damages was D. F. Anderson, an apparent plaintiffs' attorney and delegate from Youngstown.

C.   The Role of the Would-Be Tort Retractors

While the scholarly account of tort reform overlooks the political activities of the early tort expansion movement, the scholarly account utterly disregards any of the early activities of tort retractors. Contrary to the perception left by the scholarly account corporate, professional and insurance interests were not absent from the early struggle for tort expansion. Instead, predecessors-in-interest to the current tort retractors sought legislative measures similar to those sought by the tort retractors of today as early as the late Nineteenth Century. These predecessors-in-interest also resisted efforts to legislatively expand tort expansion. Finally, tort retractors challenged legislative tort expansion in the courts.

1.   The Legislative Activities of Early Tort Retractors

In the mid and late Nineteenth Century, corporate interests wielded significant power in state legislatures. Indeed, many Progressive Era reforms evidenced a distrust of legislatures because of the influence that corporations held over legislators. Many of the most recognizable Progressive Era innovations attempted to make legislative bodies more accountable to the general public rather than corporate interests. For example, Progressives were instrumental in bringing about the ratification of the Seventeenth Amendment, providing for the direct election of U.S. Senators. Progressives argued that direct election was necessary to make the Senate responsive to the popular will. They contended that appointment of Senators by state legislatures had made senators beholden to corporate interests because corporate interests wielded strong influence over the state legislators who selected senators. Most notably, in a series of articles titled "Treason of the Senate," one leading Progressive Era reformer attempted to document the influence of corporate contributions on the voting records of many sitting senators.

Progressives advocated direct democracy measures such as initiative, referendum and recall as the centerpiece of progressivism. Indeed, many states adopted such measures during the Progressive period. These measures allowed citizens to bypass the legislature and enact legislation themselves or repeal statutes enacted by the legislature. This type of direct democracy was seen as a counterbalance to corporate influence over legislators. . . .

Corporate interests wielded some of this influence to win tort retraction measures and to successfully block or limit tort expansion in state legislatures. In some states, railroad and other corporate interests won shortened statutes of limitation in personal injury actions. Tort retractors blocked, stalled or weakened workers compensation legislation. Indeed, many commentators contend that most Progressive Era legislation succeeded only after significant corporate input and ultimately represented a compromise between corporate and reform interests.

. . . .

Populist Era reformers had won enactment of a mine safety bill as early as 1880. However, mine operators won concessions to this law. For example, the mine safety code provided a cause of action for workers injured as a result of a violation of the safety code or for the families of workers killed as a result of a violation. The right to a cause of action in the mining code eliminated wrongful death claims by unmarried mine workers and underage mine workers. Such claims would have been permitted under the generally applicable wrongful death statute.

Likewise, corporate interests were able to obtain concessions in Ohio's workers' compensation act. The act permitted employers to self-insure. If an employer was able to post an adequate bond, it did not have to pay insurance premiums into the state compensation fund. Instead, an employer posting the requisite bond paid compensation directly to an injured worker. In this way, the employer only needed to pay if an employee was actually injured. This provision inured to the benefit of larger employers.

2. Judicial Challenges to Tort Expansion

Much like today's tort expansionists, early tort retractors challenged the legislative victories of the Progressive Era tort expansionists in the state and federal courts. For example, corporate and railroad interests challenged statutes abrogating the fellow-servant rule and the assumption of the risk defense on equal protection grounds and state single-subject legislation limitations. In response to a challenge by railroad interests, the U.S. Supreme Court declared unconstitutional the original version of the Federal Employers' Liability Act. Tort retractors also challenged workers' compensation statutes. In one of the most high profile decisions of the time, the New York Court of Appeals struck down New York's first workers compensation statute. In Ives v. South Buffalo Railway, the Buffalo Railway challenged New York's statute on the grounds that it violated due process. The New York Court of Appeals agreed, concluding that the statute violated due process because it required the employer to compensate the employee for his injuries even when the negligence of the employee, rather than the employer, caused the injuries. Indeed, several Progressive Era reform measures evidenced as much distrust of the judiciary, in particular the federal judiciary, as they evidenced distrust of the legislature, and conventional wisdom among historians has been that federal, and sometimes state courts, were sympathetic to tort retractors' claims.

. . . .

JULIE DAVIES, REFORMING THE TORT REFORM AGENDA[7]

. . . .

Although tort reform legislation is not limited to the medical malpractice issue, it is undeniable that much of the political impetus for reform has been spurred by the perception that tort law is hurting doctors and the delivery of health care. . . .

Although there is enormous substantive and procedural diversity in the tort reform that has been enacted, there is commonality in its premise. Most tort reform is designed to minimize the number of personal injury actions that are filed or to mitigate the damages that would be paid in a settlement or an eventual trial. The assumption, based on that premise, is that lower numbers of tort actions mean a lower risk of litigation and high

---

[7]   25 WASH. U. L. J. & POL'Y 119 (2007).

payouts, which should have the effect of lessening the costs of liability insurance. The beneficiaries of reform legislation—businesses, medical practitioners, or the insurance industry itself—should see cost savings and the intangible, psychic benefits of less litigation. In theory, these benefits would then be passed along to the ultimate consumers of various services and the American economy generally. . . .

A.   Understanding the Positions of Major Interest Groups

Physicians are a major force in issues of tort reform and health care reform. Although the health industry is broader, including hospitals, labs, pharmaceutical companies, and others involved in the delivery of care, physicians remain the most respected and visible representatives of a group with inconsistent positions. To the extent that the AMA represents physicians, the group has opposed reform to the traditional fee for service model of health care delivery since the early twentieth century. This opposition, motivated by fear that government intervention would inevitably lead to regulation of fees, used a multiplicity of arguments, ranging from interference with the doctor-patient relationship to the specter of socialism, communism, and incipient revolution.

Today, the AMA speaks with less authority than it did at one time, but its opposition to fundamental change remains. Although acknowledging the public health and economic burdens the uninsured cause, the AMA's approach to change retains a strong endorsement of private health care financing, relying on monetary assistance to the uninsured in the form of tax credits and vouchers. Ideally, the $100 billion annual federal subsidy for employment-based health insurance would be eliminated and there would be a subsidy through tax breaks to allow individuals to purchase healthcare. This echoes the Bush administration's view that each person should select and pay for that individual's own health care preferences. There are, however, physician groups that have declared their independence from the AMA on the issue of universal health care, making powerful arguments for change.

On the topic of tort reform, particularly in the medical malpractice context, the voices of physicians are much less muffled. There is particular concern about medical malpractice liability, even though according to Professor Tom Baker, the threats are not nearly as large as they are perceived to be. Physicians attribute high insurance costs to the tort system, and they believe it fuels counterproductive practices, such as defense medicine, as well.

Consumers, meaning individuals who use both the health care system and the tort system, also have somewhat inconsistent positions. Many average Americans are unconvinced that health care reform would be a good thing, particularly if government is involved. They fear that change would imperil the quality of care that the 80% of the population with health insurance now enjoys or that there will be long waits for service, worse diagnostic equipment, and higher taxes. Yet public opinion is also critical of the costs of health care, even when subsidized through employment, and there are many examples of individuals who have sought prescriptions or care in other countries because they were priced out of the market here.

Consumers' positions may also be colored by a perception that those who lack insurance through an employer are unworthy of having it, that the uninsured have deliberately chosen not to pay into insurance plans their employer offers, or that they are not entitled to help because they are immigrants and noncitizens. These assumptions enable many Americans to sleep just fine at night regardless of the fact that others lack access to health care. In fact, none of these perceptions is true, but the public is not well educated about who lacks insurance. It is ironic that the American public, so widely viewed as litigious to a fault, seems also to favor tort reform. This is possibly a product of media exaggeration and misstatement of torts issues.

Insurance companies, employers, and trade unions were all influential in assisting AMA efforts to derail earlier proposals for compulsory health insurance. Today, their interests seem to have diverged. Insurance companies remain firmly opposed to compulsory insurance and indeed to any change in the status quo. Insurance companies favor tort reform to the extent it saves money on what they must pay out in claims, but presumably they would not favor reform if it would replace the tort system and reduce or eliminate their source of profits. Business and labor both feel the impact of the extraordinary costliness of the American health care system. Indeed, labor disputes often center on the cost of health care. Thus, these groups should embrace change if it could be brought about at a lower cost than they are currently paying. Businesses are affected by litigation or threatened litigation and may therefore favor tort reform.

Trial attorneys add yet another powerful dimension to the political mix. Their self-interests have to be in protecting against changes to the common law that affect the amount of recovery or the plaintiffs' ability to collect it, because this is how they make their living. It is unlikely that any form of compromise, even if it produced traction on health care reform, would outweigh this interest.

B.   Aligning the Interests by Broadening the Agenda

Having examined the interests of various groups, it is apparent that there are some quid pro quos that could bring traditional opponents together if accompanied by accurate information about the issues. Physicians, for example, ought to favor this approach. Many physicians are enmeshed in health care bureaucracies that consume hours of administrative time to bill and collect money. They may receive underpayments from governmental agencies for some procedures and they are subject to rules and restrictions that interfere with their ability to serve patients to the extent many would like. At the same time, however, physicians are very concerned about medical malpractice premiums and the costs (monetary and emotional) of malpractice litigation. If physicians understood that some of the hard-fought objections to particular types of tort reform would be less persuasive if there were an assurance that injured parties would have access to health care, and that this access would benefit their own practices, perhaps they would, as a political force, push their leadership in a different direction.

Consumers as a group ought to favor health care reform, even if they are not altruistic enough to worry about the fate of those who lack coverage. As purchasers of insurance, most consumers would clearly benefit if costs could be lowered and services delivered efficiently. The extent to which it would be in consumers' interest to accept tort reform as a quid pro quo would depend on whether access to health services included care for long-term disability and other benefits that now are often available only by instituting a lawsuit. Consumer support would also depend on what form the reform took. However, the legal and psychological benefits consumers would gain from health care reform ought to mean there is less need to invoke tort remedies. There might be some changes to the legal system that are indeed beneficial or simply uncontroversial. But like physicians and the AMA, consumers will have to realize that their true interests may diverge from that of the consumers' attorneys—which is by far the largest and most powerful group acting on their behalf.

Employers and businesses should certainly be in favor of health care reform. They already are enmeshed in the problems inherent in the delivery of health care through employers. They face increasingly expensive commitments to employees and the prospect of an unhappy and uncompetitive workforce if benefits are cut. They participate in subsidizing the costs associated with the uninsured. Any means that could be taken to simplify the system should be welcomed. If, as a subsidiary benefit, people would have less need and incentive to litigate because they would have greater access to care, businesses and employers should embrace a change. They are common defendants in tort cases.

F. PATRICK HUBBARD, THE NATURE AND IMPACT OF THE "TORT REFORM" MOVEMENT[8]

I. Introduction

For over thirty years, repeat players on the defense side of tort litigation have undertaken to "reform" tort doctrine in their favor. Initially,

----

[8]   35 HOFSTRA LAW REVIEW 437 (2006).

these efforts consisted of ad hoc efforts to address a series of "crises," primarily in terms of the cost and availability of liability insurance. In the 1980s, the tort reform movement began to develop a more permanent institutionalized approach to the push for "reform." Not surprisingly, there has been considerable debate about the goals of this movement, the fairness or efficiency of the specific doctrinal reforms it seeks, and the methods it uses. . . .

Though there are only limited statistics on how the tort system provides compensation for "wrongs" in practice, it is possible to make some generalizations about three important issues concerning the role of tort law in providing compensation for injuries. First, what role does tort law play in compensating for accidents in the United States? Second, to what extent do potential tort claims actually become the subject of formal litigation? Third, of the cases that are litigated, what is known about the administration of these cases?

1.   Compensation Schemes for Accidental Injury

The tort system plays a relatively limited role in compensating for accidental injury in the United States. Because tort law focuses on wrongdoing, the system does not generally provide compensation where the injurer was not a wrongdoer. In addition, the system does not provide compensation where a wrongdoer has no insurance or no personal assets to pay compensation, or where the amount of loss is too small to be worth the cost of litigation. Even where a wrongdoer has assets or insurance, the tort system will not provide recovery for injury unless the victim brings a claim. As to compensation systems other than tort law, the United States has a diverse set of partially overlapping schemes. For example, nearly all workplace injuries are covered exclusively by workers compensation, not tort. The costs of accidental injuries are also covered by no-fault auto insurance schemes in some states, by private first party insurance schemes like life insurance and health insurance, and by public schemes like Medicare and Medicaid. As indicated below, coordinating these schemes with tort law is both complicated and controversial.

2.   Injuries, Grievances, Legal Wrongs, and Claims in Tort

People who have been injured can relate to the legal system in terms of three overlapping categories: (1) those who feel that they have a legal grievance in the sense that they feel they have been wrongfully injured, (2) those . . . wrongfully injured, and (3) those who make a claim in tort, either informally or formally through litigation. The categories are not the same because: (1) some persons who feel they have been wrongfully injured and some persons who have been wrongfully injured may not file a claim, and (2) some people who feel wronged or file a claim may not actually have a valid tort claim. Our understanding of tort claims is improved if we can compare the three categories in terms of the ratio of grievances to filed claims and of valid claims to filed claims. Unfortunately, it is hard to determine these ratios because there is so little data on nonclaiming by people who feel they have a grievance or people who have been wronged. To the extent data on the ratio of grievances to filed claims are available, it appears that many accidentally injured people do not make a claim of tortious injury even though they feel they have a grievance for having been wrongfully injured. In addition, it appears that the ratio of valid claims to filed claims is very high. For example, such a pattern of underclaiming is supported by studies of medical negligence, which indicate the ratios of valid claims to filed claims to be ten to one and eight to one.

3. Administration and Distributive Impact of the Tort System

Though data about litigation are easier to find than data about the ratios of claims to grievances and of claims to negligence, there are substantial shortcomings in the available litigation data. As a result, it is only possible to sketch rough approximations about tort settlements and litigation. One recent study provides the following crude overview of the tort system in terms of data for the year 2000: The number of civil suits in state courts—excluding domestic relations litigation—has been roughly the same in proportion to the population from 1987 to 2001, tort filings in state courts declined from 1992 to 2001, and the states vary considerably in terms of whether these rates have increased or decreased and in terms of the rates of increase and decrease in any given year. Another study indicated that approximately 750,000 tort suits were filed in state and federal courts in 2000; about half of these involved automobile cases. In general, about 3% of tort cases filed are actually tried. A verdict study of the nation's seventy-five largest counties in 1996 indicated that plaintiffs prevailed 48% of the time and that the median plaintiff's verdict was $30,500. Some specific median plaintiffs' verdicts were $285,576 for medical malpractice, $176,787 for nonasbestos product liability, and $17,931 for automobile accidents. This study indicated that about 3% of winning plaintiffs received punitive damages with the median punitive award being $38,000. In terms of overall costs of the tort system, one recent estimate, based on payments by liability insurance companies and by self-insured defendants as a result of both verdicts and other payments, is that $260 billion was paid out for processing and paying tort claims in 2004. A study of the distribution of these costs indicates that plaintiffs received 46% of the total costs and that 54% went to pay for plaintiffs' attorneys (19%), defense costs (14%), and for the insurance companies' administrative costs (21%). Because the 46% that goes to plaintiffs is simply a redistribution of loss, it is arguably not a cost of the tort system. By themselves, these data about the tort system do not tell us the whole story because important concerns, like the following, are not addressed: Are there indirect benefits from the redistribution to victims? Are the overall benefits of tort liability worth the costs? As to the 54%

administrative costs, how does this figure compare to the administrative costs of other compensation schemes?

As these figures indicate, the tort system is one of the basic schemes used to allocate the costs of injuries in the United States. As a result, it has a fundamental impact on the distribution of wealth because, for any injury, there are four potential bearers of the costs involved: the victim, the injurer, a third party like a private insurer, or the public through a social welfare scheme. If the costs are left on victims, they are poorer; if costs are shifted, victims are richer while injurers, third parties, or the public are poorer. In the tort system, the decision tends to be limited to whether the loss will be borne by the victim or the injurer. Third parties like liability insurers may ultimately bear the cost, but the initial judicial allocation will not usually involve the third party. . . .

C. The Goals of Tort Law

The distributional impact of the tort system's imposition of accident costs raises fundamental moral and political issues concerning the reasons for and methods of allocating the loss. The tort system's redistribution of the loss from the plaintiff to the defendant has been justified in terms of three policy goals. First, the liability for payment of compensatory damages prevents wrongdoing and thus protects rights in several ways, particularly: (1) the payment for injuries caused by wrongful conduct provides an incentive to avoid wrongful conduct; and (2) even where no wrongdoing is involved, imposing liability for accident costs provides an incentive to reduce injuries not currently 446 preventable by due care by lowering the level of activity, or by seeking innovations that result in new, more cost-effective safety measures. Second, our sense of fairness requires that, as a matter of "corrective justice," victims who suffer injury because their rights have been wrongly denied should have recourse to a system that requires injurers to pay compensation. These injurers "deserve" to bear the costs of their wrongs, not innocent victims. This concept of "just desert" also serves to limit liability from becoming disproportionately large in comparison to a defendant's wrongdoing. Third, compensation of victims is frequently said to be, by itself, a goal of tort law. Punitive damages are justified in terms of the first two goals. More specifically, these damages provide additional prevention by increasing the deterrent impact. This is particularly true in situations where compensatory damages alone may be insufficient. In terms of corrective justice, punitive awards provide vindication for the victim's rights where they have been violated by an exceptionally egregious wrong and satisfy a need for retribution for such conduct.

All three goals have been the subject of extensive debate and disagreement. For example, prevention/deterrence theories are criticized on the ground that they rely on unrealistic assumptions about human behavior—particularly given the widespread use of insurance schemes and the practical problems of suing for small losses and collecting judgments from most uninsured defendants—and about our ability to calculate costs and benefits. Corrective justice is problematic in situations where the loss is not worth the cost of litigation or where the wrongdoer lacks insurance or assets to pay a judgment. Both deterrence and corrective justice theories rely on a concept of a "wrong" to be deterred or corrected, yet both lack a generally accepted theory of rights and of correlative wrongdoing or a theory of allocation of loss where multiple wrongdoers are involved. Moreover, specific tests of wrongdoing are often extremely vague. The view that compensation is a goal of tort law is particularly questionable because the position arguably confuses goals and means. For example, compensatory damages are also used in contract law, but virtually no one asserts that compensation is a goal of contracts. As with torts, contract damages are a means of achieving goals. The role of compensation as a means can be seen more clearly if damages are contrasted with injunctions, which are sometimes granted as the remedy for a tort and thus are a means of achieving goals. Yet no one argues that injunctions are a goal of tort law. . . .

D.   The Mechanics of the System

Though many claims involving compensation for tort liability are resolved without an attorney, attorneys are central in the operation of the tort system. Plaintiffs in tort litigation are generally represented by attorneys paid on the basis of a contingency fee in the range of 30–40% of recovery, which provides an incentive for the plaintiff's attorney to maximize the amount of compensation per unit of his input. This incentive scheme operates differently with different segments of the plaintiffs' bar. For example, some attorneys specializing in plaintiffs' work handle a large number of cases involving smaller amounts of compensation that can generally be resolved without trial; other plaintiffs' attorneys specialize in trying a small number of cases involving the potential for substantial verdicts or settlements. The contingency fee system forces plaintiffs' attorneys to act as gatekeepers who only take cases likely to generate a return greater than their investment. In ordinary cases, lawyers may reject as many as nine out of ten potential cases. In complex expensive matters, like medical malpractice, the rates of rejection are likely to be much higher. The defense bar generally operates on the basis of a fee paid regardless of outcome. Because defendants in tort disputes tend to have more wealth than plaintiffs, they have an advantage in the litigation. Defendants' resources will be superior to those of the plaintiffs' side, particularly where the plaintiffs' lawyers handle a large number of cases involving relatively low damages. However, in litigation involving plaintiffs' lawyers with a small-volume, high-damages practice, the plaintiff's side may have superior resources because cost-containment measures by insurance companies often limit expenditures by the defense side. . . .

E.   Current "Tort Reform" Movement

1.   History, Agenda, and Techniques

The history of the "tort reform" movement can be divided into two overlapping dimensions. The first part, which consists of ad hoc calls for reforms to address a specific liability insurance "crisis," began in the 1970s when reforms were sought to address a "crisis" caused by large increases in medical malpractice liability premiums and in product liability insurance premiums. In the 1980s, a broader "crisis" was caused by a general increase in liability insurance premiums. Once again, reform was sought. In the late 1990s, new "crises" resulted in products liability and medical malpractice and reforms were declared necessary. Each of these "crises" generated its own response in terms of proposed legal changes and in terms of support for and against these changes.

Long-term institutionalized efforts for "reform" characterize the second dimension of the movement, which began in the 1980s. During this time, the level and intensity of the debate increased and a major ongoing long-term struggle developed between two loosely allied groups. On one side were defense-oriented groups like liability insurance companies, physicians, and business groups, which are interested in "Tort Reform "as the solution to a broad "crisis" in tort liability law and insurance. On the other side are two groups: (1) plaintiffs' attorneys, occasionally joined by a variety of consumer rights organizations, claiming to represent the position of potential victims; and (2) academics using the rational model to criticize the claims of the "tort reform" movement. The institutionalization and success of the first side are illustrated by the founding of the American Tort Reform Association ("ATRA") in 1986 and the inclusion of "tort reform" in the Republicans Party's "Contract with America" in 1994.

Where an increase in liability insurance premiums results in calls for tort reform, this institutional dimension capitalizes on the increase by labeling it a "crisis" and coordinates efforts to resolve it through reform. However, the institutional push for reform is constant regardless of whether an insurance "crisis" exists, and is phrased in broad terms as a "lawsuit crisis" that is structural, widespread, and potentially enduring unless reforms are adopted. The movement also has a continually increasing and evolving list of proposed reforms to address the "lawsuit crisis."

Although tort law is predominantly a matter of state law and the details of tort reform are often fundamentally different from state to state, it is appropriate to speak in terms of a national movement with respect to five characteristics. First, in every state, a large segment of society—including doctors, retail store owners, and manufacturers—knows it needs to self-insure or purchase liability insurance because of the risk of being sued for tortious injury. Because these "haves" know that they are repeat players on the defense side of the tort system, they have a common motive to reduce costs by reducing the amount of their potential liability in tort by changing tort law in ways that favor defendants. Thus, they define tort reform as changes in tort systems that will have the following two effects: Plaintiffs will win less often, and winning plaintiffs will get less recovery. Subgroups may differ on the relative importance of particular proposals, but all want to reduce defendants' liability costs. This shared view is reflected in the membership of ATRA, which includes physicians groups like the American Medical Association, manufacturers like DaimlerChrysler Corporation and Caterpillar Corp., and insurance companies like State Farm.

Second, these actors have embraced the political model for addressing reform and have used their considerable resources to lobby and support candidates, to conduct massive publicity campaigns, and to fund conservative think tanks in order to place their common concern for reform on the political agenda in the states and in Congress. In addition, they make campaign contributions to judges seeking election and have attacked judicial decisions that hold reform legislation unconstitutional or that interpret the legislation in a way that favors the plaintiffs' position. The funding of these various activities has created a group of people who provide these activities and who, therefore, have a strong incentive not only to further the agenda but also to reinforce and intensify the belief that a serious crisis exists.

Third, the tort reform movement shares a common ideology favoring "efficiency" and self-reliance as the bases for the allocation of the risk of injuries. From the perspective of this ideology, tort law should foster efficient behavior by having the following characteristics: (1) injured persons should be required to have primary responsibility for making decisions about risk, for avoiding injury to themselves, and for insuring against that injury; (2) plaintiffs should not recover damages unless they have satisfied their responsibility to protect themselves and unless the plaintiff has clearly shown that the defendant's conduct caused the injury; (3) the conduct by the defendant was at least negligent in the sense that the defendant should have reasonably known the conduct involved a failure to take a safety precaution that was cheaper than the accident cost resulting from the lack of the precautionary measure; and (4) the damages awarded do not exceed the amount necessary to provide "reasonable compensation." If these conditions are not met, payments to a plaintiff are viewed as both unfair and inefficient. Because of this ideology, as well as the nature of the parties in the tort reform movement and the movement's embracing of the political model, it is not surprising that the movement has, to a considerable extent, become allied with the Republican Party.

Fourth, this push for reform has attempted to gain public support of its legislative agenda and its ideology through the use of massive publicity campaigns that share a common rhetorical emphasis on the importance of widely shared values like fairness, efficiency, and personal responsibility. However, reform proponents do not address the difficult tasks of defining, applying, and justifying their use of these values in terms of a specific problem raised by a tort doctrine or of the effect of a specific change on the problem. This rhetoric is bolstered by attacks on plaintiffs and on the judicial system by means of the constant repetition of an asserted need to address a crisis and of anecdotal "horror stories" about the "tort tax," a "litigation explosion," "lawsuit abuse," "frivolous lawsuits," "judicial hellholes" and "dishonorable" courts. . . .

Traditional reform sometimes has some of these political aspects, particularly when reform is sought within a legislative context. For example, rhetoric can play a role because it can usefully communicate in concrete ways that accurately capture a policy position or motivate people through a common basis of shared values. In terms of accident law, an example of this use of rhetoric is reflected in the phrase, "the price of the product should bear the blood of the workingman," which was used to support the legislative adoption of workers compensation. This rhetorical phrase accurately captures both the risk-spreading enterprise liability theory underlying this compensation scheme and the shared concern for injured workers and their families, even though it begs the question of why workers' injuries should be viewed as a cost of the employer's enterprise of production rather than a cost of the employee's enterprise of working.

In contrast, "tort reform" rhetoric often lacks such a relationship and appears designed to persuade by misleading. It is rhetoric, in the negative sense criticized by Socrates, designed not only to appeal to shared values but also to take advantage of misconceptions so that it can be "more convincing among the ignorant than the expert." For example, ATRA and other supporters of tort reform stress the problem of "frivolous litigation" and repeat a litany of anecdotes about specific "loony lawsuits." This approach has a powerful impact on public opinion because polling data indicate that "Americans believe too many frivolous lawsuits clog our courts." However, the movement provides no definition of "frivolous lawsuits" and no measure of how many frivolous suits constitute "too many." Nor does it give data to support the claim of a problem. Instead of addressing the validity of the public belief that there is a problem of frivolous lawsuits, the movement simply utilizes the belief to support its agenda. For example, ATRA claims that it "successfully translates that frustration with frivolous lawsuits into action and reform." But ATRA's "action and reform" concerning frivolous lawsuits consists solely of legislative proposals that will reduce a plaintiff's right to compensation regardless of whether the claim is frivolous under existing substantive rules. ATRA has virtually no legislative proposal specifically directed toward frivolous litigation in the sense of claims that are defined as clearly groundless under existing rules of tort. Indeed, it is hard to know what might be proposed because, as indicated below, the federal and state systems already have several specific schemes designed to address groundless lawsuits.

The rhetorical attacks on "frivolous litigation" are part of a broader rhetorical pattern of criticizing courts by using claims that imply courts are neither competent nor trustworthy. This broader attack is reflected in recurring rhetorical phrases such as the need for "real justice in our courts" and the need to stop "lawsuit abuse," "looney lawsuits," and "judicial hellholes." It is also implicit in the "reform" position that jury verdicts for compensatory and punitive damages are "excessive" and "erratic" despite judicial control over jury verdicts. The broadest attack is to question the deterrent role of the tort system by asserting a need to stop "regulation through litigation."

These rhetorical attacks on the legitimacy of courts and on the fairness and efficiency of tort law are consistent with the interest of the "haves" supporting the tort reform movement to seek limits on legal curbs on their economic power. As indicated above, decisions of judges and juries are less subject to manipulation through the use of economic resources than are legislatures and regulatory agencies. In addition, courts prefer to use the rational model in decision-making rather than the political model. Consequently, reducing the role of courts, vis-a-vis that of legislatures and agencies, in allocating injury costs increases the ability of the "haves" to use their economic advantage in determining the rules and outcomes in particular cases. . . .

B. IS THE CIVIL JUSTICE SYSTEM IN CRISIS? THE BASIC DISPUTE AND THE NATURE OF THE FIGHT

1. The articles and interest group statements that follow continue the tort reform discourse. The contrast between CJ & D's excerpt and ATRA's excerpt could not be more profound. Not surprisingly, the literature in the field reflects strongly held opinions and beliefs. Are these opinions supported by data you find convincing?

2. On the nature of the dispute, consider just one topic: punitive damages. Beyond the excerpted articles that follow, take a look at Sheila B. Scheuerman, *Two Worlds Collide: How the Supreme Court's Recent Punitive Damages Decisions Affect Class Actions*, 60 BAYLOR L. REV. 880 (2008), and Michael P. Allen, *Of Remedy, Juries, and State Regulation of Punitive Damages: The Significance of* Philip Morris v. Williams, 63 N.Y.U. ANN. SURV. AM. L. 343 (2008). There are those who see punitive damages as a massive problem for U.S. businesses, particularly in the health care field. There are also those who assert that there is nothing close to a real

problem with punitive damages—and since the Supreme Court decision, *State Farm Mut. Auto. Ins. Co. v. Campbell*, 538 U.S. 408 (2003), there are not likely to be any meaningful punitive damages awarded in the future.

3.   Over the years, punitive damages have been a centerpiece of many tort reform proposals (either seeking to cap or eliminate punitive damages). As you read the articles that follow, what strikes you as the centerpiece of tort reform in the future—and what will be the central arguments in opposition?

Center for Justice and Democracy—Three Short CJD Information and Advocacy Articles

The web site for the Center for Justice and Democracy describes the center as follows:

The Center for Justice & Democracy is the only national consumer organization in the country exclusively dedicated to protecting our civil justice system.

We are:

— Working full-time to make sure average Americans get a fair shake in court, even against the country's most powerful special interests.

— Exposing unscrupulous attacks by special interests on judges, juries, injured consumers and the attorneys who represent them.

— Raising public awareness of the value of our civil justice system and the dangerous campaign behind the so-called "tort reform" movement.

Our Challenge

As American consumers and citizens, we are challenged as never before in history by a corporate-led attack against independent judges and on our precious right to trial by jury in civil cases.

With money and politics already dominating the executive and legislative branches of government, America's civil justice system is one of the only places left in America where individual citizens can successfully challenge powerful industries and institutions and hold them accountable.

Insurance companies, manufacturers of dangerous products and chemicals, the tobacco industry, and other major corporate interests are engaged in a nationwide campaign to weaken our civil justice system—to make it easier for them to escape responsibility for the harm they cause.

This so-called "tort reform" movement has sunk multi-millions of dollars into hundreds of industry-sponsored conservative groups. These "think-tanks," public relations, polling and lobbying firms are setting legislative agendas, devising strategies and purchasing expensive media to undermine consumer rights.

Their goals are to take power away from independent judges and juries and to enact laws that let corporations off the hook for their misconduct.

* * *

What follows are three short pieces from the CJD website, two responsive advocacy pieces and a glossary. They are: "We The Plaintiffs"—A Retort, Federal Preemption of Tort Law: No Recourse for the Injured"; "Immunity for the Wrongdoer," and "A Glossary of Common Tort Reforms," are available on the website of the *Center for Justice and Democracy*. https://www.centerjd.org/. *All internal footnotes have been deleted for this text*.

CJD Item I, "We The Plaintiffs"—A Retort
July 19, 2012

. . . .

The only "sue-happy" people in this country are banks and debt collectors.

- According to the most recent data from the National Center for State Courts (NCSC), tort [*i.e.*, personal injury] cases represent only 5% of all incoming civil cases today. On the other hand, nearly 70% of civil caseloads are contract-based. Why so many contract disputes? It is worth looking at Kansas, a state that has adopted statistical reporting which allows examination of its court data. In Kansas, only 2% of incoming civil cases involved torts, yet a whopping 80% of incoming civil cases involved contract disputes. Of that number, fully 75% of these were debt collection cases; 7% were mortgage foreclosures.

- According to an extensive study by the Rand Institute for Civil Justice, for the typical injury, "the injured person does not even consider the notion of seeking compensation from some other person or entity. . . ." Only 10 percent ever file a claim, which includes informal demands and insurance claims. *Only two percent file a lawsuit*. The study concludes that these statistics are at odds with any notion that we live in an overly litigious society.

Medical malpractice cases.

• Each year, hundreds of thousands of Americans are killed or injured by avoidable medical errors. According to a November 2010 study by the Office of Inspector General of the U.S. Department of Health and Human Services, about 1 in 7 patients in hospitals experience a serious medical error, 44 percent of which are *preventable*. Despite the amount of preventable medical negligence nationwide, very few injured patients file suit. According to the 1990 Harvard Medical Practice Study, eight times as many patients are injured by medical malpractice as ever file a claim; 16 times as many suffer injuries as receive any compensation.

• According to an April 2011 National Center for State Courts report, "despite the widespread prevalence of medical negligence," in 2008 medical malpractice case filings "represented well under 2 percent of all incoming civil cases, and less than 8 percent of incoming tort cases" in the general jurisdiction courts of 12 states reporting. In an October 2011 study, researchers found that from 2000 to 2009, med mal filings fell by 18 percent in the general jurisdiction courts of seven states reporting. In five of those states, filings fell by between 18 and 42 percent. These findings are consistent with the April 2011 National Center for State Courts report, which concluded that "[c]ontrary to the claims of some tort reform advocates, medical malpractice caseloads have been decreasing over time." And according to Public Citizen, "By almost any measure, medical malpractice payments were at their lowest level on record in 2011. . . . Both the number of medical malpractice payments made on behalf of doctors and the inflation-adjusted value of such payments were at their lowest levels since 1991, the earliest full year in which the government collected such data."

• And just to emphasize—these claims are not frivolous. As the Harvard School of Public Health put it in a 2006 study, "[P]ortraits of a malpractice system that is stricken with frivolous litigation are overblown." Specifically, "Some critics have suggested that the malpractice system is inundated with groundless lawsuits, and that whether a plaintiff recovers money is like a random 'lottery,' virtually unrelated to whether the claim has merit," said lead author David Studdert. "These findings cast doubt on that view by showing that most malpractice claims involve medical error and serious injury, and that claims with merit are far more likely to be paid than claims without merit."

Figures claiming the "cost" of our tort system is $251 billion, or 2.2% of our GDP, or $808 per person, come from a widely-discredited report by an insurance industry consulting firm.

• There is only one source for numbers like this—insurance consulting firm Towers Watson, which issues an annual report called "Tort System Costs." These numbers have been criticized and debunked for years, including in the *Wall Street Journal, Business Week*[22] and *Congressional Quarterly*, as well as by the Economic Policy Institute and academics like Daniel Capra, Philip Reed Professor of Civil Justice Reform at Fordham University School of Law, who used words like "folly," "disingenuous," "nothing but absurd and self-serving overkill" and "vastly overinclusive" to describe them.

- Towers Watson data actually have no connection whatsoever to the costs of lawsuits, litigation or the courts. By its own admission, Towers Watson does not examine jury verdicts, settlements, lawyers' fees, court costs or any actual costs of what might generally be considered the "tort" system. It examines only insurance losses, i.e., the kinds of funds that companies pay people who file insurance claims (like fender-benders)—even if no lawsuit was filed! They count this as a "cost" even though insurance companies have collected billions of dollars in premiums from everyday Americans to pay these claims. Moreover and incredibly, included in this figure are billions of dollars in bloated insurance industry overhead (salaries, bonuses, lobbying costs, perks like private jets and country club memberships, advertising expenses, rent and utilities for insurance company headquarters and commission paid to agents). This figure also entirely ignores the fact that "much of the unnecessary cost in the system results from corporate wrongdoing, causing injury, and 'hardball' litigation tactics of insurance companies that deny legitimate claims." What's more, it ignores the amount of money the civil justice system saves the economy in terms of injuries and deaths that are prevented due to safer products and practices, wages not lost, health care expenses not incurred and so on.

Most lawyers in America do not represent everyday citizens who sue; they represent corporations who either fight them or fight each other.

- In their book, *Chicago Lawyers: The Social Structure of the Bar* (1982), authors John P. Heinz and Edward O. Laumann estimated that in 1975 "more than half (53 percent) of the total effort of Chicago's bar was devoted to the corporate client sector, and a smaller but still substantial proportion (40 percent) was expended on the personal client sector. When the study was replicated twenty years later, the researchers found that about 61% of the total effort of all Chicago lawyers was devoted to the corporate sector and only 29% to the personal/small business sector. The number of lawyers in Chicago had doubled meant that the total effort devoted to the personal sector had increased by 45% but the corporate sector grew by 126%."

- As University of Wisconsin Law Professor Marc Galanter has written, "The United States is a highly legalized society that relies on law and courts to do many things that other industrial democracies do differently [like provide universal health care]. And it is worth noting that one realm in which this country has remained the leading exporter is what we may call the technology of doing law—constitutionalism, judicial enforcement of rights, organization of law firms, alternative dispute resolution, public interest law. For all their admitted flaws, American legal institutions provide influential (and sometimes inspiring) models for the governance of business transactions, the processing of disputes, and the protection of citizens in much of the world." In 2008, the National Federation of Independent Businesses, a "small business" lobby group that is one of the U.S Chamber of Commerce's closest allies in their fight to limit corporate liability for wrongdoing, released a survey of its members called *Small Business Problems & Priorities*.

Slanted corporate "polls," which say Americans *want* to relinquish their own legal rights, are biased and inaccurate; truthful surveys *even of small businesses* show a completely different picture.

•   In 2008, the National Federation of Independent Businesses, a "small business" lobby group that is one of the U.S Chamber of Commerce's closest allies in their fight to limit corporate liability for wrongdoing, released a survey of its members called *Small Business Problems & Priorities*. The survey listed 75 issues and asked members to indicate which were most important to them. Out of 75 issues, "Cost and Frequency of Lawsuits/Threatened Lawsuits" ranked #65, just below "Solid and Hazardous Waste Disposal."

•   In the 1990s, pollster John Zogby conducted a poll for New York's major business "tort reform" coalition, New Yorkers for Civil Justice Reform, which supposedly showed widespread support for "tort reform." Richard Behn, who headed another national polling organization, took a look at this poll and said, "Although John Zogby is a respected pollster, the survey he prepared for New Yorkers for Civil Justice Reform is clearly designed to test voter response to a set of arguments designed to enhance the positions of New Yorkers for Civil Justice Reform. There are no counter arguments included in the poll to provide any balance to these statements." Moreover, he called the polls "incendiary . . . filled with loaded language . . . [an effort to] move public opinion in a particular direction advantageous to the poll sponsor."

•   Similarly, in 1995, Frank Luntz, working for Newt Gingrich, conducted a similar "push-poll." Luntz admitted that he had "counted people as favoring civil law reform if they accepted, in telephone polls, the statement that 'we should stop excessive legal claims, frivolous lawsuits and overzealous lawyers.'" Diane Colasanto, former President of the American Association for Public Opinion Research, said, "You can't measure public opinion with leading questions like these." Similarly,

Donald Ferree of the University of Connecticut's Roper Center said such leading questions "sharply overstate support for the measures in question."

"Tort reformers" often use exaggerated or fabricated anecdotes to drive their message even though, as noted in the "We The Plaintiffs" chart, *cases are thrown out*!

• Our legal system has checks and balances in place so that if a person brings a case that a judge deems frivolous, the case is thrown out. This was the outcome of most examples cited on the "We The Plaintiffs" chart. But the truth is that attorneys do not bring frivolous cases, because lawyers who represent injured people only make money if they win. Even conservatives like James Gattuso, when with the Heritage Foundation, wrote in the Wall Street Journal that the contingency fee system both ensures that injured persons who could not otherwise afford legal representation obtain access to the legal system and, "rather than encourage baseless lawsuits, the contingent fee actually helps screen them out of the system." The system works. No one believes that insurance companies today are throwing money at frivolous claims.

• As described by Professors William Haltom and Michael McCann in their 2004 book *Distorting the Law; Politics, Media and the Litigation Crisis*, business lobbies often point to some extraordinary occurrence—some exaggerated or fabricated "horror story"—to symbolize what they want to call "ordinary" about the tort system. However, descriptions of these cases are always highly misleading or wrong. Egregious examples include:

o **Stella Awards.** This is a list of six crazy "real lawsuits" circulating around the Internet since May 2001, all of which are entirely made up. According to Snopes.com, a website that debunks urban legends, "All of the entries in the list are fabrications: a search for news stories about each of these cases failed to turn up anything, as did a search for each law case." In 2003, *Washington Post* media columnist Howard Kurtz reported on confronting *U.S. News & World Report* owner Mort Zuckerman about referencing these fictitious cases. "Great stuff," said Kurtz after describing two of the crazy lawsuits cited by Zuckerman. "Unfortunately for Zuckerman, totally bogus. Two Web sites—StellaAwards.com and Snopes.com—say the cases. . .are fabricated, and no public records could be found for them. Zuckerman has plenty of company. A number of newspapers and columnists have touted the phantom cases since they surfaced in 2001 in a Canadian newspaper."

o **Newsweek Cover Story.** On December 15, 2003, *Newsweek* ran a cover story called "Lawsuit Hell," a data-starved article based almost entirely on misreported or incompletely described anecdotes. The media watchdog organization, Fairness & Accuracy in Reporting, severely attacked the story in the March/April 2004 issue of its magazine, *Extra!,* in a story called "Trial by Anecdote; Newsweek's 'lawsuit explosion' blown away by facts." Author Neil deMause wrote that the story was "based on faulty assumptions and outright misstatements." *Washington Monthly* magazine also severely attacked the article's accuracy.

"Loser Pays" is a Loser Idea.

"We The Plaintiffs" suggests that someone who brings a lawsuit and loses should pay the other side's expenses. This is known as the "British rule," which the Founding Fathers had no interest in bringing to our country. It would mean that injured people who can't pay next month's rent would have to pay the enormous hourly lawyers' fees and court costs of the insurance company that they sue if they happen to lose in court. Even if injured victims have a strong legal case, they probably won't ever bring it because of the economic devastation they might face if they lose. That is why big corporations want this law.

CJD ITEM II, FEDERAL PREEMPTION OF TORT LAW: NO RECOURSE FOR THE INJURED; IMMUNITY FOR THE WRONGDOER

Monday, February 9, 2015

Providing a tort remedy is one of the most basic and traditional of state functions. For most of our nation's existence, this was a non-controversial precept.

However, beginning with the George W. Bush administration, recent Republican-led Houses of Congress and to varying degrees the Roberts Supreme Court, the concept of federally "preempting" state tort remedies has been forced into the political debate. The idea behind "federal preemption" in this context is not to replace state remedies with federal remedies. It is to leave harmed victims with no recourse at all and no ability to be compensated, while providing legal immunity to companies that do harm.

Preemption also means that the public must trust the federal government to "get it right" every time. Yet, time and again the public has seen that federal agencies do not always get it right, that regulated products and practices can still present risks, and that people can suffer extreme injuries as a result.

"Federal preemption" has historically arisen largely in the area of regulatory law, or "prescriptive" law, not tort law; even there, the Framers believed preemption should be rare.

- Sometimes Congress decides to exclusively regulate in an area and does not want states to also regulate. The

Supremacy Clause in the U.S. Constitution says that in such cases, the federal law is "supreme" and overrides, or "preempts," the state law.

- However, the Framers of the U.S. Constitution also "created a structure to ensure that the states would have an important and concurrent role protecting their residents." Protection of this state police power is enshrined in the 10th Amendment to the U.S. Constitution.

- "Congress historically has considered preemption of state law a rather drastic step that should be taken only where clearly necessary for a federal statutory program to work" because if used too casually, it greatly disturbs the balance of power between the federal and state systems.

- Preemption of state tort law is completely different from preemption of state regulations; the organized push by Big Business to expand preemption in the tort area, leaving individuals with no recourse at all, is unprecedented in our history.

- A tort remedy is not equivalent to a state regulation. "Tort remedies are primarily invoked to give citizens a remedy for an actual injury, not to prevent some predicted harm."

- State regulations specifically require or prohibit certain types of conduct, in contrast to tort lawsuits. Even though tort lawsuits can have a deterrent effect, a tort verdict "is not prescriptive" i.e., defendants are not required to change a product or practice in response to a verdict in any particular way or at all.

- In the 1983 Supreme Court case Silkwood v. Kerr-McGee, conservative Justice William Rehnquist joined the Court in upholding a $10.5 million punitive damages award by a local Oklahoma jury for the lethal contamination of a nuclear plant worker, even though the field—nuclear energy—was exclusively regulated by the federal government. The Court stressed the distinction between state regulatory law and state tort law, stating that "[i]t is difficult to believe that Congress would, without comment, remove all means of judicial recourse for those injured by illegal conduct."

- Although its rulings have vacillated in the area of preemption of tort remedies, the Roberts Court in Wyeth v. Levine upheld the importance of tort remedies against pharmaceutical companies, observing that "Congress did not provide a federal remedy for consumers harmed by unsafe or ineffective drugs. . . . Evidently, it determined that widely available state rights of action provided appropriate relief for injured consumers."

- Until very recently, Congress has never attempted to expressly preempt state tort law without providing for an alternative compensation mechanism.

Federal laws and state tort remedies have always co-existed without problem; in fact, state tort lawsuits have supported federal agencies in many important ways.

Federal agencies "are in many ways ill-equipped to gather information that firms do not want known." The reasons vary: Agencies are often captured and are controlled by the very industries they are supposed to regulate. They are also typically understaffed and underfunded. In addition, they usually lack subpoena power and sometimes cannot get information from companies that could be discovered in civil lawsuits.

In the 2009 case, *Wyeth v. Levine*, the Supreme Court ruled that in the case of pharmaceutical regulation by the FDA,

State law offers an additional, and important, layer of consumer protection that complements FDA regulation."

"State tort suits uncover unknown drug hazards and provide incentives for drug manufacturers to disclose safety risks promptly," noting that such suits "serve a distinct compensatory function that may motivate injured persons to come forward with information."

"FDA has limited resources to monitor the 11,000 drugs on the market and manufacturers have superior access to information about their drugs."

The recent General Motors ignition switch scandal is another good example.

Only because of a civil lawsuit brought by Ken and Beth Melton over the death of their daughter Brooke did the world learn that GM hid information about a massive faulty ignition defect for over a decade. The Meltons' suit and resulting publicity prompted GM to confirm that the design had been changed and triggered long-delayed action.

It was only then that NHTSA launched a full investigation into GM's failure to act on the ignition-switch problem. NHTSA's Acting Administrator David Friedman faced questions before Congress about the agency's repeated failures to both detect the defect and compel GM to act.

Preemption of tort remedies "shifts the burden of redressing injuries from the responsible party to the victims, to taxpayers, and to society as a whole."

A National Conference of State Legislatures report on NHTSA's proposed roof-crush rule during the Bush administration found that "preemption of tort suits would cost the states $60.2 million a year because some persons who would become disabled as a result of rollover accidents would be forced to resort to Medicaid (partially funded by states) because of the lack of tort compensation."

CJD ITEM III, GLOSSARY OF "TORT REFORMS"

"Tort reforms" (or tort "deforms") are cruel laws that reduce the protections and rights our country provides to those who are injured by defective products, toxic chemicals, medical malpractice, and other wrongdoing. "Tort reforms," which often change centuries-old common law, directly interfere with the independence of our nation's civil justice system, tying the hands of judges and juries who hear the evidence in a case, and undermining our country's uniquely individualized system of justice. They make it more difficult or impossible for injured consumers to hold wrongdoers accountable. Adding to the already existing barriers to court that exist for injured consumers, "tort reforms" present a peril to both family safety and democracy in our country. . . .

Collateral Source Rule—The collateral source rule prevents a wrongdoer from reducing its financial responsibility for the injuries it causes by the amount an injured party receives (or could later receive) from outside sources. Payments from outside sources are those unrelated to the wrongdoer, like health or disability insurance, for which the injured party has already paid premiums or taxes. The rule also prevents juries from learning about such collateral payments, so as not to unfairly influence with verdict. States that have modified this rule have either completely repealed it, mandating that payments received from health insurance, social security or other sources be used to reduce the wrongdoer's liability. Or, they allow juries to hear during trial about collateral payments.

Caps (on Damages)—A damages cap is an arbitrary ceiling on the amount an injured party can receive in compensation by a judge or jury, irrespective of what the evidence presented at a trial proves compensation should be. A cap is usually defined in a statute by a dollar figure ($100,000, $500,000, etc.) or by tying the cap to another type of damages (e.g. two times compensatory damages). Caps usurp the authority of judges and juries, who listen to the evidence in a case, to decide compensation based on each specific fact situation. Several states have declared caps unconstitutional.

Caps on Non-economic Damages—Non-economic damages compensate injured consumers for intangible but real injuries, like infertility, permanent disability, disfigurement, pain and suffering, loss of a limb or other physical impairment. Caps or limits on non-economic damages have a disproportionate effect on plaintiffs who do not have high wages—like women who work inside the home, children, seniors or the poor, who are thus more likely to receive a greater percentage of their compensation in the form of non-economic damages if they are injured.

Caps on Punitive Damages—Punitive damages, also known as "exemplary damages," are assessed against defendants by judges or juries to punish particularly outrageous, deliberate or harmful misconduct, and to deter the defendant and others from engaging in similar misconduct in the future. It is well recognized that the prospect of having to pay punitive damages in a lawsuit by an injured consumer causes corporations to build safer products and operate more safely. Many dangerous and defective products—including the Ford Pinto, asbestos, and the Dalkon Shield IUD—were removed from the market because of punitive damages. Companies often weigh the potential costs of liability to determine whether a defective product should be redesigned or removed from the market, or an unsafe practice should be stopped. Capping or limiting punitive damages allows companies to treat liability as a cost of doing business, weakening their deterrent impact.

Contingency Fee Limits—Under a contingency fee arrangement, a lawyer agrees to take a case on behalf of an injured client without obtaining any money up front from the client. This is a risk, because if the case is lost, the lawyer is paid nothing. In return, the lawyer is entitled to a percentage of the amount of money collected—usually one-third—if the case is successful. This system provides injured consumers who could not otherwise afford legal representation with access to the courts. Typically, states limit contingency fees by capping them sometimes way below one-third, sometimes along a sliding scale so fee percentages decrease, sometimes drastically, as judgments increases. The principal impact of contingency fee limits is to make it less likely attorneys can afford to risk bringing many cases, particularly the more costly and complex ones, providing practical immunity for many wrongdoers

Joint and Several Liability Limits—The doctrine of joint and several liability is a fairness rule, developed over centuries to protect injured consumers. It applies when more than one defendant is found fully or substantially responsible for causing an injury (not 1% or 10% responsible, as is commonly misstated). If one wrongdoer is insolvent or cannot pay their share, the other fully-responsible wrongdoers must pick up the tab, to make sure the innocent victim is fully compensated. For example, suppose three toxic polluters recklessly contaminate drinking water, causing leukemia in neighborhood children. The actions of any one of them alone would be sufficient to cause leukemia. But because three companies are involved, each one's relative share becomes only one-third.

This fortuitous circumstance allows them to split the total compensation each one owes the victims. But if one of those three companies becomes insolvent and cannot pay any compensation, who should cover it? Joint and several liability says that the other companies must cover the insolvent company's share. When joint and several liability is limited or abolished, however, these other wrongdoers are not required to cover the insolvent company's share. The wrongdoers are off the hook and the innocent victim receives far less compensation for injuries than the judge or jury determined they deserve.

Loser Pays—The English "loser pays" rule, which mandates that a losing party pay the winners' costs, is an unfair and dangerous rule. Its chief effect is discouraging important and legitimate cases. For example, imagine you are injured by a negligent or reckless corporation and believe you have a strong legal case. The economic devastation you might face upon losing your case, having to reimburse a large company for its inflated, hourly legal bills, would surely chill your right to file suit and attempt to hold that company accountable in court. That is why even in Britain, where loser pays exists, "legal expense" insurance is available, providing at least those who can afford it with the means to protect themselves against payment of an opponent's legal costs.

Prejudgment Interest—Prejudgment interest is the amount of interest that accrues on the value of an injured consumer's claim between the time he or she files a case and the final judgment. Some states penalize victims by prohibiting pre-judgment interest or by imposing very low limits on pre-judgment interest rates. Laws that limit prejudgment interest can delay timely settlements or judgments in civil cases by reducing the monetary incentive that defendants have to resolve cases expeditiously.

Product Liability Defenses—The doctrine of "strict liability" has long applied in suits involving defective products. Strict liability ensures that one who is responsible for bringing a dangerously defective product into the marketplace or workplace compensates those injured by the product. However, some states have enacted new defenses for those who manufacturer or sell defective products. For example, some laws establish a presumption that an injury-causing product, drug or medical device is not defective or unreasonably dangerous if the product complies with government standards. This benefits manufacturers that profit from weak and long out-of-date health and safety standards, like manufacturers of cars, trains, factory equipment and school buses. Other provisions require an injured consumer to prove the existence of an "alternative design" for a defective product, which would have prevented the harm but would not have hurt the product's marketability. This forces plaintiffs, who are at a distinct disadvantage when it comes to knowledge about technical design alternatives, to prove the existence of such alternatives when this defense is raised. Other laws immunize manufacturers that produce products with design defects if the products have "obvious risks," like tobacco, or are considered "unavoidably unsafe," like guns—even if a defective gun accidentally discharges and kills someone.

Statute of Repose—A statute of repose for products completely cuts off liability of the manufacturer or seller of a defective product after an arbitrarily-established number of years, such as 10 years or 15 years. (A few states have adopted statutes of repose to cut off doctors' and hospitals' liability for medical malpractice, as well.) Statutes of repose apply no matter how serious the injuries, how many injuries have been caused over the years by these products or services, or how reckless the actions of the wrongdoer were. They cover products with expected lives much longer than typical cut-off dates in the statute of repose, products like nuclear power plant components, medical devices such as pacemakers, elevators, airplanes, home appliances, playground equipment, farm equipment, freight trains, trucks, and other industrial machinery.

Structured Settlements—Also called "periodic payments," structured settlement laws either mandate, allow defendants to request, or allow courts to require that some or all payments awarded by a judge or jury be made to the injured consumer over a long period of time. In other words, the injured consumer is prohibited from receiving payments in a lump sum. These provisions increase the hardships of the most seriously injured consumers who are hit soon after an injury with large medical costs and must make adjustments in transportation and housing. Often, the law allows insurance companies to pocket the money upon the plaintiff's death, instead of paying it to a dependent spouse or child.

LARRY LYON, BRADLEY J.B. TOBEN, JAMES M. UNDERWOOD, WILLIAM D. UNDERWOOD AND JAMES WREN, STRAIGHT FROM THE HORSE'S MOUTH: JUDICIAL OBSERVATIONS OF JURY BEHAVIOR AND THE NEED FOR TORT REFORM[9]

I.   Overview

Is tort reform motivated by a legitimate tort crisis, by false perceptions, or worse—by a business and insurance lobby that is both powerful and cunning in its use of innuendo and misinformation? Ultimately this is the question that is at the core of the empirical research underlying this article. A complete answer to this question is obviously beyond the scope of this article and likely beyond the scope of any single

---

[9]   59 BAYLOR LAW REVIEW 419 (2007).

empirical research effort. However, the research described here is designed to add substance to the debate and to inform dialogue on the issue.

Tort reform has been discussed for at least the last several decades and the debate continues unabated. Tort reform legislation has been enacted federally and in at least 34 states over the past five years, with additional legislation currently pending in Congress and numerous state legislatures.

In general, the reformers argue that "the system is rife with frivolous lawsuits, unethical behavior by plaintiffs' attorneys, and runaway juries." Yet the evidence of a need for such reform remains questionable. It seems that much of what has been written in favor of a need for tort reform is premised upon anecdotal horror stories, surveys of public opinion or analysis of jury verdicts that employs qualitative second-guessing of jury verdicts by someone who was not present at trial to actually see and assess the evidence first-hand. Each of these information sources suffer serious flaws when offered in support of a significant legislative reform agenda. By contrast, the empirical research presented by this article involved going to the most credible source available for information on whether there exists within typical state courthouses a real tort crisis—the trial judges in Texas, a state variously heralded as one of the perennial "hell-holes" of litigation and simultaneously as a judicially pro-defendant venue. It is from the observations of such informed, yet impartial observers that the authors felt that one could best assess the authenticity of a general tort crisis.

One of the most popular tools utilized in support of tort reform is the litigation anecdote. As one scholar has lamented, "the use of anecdotal evidence has been unusually popular in discussions about the nature of the litigation system." These stories typically include ones such as the burglar falling through a skylight who recovered damages, the "well traveled and inaccurate story" of the medical malpractice claimant who claimed she had lost her powers of extrasensory perception as a result of a botched CAT scan, and the overweight man who suffered a heart attack while starting a Sears lawnmower and sued claiming a defective product. All true in part— yet each story leaving out important clarifying information. The premise of these stories seems to be that uneducated juries are frequently wooed by sharp plaintiff trial lawyers to reach ridiculous verdicts. The point of the stories suggests that juries can no longer be trusted to find the truth on matters of both liability and damages. While one would not believe that any serious social scientist would place much emphasis on such stories, they continue to persist in the media with the most outlandish stories being "repeated often in the media" and lay people "readily [believing] that the category of undeserving plaintiffs dominates the system." Such anecdotes obviously suffer from being unrepresentative of the entire civil litigation system, but this weakness is just the beginning of the problem. Michael Saks found:

some litigation system anecdotes are simply fabricated. Others are systematically distorted portrayals of the actual cases they claim to report. More important than what we learn about these stories, perhaps, is what we learn about ourselves and our remarkable credulity. Even when true, anecdotes enjoy a persuasive power that far exceeds their evidentiary value.

. . . .

This issue of whether a litigation crisis exists is not only important for policymakers in the executive and legislative branches but also helps, to a certain degree, to answer questions going to the very constitutionality of some tort reform measures—chiefly whether arbitrary legislative caps on the recovery of actual damages are a violation of a claimant's rights to substantive due process or right to a jury trial. In this latter regard, different judicial perceptions at the appellate level of the legitimacy of a tort crisis underlie some different conclusions as to whether damage caps violate constitutional principles of due process and the right to a jury trial. Thus, some courts have upheld damage caps while others have rejected them with the result turning on the underlying dispute of whether or not a real tort crisis exists.

Given the rather obvious problems with reliance upon anecdotal evidence of jury incompetence and of previous efforts to rely upon specific case analysis or jury verdict statistics, is there a better way to objectively determine whether an authentic tort crisis exists? The authors strongly believed that asking state court trial judges—"the daily observer of the jury system in action"—would yield the most reliable information on the state of the jury system. The trial judge is the only one in a position to have both seen the same evidence as the jury and yet to be completely non-partisan about the proceedings. Further, the trial judge has the benefit of seeing the jury system at work in many cases and is unlikely to form views about the legitimacy of a tort crisis based upon anecdotal information about one particular case.

. . . .

B.   Survey Findings

1.   Actual and Exemplary Damages

Consistent with the thought that more data on judicial observations of a possible tort crisis was necessary to the continuing debate on tort reform, trial judges were asked several questions concerning the frequency with which they had observed runaway juries. Specifically, in two separate questions, the judges were asked about the frequency with which they had observed, during the preceding four years, juries award either actual or punitive damages in an amount that they considered "disproportionately high" in light of the evidence presented at trial. Tables 1 and 2 reveal a rather large percentage who had either witnessed no such instances or a relatively small percentage.

Table 1

In what percentage of cases tried before you as presiding judge during the past 48 months, in which the jury awarded compensatory damages, do you believe that the jury's verdict on compensatory damages was disproportionately high given the evidence presented during the trial?

[Answer]	Frequency	Percentage
0%	196	83.4%
1–25%	35	14.9%
26–50%	2	.9%
51–75%	1	.4%
76–100%	1	.4%
TOTAL	235	100.0%

Table 2

In what percentage of cases tried before you as presiding judge during the past 48 months, in which the jury awarded exemplary damages, do you believe that the jury's exemplary damage award was disproportionately high given the evidence produced during trial?

[Answer]	Frequency	Percentage
0%	89	83.2%
1–25%	8	7.5%
26–50%	2	1.9%
51–75%	1	0.9%
76–100%	7	6.5%
TOTAL	107	100.0%

Thus, more than 83% of the Texas district court judges had observed not a single instance of a runaway jury verdict on either actual or exemplary damages during the preceding 48 months before the survey. Furthermore, less than 2% of the judges reported any frequency greater than 25% of the cases involving excessively high awards of actual damages, with the percentage of judges observing excessive punitive damage awards more than a quarter of the time being somewhat higher at roughly 9 %.

Even these low figures may tend to exaggerate the instance of runaway jury verdicts because a remarkably low number of judges had felt so strongly about a jury's excessive award to actually grant relief to a defendant during the preceding 48 months based upon an excessive award of actual or punitive damages. Table 3, for example, reveals that over 85% of judges had granted relief during the past four years due to an excessive award of actual damages either not at all or in only one instance. Moreover, no judge in the entire sampling had granted such relief during the prior four years in more than three cases.

Table 3

Aside from circumstances when you have been required to apply existing statutory limits on compensatory damages (*i.e.*, medical liability cases governed by Chapter 74 of the Texas Civil Practice and Remedies Code), on how many occasions during the past 48 months have you granted some form of relief based on your determination that the jury's verdict on compensatory damages was excessive?

[Answer]	Frequency	Percentage
0	24	64.9%
1	8	21.6%
2	3	8.1%
3	2	5.4%
TOTAL	37	100.0%

What is more surprising, perhaps, than how few judges had observed excessively high jury awards was that a greater number of judges observed just the opposite—that jury awards of compensatory damages that were disproportionately low was a greater problem, as revealed by Table 4.

Table 4

In what percentage of cases tried before you as presiding judge during the past 48 months, in which the jury awarded compensatory damages, do you believe that the jury's verdict on compensatory damages was disproportionately low given the evidence that was produced during trial?

[Answer]	Frequency	Percentage
0%	132	58.1%
1–25%	43	18.9%
26–50%	27	11.9%
51–75%	16	7.0%
76–100%	9	4.0%
TOTAL	227	100.0%

Thus, whereas over 83% of Texas judges had not witnessed a single jury award too much in damages, only 58% could say the same about witnessing juries being too stingy with awards of compensatory damages. Significantly, there was also a fairly high instance (approximately 15%) of

Texas trial judges observing juries refuse to make any award of punitive damages when the judge believed such an award was warranted by the evidence, as revealed in Table 5. In both instances, when asked about the reason they believed the juries had awarded too little in actual damages or had failed to award punitive damages when the judges believed they should have, the primary rationale offered was due to "media coverage of tort reform issues." In other words, even where media coverage of a tort crisis does not result in legislative action, juries tend to use that some coverage to reduce or eliminate awards of compensatory and exemplary damages on their own initiative.

Table 5

In cases tried before you as presiding judge during the past 48 months, on how many occasions when the jury refused to award exemplary damages did you believe that the jury should have awarded exemplary damages based on the evidence presented?

[Answer]	Frequency	Percentage
0	183	85.5%
1	10	4.7%
2	11	5.1%
3	3	1.4%
5	1	0.5%
7	1	0.5%
10	1	0.5%
25	2	0.9%
100	2	0.9%
TOTAL	214	100.0%

These findings suggest that far from a tort "crisis" the vast majority of Texas district judges have observed no significant evidence of a need for tort reform. And when asked specifically about the topic of extending limits for non-economic damages to areas outside of medical malpractice or imposing any further limits on punitive damages, they similarly indicate that no such further reforms are necessary. Indeed, if one were to base possible additional legislation solely on the reported observations of the Texas judiciary, one might have to consider a statutory floor on damages rather than a ceiling since Texas juries appear to have more of a problem with giving too little than too much in damages.

2.   Frivolous lawsuits

The other major category of inquiry in the survey asked Texas trial judges about instances of frivolous litigation filed in their courts. Tables 6–8 show the responses of the judges to these three remaining inquiries.

Table 6

What percentage of civil suits presented to you for a determination on the merits during the past 48 months (whether by special exception, motion for summary judgment, or trial to the bench or jury) would you characterize as frivolous?

[Answer]	Frequency	Percentage
0%	125	44.3%
1–25%	154	54.6%
26–50%	3	1.1%
51–75%	0	0%
76–100%	0	0%
TOTAL	282	100.0%

Table 7

On how many occasions during the past 48 months have you imposed sanctions under Rule 13 of the Texas Rules of Civil Procedure or Chapters 9, 10 or 11 of the Texas Civil Practice and Remedies Code for bringing frivolous claims?

[Answer]	Frequency	Percentage
0	99	65.1%
1	30	19.7%
2	11	7.2%
3	7	4.6%
4	1	1.7%
5	2	1.3%
6	1	.7%
10	1	.7%
TOTAL	152	100.0%

Table 8

Based on your experience, do you believe that there is a need for further legislation addressing frivolous lawsuits?

[Answer]	Frequency	Percentage
Yes	39	13.9%
No	242	86.1%
TOTAL	281	100.0%

While 44% of the judges had not personally observed a single frivolous lawsuit in their courtroom during the prior four years, 99% had observed no more than between 1–25% of the cases filed before them as being frivolous. Perhaps more telling—if you believe that actions speak louder than words—85% of the responding judges had at most sanctioned a lawyer under Tex. R. Civ. P. 13 only one time or less during the prior four years. Finally, over 86% of the responding judges believed that there was no need for further legislation addressing frivolous lawsuits.

III. Conclusion

When one separates fiction from fact, the tort landscape takes on a much different hue. Listeners to popular media might be convinced that too many people are suing and recovering too much money in America. The facts show otherwise. There has been a decline of more than 50% in the number of civil jury verdicts in Texas from 1985 to 2002. One study has shown, for example, that the vast majority of instances of medical malpractice never result in a claim being asserted by the victim. "A great many potential plaintiffs are never heard from by their injurers or their insurers." This study concluded that "at most only 10% of negligently injured patients sought compensation for their injuries." Our research confirms that most Texas trial judges do not see significant numbers of frivolous filings by people who have no business suing. And what happens to those 10% of the patients who do file meritorious tort suits for their personal injuries? According to our research, such victims are much more likely to be under-compensated than they are to receive any windfall. Such results fail to achieve either of the two primary goals for tort jurisprudence—the victim does not receive full compensation and the tortfeasor goes undeterred. Such facts need to receive more prominent consideration in any future debates about a tort crisis and the need for reform.

The materials that follow were prepared by the American Tort Reform Association (ATRA). Like the Center for Justice and Democracy, ATRA's position on tort reform is not subtle: they favor tort reform. ATRA's web site describes the Association as follows:

American Tort Reform Association: Commentary, Press Releases, and a White Paper

http://www.atra.org/about/

ATRA—At a Glance

Since 1986, the only national organization exclusively dedicated to reforming the civil justice system. A nationwide network of state-based liability reform coalitions backed by 135,000 grassroots supporters. An unparalleled track record of legislative success.

ATRA was founded in 1986 by the American Council of Engineering Companies. Shortly thereafter, the American Medical Association joined them. Since that time, ATRA has been working to bring greater fairness, predictability and efficiency to America's civil justice system. Those efforts have resulted in the enactment of state and federal laws that make the system fairer for everyone. Further, ATRA is a nonpartisan, nonprofit organization with affiliated coalitions in more than 40 states. We are the only national organization dedicated exclusively to tort and liability reform through public education and the enactment of legislation. ATRA's membership is diverse and includes nonprofits, small and large companies, as well as state and national trade, business, and professional associations. . . .

ATRA's Mission: Real Justice in Our Courts

ATRA is the only national organization exclusively dedicated to repairing our civil justice system. ATRA fights in Congress, in state legislatures, and in the courts to make the system fairer. We identify and champion elected officials and judges who want to fix the system. In the media, we serve as the national voice of the civil justice reform movement.

Today, America's $246 billion civil justice system is the most expensive in the industrialized world. Aggressive personal injury lawyers target certain professions, industries, and individual companies as profit centers. They systematically recruit clients who may never have suffered a real illness or injury and use scare tactics, combined with the promise of awards, to bring these people into massive class action suits. They effectively tap the media to rally sentiment for multi-million-dollar punitive damage awards. This leads many companies to settle questionable lawsuits just to stay out of court.

These lawsuits are bad for business; they are also bad for society. They compromise access to affordable health care, punish consumers by raising the cost of goods and services, chill innovation, and undermine the notion of personal responsibility. The personal injury lawyers who benefit from the status quo use their fees to perpetuate the cycle of lawsuit abuse. They have reinvested millions of dollars into the political process and in more litigation that acts as a drag on our economy. Some have compared the political and judicial influence of the personal injury bar to a fourth branch of government.

ATRA works to counter that influence by challenging this status quo and continually leading the fight for common-sense reforms in the states, the Congress, and the court of public opinion.

ATRA's Agenda: Fair Laws, Fair Judges, Fair Courts

ATRA supports an aggressive civil justice reform agenda that includes:

1. Health care liability reform

2. Class action reform

3. Promotion of jury service

4. Abolition of the rule of joint and several liability

5. Abolition of the collateral source rule

6. Limits on punitive damages

7. Limits on noneconomic damages

8. Production liability reform

9. Appeal bond reform

10. Sound science in the courtroom

11. Stopping regulation through litigation

Two recent Press Releases and one White Paper (denoted ATRA I, II, and III) from the American Tort Reform Association provide a basis to assess the perspectives and approach of ATRA on a number of tort reform issues.

ATRA I, Press Releases I

February 7, 2017

WASHINGTON, D.C., February 7, 2017—Noting "recent media coverage influenced by trial lawyers' willful efforts to mislead the public about an important policy debate," the American Tort Reform Association today urged journalists, lawmakers and academics to set the record straight."

"With plenty of help from 'Show Me Your Lawsuits State' judges, the personal injury bar has managed over the past few decades to corrupt and distort the Missouri Merchandising Practices Act (MPA) into an all-purpose tool for bringing a variety of lawsuits—many of them preposterous," began ATRA president Tiger Joyce.

He referenced a study by Emory University law professor Joanna Shepherd, showing that the number of MPA lawsuits has grown exponentially. Shepherd attributes this growth to the original 1967 statute's failure to define unlawful practices with specificity, subsequent expansions of the law by plaintiff-friendly courts, and 1973 amendments that invited private-sector lawyers to pursue attorneys' fees and punitive damages in specious class actions that can actually hurt consumers when litigation costs are passed on in the form of higher prices.

"But now that a large majority of Missouri's lawmakers and a new governor rightly see the MPA doing more to enrich trial lawyers than it does to protect consumers," Joyce continued, "those lawyers are desperately spreading misinformation through the media in an effort to scuttle reform legislation.

"The trial lawyers have focused their media misinformation campaign on a provision in the reform bill, S.B. 5, which quite reasonably protects sellers of goods and services from lawsuits over alleged conduct that is either allowed or required by state or federal regulators. Missouri's lawsuit industry is falsely claiming that this provision would wholly exempt from MPA claims any industry that is regulated by a government agency."

Offering a lengthy list of "flimsy MPA lawsuits filed in recent years that alleged various 'unfair' or 'deceptive' practices," Joyce clarified that S.B. 5 "simply seeks to keep pay-day-seeking plaintiffs' lawyers from dragging into court law-abiding merchants whose relevant conduct is considered permissible by a government agency already working at taxpayers' expense to protect consumers.

Jennifer Artman, a Kansas City-based attorney who testified in support of S.B. 5 on ATRA's behalf concurred, saying, "With this provision, our courts can rely on well thought-out decisions made by regulatory agencies and decades of guidance from the Federal Trade Commission. It removes the very real risk of a plaintiffs' lawyer bringing a private lawsuit claiming a business's action is unfair or misleading when that same action is permitted by a government agency."

Artman's colleague, James Muehlberger, a seasoned Missouri litigator added, "We are seeing a surge of cut-and-paste MPA class actions in Missouri courts," several of which he has defended. "These are lawyer-driven claims that fight over whether a company can fit more Skittles or Hot Tamales in a box, or if cupcake mix or cleaning products qualify as 'natural.'"

Agreeing with Artman's and Muehlberger's analyses, Joyce explained that, "31 other states already have such regulatory exemption language in their state consumer protection laws, including five that border Missouri: Illinois, Iowa, Nebraska, Oklahoma and Tennessee. So the notion that this element of the MPA reform bill is extraordinary or draconian is also patently false.

"For the sake of consumers, and in order to mitigate Missouri's troubling reputation as a Judicial Hellhole that's hostile to business investment, lawmakers and Governor Greitens should not be fooled by the trial lawyers' propaganda and move ahead with their reasonable and much needed civil justice reform agenda," Joyce concluded.

ATRA II, Press Releases II

December 15, 2016

Junk Science,' Outlier Verdicts Put St. Louis Atop Latest 'Judicial Hellholes' List

The American Tort Reform Foundation issued its 2016–2017 Judicial Hellholes® report, naming courts in Missouri, California, New York, Florida, New Jersey, Illinois, Louisiana, Virginia and Texas among the nation's "most unfair" in their handling of civil litigation.

"With both this annual report and a year-round website, our Judicial Hellholes program since 2002 has been documenting troubling developments in jurisdictions where civil court judges systematically apply laws and court procedures in an unfair and unbalanced manner, generally to the disadvantage of defendants," began American Tort Reform Association president Tiger Joyce.

"This year, thanks to the Show Me Your Lawsuits State's lax standard for expert testimony, 'junk science' is driving groundless lawsuits and monstrous verdicts that have made the Circuit Court for the City of St. Louis the #1 ranked Judicial Hellhole," Joyce continued. "The overwhelming majority of plaintiffs filing these suits are not from St. Louis, or even from Missouri. They travel from across the country to exploit a weak venue law as their lawyers spend heavily on television advertising that works to prejudice potential jurors against defendants.

"Ranked second this year is perennial hellhole California, where lawmakers, prosecutors and plaintiff-friendly judges inexorably expand civil liability and thus invite the nearly 1 million new lawsuits filed there each year," Joyce explained. "Of course, the politically influential personal injury bar is enriched by such litigiousness, even as tightened state budgets make it increasingly difficult for state courts to keep up with the volume.

Nonetheless, a very poorly reasoned state high court decision this year effectively invites even more out-of-state plaintiffs to clog dockets further.

"Across the country, New York City's Asbestos Litigation (NYCAL) court, our #3 Judicial Hellhole, has incredibly come to favor plaintiffs even more since the corruption conviction of former New York State Assembly Speaker Sheldon Silver, which led to the replacement of that court's top judge. But despite early signals that Justice Peter Moulton might carry out needed reforms, he has since shown his determination to ignore balanced procedural trends in asbestos litigation nationwide by reestablishing punitive damages and normalizing the consolidation of cases at the expense of defendants' due process rights.

"Next on this year's list comes Florida's Supreme Court, from which flow liability-expanding decisions that ignore state lawmakers' prerogatives and motivate South Florida's plaintiffs' bar to become even more aggressive. Meanwhile, alliances between personal injury lawyers, shady medical clinics and various service providers continue to target insurance companies, and consumer protection lawsuits seem to serve no one but the lawyers who gin them up.

"It's a similar story in New Jersey, where bad high court decisions have boosted consumer litigation and undermined arbitration agreements in seemingly lawful contracts, and a lax standard for expert testimony continues to attract many products liability plaintiffs from other states.

"Three historically litigious counties in Illinois—Cook, Madison and St. Clair—collectively comprise our sixth ranked hellhole this year," noted Joyce. "Whether it's medical malpractice, product liability or disability access lawsuits, Cook County is the wrong place to defend a lawsuit. Meanwhile, with cozy relationships between judges and local lawyers stacking the deck against defendants, largely rural Madison County still serves as the nation's asbestos lawsuit capital. Neighboring St. Clair County also hosts more than its fair share of litigation while its judges manipulate the judicial selection system to remain on the bench.

"Rounding out the latest Hellholes list are Louisiana, Newport News, Virginia, and Hidalgo County, Texas," Joyce reported. "The Pelican State's trial-lawyer-turned-governor has hired rich political donors to run specious, multibillion-dollar litigation against the energy industry, while plaintiff-favoring interpretations of maritime law in the shipbuilding town along Virginia's coast results in the nation's highest win rate at trial for asbestos plaintiffs. And at the southern tip of Texas, a flood of groundless, even fraudulent storm-damage lawsuits is prompting both judges and lawmakers to act."

Joyce said the annual report's marginally less severe "Watch List" jurisdictions this year include the supreme courts of Georgia, Montana and Pennsylvania, as well as courts in McLean County, Illinois, Philadelphia and Pittsburgh. The Watch List also critically scrutinizes a federal judge's handling of multidistrict litigation in the Northern District of Texas and, for what Joyce says "is, hopefully, the last time," the rapidly reforming but once perennial Judicial Hellhole of West Virginia.

Singularly unsound state high court decisions in Arkansas, Indiana and Maryland comprise the report's latest list of "Dishonorable Mentions." And the report's "good news," or "Points of Light," include fair and balanced judicial decisions in Arizona, Arkansas, Colorado, Delaware, the District of Columbia, Florida, Indiana, New Hampshire, North Carolina, Oklahoma, and Oregon; as well as positive statutory reforms enacted in Mississippi, New Mexico, Tennessee, Utah and West Virginia.

"Finally, this year's 'Closer Look' examines litigation under the federal False Claims Act's qui tam provision," Joyce said. "It allows private individuals to sue on behalf of the federal government and obtain a 'bounty' if successful. As a result of a series of legislative expansions and judicial rulings, this law, originally enacted to battle fraud in wartime contracting, has morphed into a trial lawyers' dream. Penalties available under the law have dramatically increased while it's become much easier to bring these claims, and the promise of more federal funding has enticed states to enact similarly problematic laws. And a recent decision by the U.S. Supreme Court, upholding a lower court award even though the whistleblower flagrantly violated the law's 60-day seal requirement, is likely to encourage more questionable claims."

The following White Paper, first reprinted in the first edition of this text, has continuing value in setting on the ATRA perspective:

ATRA III, Defrocking Tort Deform: Stopping Personal Injury Lawyers From Repealing Existing Tort Reforms and Expanding Rights to Sue in State Legislatures

A White Paper

www.atra.org/reports
© 2008 American Tort Reform Association. Excerpted and reprinted with permission.

I. INTRODUCTION

In recent years, the organized personal injury bar (the newly named American Association for Justice, formerly the Association of Trial Lawyers of America, and its state sister groups) have initiated a campaign in state legislatures to increase their business. These efforts fall into two general categories. First, bills that scale back or outright repeal common-sense reforms that reeled in an out-of-control civil justice system. Second, bills that create new types of lawsuits or increase the potential for high awards.

The legislative push for expanded liability represents a more activist strategy in state legislatures. For more than 30 years, the principal manner in which personal injury lawyers attacked legislative civil justice or tort reform was through the courts.[10] This process came to be known as "judicial nullification of tort reform." Although some state supreme courts, including California and Michigan, have followed traditional separation of powers principles and sustained the legislature's constitutional authority to enter and shape the civil justice arena, the personal injury bar has been successful in its judicial attacks on tort reform.

Now, the personal injury bar has opened up this second front to attack existing civil justice reforms through the legislature. The plaintiffs' lawyers and their allies have increased lobbying efforts, which have shown particular viability where personal injury lawyer groups have contributed substantially to the election of representatives on key legislative committees and to state legislatures as a whole. Often, these efforts toward change are not overtly led by recognized personal injury groups, but by so-called "consumer groups" who help fulfill the trial-lawyer agenda. At other times, organizations like the People for the Ethical Treatment of Animals (PETA) have their own political agenda that happens to parallel the agenda of personal injury lawyers, as is the case with proposals to expand the scope of damages available for injury to an animal.

If existing rules of tort law are unfair to citizens of the state, then it may be appropriate to legislatively expand liability rules. For example, until the late-nineteenth century, actions for wrongful death were not permitted under the common law of many states. As unfair as it may sound, one was able to obtain a recovery under the common law of torts if a person was injured, but would recover nothing if the person was killed. This was obviously unfair and, after some struggle, legislatures in almost every state enacted wrongful death and survival statutes to make the situation a fair one. Likewise, nearly every state has abandoned the absolute defense of contributory negligence, which barred a plaintiff from recovery if he or she had any degree of responsibility for the injury, in favor of a system that simply reduces a plaintiff's recoverable damages by his or her percentage of fault.

Recent personal injury lawyers' efforts, however, are less directed at "fairness" than at expanding their ability to bring lawsuits and the profitability of claims. These efforts fall into two principal categories. The first is modification of existing civil justice reforms. The second is to open up avenues for new extensions of liability.

---

[10] See Victor E. Schwartz & Leah Lorber, *Judicial Nullification of Civil Justice Reform Violates the Fundamental Federal Constitutional Principle of Separation of Powers: How to Restore the Right Balance*, 32 RUTGERS L. REV. 1005 (2001).

This paper closely examines legislation supported by the personal injury bar over the past year. Each effort to expand liability is addressed separately, with an explanation of the general issue involved, highlights of legislative attempts in the states, and a discussion of why state legislators should reject such proposals if reintroduced in the future.

II. ROLLING BACK THE CLOCK: EFFORTS TO "CHIP AWAY" AT OR REPEAL TORT REFORM

Over the past 20 years, state legislatures have taken action to address areas of the civil justice system where the unjust assignment of liability has had a harmful effect on small businesses, the availability of health care, the economy, consumers, and basic principles of fairness.

States have enacted joint and several liability reforms to ensure that defendants are responsible for their fair share of damages, not more, not less. They have placed limits on the bond needed to stay execution of a judgment during appeal so that a defendant does not lose his or her ability to obtain judicial review of an extraordinary award. State legislatures have also placed limits on punitive damage awards that had, in the words of Supreme Court Justice Sandra Day O'Connor, "run wild," and on the immeasurable pain and suffering damages in medical liability cases that had caused a crisis in the health care system.

In the past, plaintiffs' lawyers concentrated their efforts on stopping such commonsense reforms in the courts. They took advantage of lengthy state constitutions that are filled with vague clauses, such as so-called "open courts" provisions, that have no comparable equivalent under the U.S. Constitution. Indeed, a number of state courts chose to "nullify," or strike down on state constitutional grounds, the reasonable exercise of legislative public policymaking in the area of civil justice reform. These courts, often by slim majority decision, substitute their own views of public policy for those of legislatures.

While the personal injury bar continues to seek judicial nullification in the courts, it is now engaged in a frontal assault on the tort reform gains of the past two decades. They are seeking to repeal or significantly roll back such laws through their allies in state legislatures. . . .

III. MORE LAWSUITS

The personal injury bar is not just seeking to reverse the progress made in recent years, but in true entrepreneurial spirit, they also are attempting to create new ways to sue. This is understandable, as more lawsuits mean more profits for plaintiffs' lawyers. Sometimes these efforts are blatant, such as broadening the scope of what are already expansive consumer laws to allow new claims against new defendants. In other cases, the effect is more subtle, such as including language in legislation that sets the stage for courts to recognize new rights to sue where not explicitly authorized by the statute. In addition, the plaintiffs' bar has sought to empower itself to bring lawsuits as "private attorneys general," giving it the right to sue on behalf of the state or its citizens. In some instances, legislation would increase the power of the state attorneys general, allowing them to hire friends or political donors to represent that state and keep a part of the public's award through a contingency fee. . . .

B. Setting the Stage for Implied Causes of Action

One of the more subtle attempts by the personal injury bar to expand liability occurs with implied rights of action. These are private causes of action that are not expressly stated in the law, yet can be interpreted by a court to exist given the nature and intent of a particular piece of legislation. When adopted by a court, a new avenue of relief is created. This may not necessarily follow the legislature's design and could lead to an entirely new and unanticipated field of litigation.

Given the potential payoff, the personal injury bar has an incentive to place carefully crafted language in regulatory legislation to "set the stage" for subsequent attempts to bring a cause of action. In other words, language is inserted for the purpose of encouraging courts to interpret the statute in a way that creates a new private right of action under that statute. Often these attempts will occur in seemingly innocuous legislation, like a regulatory proposal, where the legislature's apparent focus is elsewhere. For example, in enacting disclosure requirements about food or mandatory requirements for the strength of a roof, a legislature's attention is on the particular safety or disclosure at issue, the law's enforcement, and the appropriate penalties for violations; it is not on whether to vest personal injury lawyers with new ways to sue.

A court's finding of an implied right of action can result in patent unfairness to litigants. Where unanticipated, an implied right of action amounts to a change in substantive law without opportunity for comment or debate, or adequate legislative process. Indeed, many of the legislators voting in favor of the bill may not be aware of its potential interpretation by a court. Defendants can similarly be surprised and forced to defend actions where there was no prior indication of liability exposure. Hence, implied rights of action can be said to reduce predictability and stability in the civil justice system.

There is, however, a relatively simple precautionary measure to deny implied rights of action. Language that states plainly, "No private cause of action is created by this legislation" will prevent a court from holding otherwise. Separate model reform legislation developed by the American Legislative Exchange Council provides that courts may not recognize new private causes of action unless the legislature expressly authorizes such suits. This effectively ensures that new ways to sue are created only with clear legislative intent, transparency, and close deliberation and debate.

C. Deputizing Private Lawyers to Sue on Behalf of the State

In 2007, spurred by financial incentives in the federal Deficit Reduction Act of 2005, many states considered adopting false claims/*qui tam* laws targeting Medicaid fraud. These laws generally authorize private civil actions alleging that a person knowingly presented a false claim and deceived the state for the purpose of getting a false claim paid.

Typically, the plaintiff receives a significant percentage of any amount recovered for the state treasury. For example, *qui tam* laws are a favorite tool for plaintiffs' lawyers to sue pharmaceutical manufacturers for allegedly committing fraud against federal and state health care programs through their marketing practices. . . .

D. Hiring of Private Lawyers by the State

With increasing frequency, state government officials are turning to outside private lawyers to pursue litigation on behalf of the state. Past experience has shown that such arrangements are too often the result of agreements made behind closed doors between public officials and private contingency fee lawyers. Attorneys may be hired by state officials primarily based on their personal and political connections and not their experience. Moreover, the use of private lawyers by the government, particularly on a contingency fee basis, raises the potential for government work to be motivated by profit, not the public interest. For this reason, it is particularly important to watch legislation that would explicitly authorize or could be used by attorneys general to hire private contingency fee lawyers.

For example, Louisiana, H.B. 360, as originally introduced, would have allowed institutions of higher education to negotiate and enter into contracts for the use of credit cards. After an amendment in the Senate, however, the bill would have authorized the state attorney general to contract with private lawyers to file suit against prescription drug manufacturers. Ultimately, the problematic language was stripped out in conference committee prior to Governor Kathleen Blanco signing the bill into law on July 11, 2007.

IV. MORE MONEY

While lawyers can create new business by creating new rights to sue, they can also expand their existing business by increasing the profit margin on claims already available.

A. Inflating Limitations on Damage Awards

One staple of the plaintiffs' bar agenda is to lift limits on damages wherever they exist. The reason for this objective is obvious—any increase in damage limits directly serves the personal injury lawyers' bottom line by inflating jury verdicts and providing greater leverage in settlement negotiations.

Legislation increasing the potential size of awards can come in a variety of contexts. In states that place caps on damages, the proposed legislation routinely seeks to arbitrarily increase those statutory amounts. In other jurisdictions, proposals might more generally expand damages to require payment of attorneys' fees or other costs where such payment is discretionary for the court and authorized only as justice demands. Legislation also may attempt to force a defendant to pay more economic damages than are necessary to "make the plaintiff whole" by denying the defendant's ability to offset expenses which are not actually incurred by the plaintiff. . . .

State legislatures have considered proposals that would increase potential damages beyond a reasonable adjustment for inflation. For example, the above Washington legislation would have amended the state's consumer protection act to increase potential damages by a factor of five. Such changes are by no means minor and can encourage additional litigation when it is not appropriate. Further, these proposed increases have no economic rationale and are not based on anything other than the general desire to increase payouts.

In addition, legislation denying defendants the ability to offset damages to account for expenses that the plaintiff did not pay out-of-pocket is similarly ill-advised. When a plaintiff receives funds from the defendant and another source for the same injury, he or she obtains a double recovery. The defendant's statutorily required payment of full damages, therefore, makes the plaintiff "more than whole."

B. Broadening the Scope of Consumer Laws or Available Damages

Consumer protection laws have emerged as a powerful tool for plaintiffs' lawyers to launch new types of litigation. These laws generally prohibit "unfair or deceptive" acts in the sale of a product or service; however, because the range of consumer products is so complex and varied, these statutes are purposely vague and broadly designed. This fact makes the law an attractive means for innovative and profit-motivated personal injury lawyers to attempt to attack a wide range of conduct to circumvent traditional requirements of product liability law or to promote their own regulatory agenda.

Overexpansion of existing consumer protection acts has led to cases, such as the Washington, D.C., "lost pants" lawsuit where a plaintiff pursued a claim against a dry cleaner for years, seeking $54 million for a misplaced pair of suit pants. While the judge ultimately ruled for the defendant after trial, the broad wording of the law, which allowed individuals to sue for $1,500 "per violation" without demonstrating injury, did not allow the judge to dismiss the case at an early stage and led to thousands of dollars in defense costs for a small business. In the end, the family-owned cleaners opted to close that shop.

While this example illustrates an attempt to test the limits of the law as currently written, proposals to broaden the scope of consumer laws seek a more certain route to more claims for more money. These attempts to stretch the boundaries of consumer protection law are most often seen through amendment of statutory definitions, recognition of specific conduct as a violation, or expansion of the act to cover industries already regulated by government agencies. . . .

Such legislation is over-expansive and often unnecessary. For example, the Michigan legislation would have created a new right to sue for allegedly deceptive advertising of prescription drugs, despite the fact that prescription drugs are already among the most regulated products, and their labeling and advertising are reviewed and approved by the FDA. Likewise, the New Hampshire bill would permit private lawsuits for alleged violations of the state's insurance law, which already provides an appropriate remedy for deceptive insurance practices. Further, insurance represents another of the most heavily regulated industries in the country.

The New Hampshire and Michigan bills are an attempt to facilitate litigation against a particular industry. It is based less on fairness than on a search for "deep pockets." Current law places reasonable limits on these types of actions that should be maintained to prevent excessive and unwarranted litigation.

C. Expanding Recovery in Wrongful Death Actions

An increasingly common approach by the personal injury bar to fundamentally alter and expand liability is through seeking an amendment to a state's wrongful death statute. Such efforts generally attempt to either: (1) expand the class of persons who may recover in the event of a wrongful death; or (2) allow for non-economic recovery under the statute.

By expanding the scope of claimants in wrongful death actions, personal injury lawyers can increase the number of potential plaintiffs in each and every case. This necessarily creates more litigation and brings more profit for the plaintiffs' bar. To compound this effect, the personal injury bar has pushed legislation to allow non-economic damages, such as pain and suffering and loss of consortium or society, in wrongful death actions. These damages are in addition to the traditional economic damages that compensate a plaintiff for all of the direct pecuniary losses incurred as a result of the decedents' wrongful death. Non-economic damages are also more subjective in nature, which can lead to higher damages and increase the potential for excessive awards. . . .

While any wrongful death is tragic, legislative amendments, such as these, are not the answer. First, as a practical matter, no amount of money can restore a life or bring about comfort to what is a true, serious, and meaningful loss of companionship of the deceased. When wrongful death statutes originally were enacted into law, damages were often capped, and, in all cases, they were limited to economic losses. The reason for this limitation was the concern that there is no objective standard for measuring loss of companionship, particularly for the loss of a loved one. If family members were permitted to recover such damages, the emotions of the moment could result in excessive awards.

At first, these statutes were narrowly construed and sometimes unfairness did result; for example, in cases of the death of a child who was never employed or a spouse who worked at home. Over time, however, courts and sometimes legislatures corrected any unfairness by providing that juries could consider losses of earnings that a child might have in the future, or, in the case of a spouse who took care of the "home front," considering the economic value of his or her caring for children, cooking, and keeping a household afloat. In some situations where a stay-at-home spouse was, in effect, managing the family's economics, this too resulted in what might be deemed substantial compensation. In essence, the words "economic loss" developed to broadly cover many aspects of a loss.

If and when a state considers expansion of damages, common sense and practical matters suggest that it needs to be curtailed to prevent verdicts that are based on passion and raw emotion, not facts. There needs to be a substantial showing that existing laws do not provide an adequate recovery in wrongful death actions before abandoning centuries of law.

Second, with regard to expanding the scope of wrongful death beneficiaries, state legislatures have carefully limited those who recover in wrongful death to immediate family, such as husbands, wives, parents, children, and sometimes grandparents and grandchildren. Some state laws set an order of priority as to who may bring the suit, permitting only the closest family members to bring a claim. More distant relatives, however, historically have not been included. As a practical matter, wrongful death statutes have been parallel to persons who might recover if a person died without leaving a will. The general policy behind such laws is an appreciation that a defendant has only a finite amount of assets from which to compensate family members when a death occurs. Thus, claims should be limited to those who have had a relationship recognized by the state in other contexts as an appropriately close blood relationship or other legal relationship.

D. Allowing Recovery for Emotional Harm in Cases of Injuries to Animals

In the search for new business opportunities, the personal injury bar has identified expanded pet damages as a potential well of litigation and concentrated efforts to pass legislation where formidable barriers to sue exist under state common law. These efforts are designed to either create a new cause of action for the injury or death of a companion animal or to expand existing remedies to include non-economic losses such as pain and suffering or loss of companionship.

Over the past year, the District of Columbia, New Jersey, and New York were among the jurisdictions that considered such legislation:

District of Columbia (B17–089): Proposed subjecting veterinarians and individuals to liability for an owner's non-economic damages, such as loss of companionship and pain and suffering, for a pet's death.

New Jersey (A. 4217): Proposed authorizing a civil action for pet injury or death from consuming or coming into contact with adulterated pet food. Damages would include loss of companionship up to $15,000.

New York (A. 2610): Proposed establishing a tort cause of action for the wrongful injury or death of a companion animal and provide for non-economic damages, including the owner's loss of companionship, society, comfort, protection, and services.

For more than 200 years, the laws governing animal ownership and animal care in this country have been remarkably consistent. These laws have created a stable legal system that promotes responsible animal ownership, deters animal abuse, and promotes innovative, affordable, and quality animal care. Under this system, which includes tort and products liability laws, pet owners are able to receive full and fair compensation when their pets are injured. States generally allow pet owners to recover all of their economic losses, including veterinarian bills and other costs incurred from an injury, as well as costs of any special training or income or services a pet may have provided to its owner. In many states, an owner also can collect the costs that might be involved in obtaining a new pet. In addition, punitive damages provide an available means to punish those who commit egregious intentional wrongful acts against pets.

Non-economic damages, however, are not permitted. These tort rules are understandable, particularly when one realizes that if a person's best friend is injured, no pain and suffering type claims are allowed. Further, when an immediate family member is injured, recovery for emotional harm is rarely permitted except in narrowly defined extreme circumstances. Indeed, an overwhelming majority of Americans, including pet owners, responded to a Gallup poll in the spring of 2007 that owners should not be entitled to pain and suffering type damages in animal injury and death cases.

Most important to debates in state legislatures, and perhaps to the general public, is that introducing pain and suffering and other non-economic damages in animal injury cases will strain not only caregivers, but also animals owners. Veterinary care and boarding services, for example, will become more expensive because even highly responsible pet care providers will have to pay much higher insurance costs because of increased liability risk. Increasing potential liability may also compromise the incentive to develop pet and animal medicines. Given the fact that the amount of money many Americans have to spend on their pets is limited, the reality is that when pet care services become unaffordable, it is the pets who suffer. More animals will face untreated ailments or, worse, be put to death.

Legislative attempts to change the rule may appear in "modest clothing." For example, a proposal may limit non-economic damages to $5,000, $10,000, or $15,000 as in the case of the New Jersey bill. In some instances, the legislation may specifically exclude veterinary services or only apply to intentional or malicious acts. Those familiar with the legislative process, however, realize that these modest changes are attempts to get the proverbial "foot in the door." Over time, limits on pet damages will rise or disappear. So, too, will exemptions for veterinary medicine and restrictions on the types of lawsuits where emotional harm damages are allowed.

V. MORE TIME TO SUE

Statutes of limitations and statutes of repose place time limits on the filing of lawsuits. Once this period expires, a person can no longer bring a claim for the injury at issue. These limitations ensure predictability and finality in the civil justice system.

Legislatures carefully determine statutes of limitations and repose to provide plaintiffs with fair and ample opportunity to file claims. Nevertheless, the plaintiffs' bar continually pushes to extend these time limits, leaving many defendants with tremendous uncertainty of their exposure to liability. In the past year, at least eight states considered legislation to arbitrarily increase statutes of limitation or repose.

A. Extending Statutes of Limitations

Statutes of limitations provide a deadline for bringing a lawsuit. These laws prohibit plaintiffs' lawyers from reviving old claims under new legal theories, bringing cases in light of new court rulings or other developments, or sitting on a case for so long that the opposing party has a more difficult time defending itself.

Statutes of limitations recognize that, over time, memories fade, witnesses become hard to find or pass away, and documents are discarded or lost. The clock ordinarily begins to run when the injury occurred or when the claimant knew or should have known of the injury giving rise to the action. Typically, these periods are several years in duration. Where the individual who is harmed is a minor, under a disability preventing him or her from pursing a claim, or the injury is latent, the period is often tolled. Without fair time limitations on lawsuits, potential liability never ends, and individuals and businesses are placed in the difficult situation of defending against charges when those who were involved and the evidence are long gone. . . .

B. Repealing or Extending Statutes of Repose

A statute of repose sets a time limit for bringing a claim based on the expected lifespan of a product or benefit of a service. Statutes of repose recognize that certain products have a finite lifetime during which the manufacturer is responsible for defects. After that period expires, it is much more likely that any failure of the equipment is a result of ordinary wear and tear than any defect in the design. . . .

C. Why Proposals to Extend or Eliminate Statutes of Limitations and Repose are Unsound Policy

The primary purpose behind statutes of limitation or repose is to settle expectations so that ordinary people and businesses can get on with their lives, without fear of prolonged and unbounded legal exposure for actions allegedly committed years before. No one can make business and personal plans or borrow money when faced with the indefinite risk of litigation or bankruptcy. This drain on initiative and enterprise is hard to quantify, but impossible to ignore.

Statutes of limitation and repose also serve a gatekeeper function in the civil justice system. They avoid trials based on evidence whose reliability necessarily deteriorates with time: recollections fade, witnesses die, and documents are misplaced or lost. Consequently, the key factual findings needed to resolve litigation become ever more untrustworthy. Without time limits, the ordinary "he said-she said" of litigation can turn into a one-sided allegation by a plaintiff that an event happened because the person says it happened, while the defendant lacks the ability to appear or muster facts that might disprove the allegation. Innocent people can be wrongly accused and have their reputations ruined.

The legislation proposed in many of these states would alter reasoned and balanced limitation periods, which have provided a sense of predictability and certainty in the civil justice system for centuries. They also would lead to greater injustice for civil defendants less able to defend accusations after considerable passage of time. Lastly, some proposals are retroactive: they could revive many time-barred claims, potentially violating the constitutional rights of civil defendants.

VI. OTHER PROPOSALS TARGETED AT CIVIL DEFENDANTS

State legislatures also considered many other proposals pushed by the personal injury bar that would have made it more difficult to mount a defense in civil litigation. Such measures include eliminating defenses, making it more difficult to keep sensitive records and trade secrets confidential during litigation, and voiding contractual rights. . . .

VII. CONCLUSION[11]

It is now more important than ever to be on guard against legislative attempts to expand liability. Plaintiffs' lawyers are not only threatening to undo recent progress towards a more stable and predictable civil justice system, but also to expand liability in a drastic and unprecedented manner. The personal injury bar and its allies are well organized, well funded, and have teamed up with their members and supporters in state legislatures. Rather than play defense, as they have over the past two decades by seeking to overturn rational tort reform measures in the courts, they are now on the offensive with a massive legislative and public relations campaign.

Going forward, it is particularly important to:

- Keep a close watch for legislation that rolls back enacted tort reforms, such as attempts to limit apportionment of damages, lift limits on non-economic damages, or repeal laws that limit liability when a defendant has faithfully adhered to government regulations.

- Closely examine legislative language to determine whether it might create a new private right of action, either explicitly or implicitly. Demand transparency.

- Scrutinize proposals that would deputize private profit-driven lawyers to sue on behalf of the state to ensure that the claims brought are in the public interest and do not provide a windfall in fees.

- Ensure that consumer protection laws continue to serve their intended purpose: to compensate individuals for actual losses caused by their reliance on a deceptive business practice. Guard against legislation that expands their reach into

---

[11]   Additional resources for this piece include: American Tort Reform Foundation, *Private Consumer Protection Lawsuit Abuse (2006), available at* http://www.atra.org/reports/consumers/consumer_protection.pdf; Joseph Carroll, *Pet Owners Not Worried That Their Pets Will Get Sick From Pet Food,* GALLUP NEWS SERVICE, Apr. 3, 2007, available at http://www.gallup.com/poll/27076/Pet-Owners-Worried-Their-Pets-Will-Get-Sick-From-Pet-Food.aspx; *See* Victor E. Schwartz & Emily J. Laird, *Non-Economic Damages in Pet Litigation: The Serious Need to Preserve a Rational Rule,* 33 PEPPERDINE L. REV. 227 (2005).

already-regulated industries, allows lawsuits without injury,
or permits damages far in excess of financial loss.

- Stop attempts to expand liability in wrongful death actions,
  such as proposals to allow recovery by distant family
  members or immeasurable emotional harm. Such changes
  will dramatically increase the potential for excessive awards.

- Adhere to traditional principles of law with respect to
  damages in cases involving the injury or death of an animal.
  Proposals that would permit recovery for an owner's
  emotional harm would lead to more lawsuits, higher
  insurance rates for veterinarians, and ultimately increase the
  cost of veterinary care, threatening its affordability.

- Prevent the chipping away of statutes of limitations and
  repose, which ensure that lawsuits are timely brought with
  the benefit of the most reliable evidence.

- Resist efforts to target particular industries that are driven
  by politics and profit, not sound public policy.

ATRA, described earlier in this text, like the Center for Justice and
Democracy, is a primary participant in the tort reform discourse. One way
they put forward their perspective on the tort system (which they see as
out-of-control and damaging) is to designate "judicial hellholes," *i.e.*, select
jurisdictions that allegedly have a pronounced proclivity to favor plaintiffs
in civil litigation, focused particularly on medical malpractice.

C. WHAT SHOULD CHANGE—IF ANYTHING: THE CONTENT OF THE TORT REFORM DISCOURSE

NOTES AND QUESTIONS

1.   In the excerpted articles that follow, focus on the way issues are
defined. What are the problems identified and what, if anything, should be
done about those problems? Some authors focus on precise topics while other
write more broadly about the field. For an example of effective scholarship with
a laser-beam focus on a specific problem, take a look at Byron G. Stier's *Now
It's Personal: Punishment and Mass Tort Litigation After* Philip Morris v.
Williams, 2 CHARLESTON L. REV. 433 (2008).

2.   Consider the federalism issues raised by tort reform. Should state
tort law and the threat of civil damages in a tort case be the dominant force
that compels safer and more efficient goods and services—or should it be
federal statutory or regulatory standards? This problem has been part of the
tort reform discourse for at least the last 25 years—at least. Each time the
Supreme Court decides a new preemption case (and they seem to do so on a

regular basis), the commentary is fierce. Is the decision the death knell for state tort law—or for effective regulatory enforcement? *See* David C. Vladeck, *Preemption and Regulatory Failure*, 33 PEPP. L. REV. 95, 102 (2005).

3.   *Wyeth v. Levine*, 129 S.Ct. 1187 (2009), set out in the final section of this text, is a major new preemption case. Ask yourself if that decision really changes the balance between state law and federal regulation—and how does it fit into the tort reform discourse? For a view on this a decade or so earlier, *see* Robert B. Leflar & Robert S. Adler, *The Preemption Pentad: Federal Preemption of Products Liability Claims after Medtronic*, 64 TENN. L. REV. 691, 696–99 (1997).

4.   As you read through the materials that follow, once again, keep track of the issues raised and the solutions proposed. These pieces talk about change. Can you identify the change they propose? Is there a basis for those changes?

CONGRESSIONAL BUDGET OFFICE, 2003,[12] THE ECONOMICS OF U.S. TORT LIABILITY: A PRIMER

Chapter 5: An Overview of Policy Options for Changing the Tort System

Various scholars and policy advocates have proposed altering the tort liability system to reduce what they see as excessive transaction costs and other problems associated with it. Those proposals are too numerous for all of them to be discussed here. Instead, this chapter examines a number of policy options to illustrate the range of choices available to lawmakers. The chapter outlines each option's potential implications for efficiency and equity. For reasons of space, however, it cannot analyze any one option in full detail. (For example, it does not consider the effects on state law or the potential transition problems associated with a particular change, nor does it discuss the many possibilities for combining policies that are not mutually exclusive.)

The options discussed here can be grouped according to their general approach. The first approach would greatly reduce the scope of the tort system and rely more heavily on other tools to control the costs of injuries. The second group contains options that are more incremental in nature but that could be applied broadly to the universe of torts. The final set comprises options targeted toward types of tort claims that have raised particular policy concerns, such as claims arising from medical malpractice or asbestos exposure and those litigated as class actions.

In all three groups, most of the proposals can be seen as addressing one or more of the fundamental barriers to efficiency. . . .

---

[12]   http://www.cbo.gov/doc.cfm?index=4641&type=0&sequence=6.

- The difficulty of giving both potential injurers and potential victims incentives to choose the efficient form and scale of their risk-related activities;

- The added difficulty of optimally distributing (insuring) the risks that remain after efficient precautions have been taken; and

- Problems relating to the cost and scarcity of information, including transaction costs, errors in judgments and in settlements, and inefficient standards for due care.

Other options respond to issues that arise from broader aspects of the legal system, such as the perceived problem that some locally elected judges are biased against out-of-state corporate defendants.

Options for Reducing the Scope of Tort Liability

The policy changes in this group—which involve replacing some or all types of tort liability with private or public insurance—generally go well beyond the kinds of proposals now being considered by the Congress. They are included here because they help clarify the strengths and weaknesses of the tort system or provide useful comparisons with other options.

Replacing Tort Liability with Private Insurance

Some academic economists favor the approach of eliminating tort liability, except perhaps for injuries between "strangers" (such as injuries from automobile accidents). Potential victims would rely to a greater extent on their own insurance for protection against injury risks. In cases in which potential injurers could cost-effectively reduce those risks, they would be motivated to do so to the extent that they could gain a marketing advantage—by advertising the safety of their products or by offering injury compensation in a warranty, purchase contract, or the like. Some increases in government regulation might also occur.

From the standpoint of efficiency, eliminating tort liability would have several desirable implications, although it would fall short of the ideal. It would give potential victims the incentive to take all cost-effective precautions and to obtain the optimal amount of risk spreading through insurance or other compensation contracts. And provided that the insurance and contract terms were clear enough, the amount of litigation would decline significantly, reducing both transaction costs and the inefficiencies associated with erroneous judgments. However, this approach would weaken incentives for potential injurers to exercise cost-effective forms of care (at least those not required by regulation) and could increase inefficiencies associated with imprecise or too-stringent regulation.

From the standpoint of equity, the implications of shifting primary responsibility for injury costs to victims could be considered both good and bad. Lower liability-related costs for businesses should lead to lower prices for many consumer goods and services and reduce the extent to which consumers are implicitly forced to pay for unwanted insurance for non-pecuniary damages. But victims would usually get compensation only for pecuniary losses, and those who had not bought insurance might get no compensation at all. Moreover, injurers would pay compensation only to the extent that they had contracted in advance to do so, and in cases of subtle, delayed, or indirect harm, some injurers' roles might go undetected because few, if any, plaintiffs' attorneys would be working to identify the causes of injuries.

A narrower variant of the same basic idea would eliminate liability only for those products (or features of products) that have been certified as safe by a federal body, such as the Food and Drug Administration, the National Highway Traffic Safety Administration, or the Consumer Product Safety Commission. Many of the arguments for and against completely eliminating tort liability would apply here as well, at least qualitatively. For example, the same efficiency and equity implications would follow from making consumers bear the risk of using the relevant products. The main immediate difference from the standpoint of efficiency is that focusing on products that satisfied federal safety regulations would presumably limit the extent of any increase in injury risks. From the perspective of equity, removing the threat of liability from firms whose products met federal standards might be particularly appropriate. Over time, however, this variant could result in a greatly expanded role for federal regulators—with potentially significant consequences for both efficiency and equity—as firms and industries seeking to exempt their products from liability pushed to broaden the scope of federal safety standards.

Replacing Tort Liability with Public Insurance

Another variant of the previous approach would eliminate (or greatly restrict) tort liability as described above but replace it with a public insurance system, like the present workers compensation system or the fund for vaccine victims. In this option, victims would receive compensation from a government fund according to a fixed schedule based on the type of injury they had and other relevant factors. To finance the fund, businesses would pay "experience-rated" premiums that reflected the previous record of injuries associated with their products. (Companies would ultimately pass on the costs of those premiums to their customers, workers, or investors in the form of higher prices, reduced wages, or lower returns on capital, respectively.) Depending on the details of the proposal, nonprofit organizations and state and local governments might also participate. But cost considerations would probably make it impractical to rate and collect premiums from individuals, so the injuries they caused might still be handled through the tort system.

Proponents of this variant hope that by standardizing the amount of compensation awarded for similar injuries, this approach would cap or reduce punitive damages and compensatory awards for pain, suffering, and other nonmonetary losses. The effects of reducing such nonpecuniary awards would be qualitatively similar to (though not as large as) the effects of simply eliminating tort liability. Again, potential victims would have better incentives to take efficient precautions, and risk would be distributed more efficiently (because consumers would not be implicitly paying for so much unwanted insurance for nonpecuniary damages). However, some injurers might not face sufficient penalties, and some victims might not receive full compensation for their pain and suffering.

Other implications of the public insurance approach flow from its shift away from litigation to an administrative mechanism. For example, one key argument made for the approach is that it would significantly reduce transaction costs from the 54 percent estimated under the current tort system. (However, transaction costs would probably remain higher than the 20 percent estimated for state workers compensation programs because of higher costs for such things as determining which injuries were compensable and associating injuries with particular injurers.) Conversely, one argument against public insurance is that the schedule of damages might not do justice to individual cases. Another is that in some cases of subtle, indirect, or delayed harm—such as cancers with long latencies caused by exposure to a particular chemical—victims might not recognize that they had suffered a compensable injury, since there would be few, if any, plaintiffs' attorneys working to identify injury causes. In addition, this option would represent a sharp departure from current practice for injuries that are judged under a negligence standard. Providers of medical care, for example, are now held liable only for injuries considered to result from negligence; but with this option, all compensable injuries to patients under their care would be reflected in their assessed premiums for the public fund.

The incentives for potential injurers to exercise care might be more or less efficient under a public insurance program than they are now. For a firm to be encouraged to take all cost-effective precautions, its assessed premiums would need to reflect all of the effects of its actions on expected future injury costs, and the experience rating would probably not be that thorough. However, even if the new incentives fell on the low side, the error could be smaller than it is now if current incentives are inefficiently high because of mistaken or excessive trial awards. . . . . .

[The report then considers the viability of controlling damage awards and attorney's fees. These sections were omitted because they are dealt with in detail in other articles within the text.]

Restricting or Eliminating Joint and Several Liability

For injuries caused by more than one party, the question arises of how much liability to assign to each party. Courts generally use one of two rules in answering that question (although other approaches can be imagined). Under joint and several liability, any one injurer or subset of injurers can be held responsible for paying all of the damages. That individual or group often has the right to seek reimbursement from the remaining injurers. Under several liability, by contrast, the court determines the relative contribution of each injurer in causing the harm and holds each one responsible for only that proportion of the damages. In the past 20 years, many states have either eliminated joint and several liability under some or all circumstances or have restricted it in various ways—for example, by limiting it to certain types of damages or to injurers whose liability exceeds a certain percentage threshold.

Whether such changes have increased or decreased efficiency is not clear. Ideal incentives require joint injurers to each face liability equal to the incremental effect of their own actions, but neither joint and several nor several liability reliably achieves that result. To illustrate, consider a case in which the actions of two injurers are both necessary to cause harm—for example, in which each one disposes of a chemical and the two chemicals then combine to produce an explosion. Avoiding the explosion is efficient if either party could do so at a cost lower than the cost of the resulting damage. But neither injurer might take care if it expected to share liability evenly under either joint and several or several liability and its prevention costs exceeded 50 percent of the damage.

What is clear is that several liability has two disadvantages for plaintiffs—and conversely, two advantages for defendants—relative to joint and several liability. First, it makes plaintiffs bear a higher share of the transaction costs. Instead of pursuing only a selected subset of the alleged injurers (often just the single party with the deepest pockets) and shifting the costs of dealing with the remaining parties to that selected group, plaintiffs must sue everyone from whom they hope to collect damages. Second, if some of the injurers are bankrupt, defunct, or otherwise unable to pay their share of the damages, several liability leaves plaintiffs partially uncompensated, whereas joint and several liability compensates them more fully, to the extent that other, deeper-pocketed injurers can be tapped for their fellow injurers' shares.

Offsetting Payments from Collateral Sources

Under the law's traditional "collateral-source rule," the fact that an injured plaintiff has received benefits from some independent source—such as an insurance policy—may not be considered in determining whether a defendant should pay damages and, if so, how much. In some cases, the collateral source exercises a lien or right of subrogation and is reimbursed for the overlap between the benefits and the damages. In many cases, however, the effect of the collateral-source rule is to allow victims to receive double compensation for their injuries.

In the past two decades, many states have revised the collateral-source rule in various ways that could serve as models for federal action. Those revisions range from merely allowing collateral payments to be introduced as evidence in certain types of cases to requiring that damages be reduced to offset such payments under all circumstances. If verdict errors never occurred, there would be no clear economic rationale for such changes—efficiency dictates that injurers should face the costs of their actions (or, at least, of their negligent actions) regardless of the other benefits available to victims. However, if judges or juries sometimes wrongly find defendants liable because of conscious or subconscious concern that plaintiffs may lack the resources to deal with their injuries, then such changes may improve efficiency. In either case, it may be more equitable for injurers not to pay victims who receive collateral benefits, at least under some circumstances—which may argue for allowing information about such benefits to be introduced as evidence and considered by juries and judges.

NANCY C. MARCUS, PHANTOM PARTIES AND OTHER PRACTICAL PROBLEMS WITH THE ATTEMPTED ABOLITION OF JOINT AND SEVERAL LIABILITY[13]

. . . .

In a 1990 law review article, one proponent of joint and several liability abolition predicted that "abrogating joint and several liability would simplify the tort process and arguably would reduce transaction costs, since contribution would not be needed." [Carol A. Mutter, *Moving to Comparative Negligence in an Era of Tort Reform: Decision for Tennessee*, 57 TENN. L. REV. 199, 307, 319 (1990)]. Seventeen years later, it is apparent that efforts to abolish joint and several liability have had the opposite effect. The process of determining damages in tort actions has become substantially more complicated as a result of efforts to replace joint and several liability with proportional allocation, resulting in unforeseen complexities which make it difficult for courts to apply the new laws in a coherent and fair manner. Rather than providing an answer to problems related to strategic or multiple lawsuits and unfair damage awards, attempts to abolish joint and several liability have only created more

---

[13]   60 ARK. L. REV. 437 (2007).

problems in these areas, forcing courts to choose between allowing unfair or inaccurate damage assessments through phantom party allocation, or in the alternative, continuing to allow multiple lawsuits while still denying contribution remedies to defendants.

The struggles of the courts in states which have attempted to abolish joint and several liability legislatively should be considered by other states weighing their options for multiple tortfeasor damages apportionment. As has been described, it is through joint and several liability with contribution, not through the myriad of alternative approaches taken by states in recent years that both plaintiffs and defendants are accorded practically realizable, consistent, and fair protections against unfair damage awards. By returning to joint and several liability with contribution, states can ensure that plaintiffs are fully compensated for their injuries, while still allowing co-defendants to apportion responsibility amongst themselves.

While the Third Restatement has been critiqued in this article for specific flaws and omissions, and criticized by others for alleged biases, it should be applauded for recognizing many of the problems with several liability and with some hybrid approaches to the allocation of damages. It should also be credited for suggesting as the fairest approach one which retains joint and several liability in the initial determination of damages. However, the Restatement falls short here, in also recommending proportional reallocation to both plaintiffs and defendants, while failing to consider joint and several liability with contribution as a more equitable approach. The Restatement offers no explanation as to why an approach which allows reallocation in a manner that leaves the tort victim potentially paying the bills of unavailable tortfeasors is a better solution than joint and several liability with contribution, which provides protections to both plaintiffs and defendants. Nonetheless, as even the Third Restatement observes, contribution continues to play an important role in the modern era of tort "reformed" states, even in those states without joint and several liability.

In conclusion, several liability has long been recognized as unfair to plaintiffs, but it is now apparent that it has failed to serve the interests of defendants as well. Several liability precludes contribution remedies for defendants and increases their likelihood of being sued, while failing to present a viable solution to the problem of unavailable tortfeasors or inaccurate apportionment. Thus, joint tortfeasors are no better off—and are arguably worse off—under modern proportional allocation systems than under joint and several liability with contribution.

Considering that no state has been willing or able to completely abandon joint and several liability, and that contribution remains a desirable remedy in the eyes of many defendants and courts, it may be time to question the continued viability of several liability. After two decades of confusion in the courts resulting from failed efforts to abolish joint and several liability or to establish in its place a coherent, effective, and equitable alternative, state legislatures may be well-advised to consider that it may be several liability, not joint and several liability, which is due for abolition. The time is ripe to reconsider joint and several liability with contribution as the most practical and equitable approach to multiple-tortfeasor damage allocation. Several liability has had its chance, and it has failed.

VICTOR E. SCHWARTZ AND CARY SILVERMAN,[14] THE CASE IN FAVOR OF CIVIL JUSTICE REFORM

In October 2015, Emory University School of Law hosted a provocatively titled symposium, "The 'War' on the U.S. Civil Justice System." The program was co-sponsored by the Pound Civil Justice Institute, a "think tank" founded and controlled by leaders of the plaintiffs' bar that advocates for expansions in liability through presenting legal education seminars and publishing papers. The distinguished law professors invited to participate in this symposium generally view tort reform as making it more challenging to bring lawsuits. Advocates for legal reform unsurprisingly have a different perspective. They view reform as creating greater fairness in the legal system, reducing unnecessary costs, and helping to assure sound results for all parties.

The introduction to the symposium edition waxes nostalgic for the civil justice system of "[a] half-century ago," which was "a much-admired, well-organized process for resolving disputes, generally in public, before juries and independent judges." As this Essay will show, at that time, the nation was in the midst of the most rapid expansion of liability exposure in its history. Civil justice reform is an effort, not to turn back the clock, but to achieve balance in areas where courts went too far in relaxing requirements for both imposing liability and awarding damages.

I. THE RAPID RISE IN LIABILITY: 1950S TO 1970S

Between the 1950s and 1970s, the civil justice system experienced unprecedented change, including expansion of liability exposure, elimination of defenses, creation of modern class action and mass tort litigation, and larger damage awards. The plaintiffs' bar proved itself adept

---

[14] Victor E. Schwartz and Cary Silverman are partners in Shook, Hardy & Bacon L.L.P.'s Public Policy Group. Mr. Schwartz coauthors the most widely used torts casebook in the United States, Prosser, Wade & Schwartz's TORTS (13th ed. 2015). Mr. Silverman is an adjunct professor at The George Washington University Law School. This reprint excludes footnotes that appeared in the original article, which can be found at http://law.emory.edu/elj/_documents/volumes/65/online/schwartz-silverman.pdf. The above piece is at: 65 EMORY L.J. ONLINE 2065 (2016).

at persuading a number of courts to shift the law to favor increased liability during this period. Below are some milestones.

1950s: The Rise of Pain and Suffering Damages. Plaintiffs' lawyers became more creative in their search for what Melvin Belli—the "King of Torts" at the time—called the "adequate award." 4 Historically, noneconomic damages were modest and rarely exceeded a claimant's economic damages. Courts typically reversed awards that were larger. Mr. Belli and other plaintiffs' lawyers changed that. They used a new type of proof in personal injury cases they labeled "demonstrative evidence." Rather than rely on the victim's testimony, the lawyers used graphic pictures and other non-testimonial means to create in juries a sense of empathy for the plaintiff and outrage against the defendant. This tactic increased the size of pain and suffering awards from modest amounts to six-figure awards that sometimes reached millions of dollars. By the 1970s, "in personal injuries litigation the intangible factor of 'pain, suffering, and inconvenience' constitutes the largest single item of recovery, exceeding by far the out-of-pocket 'specials' of medical expenses and loss of wages."

Over time, plaintiffs' lawyers created an expectation that plaintiffs in personal injury lawsuit are entitled to large pain and suffering awards, where there had been no such belief before. They were able to accomplish this even though pain and suffering awards, unlike economic damages or arguably punitive damages, are nonfunctional. There is no evidence that a noneconomic damage award reduces a person's pain and suffering. However, as Fourth Circuit Judge Paul Niemeyer has said, "[M]oney for pain and suffering . . . provides the grist for the mill of our tort industry."

1963: Strict Product Liability and Mass Tort Litigation Begins. The Supreme Court of California became the first to recognize strict product liability under tort law, allowing plaintiffs to recover for harms caused by defective products without proving that the manufacturer was negligent. The American Law Institute then adopted § 402A of the Restatement (Second) of Torts in 1965, creating strict product liability. Section 402A's authors, Deans William Prosser and John Wade, intended strict liability to apply when a product did not meet a manufacturer's own design standard (as in, for example, finding a mouse in a beverage bottle). Some courts extended strict liability to claims challenging a product's design and warnings, creating both vast, uncertain liability exposure and litigation.

Around this time, plaintiffs' lawyers succeeded in extending "mass tort" litigation, previously reserved for mass disasters such as airplane crashes where all people involved suffered the exact same fate at the same time, to cases involving a single product or substance, but with significantly different facts at different times in individual cases. While there can be benefits to coordinating procedural issues, faced with hundreds or thousands of claims, some judges adopted procedural shortcuts that placed efficiency before due process, such as bundling lawsuits and holding joint trials involving multiple plaintiffs with varying injuries and numerous defendants.

1966: The Modern Class Action Era. A newly-revised Rule 23 of the Federal Rules of Civil Procedure took effect on July 1, 1966, marking the current era of class action litigation. Development of class action doctrine in state courts followed. As University of Arizona Law Professor David Marcus colorfully put it, "To anyone interested in buccaneering attorneys, maverick judges, mind-boggling settlement sums, idealistic lawyering, or base legal corruption, the next forty-odd years have yielded a rich harvest."

The revised rule required plaintiffs to opt out of a class action rather than opt in. As a practical matter, most recipients of class action notices tossed them in the garbage, but they became part of "the class." When settlement time came, the plaintiffs' lawyers made a fortune in fees, the defendants bought peace, and the class members generally received only modest recoveries, such as the right to obtain a coupon for a product they did not like in the first place.

Late 1960s: Punitive Damages "Run Wild." American courts began to depart from the "intentional tort" moorings of punitive damages. Historically, the common law strictly limited punitive damages to a narrow category of torts involving conscious and intentional harm in which the defendant's conduct was an "affront[ ] to the honor of the victims." They later became firmly established as a means to punish the defendant and deter others from similar conduct, and typically involved situations in which one person intentionally harmed another. For much of early American jurisprudence, punitive damages awards "merited scant attention," because they "were rarely assessed and likely to be small in amount." Then, states began to allow punitive damages for reckless actions and even gross negligence. The standards fell so low that punitive damages were "awarded in cases in which liability of any sort would have been almost out of the question" a decade or two earlier. Awards became highly unpredictable and increasingly commonplace, particularly with the advent of strict product liability and mass tort litigation. The size of punitive awards "increased dramatically."

By the late 1980s, practitioners observed that "hardly a month [went] by without a multi-million dollar punitive damage verdict . . ." It was not long before the U.S. Supreme Court recognized that punitive damages had "run wild" and placed procedural and substantive due process safeguards on such awards.

1960s–1970s: Relaxation of Requirements for Consumer Lawsuits. During the heyday of consumerism, states adopted consumer protection laws that, unlike the Federal Trade Commission Act, included a private right of action. These laws allowed plaintiffs to sue for any conduct that could be viewed as "unfair" or "deceptive." They eliminated the need for the plaintiff to show that that the deception was intentional or that the consumer was actually deceived, as required under common law. Many of the statutes also authorized a plaintiff to recover statutory damages, treble damages, and attorneys' fees. Congress decided not to provide a private right of action for unfair or deceptive conduct when enacting the FTC Act both because of the vagueness of the prohibited conduct and concern that "a certain class of lawyers, especially in large communities, will arise to ply the vocation of hunting up and working up such suits."

In this instance, Congress was prophetic. Those excesses have in fact occurred under state laws. They can be seen in the surge of class actions alleging that foods are improperly advertised as "natural," that some "Footlong" subs are only eleven-and-a-half inches, or claims that Red Bull did not give a consumer "wings."

1960s–1970s: Rise of the Regulatory State. Agencies such as the FDA, EPA, and OSHA received more power and subjected businesses to increased federal oversight and complex and costly regulations. Businesses that meticulously follow government standards, however, in most cases remain subject to tort liability and even punitive damages and civil penalties. The result is today's debate over federal preemption and efforts to enact state laws that recognize regulatory compliance in determining liability and the appropriateness of punishment.

1970s: Replacement of Contributory Negligence with Comparative Fault. Courts and legislatures began replacing the contributory negligence defense with the more plaintiff-friendly comparative fault. Contributory negligence provided that a person who is partially responsible for his or her own injury cannot recover any damages in a personal injury lawsuit. Courts and legislators replaced it with comparative fault, which allows a plaintiff to recover when partially at fault for his or her own injury, but proportionally reduces the plaintiff's damages. After adopting comparative fault, some courts eliminated long-recognized affirmative defenses such as assumption of risk, the open and obvious danger rule, and product misuse, finding that a plaintiff's knowledge, carelessness, or recklessness could be factored into damages, rather than bar a claim.

1973: Asbestos Litigation, the Nation's Longest Running Mass Tort. The modern history of asbestos litigation began in 1973. Over the years, plaintiffs' lawyers generated asbestos and silica lawsuits through mass screenings. They brought thousands of lawsuits on behalf of people who have no physical impairment, causing a spiral of company bankruptcies and jeopardizing recovery for those who are sick. The asbestos litigation reached such proportions that the Supreme Court referred to the litigation as a "crisis." Some claims were exposed as potentially fraudulent. Today, the plaintiffs' bar continues to widen the next of asbestos litigation, targeting businesses with increasingly attenuated connections to the plaintiff's injury. Commentators have characterized the litigation as an "endless search for a solvent bystander."

1977: ATLA—From Trade Association to Lobbying Force. The Association of Trial Lawyers of America (now renamed the "American Association for Justice" (AAJ)) moved its headquarters from Boston to Washington, D.C. ATLA, which had acted primarily as a trade association for plaintiffs' lawyers became a lobbying force to support liability-enhancing policy and fight proposals that would reduce litigation. Its first victory was to kill a federal bill that substituted a no-fault system for automobile accidents. That legislation threatened the basic "bread-and-butter" of the plaintiffs' bar. AAJ is now one of the most powerful lobbying groups in Washington, posing an obstacle to federal civil justice reform and at the same time advancing its liability-expanding mission in both Congress and federal agencies.

Continuing: More Lawyers, More Lawsuits. In 1950, there were 221,605 active lawyers in the United States, 40 or about 1 lawyer for approximately every 700 persons in the country. By the late 1970s, it was Chief Justice Warren Burger who warned that "unless we devise substitutes for the courtroom processes—and do so quickly—we may be well on our way to a society overrun by hordes of lawyers, hungry as locusts, and brigades of judges in numbers never before contemplated." While the U.S. population has steadily grown, the number of lawyers is growing far faster. Today, there are six times as many active lawyers as in 1950—a total of 1.3 million. That is roughly 1 lawyer for every 250 people. It is no surprise that America is more litigious than ever.

II. THE RESPONSE: CIVIL JUSTICE REFORM

Newton's Third Law of Motion is that "for every action, there is an equal and opposite reaction." Civil justice reform is a reaction to the decades-long relaxation of legal standards. Calls for legal reform grow louder when excesses in liability adversely affect society, including making it difficult to find a doctor in some areas, more expensive to get certain goods and services, or difficult to manage a business or find a job. Legal reform is also motivated by meritless and frivolous claims that impose unwarranted costs, extraordinary awards, windfall attorney fees, and lawsuits that appear to serve the interests of lawyers rather than address an actual harm.

A. *State Tort Reform on the March*

Constraining Subjective Pain & Suffering Awards. Civil justice reform has moved at a steady pace at the state level. One of the earliest responses to the adverse effects of liability occurred in California in 1975, where, in response to a medical liability crisis, the state adopted the landmark Medical Injury Compensation Reform Act (MICRA). The law limits noneconomic damages to $250,000 in medical negligence cases. Following California's lead, many states have limited noneconomic damages in the healthcare liability context. Several states have a statutory limit that extends to all personal injury claims. These limits range from $250,000 to over $1 million.

Placing bounds on noneconomic damage awards does not affect an individual's ability to recover medical expenses, lost income, or other financial losses. A multi-million dollar award does nothing to ease the pain and suffering of a person who has suffered a tragic injury. Reasonable limits, however, are important for preserving access to critical medical specialists, keeping health insurance affordable and accessible, and reducing unnecessary defensive medicine. Statutory limits also promote more uniform treatment of individuals with comparable injuries, control outlier awards, and facilitate settlements. When California voters had an opportunity to significantly raise the statutory limit in 2014, two-thirds of the voters said "no," and the proposition failed in every county of the state.

Providing Procedural Safeguards and Proportionality in Punitive Damages. Another early reform required "clear and convincing" evidence of misconduct to support an award of punitive damages. This standard reflects the quasi-criminal nature of punitive damages and falls between the "preponderance of the evidence" standard of proof used to establish liability in an ordinary civil case and the "beyond a reasonable doubt" standard applied in criminal cases. States also limited the size of punitive damage awards, typically to the greater of a fixed dollar amount or a multiple of the plaintiff's compensatory damages. These laws embrace the due process principles of proportionality and notice. Florida may have been the first state to place a statutory limit on punitive damages in 1986. Today, approximately half of the states have such a law.

Turning Joint Liability into Fair Share Liability. A cascade of states has abandoned or sharply limited joint and several liability. Joint and several liability exposes any individual or business that is partially responsible for a plaintiff's harm to liability for paying the entire damage award. The unfairness of requiring a minimally at fault defendant to pay 100% of the plaintiff's damages came more into focus as states replaced the contributory negligence defense with comparative fault. Since juries could readily apportion fault between a plaintiff and a defendant, juries could do so among a plaintiff and multiple defendants. Today, only a handful of jurisdictions continue to apply full joint liability, and most of those are states that continue to recognize contributory negligence by the plaintiff as a defense to liability.

Holding Product Sellers Responsible Only for Their Actual Fault. States began to respond to court decisions that vastly expanded the liability of those who manufacture and sell products. In the late 1970s and early 1980s, many states enacted statutes of repose, which end liability exposure many years after a product is sold or its "useful safe life" expires, or after an improvement to real property is completed. Later, many states adopted "innocent seller" laws, limiting the liability of retailers, often small businesses, which had no part in designing an allegedly defective product or its warnings, to negligent conduct based on their own actions.

Removing Roadblocks to Appeal. Appeal bond reform, which took root in the 2000s, addresses the problem of civil defendants being blocked from the ability to appeal a judgment because they lack the financial wherewithal to post a bond covering an extraordinary judgment. Excessive appeal bond requirements may preclude even the largest corporations from being able to appeal an unjust verdict, forcing settlement regardless of the merits. States adopted reforms that placed reasonable limits on bond requirements so that defendants are better able to exercise their right to an appeal.

Other Reforms. Other popular and just reforms in recent years include providing an immediate appeal of class certification rulings, reducing excessive rates of interest on court judgments, allowing juries to consider compensation for an injury provided to the plaintiff from sources other than the defendant, requiring asbestos and silica claimants to present credible and objective medical evidence of physical impairment in order to bring or proceed with a claim, and requiring attorneys to file claims where their client lives or was injured. States also adopted, through legislative action and court rulings, stronger standards for admission of expert testimony intended to root out junk science.

While some states have gradually enacted reforms, others have adopted comprehensive bills or focused on civil justice reform during a particular session.

The Plaintiffs' Bar's Technique to Challenge Reform. The plaintiffs' bar has reacted by challenging the constitutionality of civil justice reforms in the courts under state constitutions, not the U.S. Constitution. State constitutions offer unique and ambiguous provisions, such as single subject rules or a right to "open courts." These provisions are open to broad interpretation. Plaintiffs' lawyers also invite state courts to read the right to jury trial, equal protection, or separation of powers under a state constitution differently than under the U.S. Constitution. Through these tactics, plaintiffs' lawyers have persuaded several state high courts to invalidate tort reforms. Since state courts base these decisions purely on state law, as the plaintiffs' bar fully appreciates, these cases are not subject to review by the U.S. Supreme Court. Many perceptive judges, however, have not let these provisions be unreasonably stretched. Most have upheld and respected the legislature's authority to establish the contours of civil claims, defenses, remedies, and penalties.

B. Federal Achievements

Civil justice reform largely occurs at the state level, but in some areas of national concern, Congress has passed targeted laws designed to address areas where expansive liability has adversely affected the public or hurt interstate commerce and thus the national economy. At the same time, Congress has also sought to encourage a wide range of socially beneficial activities.

For example, when liability concerns threatened public health by jeopardizing access to vaccines, Congress enacted the National Childhood Vaccine Injury Act of 1986. This law created a no-fault compensation program for childhood vaccine-injury victims funded by an excise tax on each dose of vaccine. During the 1990s, Congress also limited the liability of persons who donate food and grocery products to nonprofit organizations for distribution to needy individuals (Bill Emerson Good Samaritan Food Donation Act of 1996); volunteers who act on behalf of nonprofit organizations (Volunteer Protection Act of 1997); air carriers and qualified passengers who provide in-flight assistance during medical emergencies (Aviation Medical Assistance Act of 1998); and companies that provide raw materials and component parts needed for medical devices (Biomaterials Access Assurance Act of 1998). Congress also protected teachers and principals who follow school rules from lawsuits (Paul D. Coverdell Teacher Protection Act of 2001).

When lawsuits based on accidents involving very old planes threatened to destroy America's light aircraft industry, Congress enacted the General Aviation Revitalization Act of 1994. The law created an 18-year statute of repose. It successfully resulted in a revitalization of the piston-driven aircraft industry and helped create thousands of well-paying jobs.

In response to reports from families of those killed in the 1996 crashes of TWA Flight 800 off the coast of New York and ValuJet Flight 592 in the Florida Everglades, Congress passed the Aviation Disaster Family Assistance Act of 1996 to restrict lawyers from contacting family members immediately after a crash.

When a surge of securities-fraud lawsuits against public companies and accounting firms deterred companies from voluntarily disclosing information to their investors or shareholders and led to loss of productivity and jobs, Congress passed the Private Securities Litigation Reform Act in 1995 and the Securities Litigation Uniform Standards Act in 1998. These reforms established important procedural and substantive restrictions on securities lawsuits, including the creation of a heightened pleading standard that generally makes it more difficult for plaintiffs to file allegations of securities fraud without having solid information beforehand on which to base such a claim.

In the late 1990s and early 2000s, it became apparent that plaintiffs' lawyers were abusing the class action procedural tool. Class actions are intended to make it worthwhile to bring small claims stemming from a common practice or incident. Plaintiffs' lawyers, however, were stretching the class action device by bringing massive lawsuits on behalf of thousands of individuals nationwide based on different laws and different factual situations. They filed these lawsuits before friendly judges in local courts, such as Madison County, Illinois, which became known as "magnets" for class action litigation. Many of these cases were called "coupon class actions," because the plaintiffs' lawyers often took home millions of dollars in fees, while the consumers they purportedly represented received coupons from the targeted company as their recovery. Congress responded by passing the Class Action Fairness Act of 2005 (CAFA). CAFA's expansion of federal diversity jurisdiction moved class actions of national importance from state to federal court—and the more rigorous application of class-certification standards that exists in most federal courts.

III. TODAY'S LEGAL REFORM PRIORITIES

While states such as Tennessee and Wisconsin (2011), South Carolina (2012), Oklahoma (2013), and West Virginia (2015) continue to make progress in enacting the types of laws above, today's civil justice reforms are largely not the reforms of the 1980s. They respond to new areas of excess and abuse in the liability system. Below are examples of priorities on the legal reform agenda both at the federal and state level.

Transparency in state retention of lawyers on a contingency-fee basis. Plaintiffs' lawyers are increasingly reaching out to state attorneys general and other state and local officials to offer their services. In these cases, private attorneys often develop the innovative theories of liability, approach AGs, and then litigate the state's enforcement action in exchange for a contingency fee. Placing the government's power to investigate business and bring enforcement actions in private individuals whose compensation increases based on the amount of damages or fines imposed raises serious ethical and constitutional concerns. The history of AGs hiring lawyers and firms that heavily contribute to their campaigns through no-bid contracts contributes to a "pay-to-play" culture. Such arrangements hurt the public, since a significant portion of the recovery that would have otherwise gone to the state had the government pursued the action with its own attorneys, goes to a few private lawyers. For these reasons scholarship, think tank papers, reports, congressional testimony, and the mainstream media have widely criticized state hiring of outside counsel on a contingency-fee basis.

To address concern with state retention of private attorneys on a contingency-fee basis, since 2010, fifteen state legislatures have adopted safeguards providing for transparency in government hiring and payment of outside counsel, and adopting a sliding scale for fee awards. Some state laws go further to protect the legislature's appropriation authority by requiring the AG to obtain legislative approval before retaining an attorney on a contingency-fee basis.

Asbestos trust transparency. As a result of asbestos-related bankruptcies, trusts collectively hold over $30 billion to pay for harms caused by former insulation defendants. The asbestos litigation has morphed into a two-tiered system of bankruptcy trust claims and tort claims against still-solvent defendants. The lack of transparency between these two systems has led to abuse. For example, in a January 2014 ruling involving Garlock Sealing Technologies, LLC, a federal bankruptcy judge described how Garlock became a target defendant after asbestos plaintiffs' lawyers bankrupted the primary historical insulation defendants. According to the federal judge, Garlock's participation in the tort system became "infected by the manipulation of exposure evidence by plaintiffs and their lawyers." Evidence that Garlock needed to attribute plaintiffs' injuries to the insulation companies' products "disappeared." The judge said this "occurrence was a result of the effort by some plaintiffs and their lawyers to withhold evidence of exposure to other asbestos products and to delay filing claims against bankrupt defendants' asbestos trusts until after obtaining recoveries from Garlock (and other viable defendants)."

Legislatures are responding to this gamesmanship by providing defendants with greater access to asbestos bankruptcy trust claim submissions by plaintiffs. These materials contain important exposure history information, giving tort defendants a tool to identify fraudulent or exaggerated exposure claims, and to establish that trust-related exposures were partly or entirely responsible for the plaintiff's harm.

Third-party litigation funding. Third parties have increasingly invested money into litigation. This lending comes in two forms: (1) companies that promise quick cash to consumers while they await their day in court or payment of a settlement; and (2) investment firms that infuse money into mass tort and other large-scale cases, contributing not only to legal costs, but also plaintiff recruitment and other litigation advertising costs, in return for a portion of any recovery. Both types of arrangements have negative consequences.

The first variant takes advantage of the most vulnerable people, often subjecting them to exorbitant interest rates and fees that may leave them with little, if any, recovery after taking a relatively small loan. Rates charged by lenders often exceed 100% annually, according to a review by the New York Times and the Center for Public Integrity. Some states are taking action by limiting interest rates, requiring disclosure of information to consumers, and adopting other safeguards.

The second variant can prolong questionable litigation, inject a third party with its own financial interests into litigation-related decisions, and pose an obstacle to settlement. At minimum, requiring disclosure of third-party investments in litigation would begin to address the inherent risks of these arrangements.

Class action abuse. While CAFA has helped provide a neutral federal forum for multi-state class actions and eliminated "coupon" recovery for consumers in federal courts, new abuses have emerged. Lawyers often sue on behalf of classes so broad that they include people who have experienced no injury—they had no problem with the product at issue, were not influenced by labeling or an advertisement that lawyers claim was misleading, or otherwise experienced no financial loss from the allegedly improper practice at issue. These "no injury" claims are lucrative for the lawyers who bring them, often with the aid of hired-gun experts that develop creative theories of damages as a substitute for an actual loss. But consumers, who typically are offered the opportunity to file paperwork for a nominal sum, view them as worthless.

A recent U.S. Supreme Court ruling reaffirming that Article III standing requires all private plaintiffs to allege a concrete injury in fact may curb class actions that allege a mere technical statutory violation that caused no real harm. States are tightening consumer and other laws to require private plaintiffs who seek monetary damages to show an actual injury. Congress is also considering legislation that would instruct federal courts not to certify class actions where the class includes individuals who have not experienced an injury.

Another area of concern is the archaic Telephone Consumer Protection Act (TCPA), a federal law that has given rise to a cottage industry for lawyers and serial plaintiffs who take advantage of the statute's uncapped $500 statutory damage provision. TCPA filings went from 14 in 2007 to 3,710 in 2015. Under this law, a business that intends to communicate with its customers or employees through a phone, fax, or text message, but inadvertently reach others, is subject to millions of dollars in liability. As Professor Adonis Hoffman, a former FCC lawyer, has observed, when the average consumer receives $4.12 in a settlement and lawyers receive an average of $2.4 million, "[s]omething is wrong with this picture." While the FCC could have clarified the law to reduce litigation, it instead issued a ruling in 2015 that observers expect to be a gold mine for plaintiffs' lawyers.

Congress should update the antiquated law and reduce the opportunity for abuse. It can do so through such measures as an aggregate cap on statutory damages recoverable in class actions, a defense for calls placed to reassigned numbers, and carefully considering how the TCPA applies to technology that did not exist when Congress enacted the law, such as text messaging.

Misleading lawsuit advertising. Americans are increasingly bombarded on television and the internet with advertising urging them to file lawsuits. A recent analysis found that lawsuit advertising on television rose 68% from $531 million in 2008 to a projected $892 million in 2015. Such aggressive recruitment of clients leads to many claims that are meritless. Some may even be fraudulent. Individuals and firms known as "lead generators" use call-centers, some located abroad, to find, trade, bundle, and sell potential mass tort claims—with the goal of generating so many claims that businesses feel compelled to settle.

These advertisements not only generate questionable litigation, but growing evidence suggests that they may adversely affect public health. Scientifically unsupported or exaggerated claims that drugs or medical devices cause serious injury or death may frighten people, leading them to not seek treatment that would improve their lives. Even worse, misleading advertising could lead patients to stop taking a prescribed drug without consulting their doctors, posing a risk of harm. The FDA, FTC, and state officials should consider taking action to stop deceptive lawsuit advertising.

Fraudulent joinder. Plaintiffs' lawyers frequently drag in an individual or local business as additional defendants in a case targeting an out-of-state business. Doing so destroys "complete diversity," thwarting the ability of the out-of-state business to have its case decided in a neutral federal court. Examples include local store managers, salespeople, retailers, distributors, pharmacies, claims adjusters, and small businesses that, under applicable state law, are not legally responsible for an injury. Once the case is remanded to a state court viewed favorable to a plaintiff, the local defendant is typically dropped from the case or not pursued. The doctrine of fraudulent joinder allows federal courts to retain jurisdiction when the plaintiff has no viable claim against the local defendant. The standard for finding fraudulent joinder, however, it remarkably high, requiring remand to state court if the plaintiff has even a "glimmer of hope," 104 and it is inconsistently applied.

Proposed federal legislation would provide a uniform approach to deciding fraudulent joinder, eliminating confusion and unnecessary litigation. It will also adopt a more realistic and fair assessment of whether a plaintiff has stated a viable claim against a local defendant and intends to pursue a judgment against that person.

"Phantom damages." Plaintiffs' lawyers argue in personal injury cases that their clients should receive damages for medical expenses for the amount billed by their healthcare providers, even when providers accepted a substantially lower amount as payment in full. It has become common for billed rates to be three to four times higher than the amounts paid by patients or their insurers (including private insurers, Medicare, or Medicaid) due to negotiated rates, discounts, and write-offs. This difference, the amount that no one ever paid but is sought in personal injury litigation, is sometimes referred to as "phantom damages."

As a result, defendants pay significantly inflated judgments and settlements to reimburse a plaintiff for nonexistent medical expenses. Such damages serve no compensatory purpose. These phantom damages can unjustly place costs on small businesses and nonprofits that are sued for common accidents such as slip-and-falls. States have responded by enacting legislation providing that only amounts actually paid for medical bills, not the billed rates, are admissible at trial. Some state courts have interpreted the collateral source rule to reach the same result.

Other civil justice priorities include providing a remedy to those who are harmed by frivolous claims and defenses, and facilitating consistency between regulatory obligations and the liability system. In addition, civil justice reform advocates will continue to respond to attempts to restrict alternatives to litigation, misuse public nuisance law to impose liability on entire industries when legal activities have societal costs, or impose excessive liability on companies that experience a data breach.

CONCLUSION

Civil justice reform should not be viewed through a trial-lawyer prism. It does not create unreasonable barriers to recovery. To the contrary, civil justice reform is designed to preserve legitimate claims while putting a damper on excesses in the system. As this Essay shows, those excesses are decades in the making.

When aspects of the civil justice system become imbalanced, society experiences adverse effects. Businesses cannot expand and grow. Doctors face challenges when practicing medicine. Innocent people are saddled with unrecoverable defense costs. Ridiculous lawsuits and extraordinary awards take a toll on the public's faith in the judicial system.

When litigation shifts from helping people to primarily benefiting attorneys, correction is needed. Civil justice reform makes modest changes to address patterns of abuse and unevenness in the law. It does so while ensuring that people receive fair recovery from those who are responsible, that punishment for misconduct is consistent principles of due process, and that the civil justice system treats all parties fairly.

––––––––––

D. CAPS AND OTHER TORT REFORMS DISPUTES

LEE HARRIS AND JENNIFER LONGO, FLEXIBLE TORT REFORM[15]

Introduction

Tort reform is controversial, to put it tamely. But, at least it is easy to understand. In this Article, we refer to some doctors, insurers, and conservatives as the "reformers." They believe the current tort system is in an impoverished state, with increasing insurance costs for providers, partly due to the high costs of medical malpractice suits. The increasing costs are straining the system, they posit, by pressuring doctors out of some practice areas and increasing their costs of providing care. Consequently, the reformers push for state and federal legislative measures that would limit the liability of providers. Others, who throughout this Article we shall call the "Expanders," push back. Some trial lawyers, academics, patient advocates, and generally left-leaning interest groups argue that such measures do not work. At bottom, they not only want to derail the reformers' efforts to limit provider liability, but they also have pitched some changes of their own. Namely, the Expanders, at least some of them, seem to prefer to expand liability in cases of alleged medical malpractice. For instance, some of them have promoted a no-fault compensation system in which victims of certain injuries are always compensated.

These arguments usually play out in the rough-and-tumble political atmosphere, not in the pages of law reviews. The American Medical Association (AMA), the primary policy interest group representing doctors and other providers, appears to be on the hunt. The group can be seen asserting that the country faces a "crisis" if reforms are not approved widely and swiftly. Their ominous findings allege the skyrocketing litigation costs have caused at least twenty-one states to face a medical malpractice crisis due to increased insurance premiums. Meanwhile, we think of the American Association for Justice (AAJ), which lobbies for the trial lawyers, as the wily prey. Members of the AAJ attempt to evade the AMA's rhetoric about a "crisis" and fire back their own claims. According to them, litigation costs are hardly to blame for soaring premiums. Even in cases in which tort reform measures are passed, insurance companies cannot be trusted to pass along savings to their insured. Further, they argue that insurance premiums are a function of investment decisions by insurance companies. When insurance companies wisely invest the premiums they receive in the market, these companies have little pressure to raise premiums to meet earnings objectives. However, when the insurers' investment decisions turn out poorly, insurers frequently increase premiums to make up earnings shortfalls. In this view, declines

---

[15]   29 HAMLINE JOURNAL OF PUBLIC LAW AND POLICY 61 (2007).

in investment returns because of a floundering economy are among the main reasons insurance companies raise premiums. In short, "It's the economy, stupid," an argument the Expanders have lobbed back.

In the policy war, the reformers are winning in the sense that many state legislatures are listening and agreeing. Although federal reform measures have been elusive, the reformers have convinced the vast majority of state legislatures to approve legislation that directly affects providers, plaintiffs, and plaintiff's lawyers. A majority of states, for instance, have passed damage "caps," which limit the amount to which providers may be liable in certain damage categories. Also, plaintiffs have seen some of their traditional rights to sue limited by still other tort reform measures. For example, many state legislatures have approved changes to the procedure for filing a medical malpractice lawsuit, which have the effect of making it more difficult for plaintiffs to get their proverbial day in court. These reform measures include devices like requiring plaintiffs to participate in alternative dispute resolution prior to filing suit. Last, through still other tort reform measures, state legislatures have regulated the activity of lawyers who represent plaintiffs in medical malpractice lawsuits. State legislation regulating attorney fee arrangements has made the practice of representing plaintiffs in medical malpractice less lucrative.

Thus, the conduct of several of the most relevant actors—providers, plaintiffs, and plaintiffs' lawyers—has been regulated by state tort reform efforts. The objectives to be served by such efforts are varied. Some state legislative officials likely thought tort reforms limiting the amount that one can recover against a provider would stabilize malpractice insurance premiums. Whether the initial objectives of tort reform measures were the right ones is something that has been argued ad nauseam and will likely continue to be argued *ad infintium*.

This paper takes a different tack. Whether the initial impulse of states in passing many of these reforms was grounded in reality or simply rhetoric is, in some ways, beside the point. If tort reform measures, such as those mentioned, are continued to be supported by state legislatures, a discussion about how such measures might be better designed is in order. Many of the reform measures that state legislatures have approved might be improved. Done right, tort reform measures, like any regulatory effort, can accomplish multiple objectives. For instance, state legislatures considering some of the most popular measures might consider how such measures may be modified to promote better treatment for patients and improve healthcare quality. The next three parts discuss how some of the most popular tort reform measures enacted by state legislatures might be changed in order to create new incentives for improving healthcare quality.

1. Providers

Some of the tort reform measures operate expressly to insulate providers from liability in medical malpractice lawsuits. In this regard, state legislatures around the country have passed so-called medical liability caps, which limit provider liability in medical malpractice lawsuits. These caps bar recoveries in such suits over a prescribed amount for pain, suffering, or other non-economic losses.

As mentioned, medical liability caps usually allow for unlimited recovery on economic damages (*e.g.*, lost earnings and medical expenses) and place a limit or cap on non-economic damages (*e.g.* pain & suffering, disfigurement, and loss of consortium). Reformers maintain that caps reduce medical malpractice costs, expand access to healthcare, and improve the quality of care. Additionally, reform advocates maintain caps will head-off outsized jury awards. Furthermore, through predictability and limits, reform advocates argue that caps treat similarly-situated plaintiffs equitably. That is, proponents of tort reform note that without caps, non-economic damage awards are purely subjective, with the most well-educated, sympathetic, attractive plaintiff recovering more than others.

On the other hand, Expanders have countered that such a cap would encourage physician misconduct. In this light, medical malpractice lawsuits with unlimited recovery work to police misconduct. Furthermore, damage caps produce their own inequity. In effect, caps leave the injured bearing the losses above the cap amount, while the injurer avoids those same losses. Related to this last point, damage caps might change the composition of medical malpractice liability cases, as plaintiffs' lawyers would screen out plaintiffs likely to generate high non-economic damages but little in terms of economic damages.

More than half the states have adopted some sort of cap on damages for medical malpractice claims. California set the first damage cap with its Medical Injury Compensation Reform Act of 1975 (MICRA). MICRA capped non-economic damages at $250,000. While a number of states have adopted some form of damage cap, not all limit the cap to non-economic damages at $250,000. Some states, including New Mexico and Nebraska, go further and set a cap on total damages.

With a majority of states already adopting some sort of cap, it appears that the desirability of this reform measures (at least for now) has been decided politically. Consequently, we put to one side our arguments about whether states should adopt this type of reform, since we presume some states will continue to rely on caps. Instead, we think a more important inquiry is whether (and how) this reform measure might be improved. If designed flexibly, this reform can do more than simply insulate providers from liability. Caps might also improve healthcare quality. For instance, states inclined to approve caps, might also take an opportunity to use damages caps to create a new incentive for providers to make good treatment choices.

To accomplish this, state legislatures would have to look to ways to make cap legislation more flexible—that is, responsive to swings in healthcare quality. For instance, damages cap legislation could be hinged with provider performance. Thus, only top-performing providers would have the benefit of cap protection in the case of medical malpractice suits. Interestingly, state legislatures already have shown at least some penchant for making damages cap legislation more flexible. In some cases, for example, states have passed damages caps legislation that is responsive to swings in the economy. 36 In fact, one of the early criticisms of these liability caps is that state legislatures do not peg the cap to inflation. As a result, some states passed liability caps that automatically adjust for inflation.

In a similar vein, such statutes might also "adjust" for performance. In a previous paper, Lee Harris argues, for instance, that only high-quality providers who have reached a certain level of compliance with state quality measures ought to be eligible for a medical liability cap. Specifically in that piece, Harris argues that hospitals should be given the benefit of a medical liability cap, but only if they could show that they reached a certain level of quality. Hospitals that reach a certain benchmark would be eligible; others would not. Thus, hospitals that are sued in a medical malpractice liability would be subject to unlimited damages, unless such hospital could show high quality based on state and federal measures. Quality might be measured initially based on data that the vast majority of hospital providers already collect as part of their participation in the Medicaid and Medicare programs, along with the potential for legislatures to include additional measures devised at the state level. A hospital that, say, rarely follows Medicaid-endorsed clinical guidelines for certain treatments would not be eligible for insulation from a liability cap. This type of flexible regulation would give providers, like hospitals, a new incentive to improve treatment.

Additionally, state legislatures have even more flexibility to create a medical liability cap that takes into account provider quality. For instance, although this is not discussed in the current literature, the state might even make eligibility for medical liability contingent on a relative standard. In this view, good providers would still be rewarded with cap eligibility. However, providers would not be eligible simply because they reached some threshold level of quality. They would have to compete for eligibility against other providers. Thus, establishing the very top could be based on a comparative analysis of provider performance. The state could approve a cap only for, say, the top twenty-five percent or even top ten percent of top-performing providers. . . .

. . . . Reformers have argued that the regulation of plaintiff's lawyers might be looked at in order to solve the medical liability crisis. Among other reforms that might affect lawyer behavior, state legislatures have considered limits on attorney fees, which would make medical malpractice liability cases less appealing to the plaintiff's bar. However, as with medical liability caps, it seems that a wiser state legislature would attempt to tie these reform efforts to indicators of quality. First, we will say a word about how this tort reform measure currently works. Next, we shall move to how this reform might be improved. In a contingency fee arrangement, which represents a significant share of medical malpractice litigation, the plaintiff's attorney assumes the risk of non-recovery. The attorney or firm advances all costs for discovery, expert witnesses, and other expenses. More substantially, the attorney collects no upfront fee for her time and has no retainer of any note to draw down. As a result of this assumption of risk, a personal injury lawyer typically takes thirty-three to forty percent of any award or settlement.

Simply put, some reformers want to limit the amount a lawyer could recover in these cases. Reformers argue that in a contingency fee system, the attorneys pocket a significant share of the award and do not leave their clients, the injured patient, with enough money for their medical expenses. Further, they argue that reforms to the contingency-fee system would make it more difficult for attorneys to finance non-meritorious cases and would enable more of the jury award to directly benefit the injured patient. However, Expanders counter that a contingency fee, by itself, operates as disincentive for taking on non-meritorious cases. That is, not only would it be unethical for lawyers to take on obviously frivolous cases, it would also be an unprofitable strategy. Medical malpractice cases are time-consuming and expensive, and an attorney would be unwise to front all the expenses for a case without reasonably sufficient legal support (or settlement value). Furthermore, as it stands right now the overall cost of a plaintiff's attorney fees is similar to that of a defendant's attorney fees. Expanders posit it would be inequitable to limit the plaintiff's attorney fees and not the defendant's.

In the area of contingency fee legislation, a preliminary analysis indicates, again, that reformers have been successful in a significant number of the states. Approximately twenty-three states have passed contingency fee reform while others have either no limit or only allow courts to review the fees. States vary in the amount they restrict attorney fees. California, for example, sets reasonable limits on a sliding scale. Some states, like Utah and Tennessee, set an absolute limit of one-third on total amount recovered. Oklahoma adopted a more generous absolute contingency fee reform: An attorney's share cannot exceed fifty percent of any award.

Significantly, many state legislatures working on this reform have already taken an eye to flexibility. For instance, one of the most common limits would be to restrict the contingent fee in relatively high award cases. Under these reforms, the contingency fee and the ultimate award (or settlement) would bear an inverse relationship; the higher the award, the lower the permitted contingency recoverable by the attorney (or her firm). For instance, consider Nevada's statutory limit on contingency fees, which sets its limits on a sliding scale:

An attorney shall not contract for or collect a fee contingent on the amount of recovery for representing a person seeking damages in connection with an action for injury or death against a provider of health care based upon professional negligence in excess of: (a) Forty percent of the first $50,000 recovered; (b) Thirty-three and one-third percent of the next $50,000 recovered; (c) Twenty-five percent of the next $500,000 recovered; and (d) Fifteen percent of the amount of recovery that exceeds $600,000.

Thus, in Nevada, lawyers representing plaintiffs in medical malpractice cases face a wide range of limits on their fees, from a high of forty percent of their client's recovery to a low of fifteen percent of such recovery. But, while the Nevada statute (and others like it) is flexible, it appears to produce incentives cutting in the wrong direction. In Nevada (and other states), top-performing attorneys are "rewarded" with lower effective fees. Thus, ironically, the Nevada statute (and others like it) appears to tie recovery limits to performance—that is, the performance of the attorney relationship is exactly the opposite of what one would expect.

If state legislatures want to consider limiting contingency fees, we would argue that they should consider designing a limit that pays attention to performance and perhaps creates an incentive for lawyers to play a new role in policing provider misconduct. Thus, the state might provide that attorney fee arrangements greater than one-third are prohibited in cases of high-quality providers. Under this arrangement, other providers would not be able to quibble over the fee arrangement between the attorney and the injured client. Alternatively, state legislatures should pass tort reform measures with an eye toward making it more lucrative for attorneys to sue bad providers. In other areas, state legislatures have attempted to encourage attorneys to take certain types of otherwise low-value cases by enhancing the possible recoveries. In landlord-tenant cases, in particular, a successful claimant can frequently receive enhanced (three times their usual) damages for specific misconduct on the part of the landlord. Similarly, state legislatures may attempt to encourage attorneys to take on low-quality providers (*i.e.*, those unable to meet state quality guidelines) by creating a mechanism for enhanced penalties if the suits are successful.

Conclusion

State legislatures have approved a wide range of tort reform measures directly affecting each of the parties (providers, plaintiffs, and their attorneys) in a medical malpractice action. The vast majority of states have approved medical liability caps, which serve to insulate providers from several types of large damage awards. Additionally, some states have approved limits on contingency fee cases, which reduce the potential profits that plaintiffs' attorneys can expect to generate from such suits. Still other reforms have gone so far as to limit a plaintiff's ability to have her day in court. In each of these regards, one could argue about whether the reforms are desirable in the first place. Regardless, as long as such reforms continue to have political appeal, state legislatures (and commentators) should begin to consider how such reforms might be used to improve the treatment of future patients. Significantly, by tying the various tort reform measures to quality, state legislatures could create new incentives for improving healthcare.

LEE HARRIS, TORT REFORM AS A CARROT-AND-STICK[16]

. . . .

II. A Primer on "Tort Reform"

. . . .

A. Scope of Medical Error

Several studies have found that a significant share of patients do not receive the best treatment and are injured by medical error. For instance, several accounts suggest that patients routinely receive care at odds with the medical literature or clinical guidelines. One report suggests that two out of five chronically ill patients receive care inconsistent with medical literature. Another study shows that close to one in five surgical patients experiences a serious error while receiving care. Indeed the numbers may be even worse for patients generally. One fifteen-year observational study reports that 45.8% of patients experience at least some error while receiving medical treatment. Even worse, researchers have found that many patients suffer serious injury or die from misguided care and medical error. A Harvard University study found that patients had a 4% chance of being injured by their providers. Further, the Institute of Medicine, a nonprofit research organization, has reported that between 44,000 and 98,000 people die annually in hospitals from preventable medical error.

Many of the causes of medical error go uncorrected and unnoticed. In particular, most commentators agree that system-level problems also seem to play a role in medical error and injury, but are too rarely remedied. Some

---

[16]   46 HARVARD JOURNAL ON LEGISLATION 163, 168 *et. seq.* (2009).

injuries might be prevented, for example, by simply maintaining sufficient supply of antibiotics, like penicillin, near a patient's bedside. Other errors are caused by faulty equipment, which could be readily replaced. One study of hospitals' responses to error provides that hospitals respond in a way that attempts to correct for future errors in only 1% of error cases. As the Institute of Medicine finds, errors in treatment are caused by things like poor hospital planning: "Errors are caused by faulty systems, processes, and conditions that lead people to make mistakes or fail to prevent them. For example, stocking patient-care units in hospitals with certain full-strength drugs, even though they are toxic unless diluted, has resulted in deadly mistakes."

Systemic errors are particularly disquieting because they are likely to be repeated with future patients so long as the poorly designed system remains intact. Thus, medical error is relatively widespread, suggesting that under the current system hospitals have insufficient incentives to correct such errors. . . .

B.   Proposals for Reform

As can be expected given the widespread incidence of medical error, several legal academics have previously proposed reforms to the current medical malpractice system. Many of these proposals for reforming liability for medical malpractice focus on expanding liability. One of the underlying principles here is that if healthcare providers face expanded liability for their conduct, it may create incentives for those same actors to take due precautions. For instance, Kenneth Abraham and Paul Weiler, among others, have advocated entity liability for hospitals on the belief that hospitals will police misconduct if they could be liable for medical error. Michelle Mello and Troyen Brennan have gone even further and argued for entity liability for hospitals and a no-fault compensation scheme. Under such proposals, a specifically enumerated class of claims would automatically be compensated regardless of proof of fault. Another line of reasoning, articulated recently by New York University professors Jennifer Arlen and W. Bentley MacLeod, argues that third-party insurers, such as managed care organizations ("MCOs"), should have liability for medical malpractice. In this view, managed care organizations increasingly play an active role in the selected treatment of patients. Through utilization review, which MCOs use to rein in medical costs, they make a determination whether a treatment is medically justified. In Arlen and MacLeod's view, MCOs should be liable if their treatment choice leads to injury. Further, MCOs should be liable for the failures in care among their affiliated physicians. Thus, in one form or another, many legal commentators on tort reforms advocate expanding liability.

C.   Politics of Reform

Legal academics are not the only group supportive of expanding liability in the case of medical malpractice. For instance, other important constituencies—patient-victims of medical malpractice and trial lawyers—are also in favor of some expansions of liability. However, the politics of tort reform currently cut in exactly the opposite direction. The politics of tort reform suggest that legislators, particularly on the state level, are more likely to restrict liability on providers, rather than endorse any of the aforementioned proposals.

Specifically, as malpractice insurance premiums rose in the last quarter century, physicians protested against the tort system and demanded medical malpractice reform in the form of restrictions on liability. At the height of their activism, physicians threatened work stoppages across the country. By some indications, voters, legislators, and some mainstream publications identified with the perceived plight of doctors. At the end of the 1980s, for instance, Time ran a cover story which was sympathetic to physicians facing increasingly high malpractice premiums. According to Time, rising premiums were a "national crisis" affecting both physicians and patients:

> Given the litigious nature of American society these days, just about any kind of business, profession or government agency is likely to become the target of a suit alleging malpractice or negligence resulting in personal injury. That makes liability insurance, the kind that pays off on such claims, just about as vital as oil in keeping the economy functioning. But in the past two years, liability insurance has become the kind of resource that oil was in the 1970s: prohibitively expensive, when it can be bought at all.

More recently, a Gallup poll suggests that most Americans support limits on the amount a claimant can recover in a medical liability lawsuit. For instance, one commentator aptly encapsulates the political state of reform:

> The emotional trauma of having to defend against what often turn out to be misguided malpractice claims, together with the financial trauma of occasional jumps in their malpractice premiums, periodically sends doctors to state capitals—and now the nation's capital—for relief. Because both legislators and voters can more readily empathize with the plight of their family doctor than, for example, drug manufacturers or asbestos producers, such statutory relief has regularly been forthcoming. [Paul C. Weiler, *The Case for No-Fault Medical Liability,* 52 MD. L. REV. 908, 910 (1993)]

Healthcare providers continue their political advocacy for tort reform, forming coalitions, lobbying, and writing letters to major media outlets. In

Texas, as one commentator recently noted, some agitators for tort reform, in order to boost Republican votes, sent out a mailer that suggested that 86% of lawsuits for medical malpractice were frivolous. In some sense, even liberal advocacy groups have suggested measures aimed at reducing provider exposure, partly perhaps as a result of public opinion. For instance, the Trial Lawyers Association, a typically Democratic group, has proposed medical malpractice reform measures that will likely reduce the number of medical malpractice suits that providers face. Consequently, despite pitches from academics and some other groups for expanding liability, much of the political rhetoric and legislative reform in the area of medical malpractice has focused on reducing liability for health care providers.

In this regard, the reform most widely endorsed by legislators is a limit on damages that a plaintiff or his or her family can recover in a medical malpractice suit. Beginning with California's Medical Injury Compensation Reform Act of 1975, 53 thirty-nine states have replaced the common law rule and passed some form of liability limit under the guise of general tort reform, as shown in Tables 1 and 2. Twenty-eight states have capped awards for punitive damages, twenty-eight states have capped awards for non-economic damages, and sixteen states have approved limits on both. Some states have even extended caps on damages beyond medical malpractice to cover all civil tort cases.

State liability limits on recovery in malpractice cases come in many guises with varying caps. 56 For instance, California and Georgia have limits on recovery of non-economic damages and punitive damages set at $250,000. Some states, like Colorado, Idaho, and Arkansas, fix a maximum dollar amount, but set it to increase with inflation. Some limit the ratio of punitive damages to actual damages or relate permissible recovery to the defendant's profit margin or wealth. For instance, in Mississippi, a plaintiff's recovery for punitive damages can be as much as $20 million if the defendant's net worth is over $1 billion, but recovery cannot be more than $5 million if the defendant's net worth is less than $100 million.

[Tables omitted]

D.   Against Today's Tort Reform

Tort reform, as currently designed, is bad policy for several reasons. Since many of these areas have had sufficient treatment elsewhere in the literature, this Part takes the liberty of moving lightly and briskly.

1.   Physician Conduct

Efforts at general tort reform are inadequate because they fail to take seriously the prospect of physician misconduct. The potential of an unlimited or "uncapped" damage award deters misconduct from healthcare providers.

Medical malpractice lawsuits with unlimited recovery are a way of policing misconduct and weeding out bad doctors, which neither insurance companies nor physician organizations track satisfactorily. Unlike other forms of insurance, such as auto insurance, past performance does not affect how much medical liability insurance a private physician pays. Bad doctors are not penalized by insurance companies, which do not normally take into account previous performance when assessing medical malpractice insurance rates. Instead, insurance companies usually charge premiums based on general factors like physician specialty. Thus, insurance companies largely do not account for the competence, skill, and quality of medical services provided by the physician.

At the same time, advocates of unlimited recovery mention that state disciplinary boards may also insufficiently police the conduct of healthcare providers. For instance, according to one report, more than 35,000 doctors had more than one medical malpractice payout between 1990 and 2002. Of those, only 7.6% were disciplined by their respective state disciplinary board. According to this same data, state boards disciplined less than 17% of doctors with five or more medical malpractice payouts. Since these doctors—doctors likely to commit multiple acts of malpractice—do not necessarily face higher insurance premiums or sanction by peer organizations when they demonstrate incompetence, they may be under-deterred.

2.   Allocation of Losses

General tort reforms are poorly designed because they tilt the scales, placing undue and unwanted burdens on the injured. Current tort reform limits on provider liability are unfair because they, in effect, transfer losses from the deserving to the undeserving. The problem with liability caps is that they often operate to prevent full recovery among the parties that are in need of compensation, the recently injured, while permitting the negligent to partially escape liability. Furthermore, according to some commentators, caps on liability, like non-economic damage caps, disproportionately penalize members of vulnerable groups, such as women, children, and minorities, all of whom are more likely to realize comparatively substantial non-economic loss. Lucinda Finley argues that a cap on non-economic damages has a particularly harsh effect on women who experience unique harm from injuries that impair fertility, sexual function, continence and ability to reproduce, but might not necessarily suffer from lost wages or other traditional economic harm. A similar argument is that an overreliance on work-life expectancy to calculate economic damages, and exclusion of non-economic damages under cap legislation, might have an adverse impact on minorities and women who might have, on average, shorter work-life expectancy. Thus, while the losses of cap legislation accrue to the injured, the gains from damage caps accrue to the most negligent physicians. Perversely, doctors who cause the worst injuries are the ones who benefit from a damage cap. . . .

4. Medical Malpractice Costs

General tort reforms are unlikely to significantly moderate the cost of healthcare, though this claim has been strongly disputed. Opponents of liability caps disbelieve the presupposed relationship between liability caps and medical malpractice insurance premiums. Rather, in their view, insurance premiums are the upshot of investment decisions of insurers. They also point out that this supposed connection between insurance premiums and lawsuits is weak because very few medical malpractice lawsuits actually result in a decision that would implicate a liability cap.

One rebuttal to the assumed relationship between liability caps and medical malpractice insurance premiums attempts to show that healthcare premiums are primarily affected by insurance companies' ability to manage their cash reserves. The consumer group Americans for Insurance Reform argues that in times of rising interest rates insurance companies are able to use their premiums to realize high investment returns. In times of declining interest rates, the opposite is true. Along the same line, opponents of caps would argue that the increases in insurance premiums are a result not just of the economic environment, but also of the investment decisions of insurance companies. They would accuse these companies of too often mismanaging their money and attempting to raise premiums to make up for investment losses.

Critics of caps also argue that the supposed relationship between jury awards and malpractice insurance premiums is a canard, since many medical malpractice cases settle and few go to trial. They argue that few trials for medical malpractice go to verdict, even fewer result in a plaintiff's verdict, and only a tiny minority of those result in a plaintiff's verdict large enough to implicate the cap. Thus, these critics posit, the universe of cases that might actually be subject to a liability cap is microscopic. One study found that from 1985 to 1999, fewer than 7% of medical malpractice claims went to verdict and only 1.3% produced verdicts for the plaintiff. Another study finds that only about one in eight patients injured by negligence files a claim. The study concludes that the problem is "not too many claims, but, if anything, too few claims." Of those plaintiff/claimants who actually recover from a malpractice insurer, most do not recover an amount large enough to be reduced by a liability cap. Consequently, opponents of caps would argue that there is little relationship between medical malpractice liability caps and medical malpractice insurance premiums.

Nevertheless, opponents of tort reform are unsuccessfully fighting a two-front war. On one front, they must present the empirical case that major medical malpractice judgments are so few in number as not to make a difference for the insured. Although beyond the scope of this article, the data on this point appears mixed. However, on the other, they must also overcome the belief among many, whether empirically based or not, that medical malpractice awards are bankrupting providers and playing a role in swelling insurance premiums. Even if the opponents of caps are right and the effects of medial malpractice cases on the insured are limited, opponents still must deal with the political appeal of tort reform.

E.   [Section] Summary

To conclude, although the number of medical errors has been significant, it has not stemmed the demand for tort reform. Most reform efforts to date have aimed to reduce provider liability for medical malpractice, usually in the form of liability limits enacted by state legislatures. Although these efforts contrast noticeably with the types of reform advocated by several notable legal scholars on the subject—many of whom have suggested expanding liability on providers—they remain wildly popular among legislators. As a consequence, it appears that for any reform to have a chance of mobilizing a significant constituency politically, it likely must include some limitation or cap on recovery against healthcare providers.

The idea of creating a tort reform rule based on provider performance has the advantage, therefore, of acknowledging the political reality that liability caps have tremendous appeal and that any proposal that entirely abandon limits on liability would likely be politically unfeasible. This Article proposes instead that state legislatures should continue to embrace liability caps for providers, along with other tort reforms, but also tweak their cap rules to take into account provider performance. In this view, only providers with solid track records of high-quality performance would be eligible for the benefit of a limit on liability.

. . . .

[Article] Conclusion

The problem in the current tort reform debate is this: the most prominent reform—general limits on liability—does not work. Such limits fail to reward good behavior or punish misconduct. As a result, general liability limits help protect providers who perform well, but also protect providers prone to incompetence. Yet previous reform-minded commentators have failed to offer a solution that both creates better incentives to behave well and recognizes the political appeal of limits on damages. As an alternative, this Article argues that state legislatures should tie liability limits to conduct and incentivize providers to pursue the best available treatments. Rather than legislating general liability limits, states should seek to reward hospitals that reach a predetermined quality level with a limit on their liability and penalize all others by forcing them to operate in a world of unlimited damages. Accordingly, state legislatures have more to consider than a simple dyad of approving limits on liability or not. They should instead consider tying liability limits to the most valued attribute of medical care: performance.

————

JOANNA M. SHEPHERD, TORT REFORMS' WINNERS AND LOSERS: THE COMPETING EFFECTS OF CARE AND ACTIVITY LEVELS[17]

This Article explores the relationship between medical malpractice tort reforms and death rates. Investigating this relationship is important both because of the frequent political conflict over such reforms and because medical malpractice causes tens of thousands of deaths each year. I first develop predictions from law and economics theory about medical malpractice tort reforms' care-level and activity-level impacts on death rates. I test the theoretical predictions using extensive data and sophisticated regressions. I find that the net effect varies by reform: Some reforms are associated with increases in death rates, while others are associated with decreases in death rates. These results confirm that the tort reforms' care-level effects and activity-level effects are both important. My results also suggest that the reforms may produce three unintended consequences. First, two of the reforms are associated with increases in death rates. Second, because doctors relocate to tort reform states, tort reforms in one state are associated with increases in deaths in neighboring non-reform states. Third, these reforms disproportionately harm women. They not only disproportionately reduce women's tort judgments, but they are also associated with increases in women's death rates. . . .

. . . .

Table 3: Real-World Magnitudes of the Relationship Between Tort Reforms and Death Rates

Tort Reform	Average Change in Annual Death Rates	Average Change in the Number of Deaths in 2000
Noneconomic Damage Cap	-5.1%	797 fewer deaths
Punitive Damage Reform	-2.5%	1282 fewer deaths
Total Damage Cap	+7.7%	416 more deaths
Collateral Source Reform	+4.9%	1498 more deaths
Net Effect		165 fewer deaths

I now discuss briefly why total damage caps and collateral source reforms may be associated with increases in deaths, rather than decreases as for the other reforms. Total damage caps are a severe tort reform because they cap all damages. This contrasts with caps on noneconomic

---

[17]   55 UCLA LAW REVIEW 905 (2008).

damages and reforms of punitive damages, which limit only one part of a plaintiff's recovery. My results support the argument that the severity of total damage caps creates a dramatic reduction in care levels that overwhelms any beneficial increase in physicians' activity levels— increases in the number of either physicians or medical procedures.

Similarly, collateral source reform may reduce care levels substantially and thereby harm health outcomes, because it is also a relatively severe reform, perhaps more severe even than total damage caps. It often may eliminate most, or even all, of the liability costs for defendant hospitals and physicians. Because collateral source reforms in several states do not give to collateral sources, such as insurers, a right of subrogation, defendants in these states pay only the portion of the total harm that is not paid by the collateral source. Thus, if health insurance, disability insurance, or workers compensation insurance has already paid the costs incurred by a victim of medical malpractice, then, even if a hospital or doctor is found liable for the malpractice, neither the victim nor the insurers can collect from the defendants. Because so many victims of medical malpractice receive collateral source payments from their insurers, this reform may result in many tortfeasors paying no, or greatly reduced, damage awards.

. . . .

[Drawing on the results of this study, the] evidence suggests that having a neighboring state reform its noneconomic damages law may harm the health of the non-reform state's citizens. Thus, at least for this reform, the harms from reduced activity levels in non-reform states dominate the benefits from higher care levels. This may also be the case for the other reforms, but there are not enough data to prove this statistically.

This increase in deaths in neighboring non-reform states almost completely offsets the decrease in deaths associated with noneconomic damage caps in reform states: This tort reform is associated with approximately 790 fewer deaths in reform states, but with an additional 726 deaths in the neighboring non-reform states. This evidence is consistent with tort reform draining doctors away from non-reform states and into reform states. If this doctor drain is indeed occurring, then most of the benefits from a state adopting noneconomic damage caps represent a transfer, not a true benefit.

. . . .

We have seen that tort reforms' impacts on health outcomes depend on the relative sizes of two conflicting forces: harms from doctors' reduced level of care and benefits from their increased activity levels. The results in Part II for the population as a whole showed that two reforms that imposed only modest reductions in liability were associated with improved health outcomes, while two more severe reforms were associated with worse health outcomes. It appears then that the more that a reform decreases liability, the more that harms from the reduced level of care dominate benefits from the increased activity level.

Likewise, because reforms to noneconomic damages and punitive damages disproportionately reduce physicians' and hospitals' liability to women, adoption of these reforms should cause women's health outcomes to worsen disproportionately. In contrast, caps on total damages and reforms to the collateral source rule should have a disproportionately positive effect on women's health.

. . . .

Table 6: Real-World Magnitudes

Average Change in the Number of Deaths in 2000 Associated With Each Tort Reform

Tort Reform	Men	Women
Noneconomic Damage Caps	-534	-190
Punitive Damage Reform	-1007	--
Total Damage Caps	234	127
Collateral Source Reform	802	663
J&S Liability Reform		
Periodic Payments	--	--
Net Effect	-505	600

The results are consistent with my theoretical predictions. Noneconomic damage caps and punitive damage reforms benefit women less than men; these reforms should disproportionately reduce care levels for women, and women should benefit less from these reforms' increases in activity levels. Conversely, total damage caps and collateral source reforms harm men more than women; these reforms should disproportionately reduce care levels for men, and men should be harmed more by these reforms because they are the primary clients of the doctors affected by these tort reforms.

Most significantly, using Table 6 to add up the changes associated with the various reforms demonstrates that all the tort reforms together are associated with a net decrease in male deaths but a net increase in female deaths. The results suggest that the harm from tort reforms' disproportionate reduction in compensation to women is not offset by disproportionate benefits to women in health outcomes. Instead, the tort reforms appear to harm women both by reducing their compensation and by leading to more women's deaths.

. . . .

RICHARD C. GROSS[18], CAPS ON MEDICAL MALPRACTICE DAMAGES CUT DOCTORS' INSURANCE COSTS MAY 2007

Caps on medical malpractice damages mean lower insurance premiums for doctors, according to a new review from two Alabama universities. How these caps affect patient care or costs is less certain.

"There's been substantial controversy over whether caps do what they're supposed to—reduce malpractice insurance premiums," said lead author Leonard J. Nelson III, of the Cumberland School of Law at Samford University in Birmingham. "The rates of increase in malpractice insurance premiums are lower in states that have caps."

In their analysis of 10 studies conducted since 1990, Nelson and co-authors from the Lister Hill Center for Health Policy at the University of Alabama found no evidence that caps affect consumers' health insurance costs.

However, they did say there is evidence of "small-to-modest effects" of damages caps on so-called defensive medicine and some evidence that more physicians will practice in areas where there are caps. Doctors practice defensive medicine when they avoid high-risk patients or procedures to reduce their exposure to malpractice suits.

The study appears in the latest issue of *The Milbank Quarterly*.

In one study that examined 12 years of data, researchers found that damages caps reduced premiums for general practitioners, general surgeons and OB/GYNs by 13.4 percent, 14.3 percent and 16.9 percent, respectively, in the short term and by 40 percent to 58 percent longer term.

Lower malpractice insurance premiums for physicians indirectly help patients, said David Studdert, adjunct professor at the Harvard School of Public Health.

"If doctors' fear of litigation, stimulated in part by pricey premiums, prompts them to deliver treatments and order tests designed to cover them—not improve the patient's care—then the patient may suffer," Studdert said. "Lower premiums may, and probably do, reduce the incidence of such defensiveness."

Nelson said that caps might have "some good effects," but that "they can be unfair because people who are severely injured don't get adequately compensated." One effect of caps, he said, is that they discourage lawsuits.

---

[18]   Health Behavior News Service, May 2007.

More than half of the states have damages caps. Thirteen states and the District of Columbia never passed laws instituting caps and they were ruled unconstitutional in nine other states.

CENTER FOR JUSTICE & DEMOCRACY, SNAPSHOT OF JUSTICE 2008: "CAPS" DO NOT CAUSE INSURANCE RATES TO DROP[19]

© 2008 Center for Justice & Democracy. Excerpted and reprinted with permission

"CAPS" DO NOT CAUSE INSURANCE RATES TO DROP

In recent years, during the medical malpractice insurance "crisis" for doctors, great pressure was brought to bear on state legislatures to restrict the rights of injured patients to be compensated for their injuries. As during past insurance "crises," the insurance industry told lawmakers that enacting "tort reform," particularly caps on compensation for patients, was the only way to reduce skyrocketing insurance rates—even though other statements by industry insiders repeatedly contradict this.

Today, medical malpractice rates have stabilized and availability has improved around the country. The flattening of rates had nothing to do with tort law restrictions enacted in particular states, but rather to modulations in the insurance cycle everywhere. Whether a state has enacted strong insurance regulatory laws has also helped. The following are a few examples:

- **Illinois.** In October 2006, Illinois Division of Insurance announced that an Illinois malpractice insurer, Berkshire Hathaway's MedPro, would be expanding its coverage and cutting premiums for doctors by more than 30 percent. According to state officials and the company itself, this was made possible because of new *insurance* reforms enacted by Illinois lawmakers in 2005, and expressly *not* the cap on compensation for patients that was enacted at the same time. The law requires malpractice insurers to disclose data on how to set their rates. This, according to Michael McRaith, director of the state's Division of Insurance, allows MedPro to "set rates that are more competitive than they could have set before."

- **Connecticut.** "Rate increases are even slowing or stopping in some states that have not limited awards for pain and suffering, including Connecticut, where premium increases in

---

[19] www.centerjd.org.

the past have soared as much as 90 percent in a single year." Connecticut has no cap on damages.

- **Maryland.** "[T]he state's largest malpractice insurer said it does not need a rate increase for next year, leading some to question whether the much-debated malpractice crisis ever existed." In 2006, Maryland's largest malpractice insurer, Med Mutual, announced plans to cut their malpractice rates by 8 percent in 2007. Maryland has had a cap on damages since 1986. Sixteen years later, during the most recent insurance crisis, the state still experienced premiums that "rose by more than 70 percent in the last two years."

- **Pennsylvania.** In Pennsylvania in recent years, rates across the med mal marketplace "have found a new plateau," according to an associate counsel and director of patient safety and risk management at the University of Pittsburgh Medical Center, Richard P. Kidwell. Pennsylvania has no cap.

- **Massachusetts.** In early 2005, "[T]he state's largest malpractice insurer said it will not raise doctors' premiums. . ." Massachusetts has had a cap, but with significant exceptions, since 1986.

- **Washington.** In 2005, the state's largest med mal insurer Physicians Insurance, which is owned by doctors, requested a 7.7 percent reduction in medical malpractice rates, with the company reporting record-breaking net income. Washington does not have a cap on damages.

THE CALIFORNIA EXPERIENCE

- Thirteen years after the state's severe $250,000 cap on damages was enacted (MICRA, passed in 1975), "doctors' premiums had increased by 450 percent and reached an all-time high in California." But in 1988 California voters passed a stringent insurance regulatory law, Proposition 103, which "reduced California doctors' premiums by 20 per within three years," and stabilized rates.

- In the thirteen years after MICRA, but before the insurance reforms of Prop. 103, California medical malpractice premiums rose faster than the national average. In the twelve years after Prop. 103 (1988–2000), malpractice premiums dropped 8 percent in California, while nationally they were up 25 percent. Moreover, the law has led to public hearings on recent rate requests by medical malpractice insurers in California, which resulted in rate hikes being lowered three times.

The "liability insurance crisis" of the mid-1980s was ultimately found to be caused not by legal system excesses but by the economic cycle of the insurance industry. Just as the liability insurance crisis was found to be driven by this cycle and not a tort law cost explosion as many insurance companies and others had claimed, the "tort reform" remedy pushed by these advocates failed. It has failed again.

Only effective insurance reforms will stop these cyclical insurance crises.

THE HONORABLE RICHARD POSNER, UNITED STATES COURT OF APPEALS FOR THE 7TH CIRCUIT PROFESSOR OF LAW, UNIVERSITY OF CHICAGO LAW SCHOOL, POSNER ON TORT REFORM

Hotline Comment
The Jurist, January 17 (2005)[20]
© Richard Posner. Excerpted and reprinted with permission.

"There is a movement afoot, assisted by the strengthening of Republican control over Congress, to impose federal limits on tort litigation, particularly medical malpractice; premiums for malpractice insurance have soared in the last two years and physicians are protesting vigorously.

The costs of malpractice premiums are only about 1 percent of total U.S. health-care costs. Moreover, insofar as physicians are forced to swallow the cost of the premiums rather than being able to pass them on to their patients or their patients' insurers in the form of higher prices, the premiums do not actually increase total health-care costs. There is an indirect effect, however, insofar as malpractice liability causes doctors to practice defensive medicine. But there may be offsetting benefits, to the extent that defensive medicine actually improves outcomes for patients; and surely it does for at least some. What is more, because malpractice insurance is not experience-rated—physicians are not charged premiums based on their personal liability experience—malpractice liability may have only a slight effect on physicians' methods or carefulness, except insofar as physicians are pressured by their insurers to change their methods in order to reduce the amount of malpractice litigation.

The relation between malpractice premiums and malpractice judgments is also uncertain. No doubt capping judgments, which is the principal reform that is advocated, has some tendency to reduce premiums, but perhaps not much, because there is evidence that premiums are

---

[20]   http://www.becker-posner-blog.com/2005/01/tort-reform--posner/comments/page/2/.

strongly influenced by the performance of the insurance companies' investment portfolios.

A better reform would be to permit, encourage, or even require insurance companies to base malpractice premiums on the experience of the insured physician, much as automobile liability insurance is based on the driver's experience of accidents. That would make malpractice liability a better engine for deterring malpractice—which in turn would reduce malpractice premiums by reducing the amount of malpractice. Capping judgments, in contrast, would reduce the incentive of insurance companies and their regulators to move to a system of experience-rated malpractice insurance.

It is always important to distinguish between financial and real costs. Insofar as malpractice liability merely transfers wealth from physicians to (some) patients, aggregate costs are unaffected. The real cost of malpractice liability is limited to the cost of the actual resources consumed by such liability, principally the time of lawyers and expert witnesses (roughly half the total amount awarded in judgments goes to pay lawyers and expert witnesses), unless defensive medicine is assumed to cost more than its benefits in improving treatment outcomes. The real benefit of malpractice liability is its effect if any in deterring medical negligence; reducing that benefit would impose a real cost. Hence it is simplistic to assume that the total annual malpractice premiums paid is a good index of the net social cost of malpractice liability, or that measures to reduce those premiums by capping malpractice liability would result in a net improvement in welfare. To repeat, part of the premiums represent simply a wealth transfer from physicians to the patients who receive malpractice judgments or settlements paid by insurers. The part (roughly half) that pays for lawyers and expert witnesses should be understood as the cost of maintaining a system for increasing medical safety; the efficacy of the system could be improved, I have argued, by experience rating, but not by capping judgments.

In any event, there is no compelling case for federal limitations on malpractice liability. The issue belongs at the state level, and as reported in a *New York Times* article last Friday, a number of states have adopted or are seriously considering adopting the kind of caps being advocated in Congress. Federal legislation would simply stifle state experimentation with different methods of regulating physicians and prevent us from learning which is best.

There is a stronger case for federal regulation of class actions, as in the case of suits against asbestos manufacturers. When the members of a plaintiff class are scattered across the country, the class lawyer has a wide range of places in which to sue, and there are certain counties in the United States in which judges and juries are disproportionately generous to tort plaintiffs. Most of the costs of a large judgment or settlement in such a case are exported to other states, while the benefits are concentrated in the locale where the suit was litigated, because of the business generated for local lawyers, as well as the judgments or settlements received by the members of the class in the locale. This is a formula for abuse, concretely for a tendency for such judgments and settlements to exceed an unbiased estimate of the true costs imposed on the class by the defendants' misconduct. Malpractice litigation does not give rise to such an abuse to any very great extent, because patient and physician are usually in the same state, and a single plaintiff has only a limited choice of courts in which to sue. This is another reason not to make medical malpractice the principal object of federal tort reform.

We should be cautious about tort reform. It would be unfortunate if interest-group politics, and anecdotes concerning outlandish lawsuits (such as the suit against McDonald's by the customer who spilled hot coffee in her lap), were allowed to obscure the difficult policy issues.

PART III

A VERY BRIEF LOOK AT THE CASELAW

■ ■ ■

Like scholarship in the tort reform field, judicial decisions are plentiful, varied, and compelling. Many tort decisions handed down in the last 25 years could be seen as tort reform cases. Tort reform issues cut across—and straight through—many of the most basic issues in the field. Twenty years ago, commentators reported that some type of tort reform legislation had been adopted in the vast majority of states. Nancy L. Manzer, *1986 Tort Reform Legislation: A Systematic Evaluation of Caps on Damages and Limitations on Joint and Several Liability*, 73 CORNELL L. REV. 628, 632, 656 (1988); Mitchell S. Berger, *Following the Doctor's Orders—Caps on Non-Economic Damages in Medical Malpractice Cases*, 22 RUTGERS L.J. 173, 179 (1991).

State courts began to assess these initiatives not long after they were passed, more often than not upholding the new provisions. There are dozens of cases and articles one could read on this point. A review of the literature summarizing this material might be a more efficient way to proceed. Victor E. Schwartz & Leah Lorber, *Judicial Nullification of Civil Justice Reform Violates the Fundamental Federal Constitutional Principle of Separation of Powers: How to Restore the Right Balance*, 32 RUTGERS L. REV. 907, 952 et seq. (2001) (listing 82 decisions focused on the constitutionality of state tort reform); John C.P. Goldberg, *The Constitutional Status of Tort Law: Due Process and the Right to a Law for the Redress of Wrongs*, 115 YALE L.J. 524 (2005); John Fabian Witt, *The Long History of State Constitutions and American Tort Law*, 36 RUTGERS L. REV. 1159 (2004–2005).

The cases that follow do not address exclusively the question of constitutionality of state tort reform. They were selected to give you a sense of the Supreme Court's more recent decisions on punitive damages and preemption and to provide a look at several state cases that discuss common and important tort reform issues. For an in-depth study of the way in which states and state courts have dealt with tort reform, *see* Alexandra B. Klass, *Tort Experiments in the Laboratories of Democracy*, 50 WILLIAM AND MARY L. REV. 1501 (2009); Gary T. Schwartz, *Considering the Proper Federal Role in American Tort Law*, 38 ARIZ. L. REV. 917 (1996).

Tort reform challenges the power, purpose, and effectiveness of state and federal courts. It questions the system of trial by jury. It questions the procedures selected by state legislatures and the Congress. It challenges some of the most basic premises of the common law. In short, it poses critical public policy questions. These matters present separation of powers issues.

Without belaboring the obvious republicanism, accountability, and public choice rationales, the policymaking functions of the federal government are vested to the Congress and similar powers are vested to the state legislatures. When state court judges decide tort reform questions, should their opinions be limited solely to legal interpretation of statutes, common law, and the state and federal constitutions? Read any of the major state cases (from Ohio and Michigan in particular), and you will be hard-pressed to see that limitation. State courts often articulate public policy—but should they? Does your answer to this question depend on whether the judges are elected or appointed?

BMW OF NORTH AMERICA, INC. V. GORE
517 U.S. 559 (1996)

OPINION BY JUSTICE STEVENS

. . . .

[Nine months after Dr. Ira Gore bought a "new" BMW, he learned that prior to purchase, the car had been repainted, apparently covering scratches or other irregularities in the finish of the car. The repainting was not disclosed to Gore by the dealer. Moreover, Gore discovered that BMW had engaged in similar behavior with other vehicles in other states. Gore alleged, inter alia, that this was intentional misrepresentation and required both compensatory and punitive damages. He prevailed at trial and was awarded $4000 in compensatory damages and $4 million in punitive damages. The award was reduced to $2 million by the Alabama Supreme Court. On appeal to the U.S. Supreme Court, the Court reversed the Alabama Supreme Court, finding the award excessive and thus a violation of BMW's substantive Due Process rights. The case is of consequence because it opened the door to Supreme Court review of the amount a state court awards in a jury trial.

You might ask if this means the Court can or should sit as a "super jury," re-evaluating the size of a judgment, something the Court had avoided prior to this case. Central to the holding was the question of the ratio between compensatory and punitive damages.]

Ratio

The second and perhaps most commonly cited indicium of an unreasonable or excessive punitive damages award is its ratio to the actual harm inflicted on the plaintiff. The principle that exemplary damages must bear a "reasonable relationship" to compensatory damages has a long pedigree. Scholars have identified a number of early English statutes authorizing the award of multiple damages for particular wrongs. Some 65 different enactments during the period between 1275 and 1753 provided for double, treble, or quadruple damages. Our decisions in both *Haslip* and *TXO* endorsed the proposition that a comparison between the compensatory award and the punitive award is significant.

In *Haslip* we concluded that even though a punitive damages award of "more than 4 times the amount of compensatory damages" might be "close to the line," it did not "cross the line into the area of constitutional impropriety." 499 U.S., at 23–24, 111 S.Ct., at 1046. *TXO,* following dicta in *Haslip,* refined this analysis by confirming that the proper inquiry is " 'whether there is a reasonable relationship between the punitive damages award and *the harm likely to result* from the defendant's conduct as well as the harm that actually has occurred.' " *TXO,* 509 U.S., at 460, 113 S.Ct., at 2721 (emphasis in original). Thus, in upholding the $10 million award in *TXO,* we relied on the difference between that figure and the harm to the victim that would have ensued if the tortious plan had succeeded. That difference suggested that the relevant ratio was not more than 10 to 1.

The $2 million in punitive damages awarded to Dr. Gore by the Alabama Supreme Court is 500 times the amount of his actual harm as determined by the jury. Moreover, there is no suggestion that Dr. Gore or any other BMW purchaser was threatened with any additional potential harm by BMW's nondisclosure policy. The disparity in this case is thus dramatically greater than those considered in *Haslip* and *TXO.*

Of course, we have consistently rejected the notion that the constitutional line is marked by a simple mathematical formula, even one that compares actual *and potential* damages to the punitive award. *TXO,* 509 U.S., at 458, 113 S.Ct., at 2720. Indeed, low awards of compensatory damages may properly support a higher ratio than high compensatory awards, if, for example, a particularly egregious act has resulted in only a small amount of economic damages. A higher ratio may also be justified in cases in which the injury is hard to detect or the monetary value of noneconomic harm might have been difficult to determine. It is appropriate, therefore, to reiterate our rejection of a categorical approach. Once again, "we return to what we said . . . in *Haslip:* 'We need not, and indeed we cannot, draw a mathematical bright line between the constitutionally acceptable and the constitutionally unacceptable that would fit every case. We can say, however, that [a] general concer[n] of reasonableness . . . properly enter[s] into the constitutional calculus.' " *Id.,* at 458, 113 S.Ct., at 2720 (quoting *Haslip,* 499 U.S., at 18, 111 S.Ct., at 1043). In most cases, the ratio will be within a constitutionally acceptable range, and remittitur will not be justified on this basis. When the ratio is a breathtaking 500 to 1, however, the award must surely "raise a suspicious judicial eyebrow."

. . . .

[In finding for BMW, the Court announced that it was] not prepared to draw a bright line marking the limits of a constitutionally acceptable punitive damages award. . . . [However] we are fully convinced that the grossly excessive award imposed in this case transcends the constitutional limit. . . .

The judgment is reversed, and the case is remanded for further proceedings not inconsistent with this opinion.

It is so ordered.

[The dissenting opinions of JUSTICES BREYER, O'CONNOR, and SOUTER are omitted.]

JUSTICE SCALIA, with whom JUSTICE THOMAS joins, dissenting.

. . . .

In earlier cases that were the prelude to this decision, I set forth my view that a state trial procedure that commits the decision whether to impose punitive damages, and the amount, to the discretion of the jury, subject to some judicial review for "reasonableness," furnishes a defendant with all the process that is "due." I do not regard the Fourteenth Amendment's Due Process Clause as a secret repository of substantive guarantees against "unfairness"—neither the unfairness of an excessive civil compensatory award, nor the unfairness of an "unreasonable" punitive award. What the Fourteenth Amendment's procedural guarantee assures is an opportunity to contest the reasonableness of a damages judgment in state court; but there is no federal guarantee a damages award actually *be* reasonable.

. . . . The Constitution provides no warrant for federalizing yet another aspect of our Nation's legal culture (no matter how much in need of correction it may be), and the application of the Court's new rule of constitutional law is constrained by no principle other than the Justices' subjective assessment of the "reasonableness" of the award in relation to the conduct for which it was assessed.

. . . .

NOTES, COMMENTS, AND QUESTIONS

1.   One commentator concludes that punitive damages, once the province of juries and state courts, are now "under exacting federal constitutional due process review." Alexandra B. Klass, *Punitive Damages and Valuing Harm*, 92 MINN. L. REV. 83, 160 (2007). First, is that your reading of the *BMW* case? Does the advent of the application of substantive due process

produce such a complete change in this field? Second, there is no question that punitive damages are being scrutinized with great care at every level. Does this suggest that we have lost faith in their value, *i.e.*, do punitive damages no longer serve the purposes for which they were intended, punishment and deterrence? Consider the following: Mark Geistfeld, *Constitutional Tort Reform,* 38 LOY. L.A. L. REV. 1093 (2005); Howard A. Denemark, *Seeking Greater Fairness When Awarding Multiple Plaintiffs Punitive Damages for a Single Act by a Defendant,* 63 OHIO ST. L.J. 931 (2002); Rachel M. Janutis, *Reforming Reprehensibility: The Continued Viability of Multiple Punitive Damages After* State Farm v. Campbell, 41 SAN DIEGO L. REV. 1465 (2004).

2.   Should the Court be in the position of serving as an appellate court reviewing the reasonability of the size of jury verdicts? Do the standards in *BMW* make initial awards as well as judicial review more clear? F. Patrick Hubbard, *In Honor of Walter O. Weyrauch: Substantive Due Process Limits on Punitive Damages Awards: "Morals With Technique?",* 60 FLA. L. REV. 349, 352 (2008). "[T]he Court should be more deferential to state courts and legislatures, and more concerned with developing a coherent framework."

3.   The BMW decision is predicated on the Court's concern about the reasonability of punitive damages, particularly since the initial award was designed to punish BMW for its action, not just as those acts affected Dr. Gore but on a far boarder basis, *i.e.,* in all states where similar misconduct had occurred. The economic assumptions in the opinion are worthy of scrutiny. For a lucid and thorough economic assessment of punitive damages, take a look at A. Mitchell Polinsky & Steven Shavell, *Punitive Damages: An Economic Analysis,* 111 HARV. L. REV. 869 (1998).

STATE FARM MUT. AUTO. INS. CO. V. CAMPBELL
538 U.S. 408 (2003)

OPINION BY JUSTICE KENNEDY

We address once again the measure of punishment, by means of punitive damages, a State may impose upon a defendant in a civil case. The question is whether, in the circumstances we shall recount, an award of $145 million in punitive damages, where full compensatory damages are $1 million, is excessive and in violation of the Due Process Clause of the Fourteenth Amendment to the Constitution of the United States.

I

In 1981, Curtis Campbell (Campbell) was driving with his wife, Inez Preece Campbell, in Cache County, Utah. He decided to pass six vans traveling ahead of them on a two-lane highway. Todd Ospital was driving a small car approaching from the opposite direction. To avoid a head-on collision with Campbell, who by then was driving on the wrong side of the highway and toward oncoming traffic, Ospital swerved onto the shoulder, lost control of his automobile, and collided with a vehicle driven by Robert G. Slusher. Ospital was killed, and Slusher was rendered permanently disabled. The Campbells escaped unscathed.

In the ensuing wrongful death and tort action, Campbell insisted he was not at fault. Early investigations did support differing conclusions as to who caused the accident, but "a consensus was reached early on by the investigators and witnesses that Mr. Campbell's unsafe pass had indeed caused the crash." 65 P.3d 1134, 1141 (Utah 2001). Campbell's insurance company, petitioner State Farm Mutual Automobile Insurance Company (State Farm), nonetheless decided to contest liability and declined offers by Slusher and Ospital's estate (Ospital) to settle the claims for the policy limit of $50,000 ($25,000 per claimant). State Farm also ignored the advice of one of its own investigators and took the case to trial, assuring the Campbells that "their assets were safe, that they had no liability for the accident, that [State Farm] would represent their interests, and that they did not need to procure separate counsel." *Id.,* at 1142. To the contrary, a jury determined that Campbell was 100 percent at fault, and a judgment was returned for $185,849, far more than the amount offered in settlement.

At first State Farm refused to cover the $135,849 in excess liability. Its counsel made this clear to the Campbells: " 'You may want to put for sale signs on your property to get things moving.' " *Ibid.* Nor was State Farm willing to post a supersedeas bond to allow Campbell to appeal the judgment against him. Campbell obtained his own counsel to appeal the verdict. During the pendency of the appeal, in late 1984, Slusher, Ospital, and the Campbells reached an agreement whereby Slusher and Ospital agreed not to seek satisfaction of their claims against the Campbells. In exchange the Campbells agreed to pursue a bad faith action against State Farm and to be represented by Slusher's and Ospital's attorneys. The Campbells also agreed that Slusher and Ospital would have a right to play a part in all major decisions concerning the bad-faith action. No settlement could be concluded without Slusher's and Ospital's approval, and Slusher and Ospital would receive 90 percent of any verdict against State Farm.

. . . .

. . . . The jury awarded the Campbells $2.6 million in compensatory damages and $145 million in punitive damages, which the trial court reduced to $1 million and $25 million respectively. Both parties appealed.

[Applying *BMW v. Gore,* the Utah Supreme Court reinstated the $145 million punitive damages award.]

II

In light of these concerns, in *Gore, supra,* we instructed courts reviewing punitive damages to consider three guideposts: (1) the degree of reprehensibility of the defendant's misconduct; (2) the disparity between the actual or potential harm suffered by the plaintiff and the punitive damages award; and (3) the difference between the punitive damages awarded by the jury and the civil penalties authorized or imposed in comparable cases. *Id.,* at 575, 116 S.Ct. 1589. We reiterated the importance of these three guideposts in *Cooper Industries* and mandated appellate courts to conduct *de novo* review of a trial court's application of them to the jury's award. 532 U.S. 424, 121 S.Ct. 1678. Exacting appellate review ensures that an award of punitive damages is based upon an " 'application of law, rather than a decisionmaker's caprice.' " *Id.,* at 436, 121 S.Ct. 1678 (quoting *Gore, supra,* at 587, 116 S.Ct. 1589 (BREYER, J., concurring)).

III

Under the principles outlined in *BMW of North America, Inc. v. Gore,* this case is neither close nor difficult. It was error to reinstate the jury's $145 million punitive damages award. We address each guidepost of *Gore* in some detail.

"[T]he most important *indicium* of the reasonableness of a punitive damages award is the degree of reprehensibility of the defendant's conduct." *Gore,* 517 U.S., at 575, 116 S.Ct. 1589. We have instructed courts to determine the reprehensibility of a defendant by considering whether: the harm caused was physical as opposed to economic; the tortious conduct evinced an indifference to or a reckless disregard of the health or safety of others; the target of the conduct had financial vulnerability; the conduct involved repeated actions or was an isolated incident; and the harm was the result of intentional malice, trickery, or deceit, or mere accident. *Id.,* at 576–577, 116 S.Ct. 1589. The existence of any one of these factors weighing in favor of a plaintiff may not be sufficient to sustain a punitive damages award; and the absence of all of them renders any award suspect. It should be presumed a plaintiff has been made whole for his injuries by compensatory damages, so punitive damages should only be awarded if the defendant's culpability, after having paid compensatory damages, is so reprehensible as to warrant the imposition of further sanctions to achieve punishment or deterrence. *Id.,* at 575, 116 S.Ct. 1589.

Applying these factors in the instant case, we must acknowledge that State Farm's handling of the claims against the Campbells merits no praise. The trial court found that State Farm's employees altered the company's records to make Campbell appear less culpable. State Farm disregarded the overwhelming likelihood of liability and the near-certain probability that, by taking the case to trial, a judgment in excess of the policy limits would be awarded. State Farm amplified the harm by at first assuring the Campbells their assets would be safe from any verdict and by later telling them, post-judgment, to put a for-sale sign on their house. While we do not suggest there was error in awarding punitive damages based upon State Farm's conduct toward the Campbells, a more modest punishment for this reprehensible conduct could have satisfied the State's legitimate objectives, and the Utah courts should have gone no further. . . .

B

Turning to the second *Gore* guidepost, we have been reluctant to identify concrete constitutional limits on the ratio between harm, or potential harm, to the plaintiff and the punitive damages award. 517 U.S., at 582, 116 S.Ct. 1589 ("[W]e have consistently rejected the notion that the constitutional line is marked by a simple mathematical formula, even one that compares actual *and potential* damages to the punitive award"); *TXO, supra,* at 458, 113 S.Ct. 2711. We decline again to impose a bright-line ratio which a punitive damages award cannot exceed. Our jurisprudence and the principles it has now established demonstrate, however, that, in practice, few awards exceeding a single-digit ratio between punitive and compensatory damages, to a significant degree, will satisfy due process. In *Haslip,* in upholding a punitive damages award, we concluded that an award of more than four times the amount of compensatory damages might be close to the line of constitutional impropriety. 499 U.S., at 23–24, 111 S.Ct. 1032. We cited that 4-to-1 ratio again in *Gore.* 517 U.S., at 581, 116 S.Ct. 1589. The Court further referenced a long legislative history, dating back over 700 years and going forward to today, providing for sanctions of double, treble, or quadruple damages to deter and punish. *Id.,* at 581, and n. 33, 116 S.Ct. 1589. While these ratios are not binding, they are instructive. They demonstrate what should be obvious: Single-digit multipliers are more likely to comport with due process, while still achieving the State's goals of deterrence and retribution, than awards with ratios in range of 500 to 1, *id.,* at 582, 116 S.Ct. 1589, or, in this case, of 145 to 1.

Nonetheless, because there are no rigid benchmarks that a punitive damages award may not surpass, ratios greater than those we have previously upheld may comport with due process where "a particularly egregious act has resulted in only a small amount of economic damages." *Ibid.*; see also *ibid.* (positing that a higher ratio *might* be necessary where "the injury is hard to detect or the monetary value of noneconomic harm might have been difficult to determine"). The converse is also true, however. When compensatory damages are substantial, then a lesser ratio, perhaps only equal to compensatory damages, can reach the outermost limit of the due process guarantee. The precise award in any case, of course, must be based upon the facts and circumstances of the defendant's conduct and the harm to the plaintiff.

In sum, courts must ensure that the measure of punishment is both reasonable and proportionate to the amount of harm to the plaintiff and to the general damages recovered. In the context of this case, we have no doubt that there is a presumption against an award that has a 145-to-1 ratio. The compensatory award in this case was substantial; the Campbells were awarded $1 million for a year and a half of emotional distress. This was complete compensation. The harm arose from a transaction in the economic realm, not from some physical assault or trauma; there were no physical injuries; and State Farm paid the excess verdict before the complaint was filed, so the Campbells suffered only minor economic injuries for the 18–month period in which State Farm refused to resolve the claim against them. The compensatory damages for the injury suffered here, moreover, likely were based on a component which was duplicated in the punitive award. Much of the distress was caused by the outrage and humiliation the Campbells suffered at the actions of their insurer; and it is a major role of punitive damages to condemn such conduct. Compensatory damages, however, already contain this punitive element. . . .

C

The third guidepost in *Gore* is the disparity between the punitive damages award and the "civil penalties authorized or imposed in comparable cases." *Id.,* at 575, 116 S.Ct. 1589. We note that, in the past, we have also looked to criminal penalties that could be imposed. *Id.,* at 583, 116 S.Ct. 1589; *Haslip,* 499 U.S., at 23, 111 S.Ct. 1032. The existence of a criminal penalty does have bearing on the seriousness with which a State views the wrongful action. When used to determine the dollar amount of the award, however, the criminal penalty has less utility. Great care must be taken to avoid use of the civil process to assess criminal penalties that can be imposed only after the heightened protections of a criminal trial have been observed, including, of course, its higher standards of proof. Punitive damages are not a substitute for the criminal process, and the remote possibility of a criminal sanction does not automatically sustain a punitive damages award.

Here, we need not dwell long on this guidepost. The most relevant civil sanction under Utah state law for the wrong done to the Campbells appears to be a $10,000 fine for an act of fraud, 65 P.3d, at 1154, an amount dwarfed by the $145 million punitive damages award. The Supreme Court of Utah speculated about the loss of State Farm's business license, the disgorgement of profits, and possible imprisonment, but here again its references were to the broad fraudulent scheme drawn from evidence of out-of-state and dissimilar conduct. This analysis was insufficient to justify the award.

IV

An application of the *Gore* guideposts to the facts of this case, especially in light of the substantial compensatory damages awarded (a portion of which contained a punitive element), likely would justify a punitive damages award at or near the amount of compensatory damages.

The punitive award of $145 million, therefore, was neither reasonable nor proportionate to the wrong committed, and it was an irrational and arbitrary deprivation of the property of the defendant. The proper calculation of punitive damages under the principles we have discussed should be resolved, in the first instance, by the Utah courts.

The judgment of the Utah Supreme Court is reversed, and the case is remanded for further proceedings not inconsistent with this opinion.

It is so ordered.

JUSTICE SCALIA, dissenting.

I adhere to the view expressed in my dissenting opinion in *BMW of North America, Inc. v. Gore,* 517 U.S. 559, 598–99, 116 S.Ct. 1589, 134 L.Ed.2d 809 (1996), that the Due Process Clause provides no substantive protections against "excessive" or " 'unreasonable' " awards of punitive damages. I am also of the view that the punitive damages jurisprudence which has sprung forth from *BMW v. Gore* is insusceptible of principled application; accordingly, I do not feel justified in giving the case *stare decisis* effect. See *id.,* at 599, 116 S.Ct. 1589. I would affirm the judgment of the Utah Supreme Court.

JUSTICE THOMAS, dissenting.

I would affirm the judgment below because "I continue to believe that the Constitution does not constrain the size of punitive damages awards." *Cooper Industries, Inc. v. Leatherman Tool Group, Inc.,* 532 U.S. 424, 443, 121 S.Ct. 1678, 149 L.Ed.2d 674 (2001) (THOMAS, J., concurring) (citing *BMW of North America, Inc. v. Gore,* 517 U.S. 559, 599, 116 S.Ct. 1589, 134 L.Ed.2d 809 (1996) (SCALIA, J., joined by THOMAS, J., dissenting)). Accordingly, I respectfully dissent.

JUSTICE GINSBURG, dissenting.

. . . . I remain of the view that this Court has no warrant to reform state law governing awards of punitive damages. *Gore,* 517 U.S., at 607, 116 S.Ct. 1589 (GINSBURG, J., dissenting). Even if I were prepared to accept the flexible guides prescribed in *Gore,* I would not join the Court's swift conversion of those guides into instructions that begin to resemble marching orders. For the reasons stated, I would leave the judgment of the Utah Supreme Court undisturbed.

NOTES, COMMENTS, AND QUESTIONS

1.   Careful scholarship regarding *State Farm* suggests that the decision in no way put an end to the complexity of assessing punitive damages. Laura J. Hines, *Due Process Limitations on Punitive Damages: Why State Farm Won't Be the Last Word,* 37 AKRON L. REV. 779 (2004). However, from the perspective

of the tort reform agenda, getting punitive damages down to the levels suggested in *State Farm* has to be considered a victory. Is it? Some scholars see the decision as ineffectual and call for a return to state autonomy over punitive damages.[1]

2.   While there is little question that a massive punitive damage award, completely disproportional to the wrongdoing (or the compensatory damages for that matter), would be set aside, there is considerable debate on the frequency and actual impact of such cases.[2] If the problem is just not all that great, was it wise for the Court to resort to substantive process review? "Every empirical study of punitive damages demonstrates that there is no nationwide punitive damages crisis. The research shows that punitive damages cluster in business tort and intentional tort cases, not personal injury. The increase in punitive damages is largely confined to a few jurisdictions."[3]

3.   Perhaps it is time for you to ask: why all the fuss? In a recent decision, *Exxon Shipping Co. v. Baker*, 128 S.Ct. 2605, 2624 (2008), the Court held:

> American punitive damages have been the target of audible criticism in recent decades . . . but the most recent studies tend to undercut much of it. . . . A survey of the literature reveals that discretion to award punitive damages has not mass-produced runaway awards, and although some studies show the dollar amounts of punitive-damages awards growing over time, even in real terms, by most accounts the median ratio of punitive to compensatory awards has remained less than 1:1.

Assuming the statistical assessment of the Court is accurate, have punitive damage awards become predictable—and if so, is their deterrent value lost?

WYETH V. LEVINE
555 U.S. 555, 129 S.Ct. 1187 (2009)

OPINION BY JUSTICE STEVENS

Directly injecting the drug Phenergan into a patient's vein creates a significant risk of catastrophic consequences. A Vermont jury found that petitioner Wyeth, the manufacturer of the drug, had failed to provide an adequate warning of that risk and awarded damages to respondent Diana Levine to compensate her for the amputation of her arm. The warnings on

---

[1]   Tracy A. Thomas, *Proportionality and the Supreme Court's Jurisprudence of Remedies*, 59 HASTINGS L.J. 73 (2007).

[2]   See generally, Thomas H. Koenig & Michael Rustad, IN DEFENSE OF TORT LAW (2001); Anthony J. Sebok, *Punitive Damages: From Myth to Theory*, 92 IOWA L. REV. 957, 960 (2007); Theodore Eisenberg, *Measuring The Deterrent Effect of Punitive Damages*, 87 GEO. L.J. 347 (1998).

[3]   Michael L. Rustad, *Unraveling Punitive Damages: Current Data and Further Inquiry*, 1998 WIS. L. REV. 15, 69.

Phenergan's label had been deemed sufficient by the federal Food and Drug Administration (FDA) when it approved Wyeth's new drug application in 1955 and when it later approved changes in the drug's labeling. The question we must decide is whether the FDA's approvals provide Wyeth with a complete defense to Levine's tort claims. We conclude that they do not.

I

. . . .

[Levine prevailed at trial and was awarded $7.4 million in damages which was later reduced by the trial judge. The award was affirmed by the Vermont Supreme Court. The tort reform issue in this case is not damages— it is preemption: When does the presence and application of federal regulations preempt the application of state tort law?]

II

. . . . The [narrow] question presented is whether federal law pre-empts Levine's claim that Phenergan's label did not contain an adequate warning about using the IV-push method of administration.

Our answer to that question must be guided by two cornerstones of our pre-emption jurisprudence. First, "the purpose of Congress is the ultimate touchstone in every pre-emption case." *Medtronic, Inc. v. Lohr,* 518 U.S. 470, 485, 116 S.Ct. 2240, 135 L.Ed.2d 700 (1996) (internal quotation marks omitted). Second, "[i]n all pre-emption cases, and particularly in those in which Congress has 'legislated . . . in a field which the States have traditionally occupied,' . . . we 'start with the assumption that the historic police powers of the States were not to be superseded by the Federal Act unless that was the clear and manifest purpose of Congress.' " *Lohr,* 518 U.S., at 485, 116 S.Ct. 2240 (quoting *Rice v. Santa Fe Elevator Corp.,* 331 U.S. 218, 230, 67 S.Ct. 1146, 91 L.Ed. 1447 (1947)).

. . . .

As it enlarged the FDA's powers to "protect the public health" and "assure the safety, effectiveness, and reliability of drugs," *id.,* at 780, Congress took care to preserve state law. The 1962 amendments added a saving clause, indicating that a provision of state law would only be invalidated upon a "direct and positive conflict" with the FDCA. . . . And when Congress enacted an express pre-emption provision for medical devices in 1976, . . . it declined to enact such a provision for prescription drugs.

. . . .

III

Wyeth first argues that Levine's state-law claims are pre-empted because it is impossible for it to comply with both the state-law duties underlying those claims and its federal labeling duties. The FDA's premarket approval of a new drug application includes the approval of the exact text in the proposed label. Generally speaking, a manufacturer may only change a drug label after the FDA approves a supplemental application. There is, however, an FDA regulation that permits a manufacturer to make certain changes to its label before receiving the agency's approval. Among other things, this "changes being effected" (CBE) regulation provides that if a manufacturer is changing a label to "add or strengthen a contraindication, warning, precaution, or adverse reaction" or to "add or strengthen an instruction about dosage and administration that is intended to increase the safe use of the drug product," it may make the labeling change upon filing its supplemental application with the FDA; it need not wait for FDA approval.

Wyeth argues that the CBE regulation is not implicated in this case because a 2008 amendment provides that a manufacturer may only change its label "to reflect newly acquired information." 73 Fed.Reg. 49609. Resting on this language (which Wyeth argues simply reaffirmed the interpretation of the regulation in effect when this case was tried), Wyeth contends that it could have changed Phenergan's label only in response to new information that the FDA had not considered. And it maintains that Levine has not pointed to any such information concerning the risks of IV-push administration. Thus, Wyeth insists, it was impossible for it to discharge its state-law obligation to provide a stronger warning about IV-push administration without violating federal law. Wyeth's argument misapprehends both the federal drug regulatory scheme and its burden in establishing a pre-emption defense.

. . . . As the FDA explained in its notice of the final rule, " 'newly acquired information' " is not limited to new data, but also encompasses "new analyses of previously submitted data." *Id.*, at 49604. . . .

. . . . [A]s amputations continued to occur, Wyeth could have analyzed the accumulating data and added a stronger warning about IV-push administration of the drug.

Wyeth argues that if it had unilaterally added such a warning, it would have violated federal law governing unauthorized distribution and misbranding. Its argument that a change in Phenergan's labeling would have subjected it to liability for unauthorized distribution rests on the assumption that this labeling change would have rendered Phenergan a new drug lacking an effective application. But strengthening the warning about IV-push administration would not have made Phenergan a new drug. Nor would this warning have rendered Phenergan misbranded. The FDCA does not provide that a drug is misbranded simply because the manufacturer has altered an FDA-approved label; instead, the misbranding provision focuses on the substance of the label and, among other things, proscribes labels that fail to include "adequate warnings." 21 U.S.C. § 352(f). Moreover, because the statute contemplates that federal juries will resolve most misbranding claims, the FDA's belief that a drug is misbranded is not conclusive. And the very idea that the FDA would bring an enforcement action against a manufacturer for strengthening a warning pursuant to the CBE regulation is difficult to accept-neither Wyeth nor the United States has identified a case in which the FDA has done so.

. . . .

Impossibility pre-emption is a demanding defense. On the record before us, Wyeth has failed to demonstrate that it was impossible for it to comply with both federal and state requirements. The CBE regulation permitted Wyeth to unilaterally strengthen its warning, and the mere fact that the FDA approved Phenergan's label does not establish that it would have prohibited such a change.

IV

Wyeth also argues that requiring it to comply with a state-law duty to provide a stronger warning about IV-push administration would obstruct the purposes and objectives of federal drug labeling regulation. Levine's tort claims, it maintains, are pre-empted because they interfere with "Congress's purpose to entrust an expert agency to make drug labeling decisions that strike a balance between competing objectives." Brief for Petitioner 46. We find no merit in this argument, which relies on an untenable interpretation of congressional intent and an overbroad view of an agency's power to pre-empt state law.

Wyeth contends that the FDCA establishes both a floor and a ceiling for drug regulation: Once the FDA has approved a drug's label, a state-law verdict may not deem the label inadequate, regardless of whether there is any evidence that the FDA has considered the stronger warning at issue. The most glaring problem with this argument is that all evidence of Congress' purposes is to the contrary. Building on its 1906 Act, Congress enacted the FDCA to bolster consumer protection against harmful products. Congress did not provide a federal remedy for consumers harmed by unsafe or ineffective drugs in the 1938 statute or in any subsequent amendment. Evidently, it determined that widely available state rights of action provided appropriate relief for injured consumers. . . .

If Congress thought state-law suits posed an obstacle to its objectives, it surely would have enacted an express pre-emption provision at some point during the FDCA's 70-year history. But despite its 1976 enactment of an express pre-emption provision for medical devices, see § 521, 90 Stat. 574 (codified at 21 U.S.C. § 360k(a)), Congress has not enacted such a provision for prescription drugs. Its silence on the issue, coupled with its certain awareness of the prevalence of state tort litigation, is powerful evidence that Congress did not intend FDA oversight to be the exclusive means of ensuring drug safety and effectiveness. . . .

Despite this evidence that Congress did not regard state tort litigation as an obstacle to achieving its purposes, Wyeth nonetheless maintains that, because the FDCA requires the FDA to determine that a drug is safe and effective under the conditions set forth in its labeling, the agency must be presumed to have performed a precise balancing of risks and benefits and to have established a specific labeling standard that leaves no room for different state-law judgments. In advancing this argument, Wyeth relies not on any statement by Congress, but instead on the preamble to a 2006 FDA regulation governing the content and format of prescription drug labels. In that preamble, the FDA declared that the FDCA establishes "both a 'floor' and a 'ceiling,'" so that "FDA approval of labeling . . . preempts conflicting or contrary State law." *Id.*, at 3934–3935. It further stated that certain state-law actions, such as those involving failure-to-warn claims, "threaten FDA's statutorily prescribed role as the expert Federal agency responsible for evaluating and regulating drugs." *Id.*, at 3935.

This Court has recognized that an agency regulation with the force of law can pre-empt conflicting state requirements. In such cases, the Court has performed its own conflict determination, relying on the substance of state and federal law and not on agency proclamations of pre-emption. We are faced with no such regulation in this case, but rather with an agency's mere assertion that state law is an obstacle to achieving its statutory objectives. Because Congress has not authorized the FDA to pre-empt state law directly, . . . the question is what weight we should accord the FDA's opinion.

In prior cases, we have given "some weight" to an agency's views about the impact of tort law on federal objectives when "the subject matter is technical[ ] and the relevant history and background are complex and extensive." *Geier*, 529 U.S., at 883, 120 S.Ct. 1913. Even in such cases, however, we have not deferred to an agency's *conclusion* that state law is pre-empted. Rather, we have attended to an agency's explanation of how state law affects the regulatory scheme. While agencies have no special authority to pronounce on pre-emption absent delegation by Congress, they do have a unique understanding of the statutes they administer and an attendant ability to make informed determinations about how state requirements may pose an "obstacle to the accomplishment and execution of the full purposes and objectives of Congress." *Hines*, 312 U.S., at 67, 61 S.Ct. 399; see *Geier*, 529 U.S., at 883, 120 S.Ct. 1913; *Lohr*, 518 U.S., at 495–496, 116 S.Ct. 2240. The weight we accord the agency's explanation of state law's impact on the federal scheme depends on its thoroughness, consistency, and persuasiveness.

Under this standard, the FDA's 2006 preamble does not merit deference. When the FDA issued its notice of proposed rulemaking in December 2000, it explained that the rule would "not contain policies that have federalism implications or that preempt State law." 65 Fed.Reg. 81103; see also 71, *id.*, at 3969 (noting that the "proposed rule did not propose to preempt state law"). In 2006, the agency finalized the rule and, without offering States or other interested parties notice or opportunity for comment, articulated a sweeping position on the FDCA's pre-emptive effect in the regulatory preamble. The agency's views on state law are inherently suspect in light of this procedural failure.

. . . .

In keeping with Congress' decision not to pre-empt common-law tort suits, it appears that the FDA traditionally regarded state law as a complementary form of drug regulation. The FDA has limited resources to monitor the 11,000 drugs on the market, and manufacturers have superior access to information about their drugs, especially in the post-marketing phase as new risks emerge. State tort suits uncover unknown drug hazards and provide incentives for drug manufacturers to disclose safety risks promptly. They also serve a distinct compensatory function that may motivate injured persons to come forward with information. Failure-to-warn actions, in particular, lend force to the FDCA's premise that manufacturers, not the FDA, bear primary responsibility for their drug labeling at all times. Thus, the FDA long maintained that state law offers an additional, and important, layer of consumer protection that complements FDA regulation. The agency's 2006 preamble represents a dramatic change in position.

. . . .

In short, Wyeth has not persuaded us that failure-to-warn claims like Levine's obstruct the federal regulation of drug labeling. Congress has repeatedly declined to pre-empt state law, and the FDA's recently adopted position that state tort suits interfere with its statutory mandate is entitled to no weight. Although we recognize that some state-law claims might well frustrate the achievement of congressional objectives, this is not such a case.

V

We conclude that it is not impossible for Wyeth to comply with its state and federal law obligations and that Levine's common-law claims do not stand as an obstacle to the accomplishment of Congress' purposes in the FDCA. Accordingly, the judgment of the Vermont Supreme Court is affirmed.

It is so ordered.

[JUSTICE BREYER'S concurring opinion is omitted.]

JUSTICE THOMAS, concurring

I agree with the Court that the fact that the Food and Drug Administration (FDA) approved the label for petitioner Wyeth's drug Phenergan does not pre-empt the state-law judgment before the Court. . . .

I write separately, however, because I cannot join the majority's implicit endorsement of far-reaching implied pre-emption doctrines. In particular, I have become increasingly skeptical of this Court's "purposes and objectives" pre-emption jurisprudence. . . .

. . . .

. . . . Under the vague and "potentially boundless" doctrine of "purposes and objectives" pre-emption . . . the Court has pre-empted state law based on its interpretation of broad federal policy objectives, legislative history, or generalized notions of congressional purposes that are not contained within the text of federal law.

. . . .

. . . . Because such a sweeping approach to pre-emption leads to the illegitimate-and thus, unconstitutional-invalidation of state laws, I can no longer assent to a doctrine that pre-empts state laws merely because they "stan[d] as an obstacle to the accomplishment and execution of the full purposes and objectives" of federal law, *Hines,* 312 U.S., at 67, 61 S.Ct. 399, as perceived by this Court. I therefore respectfully concur only in the judgment.

JUSTICE ALITO, with whom THE CHIEF JUSTICE and JUSTICE SCALIA join, dissenting.

. . . .

A faithful application of this Court's conflict pre-emption cases compels the conclusion that the FDA's 40-year-long effort to regulate the safety and efficacy of Phenergan pre-empts respondent's tort suit. Indeed, that result follows directly from our conclusion in *Geier.*

. . . .

Notwithstanding the statute's saving clause, and notwithstanding the fact that Congress gave the Secretary authority to set only "minimum" safety standards, we held Geier's state tort suit pre-empted. In reaching that result, we relied heavily on the view of the Secretary of Transportation. . . . Because the Secretary determined that a menu of alternative technologies was "safe," the doctrine of conflict pre-emption barred Geier's efforts to deem some of those federally approved alternatives "unsafe" under state tort law.

The same rationale applies here. Through Phenergan's label, the FDA offered medical professionals a menu of federally approved, "safe" and "effective" alternatives-including IV push-for administering the drug. Through a state tort suit, respondent attempted to deem IV push "unsafe" and "ineffective." To be sure, federal law does not prohibit Wyeth from contraindicating IV push, just as federal law did not prohibit Honda from installing airbags in all its cars. But just as we held that States may not compel the latter, so, too, are States precluded from compelling the former. If anything, a finding of pre-emption is even more appropriate here because the FDCA-unlike the National Traffic and Motor Safety Vehicle Act-contains no evidence that Congress intended the FDA to set only "minimum standards," and the FDCA does not contain a saving clause.

　. . . .

To be sure, state tort suits can peacefully coexist with the FDA's labeling regime, and they have done so for decades. But this case is far from peaceful coexistence. The FDA told Wyeth that Phenergan's label renders its use "safe." But the State of Vermont, through its tort law, said: "Not so."

The state-law rule at issue here is squarely pre-empted. Therefore, I would reverse the judgment of the Supreme Court of Vermont.

NOTES, COMMENTS, AND QUESTIONS

1.　The politics of preemption are not entirely predictable. Those favoring aggressive federal regulation (sometimes characterized as liberal) will, on occasion, oppose coexistence application of state tort law on the premise that it is at odds with the federal regulatory effort. Marin R. Scordato, *Federal Preemption of State Tort Claims*, 35 U.C. DAVIS L. REV. 1, 3 (2001); Jean Macchiaroli Eggen, *The Normalization of Product Preemption Doctrine*, 57 ALA. L. REV. 725 (2006).

2.　While the Supreme Court is criticized on occasion for leaning too heavily on the side of tort reform or defendants in white collar cases,[4] *Wyeth* is hardly a pro-tort reform case. It is one of a series of recent decisions that attempt to balance federal regulation and state tort liability. In rejecting defendant Wyeth's claim for preemption protection and upholding the Vermont judgment, the Court allowed to stand a "failure to warn" case—and failure to warn cases are most assuredly problematic from a tort reform perspective. When one is harmed by a product, in hindsight, it is not all that unusual to assert that a warning might have helped. When there is a governmentally approved warning, as in *Wyeth*, it is understandable that a defendant would

---

[4]　*See, e.g.*, Tracy A. Thomas, *Proportionality and the Supreme Court's Jurisprudence of Remedies*, 59 HASTINGS L.J. 73, 131 (referring to the Court's "remedial bias,"); Faith Stevelman Kahn, *Bombing Markets, Subverting the Rule of Law: Enron, Financial Fraud, and September 11, 2001*, 76 TUL. L. REV. 1579, 1619–21 (2002).

argue it has done all it is supposed to do—but, according to this decision, the defendant would be wrong.[5]

3.   For those studying tort reform as part of a first-semester Torts course, it might be helpful to have a working understanding of the origin of preemption as well as a straightforward statement of the doctrine itself:

> Preemption of state law stems from the Supremacy Clause of the United States Constitution which the Court has long held requires an assessment of Congressional purpose. To that end, the Court has defined express and implied preemption doctrines. Express preemption exists when a statutory provision provides the scope of Congress' intent to preempt, and its scope must be evaluated through an assessment of the statutory language, its structure, and, there is disagreement here, its purpose as discerned through the legislative history. Implied preemption doctrines substitute for Congress' express intent to preempt a judicial determination that Congress would have wanted federal laws to govern when state laws create an actual conflict with federal objectives or make it impossible to comply with both federal and state obligations.

Mary J. Davis, *Symposium: The Products Liability Restatement: Was It a Success?: On Restating Products Liability Preemption*, 74 BROOKLYN L. REV. 759, 761–62 (2009).

4.   *Wyeth* is one of a series of recent cases that seeks to clarify federal preemption. In *Riegel v. Medtronic*,[6] decided less than a year before *Wyeth*, the Court found express preemption for Class III products approved under the Medical Devices Amendment Act of 1976, 21 U.S.C. § 360k(a) (2006) (MDA). Preemption of state tort law was premised in part on the extensive testing required prior to FDA approval under the MDA and the fact that subsequent manufacture of a product approved under this provision could not vary from the specifications established in the MDA review process. The Court found that

> Class III devices undergo a "rigorous regime of premarket approval." In the premarket approval process, the FDA reviews the device design, labeling, and manufacturing specifications and makes a determination as to whether the specifications provide a "reasonable assurance of safety and effectiveness."

Based on *Wyeth*, one could conclude that the presence of state tort litigation options played a role in protecting the consumer. Interestingly enough, some commentators find the exact opposite to be true in *Medtronic*.

[T]he opinion reflects a concern for consumer welfare. In Justice Antonin Scalia's majority opinion, the Court stressed that expert regulators are better-

---

[5]   Richard L. Cupp, Symposium: *The Products Liability Restatement: Was It a Success?: Preemption's Rise (and Bit of a Fall) as Products Liability Reform Wyeth, Riegel, Altria, and the Restatement (Third)'s Prescription Product Design Defect Standard*, 74 BROOKLYN L. REV. 727 (2009) (discussing the RESTATEMENT (THIRD) provision on pharmaceuticals, Sec. 6(c) and the impact of Wyeth and other recent preemption cases).

[6]   552 U.S. 312.

suited than juries to balance the safety risks of a particular medical device against the potential health benefits of the product. The Court pointed out that state tort litigation might very well force life-saving products off the market and thus hurt public health. From this perspective, *Riegel* . . . reflects the Court's skepticism of litigation as an effective tool for regulation and for protecting consumer welfare.

Robin S. Conrad, *The Roberts Court and the Myth of a Pro-Business Bias*, 49 SANTA CLARA L. REV. 997, 1007 (2009).

Can one generalize about consumer protection and conclude that a comprehensive federal regulatory scheme is superior to state tort law if the goal is to protect the consumer? Take a look at the *Medtronic* case and ask yourself if the process the Court describes is more likely to protect consumer interests than the incentives for safer and more efficacious products generated by the possibility of a multi-million dollar damage award.

ONEOK V. LEARJET
135 S. Ct. 1591, 191 L. Ed. 2d 511 (2015)

JUSTICE BREYER delivered the opinion of the Court.

In this case, a group of manufacturers, hospitals, and other institutions that buy natural gas directly from interstate pipelines sued the pipelines, claiming that they engaged in behavior that violated state antitrust laws. The pipelines' behavior affected both federally regulated wholesale natural-gas prices and nonfederally regulated retail natural-gas prices. The question is whether the federal Natural Gas Act pre-empts these lawsuits. We have said that, in passing the Act, "Congress occupied the field of matters relating to wholesale sales and transportation of natural gas in interstate commerce." Schneidewind v. ANR Pipeline Co., 485 U. S. 293, 305, 108 S. Ct. 1145, 99 L. Ed. 2d 316 (1988). Nevertheless, for the reasons given below, we conclude that the Act does not pre-empt the state-law antitrust suits at issue here.

A

The Supremacy Clause provides that "the Laws of the United States" (as well as treaties and the Constitution itself) "shall be the supreme Law of the Land . . . any Thing in the Constitution or Laws of any state to the Contrary notwithstanding." Art. VI, cl. 2. Congress may consequently pre-empt, i.e., invalidate, a state law through federal legislation. It may do so through express language in a statute. But even where, as here, a statute does not refer expressly to pre-emption, Congress may implicitly pre-empt a state law, rule, or other state action. See Sprietsma v. Mercury Marine, 537 U. S. 51, 64, 123 S. Ct. 518, 154 L. Ed. 2d 466 (2002).

It may do so either through "field" pre-emption or "conflict" pre-emption. As to the former, Congress may have intended "to foreclose any state regulation in the area," irrespective of whether state law is consistent or inconsistent with "federal standards." Arizona v. United States, 567 U. S. ___, ___, 132 S. Ct. 2492, 2502, 183 L. Ed. 2d 351, 370 (2012) (emphasis added). In such situations, Congress has forbidden the State to take action in the field that the federal statute pre-empts.

By contrast, conflict pre-emption exists where "compliance with both state and federal law is impossible," or where "the state law 'stands as an obstacle to the accomplishment and execution of the full purposes and objectives of Congress.'" California v. ARC America Corp., 490 U. S. 93, 100, 101, 109 S. Ct. 1661, 104 L. Ed. 2d 86 (1989). In either situation, federal law must prevail.

No one here claims that any relevant federal statute expressly pre-empts state antitrust lawsuits. Nor have the parties argued at any length that these state suits conflict with federal law. Rather, the interstate pipeline companies (petitioners here) argue that Congress implicitly "'occupied the field of matters relating to wholesale sales and transportation of natural gas in interstate commerce.'" . . . And they contend that the state antitrust claims advanced by their direct-sales customers (respondents here) fall within that field. The United States, supporting the pipelines, argues similarly. . . . Since the parties have argued this case almost exclusively in terms of field pre-emption, we consider only the field pre-emption question.

. . . .

C

. . . . Respondents, as we have said, bought large quantities of natural gas directly from interstate pipelines for their own consumption. They believe that they overpaid in these transactions due to the interstate pipelines' manipulation of the natural-gas indices. Based on this belief, they filed state-law antitrust suits against petitioners in state and federal courts. . . . The pipelines removed all the state cases to federal court, where they were consolidated and sent for pretrial proceedings to the Federal District Court for the District of Nevada. See 28 U. S. C. § 1407.

The pipelines then moved for summary judgment on the ground that the Natural Gas Act pre-empted respondents' state-law antitrust claims. The District Court granted their motion. It concluded that the pipelines were "jurisdictional sellers," i.e., "natural gas companies engaged in" the "transportation of natural gas in interstate commerce." . . . And it held that respondents' claims, which were "aimed at" these sellers' "alleged practices of false price reporting, wash trades, and anticompetitive collusive behavior" were pre-empted because "such practices," not only affected nonjurisdictional direct-sale prices but also "directly affect[ed]" jurisdictional (i.e., wholesale) rates.

The Ninth Circuit reversed. It emphasized that the price-manipulation of which respondents complained affected not only jurisdictional (i.e., wholesale) sales, but also nonjurisdictional (i.e., retail) sales. The court construed the Natural Gas Act's pre-emptive scope narrowly in light of Congress' intent—manifested in § 1(b) of the Act—to preserve for the States the authority to regulate nonjurisdictional sales. And it held that the Act did not pre-empt state-law claims aimed at obtaining damages for excessively high retail natural-gas prices stemming from interstate pipelines' price manipulation, even if the manipulation raised wholesale rates as well. See In re Western States Wholesale Natural Gas Antitrust Litigation, 715 F. 3d 716, 729–736 (2013).

The pipelines sought certiorari. . . .

II

Petitioners, supported by the United States, argue that their customers' state antitrust lawsuits are within the field that the Natural Gas Act pre-empts. . . . They point out that respondents' antitrust claims target anticompetitive activities that affected wholesale (as well as retail) rates. See Brief for Petitioners 2. They add that the Natural Gas Act expressly grants FERC authority to keep wholesale rates at reasonable levels. See ibid. (citing 15 U. S. C. §§ 717(b), 717d(a)). In exercising this authority, FERC has prohibited the very kind of anticompetitive conduct that the state actions attack. See Part I–B–3, supra. And, petitioners contend, letting these actions proceed will permit state antitrust courts to reach conclusions about that conduct that differ from those that FERC might reach or has already reached. Accordingly, petitioners argue, respondents' state-law antitrust suits fall within the pre-empted field.

A

Petitioners' arguments are forceful, but we cannot accept their conclusion. As we have repeatedly stressed, the Natural Gas Act "was drawn with meticulous regard for the continued exercise of state power, not to handicap or dilute it in any way." Panhandle Eastern Pipe Line Co. v. Public Serv. Comm'n of Ind., 332 U. S. 507, 517–518, 68 S. Ct. 190, 92 L. Ed. 128 (1947). . . . Accordingly, where (as here) a state law can be applied to non-jurisdictional as well as jurisdictional sales, we must proceed cautiously, finding pre-emption only where detailed examination convinces us that a matter falls within the pre-empted field as defined by our precedents. . . .

Antitrust laws, like blue sky laws, are not aimed at natural-gas companies in particular, but rather all businesses in the marketplace. . . . They are far broader in their application than, for example, the regulations at issue in Northern Natural, which applied only to entities buying gas from fields within the State. See 372 U. S., at 85–86, n. 1, 83 S. Ct. 646, 9 L. Ed. 2d 601; contra, [* * *22] post, at ___, 191 L. Ed. 2d, at 529 (stating that Northern Natural concerned "background market conditions"). This broad applicability of state antitrust law supports a finding of no pre-emption here. . . .

D

We note that petitioners and the Solicitor General have argued that we should defer to FERC's determination that field pre-emption bars the respondents' claims. . . . But they have not pointed to a specific FERC determination that state antitrust claims fall within the field pre-empted by the Natural Gas Act. Rather, they point only to the fact that FERC has promulgated detailed rules governing manipulation of price indices. Because there is no determination by FERC that its regulation pre-empts the field into which respondents' state-law antitrust suits fall, we need not consider what legal effect such a determination might have. And we conclude that the detailed federal regulations here do not offset the other considerations that weigh against a finding of pre-emption in this context.

* * *

For these reasons, the judgment of the Court of Appeals for the Ninth Circuit is affirmed.

It is so ordered.

Concurring and dissenting opinions omitted

_____

NOTES AND QUESTIONS

1.   While the Supreme Court has not been a paragon of consistency in the field of preemption, there are certain uniform principles the Court respects. Looking at the above case, can you identify those principles? Why would the Court allow a state antitrust claim in a field like natural gas where there is both extensive federal regulation and extensive federal antitrust law. Based on your reading of the case, what is the value of a state antitrust claim?

2.   The uneasy balance between federal energy regulation and antitrust law is discussed in a thorough and insightful piece by Professor Jim Rossi, "The Brave New Path of Energy Federalism," 95 TEX. L. REV. 399 (2016). The article explores the problem of dual sovereignty and the federalism/preemption puzzle. A similarly compelling piece by Daniel Crane and Adam Hester provides an interesting comparison focused more on traditional preemption arguments.   Daniel Crane and Adam Hester, "State-Action Immunity and Section 5 of the FTC Act," 115 MICH. L. REV. 365 (2016).

3. Preemption in the tort reform world seems to be more about the desire to limiting state tort law liability than limiting state initiated antitrust exposure. One assumption to be derived from this is that defendants will fare better working their way through the federal regulatory process than when they are exposed to state tort law. Do you agree? Are those involved in federal regulation more likely to protect industry interests than state courts and state juries?

PLIVA, INC. V. MENSING
564 U.S. 604 (2011)

Opinion by JUSTICE THOMAS

These consolidated lawsuits involve state tort-law claims based on certain drug manufacturers' alleged failure to provide adequate warning labels for generic metoclopramide. The question presented is whether federal drug regulations applicable to generic drug manufacturers directly conflict with, and thus pre-empt, these state-law claims. We hold that they do.

I

Metoclopramide is a drug designed to speed the movement of food through the digestive system. The Food and Drug Administration (FDA) first approved metoclopramide tablets, under the brand name Reglan, in 1980. Five years later, generic manufacturers also began producing metoclopramide. The drug is commonly used to treat digestive tract problems such as diabetic gastroparesis and gastroesophageal reflux disorder.

Evidence has accumulated that long-term metoclopramide use can cause tardive dyskinesia, a severe neurological disorder. Studies have shown that up to 29% of patients who take metoclopramide for several years develop this condition. . . .

Accordingly, warning labels for the drug have been strengthened and clarified several times. . . . [In] 2009, the FDA ordered a black box warning—its strongest—which states: "Treatment with metoclopramide can cause tardive dyskinesia, a serious movement disorder that is often irreversible. . . . Treatment with metoclopramide for longer than 12 weeks should be avoided in all but rare cases." . . . Mensing and Julie Demahy, the plaintiffs in these consolidated cases, were prescribed Reglan in 2001 and 2002, respectively. Both received generic metoclopramide from their pharmacists. After taking the drug as prescribed for several years, both women developed tardive dyskinesia.

In separate suits, Mensing and Demahy sued the generic drug manufacturers that produced the metoclopramide they took (Manufacturers). Each alleged . . . the Manufacturers were liable under state tort law (specifically, that of Minnesota and Louisiana) for failing to provide adequate warning labels. . . .In both suits, the Manufacturers urged that federal law pre-empted the state tort claims. . . .[T]hey argued, that it was impossible to simultaneously comply with both federal law and any state tort-law duty that required them to use a different label.

The Courts of Appeals for the Fifth and Eighth Circuits rejected the Manufacturers' arguments . . . . . We granted certiorari . . . consolidated the cases, and now reverse each.

II

Pre-emption analysis requires us to compare federal and state law. . . . It is undisputed that . . . Minnesota and Louisiana tort law require a drug manufacturer that is or should be aware of its product's danger to label that product in a way that renders it reasonably safe. . . . Mensing and Demahy have pleaded that the Manufacturers knew or should have known of the high risk . . . inherent in the long-term use of their product. They have also pleaded that the Manufacturers knew or should have known that their labels did not adequately warn of that risk.

Federal law imposes . . . complex drug labeling requirements. . . . [However] brand-name and generic drug manufacturers have different federal drug labeling duties. A brand-name manufacturer seeking new drug approval is responsible for the accuracy and adequacy of its label. . . . A manufacturer seeking generic drug approval, on the other hand, is responsible for ensuring that its warning label is the same as the brand name's. . . .

. . . . What is in dispute is whether, and to what extent, generic manufacturers may change their labels after initial FDA approval. Mensing and Demahy contend that federal law provided several avenues through which the Manufacturers could have altered their metoclopramide labels in time to prevent the injuries here. The FDA, however, tells us that it interprets its regulations to require that the warning labels of a brand-name drug and its generic copy must always be the same—thus, generic drug manufacturers have an ongoing federal duty of "sameness." U.S. Brief 16; see also 57 Fed. Reg. 17961 (1992) ("[T]he [generic drug's] labeling must be the same as the listed drug product's labeling because the listed drug product is the basis for [generic drug] approval"). . . .The FDA's views are "controlling unless plainly erroneous or inconsistent with the regulation[s]" . . .

The FDA denies that the Manufacturers could have . . . unilaterally strengthen[ed] their warning labels. The agency . . . allow[s] changes to generic drug labels only when a generic drug manufacturer changes its label to match an updated brand-name label or to follow the FDA's instructions. . . .

Next, Mensing and Demahy contend that the Manufacturers could have used "Dear Doctor" letters to send additional warnings to prescribing physicians and other healthcare professionals. . . .

A Dear Doctor letter that contained substantial new warning information would not be consistent with the drug's approved labeling. Moreover, if generic drug manufacturers, but not the brand-name manufacturer, sent such letters, that would inaccurately imply a therapeutic difference between the brand and generic drugs and thus could be impermissibly "misleading." . . .

   . . . .

To summarize . . . State tort law places a duty directly on all drug manufacturers to adequately and safely label their products. Taking Mensing and Demahy's allegations as true, this duty required the Manufacturers to use a different, stronger label than the label they actually used. Federal drug regulations, as interpreted by the FDA, prevented the Manufacturers from independently changing their generic drugs' safety labels. . . .

The Supremacy Clause establishes [that federal law "shall be the supreme Law of the Land . . . any Thing in the Constitution or Laws of any State to the Contrary notwithstanding." U.S. Const., Art. VI, cl. 2. Where state and federal law "directly conflict," state law must give way. . . . We have held that state and federal law conflict where it is "impossible for a private party to comply with both state and federal requirements."

We find impossibility here. It was not lawful under federal law for the Manufacturers to do what state law required of them. And even if they had fulfilled their federal duty to ask for FDA assistance, they would not have satisfied the requirements of state law.

If the Manufacturers had independently changed their labels to satisfy their state-law duty, they would have violated federal law. [emphasis added] Taking Mensing and Demahy's allegations as true, state law imposed on the Manufacturers a duty to attach a safer label to their generic metoclopramide. Federal law, however, demanded that generic drug labels be the same at all times as the corresponding brand-name drug labels. . . . Thus, it was impossible for the Manufacturers to comply with both their state-law duty to change the label and their federal-law duty to keep the label the same.

   . . . . Mensing and Demahy argue that if the *Manufacturers had asked the FDA for help in changing the corresponding brand-name label, they might eventually have been able to accomplish under federal law what state law requires.* That is true enough. . . .

This raises the novel question whether conflict pre-emption should take into account these *possible* actions by the FDA and the brand-name manufacturer. . . . [emphasis added]

[It] is certainly possible that, had the Manufacturers asked the FDA for help, they might have eventually been able to strengthen their warning label. . . .

If these conjectures suffice to prevent federal and state law from conflicting for Supremacy Clause purposes, it is unclear when, outside of express pre-emption, the Supremacy Clause would have any force. . . .

Here, state law imposed a duty on the Manufacturers to take a certain action, and federal law barred them from taking that action. . . . [Regarding the labeling variation between generic and brand-name drugs] "it is not this Court's task to decide whether the statutory scheme established by Congress is unusual or even bizarre." . . . . It is beyond dispute that the federal statutes and regulations that apply to brand-name drug manufacturers are meaningfully different than those that apply to generic drug manufacturers.

* * *

The judgments of the Fifth and Eighth Circuits are reversed, and the cases are remanded for further proceedings consistent with this opinion.

[JUSTICE KENNEDY joined all but Part III–B–2 of this opinion; JUSTICE SOTOMAYOR dissented. That dissent is omitted.]

NOTES AND QUESTIONS

1.   Is the only difference between *Wyeth* and this decision the fact that one case involved brand-name drugs while the other involved the generic replicant? Arlen W. Langvardt, *Generic Pharmaceuticals and the "Unfortunate Hand" Dealt to Harmed Consumers: The Emerging State Court Resistance*, 17 MINN. J.L. SCI. & TECH. 565 (2016) (discussing the distinction between generic and brand-name labeling and preemption).

2.   Putting aside the distinction between generic and brand-name products, what is your reaction to the Court's dismissal of the plaintiffs argument that there were options the defendant could exercise that would have prevented the case from being preempted? If your response to this is, "Why should the defendant be required take voluntary steps to make itself available for suit in state court?" I suggest you look at some of the arguments early in this text regarding "fraudulent joinder." When plaintiffs include parties that keep them in state court, thus avoiding removal to federal court, those pursuing tort reform cry "foul!" For a general discussion of parts of this problem, take a look at Professor Catherine M. Sharkey's "States vs. FDA," 83 GEO. WASH. L. REV. 1609 (2015).

3.   The "impossibility" construct in this case is not difficult to articulate. If compliance with federal regulatory imperatives would make it impossible for a defendant to conform with the requirements of state common law expressed in the tort system, the Supremacy Clause comes into play. This raises a question—just how "impossible" must the situation be for a plaintiff to be denied access to justice in the plaintiff's home state?

Does impossibility mean imprudent? Impracticable? Physically impossible? Unreasonable? As with so many things in the legal system, if your answer to this is, "it depends," you have responded in a way that other lawyers and law students understand but clients, judges, juries, and others would find downright irritating. On the basics of the use of the impossibility prong of preemption, take a look at *Florida Lime & Avocado Growers, Inc. v. Paul*, 373 U.S. 132, 142–43 (1963) (particularly for the "physical impossibility" prong), and *Geier v. Am. Honda Motor Co.*, 529 U.S. 861, 899 (2000).

ZEIER V. ZIMMER, INC.

152 P.3d 861 (Okla. 2006)

WATT, C.J.

. . . .

On August 9, 2004, the defendant/appellee, Theron S. Nichols (Nichols/physician/doctor), performed knee replacement surgery on the plaintiff/appellant, Monica Belinda Zeier (Zeier/patient), implanting a device manufactured by Zimmer, Inc. (Zimmer/manufacturer). Zeier filed suit against the physician and the manufacturer on May 5, 2005, alleging negligence, manufacturer's products liability and breach of warranty. The petition provided that: 1) the wrong knee replacement parts were utilized during surgery, 2) the device was defective in design; and 3) the instrument was in the exclusive control of Nichols and Zimmer at all relevant times.

The patient neither attached an affidavit of medical negligence, as required by 63 O.S. Supp.2003 § 1–1708.1E, nor did Zeier request an extension to comply with the statutory requirement. On June 1, 2005, the doctor filed a motion to dismiss for the patient's failure to provide the medical negligence affidavit. Zeier did not respond and Nichols filed a motion to deem the cause confessed which was mailed to the patient on June 29, 2005. On the same date, Zeier responded to the motion to dismiss asserting that the petition stated a cause of action for negligence under the principle of *res ipsa loquitur*. Furthermore, she argued that the affidavit requirement of 63 O.S. Supp.2003 § 1–1708.1E constituted an unconstitutional special law under the Oklahoma Constitution art. 5, §§ 46 and 59 and that it violated the constitutional guarantee of access to the courts contained in art. 2, § 6 of the Oklahoma Constitution and the Fourteenth Amendment to the United States Constitution.

. . . .

Zeier contends that 63 O.S. Supp.2003 § 1–1708.1E violates art. 5, § 46 in that it is a special law affecting only medical malpractice plaintiffs rather than all individuals seeking redress for negligent acts. The doctor insists that the statute is a general law encompassing all of the class-medical providers-and that it is general in its application. We disagree with the doctor.

Art. 5, § 46 of the Oklahoma Constitution provides that the Legislature may not pass special laws affecting certain subjects. The constitutional provision contains twenty eight areas where general laws shall always be applicable. Included within the list of categories is a prohibition against regulating the practice or jurisdiction of, or changing the rules of evidence in judicial proceedings or inquiry before the courts. The language utilized in art. 5, § 46 is a mandatory prohibition against special laws-it provides in pertinent part:

> "The Legislature shall not except as otherwise provided in this Constitution, pass any local or special law authorizing:
>
> > . . . Regulating the practice or jurisdiction of, or changing the rules of evidence in judicial proceedings or inquiry before the courts. . . ."

Title 63 O.S. Supp.2003 § 1–1708.1E requires that a plaintiff alleging medical malpractice attach an affidavit to the petition stating that the plaintiff: 1) has consulted with a qualified expert; 2) has obtained a written opinion from a qualified expert that the facts presented constitute professional negligence; and 3) has determined, on the basis of the expert's opinion, that the malpractice claim is meritorious and based on good cause. . . .

. . . .

The terms of art. 5, § 46 command that court procedure be symmetrical and apply equally across the board for an entire class of similarly situated persons or things. In a special laws attack under art. 5, § 46, the only issue to be resolved is whether a statute upon a subject enumerated in the constitutional provision targets for different treatment less than an entire class of similarly situated persons or things. The test is whether the provision fits into the structured regime of established procedure as part of a symmetrical whole. If an enactment injects asymmetry, the § 46 interdiction of special law has been offended.

The affidavit of merit requirement immediately divides tort victims alleging negligence into two classes-those who pursue a cause of action in negligence generally and those who name medical professionals as defendants. In 1984, Oklahoma became a notice pleading state with the adoption of the Oklahoma Pleading Code. The pleading code does not require negligence claimants generally to have an affidavit supporting the facts alleged and the anticipated basis for the right of recovery to be filed along with the petition. Plaintiffs alleging anything other than medical negligence need only file a petition giving fair notice of the plaintiff's claim and the grounds upon which it rests. These claimants have no affidavit requirement and may commence a cause of action with the filing of a petition, while those alleging medical malpractice must obtain a professional opinion that their cause is meritorious as a prerequisite to pursuing suit or be subject to dismissal.

. . . .

. . . . The affidavits of merit requirement obligates plaintiffs to engage in extensive pre-trial discovery to obtain the facts necessary for an expert to render an opinion resulting in most medical malpractice causes being settled out of court during discovery. Rather than reducing the problems associated with malpractice litigation, these provisions have resulted in the dismissal of legitimately injured plaintiffs' claims based solely on procedural, rather than substantive, grounds.

Another unanticipated result of statutes similar to Oklahoma's scheme has been the creation of a windfall for insurance companies who benefit from the decreased number of causes they must defend but which are not required to implement post-tort reform rates decreasing the cost of medical malpractice insurance to physicians. These companies happily pay less out in tort-reform states while continuing to collect higher premiums from doctors and encouraging the public to blame the victim or attorney for bringing frivolous lawsuits.

. . . .

The Okla. Const. art. 2, § 6 provides:

"The courts of justice of the State shall be open to every person, and speedy and certain remedy afforded for every wrong and for every injury to person, property, or reputation; and right and justice shall be administered without sale, denial, delay, or prejudice." [Emphasis provided.]

The clear language of Art. 2, § 6 requires that the courts must be open to all on the same terms without prejudice. The framers of the Constitution intended that all individuals, without partiality, could pursue an effective remedy designed to protect their basic and fundamental rights. Although we recognize that the Legislature may facilitate speedy resolution of differences, legislation cannot be used to deny the constitutional guarantee of court access-a fundamental right. Therefore, this Court strictly scrutinizes actions which deny such opportunity.

Access to courts must be available to all through simple and direct means and the right must be administered in favor of justice rather than being bound by technicalities. Claimants may not have the fundamental right of court access withheld for nonpayment of some liability or conditioned on coercive collection devices. Here, medical malpractice plaintiffs are singled out and must stand the cost of an expert opinion, which may range from $500 to $5,000, before they may proceed to have their rights adjudicated. In at least one instance, an affidavit of merit cost the litigant $12,000. A statute that so conditions one's right to litigate impermissibly denies equal protection and closes the court house doors to those financially incapable of obtaining a pre-petition medical opinion. Therefore, we determine that 63 O.S. Supp.2003 § 1–1708.1E creates an unconstitutional monetary barrier to the access to courts guaranteed by art. 2, § 6 of the Oklahoma Constitution.

. . . .

This Court does not correct the Legislature, nor do we take upon ourselves the responsibility of legislating by judicial fiat. However, we are compelled to apply Oklahoma's Constitution. It has long been the policy of the Oklahoma Constitution, the statutes and this Court to open the doors of justice to every person without distinction or discrimination for redress of wrongs and reparation for injuries. Although art. 2, § 6 does not promise a remedy for every wrong, it requires that a complainant be given access to court when a wrong suffered is recognized in the law.

Treating medical malpractice plaintiffs with rules inapplicable to all other negligence claimants interjects a degree of arbitrariness which sabotages equal access to the courts. Section 1–1708.1E creates the potential for a medical expert to usurp the functions of the judiciary and the trier of fact. The requirement that a medical malpractice claimant obtain a professional's opinion that the cause is meritorious at a cost of between $500.00 and $5,000.00 creates an unconstitutional monetary barrier to the access to courts guaranteed by art. 2, § 6 of the Oklahoma Constitution.

REVERSED.

[Concurring and dissenting opinions omitted]

NOTES AND QUESTIONS

1.   Not all "affidavits of merit" have been set aside by reviewing courts. For example, see MICH. COMP. LAWS ANN. § 600.2912d (West 2000); N.J. Stat. Ann. § 2A:53A–27 (West 2004):

> [A] plaintiff shall . . . provide each defendant with an affidavit of an appropriate licensed person that there exists a reasonable probability that the care, skill or knowledge exercised or exhibited in the treatment, practice or work that is the subject of the complaint, fell outside acceptable professional or occupational standards or treatment practices.

2.   When a state legislature adopts a tort reform provision at odds with the state constitution, decisions like *Zimmer* should come as no surprise. In other cases, while the state constitution is not transgressed overtly by a newly enacted tort reform provision, the basic concept of separation of powers can be an obstacle to tort reform. For example, in *Johnson v. Rockwell Automation*, 2009 Ark. 241, 308 S.W.3d 135, 2009 WL 1218362, the court addressed tort reform legislation dealing with two changes in the law: (1) rules regarding multiple defendants (joint and several liability) as well as persons who may have responsibility for the plaintiff's harms but are not named as parties, and (2) evidence of damages for the cost of medical care. Guarding its jurisdiction carefully regarding its rules of procedure, the court held:

> Rules regarding pleading, practice, and procedure are solely the responsibility of this court.
>
> Law is substantive [and within the province of the courts and the legislature] when it is "[t]he part of the law that creates, defines, and regulates the rights, duties, and powers of parties." Procedural law is defined as "[t]he rules that prescribe the steps for having a right or duty judicially enforced, as opposed to the law that defines the specific rights or duties themselves."
>
> Clearly the law modifying joint and several liability, defines the right of a party, a defendant, and is substantive. However . . . it is clear to this court that the legislature has, without regard to this court's "rules of pleading, practice and procedure," established its own procedure by which the fault of a nonparty shall be litigated. While respondents argued in oral argument that a defendant has always been able to "point to the empty chair," the "phantom defendant" [the tort reform provision] is different. The nonparty-fault provision bypasses our "rules of pleading, practice and procedure" by setting up a procedure to determine the fault of a nonparty and mandating the consideration of that nonparty's fault in an effort to reduce a plaintiff's recovery.
>
> Additionally, the plain language of the statute . . . is in direct conflict with our [Rules of Procedure] which specifically set[ ] forth the pleadings and instructs that "[n]o other pleadings shall be

allowed.". . . . Because the nonparty provision is procedural, it offends the principle of separation of powers. . . .

On the matter of the admissibility of evidence pertaining to medical costs, the court held:

It is undisputed that the rules of evidence are "rules of pleading, practice and procedure." Moreover, we have held that the rules of evidence are rules falling within this court's domain. Our review of the plain language of the medical-costs provision reveals that the instant statute promulgates a rule of evidence. Here, the provision clearly limits the evidence that may be introduced relating to the value of medical expenses to the amount of medical expenses paid or the amount to be paid by a plaintiff or on a plaintiff's behalf, thereby dictating what evidence is admissible. Because rules regarding the admissibility of evidence are within our province, we hold that the medical-costs provision also violates separation of powers . . . and, therefore, is unconstitutional.

3.   Is the above delineation of the limits on the power of state legislatures an accurate statement of law as you understand it? Does the substance/procedure distinction ring true? Is it possible that this is a matter of turf, power, identity, or an assertion of judicial autonomy? For a somewhat related set of thoughts, see Basil M. Loeb, *Comment, Abuse of Power: Certain State Courts Are Disregarding Standing and Original Jurisdiction Principles So They Can Declare Tort Reform Unconstitutional*, 84 MARQ. L. REV. 491, 508–13 (2000).

4.   The *Zimmer* case was not based on a right-to-a-remedy provision, similar to those in the vast majority of state constitutions—but it could have been. See Thomas R. Phillips, *The Constitutional Right to a Remedy*, 78 N.Y.U. L. REV. 1309 (2003). State court litigation regarding the efficacy of tort reform legislation is fairly common, whether the challenge is to the state or federal constitution. Carly N. Kelly & Michelle M. Mello, *Are Medical Malpractice Damages Caps Constitutional? An Overview of State Litigation*, 33 J. L. MED. & ETHICS 515 (2005).

5.   The question of remedial entitlement is perplexing when a product is produced by a foreign manufacturer. Should state courts provide a forum for U.S. citizens injured by goods made abroad? Mark P. Chalos, *Successfully Suing Foreign Manufacturers*, TRIAL, Nov. 2008, at 32, 33–35; Andrew F. Popper, *Unavailable and Unaccountable: A Free Ride for Foreign Manufacturers of Defective Consumer Goods*, 36 THE PRODUCT SAFETY & LIABILITY REPORTER 219 (2008).

MURPHY V. RUSSELL
167 S.W.3d 835 (Tex. 2005)

. . . .

In September 1998, Russell went to the Zale Lipshy Hospital in Dallas for a biopsy. She told a nurse, who had approached her to insert an intravenous line, that she would only permit the administration of a local anesthetic. She asked to discuss the matter with the anesthesiologist, Dr. Mark Murphy, and told him she did not want to be sedated or to lose consciousness. Murphy assured her that he would not sedate her but told her he still wanted to insert an IV line to administer a saline solution and perhaps antibiotics. Once she was in the operating room, the hospital staff inserted an air tube in her nose, and she lost consciousness. When she awoke in the recovery room, Murphy admitted he had sedated her contrary to her instructions.

Russell sued Murphy, asserting battery, breach of contract, and violations of the Deceptive Trade Practices Act (DTPA), seeking actual, exemplary, and additional DTPA damages. Russell did not file an expert report within 180 days of filing suit or at any time thereafter, and Murphy moved to dismiss her lawsuit, arguing that the claims are "health care liability claims" subject to the requirements of former article 4590i. The trial court granted the motion and dismissed the case. The court of appeals reversed the trial court's judgment, reasoning that "Russell does not allege and need not prove that Murphy deviated from any standard of medical care, health care, or safety", and therefore no expert medical report was required. This was incorrect.

Former article 4590i and its expert report requirements apply to a patient's claims, regardless of whether they are tort or contract claims, when those claims come within the statutory definition of a "health care liability claim." That definition is:

"Health care liability claim" means a cause of action against a health care provider or physician for treatment, lack of treatment, or other claimed departure from accepted standards of medical care or health care or safety which proximately results in injury to or death of the patient, whether the patient's claim or cause of action sounds in tort or contract.

. . . .

[A]rticle 4590i's expert report requirement establishes a threshold over which a claimant must proceed to continue a lawsuit. It does not establish a requirement for recovery. It may be that once discovery is complete and the case is tried, there is no need for expert testimony. . . . [T]he Legislature envisioned that discovery and the ultimate determination of what issues are submitted to the fact-finder should not go forward unless at least one expert has examined the case and opined as to the applicable standard of care, that it was breached, and that there is a causal relationship between the failure to meet the standard of care and the injury, harm, or damages claimed. The fact that in the final analysis, expert testimony may not be necessary to support a verdict does not mean the claim is not a health care liability claim. . . .

Russell cannot circumvent an expert examination of her claims simply by asserting that she did not consent to a general anesthetic and that the physician admitted he failed to follow her wishes regarding anesthesia, because there may be reasons why the administration of a general anesthetic did not breach any applicable standard of care. It might be that there were emergency circumstances that arguably warranted general anesthesia without Russell's consent, or that a general anesthetic was administered without Murphy's actual knowledge at the time it was done. Under such circumstances, expert testimony about the standard of care and breach of that standard might be necessary at trial, yet if we were to accept Russell's cribbed interpretation of the term "health care liability claim," her suit would proceed without the threshold expert report contemplated by former article 4590i. . . .

Because Russell's suit asserted health care liability claims, she was required to provide Murphy with an expert report in order to proceed with those claims. Because Russell failed to do so within the statutory period, we reverse the court of appeals' judgment without hearing oral argument and dismiss Russell's suit.

NOTES AND QUESTIONS

1.   How is an "expert's report" different from a medical affidavit? What effect do these requirements have on the number and nature of medical malpractice cases filed? One commentator noted:

> People should commend this requirement because it tends to eliminate the truly weak claims. However, medical experts engaged by either side have less credibility than a court-sanctioned independent expert. For states without the pre-litigation affidavit requirement, use of a court-appointed medical expert to review the claim at the litigation's outset (or even before) would serve a similar purpose.

Ellwood F. Oakley, III, *The Next Generation of Medical Malpractice Dispute Resolution: Alternatives to Litigation*, 21 GA. ST. U.L. REV. 993, 1005 (2005).

2.   For a general discussion of the use of reports, affidavits, or other pre-litigation certification requirements, see Mitchell J. Nathanson, *It's the Economy (and Combined Ratio), Stupid: Examining the Medical Malpractice*

Litigation Crisis Myth and the Factors Critical to Reform, 108 PENN ST. L. REV. 1077, 1118–19 (2004).

3.   The assumption underlying the requirement of an expert's report or a medical affidavit is that the doctor (or other expert) signing the statement is fair, unbiased, and objective—an assumption some question. In a student note, Kimberly J. Frazier, *Arkansas's Civil Justice Reform Act of 2003: Who's Cheating Who?,*[7] the author suggests these requirements systems have created a "cottage industry." It is a darker view of the tort system, one in which expert opinions are saleable commodities—and presumably so are pre-litigation reports and affidavits.

4.   In addition to filtering cases based on an affidavit or expert report, tort reform at the state level can affect the time frame in which cases can be filed. In *Diversicare General Partner, Inc. v. Rubio,*[8] an elderly plaintiff suffering from Dementia and Alzheimer's disease was sexually assaulted while in the care of the defendant nursing facility. For a variety of reasons, some related to the plaintiff's disorientation, the claim was not filed within the relatively inflexible Texas tort reform law which has a two-year statute of limitations. According to the court, this law:

> [H]eightened requirements for filing and maintaining lawsuits that assert professional liability claims against health care providers, shortened the statute of limitations and restricted tolling for such claims, and capped certain types of damages recoverable from these lawsuits. . . . Diversicare argues that these claims are barred by the two-year statute of limitations under the MLIIA, which does not provide for tolling based on mental incapacity. The parties agree that Rubio was mentally incapacitated during her entire stay. . . . Because Rubio filed suit in 1999 and the sexual assault occurred in 1995, Rubio's claims are barred by the two-year statute of limitations. . . .

For those interested in the applicability of a state tort reform provision to nursing care treatment, this is an interesting and worthwhile case.

———————

One of the central tenets of tort reform has been to require a showing of fault prior to imposing tort liability, *i.e.,* the abolition of strict liability in tort. Strict liability cases can entail either the application of Sec. 402(a) of the RESTATEMENT (SECOND) or arise in implied warranty cases, as in the decision below.

———————

---

[7]   57 ARK. L. REV. 651, 690 (2003).

[8]   185 S.W.3d 842 (Tex. 2005).

COLEMAN V. MAXWELL SHOE COMPANY, INC.

475 F. Supp. 2d 685 (E.D. Mich. 2007)

By THE HONORABLE LAWRENCE P. ZATKOFF

. . . .

On June 15, 2004, Plaintiff went shopping at Defendant J.C. Penney's store in Westland, Michigan. Plaintiff saw the "Mootsie Tootsie" shoe on display, and asked the sales clerk to bring her a size 8–1/2. The "Mootsie Tootsie" shoe is manufactured by Defendant Maxwell. Plaintiff purchased the shoes and brought them home. Two days later, the strap on the left shoe broke as Plaintiff was walking down a staircase in her home. Plaintiff fell down the stairs, sprained her left ankle, and tore the rotator cuff in her left shoulder.

Plaintiff returned the shoes to J.C. Penney. An employee refunded the purchase price, and took a picture of the unbroken right shoe. There do not appear to be any pictures of the left shoe. J.C. Penney retained the shoes, and placed them in the loss prevention office. However, at some point the shoes were either moved or disposed of, and J.C. Penney does not know where they currently are.

Plaintiff brought claims of negligence and breach of implied warranty against J.C. Penney and Maxwell. Plaintiff brought a claim of "negligence and fraud by spoliation of evidence" against J.C. Penney. Plaintiff has moved for summary judgment against J.C. Penney on the implied warranty and spoliation of evidence issues. J.C. Penney has also moved for summary judgment.

. . . .

B.   Implied Warranty

The traditional rule in Michigan was that a plaintiff did not have to show negligence on the part of the seller to recover under an implied warranty theory. The plaintiff needed to show that the product was sold in a defective condition and the defect caused the plaintiff's injury. *Piercefield v. Remington Arms Co.*, 375 Mich. 85, 133 N.W.2d 129 (1965). The Michigan Tort Reform Act, which became effective in 1996, contained a section dealing with the liability of sellers for items they sold, but did not manufacture: a product liability action, a seller other than a manufacturer is not liable for harm allegedly caused by the product unless either of the following is true:

(a)   The seller failed to exercise reasonable care, including breach of any implied warranty, with respect to the product and that failure was a proximate cause of the person's injuries.

(b)   The seller made an express warranty as to the product, the product failed to conform to the warranty, and the failure to conform to the warranty was a proximate cause of the person's harm. M.C.L. § 600.2947(6).

Plaintiff and J.C. Penney offer differing interpretations of this section. J.C. Penney claims that the Tort Reform Act added an element of fault to the traditional test for breach of implied warranty. In other words, the plaintiff must show that the product was sold in a defective condition, the defect caused her injury, and the seller failed to exercise reasonable care.

In contrast, Plaintiff argues that the Tort Reform Act did not change the traditional test for breach of implied warranty. Thus, pursuant to § 600.2947(6), the plaintiff can either show that the seller failed to exercise reasonable care, or that the product was sold in a defective condition, and the defect caused her injury.

The resolution of both Plaintiff's and J.C. Penney's motions for summary judgment hinges on the interpretation of § 600.2947(6). J.C. Penney notes that according to Plaintiff's own testimony, the shoe appeared to be in perfect condition when she purchased it. Plaintiff has failed to produce any evidence showing that J.C. Penney was negligent in failing to detect the defect in the shoe. Thus, if J.C. Penney is correct, and § 600.2947(6) requires a showing of fault on the part of the seller, it is entitled to summary judgment.

Likewise, J.C. Penney has not challenged Plaintiff's claim that a strap on the shoe broke, causing her to fall down the stairs. Plaintiff has shown that the shoe was defective, and the defect caused her injury. Thus, if Plaintiff's interpretation of § 600.2947(6) is correct, she is entitled to summary judgment on the issue of liability for breach of implied warranty.

The Michigan Supreme Court has not ruled on the issue, and the Michigan Court of Appeals, in two unpublished opinions, has issued contradictory statements on the statute. In 2001, the Court of Appeals stated that:

> [A] plaintiff seeking to recover from a retailer must establish: (1) that the seller failed to exercise reasonable care relative to the product at issue and (2) that the seller's conduct proximately caused the plaintiff's injuries. Additionally, the statute provides that if a plaintiff can establish a breach of any implied warranty, that will suffice for purposes of showing that the seller failed to "exercise reasonable care" as regards the product.

Adams v. Meijer, Inc., No. 224213, 2001 Mich. App. LEXIS 298, (2001).

This statement clearly supports Plaintiff's interpretation of the statute. In 2005, however, a different panel of the Court of Appeals held that:

The plain language MCL 600.2947 states that, in cases where a plaintiff brings a product liability action based on harm allegedly caused by a product, the only claims that may lie against a non-manufacturing seller are those based on a failure to exercise reasonable care and those based on breach of an express warranty. If the language of a statute is clear and unambiguous, no interpretation is necessary and the court must follow the clear wording of the statute. The clear and unambiguous language of MCL 600.2947 precludes an ordinary manufacturing defect claim against a non-manufacturing seller because such a claim does not involve an allegation that the seller failed to exercise reasonable care or made an express warranty.

Hastings Mut. Ins. v. GMC, No. 252427, 2005 Mich. App. LEXIS 849, *7–*8 (2005) (citation omitted).

This holding clearly supports J.C. Penney's interpretation.

. . . .

The Court finds that Mills provides the best interpretation of the statutory language. The Siedlik court based its decision in large part on a Sixth Circuit case, *Hollister v. Dayton Hudson Corp.*, 201 F.3d 731, 737 (6th Cir. 2000), and a Michigan Supreme Court case, *Piercefield v. Remington Arms Co.*, 375 Mich. 85, 133 N.W.2d 129 (1965). However, although Hollister was decided in 2000, the case was filed in 1996, before the Tort Reform Act took effect. Thus, § 600.2947(6) was not relevant to the case, and the Sixth Circuit did not discuss the statute. Likewise, Piercefield was decided before the Tort Reform Act was passed. While these cases explain the traditional rule for breach of implied warranty claims, they do not shed light on how the Tort Reform Act altered those claims.

The plain language of § 600.2947(6) indicates that the legislature did not intend for failure to exercise reasonable care and breach of implied warranty to be separate [* *13] products liability claims. § 600.2947(6)(a) states that a non-manufacturing seller is not liable unless "[t]he seller failed to exercise reasonable care, including breach of any implied warranty, with respect to the product and that failure was a proximate cause of the person's injuries." (emphasis added). Had the legislature intended this section to allow for two separate claims, it would have used the conjunction "or": "the seller failed to exercise reasonable care, or breached any implied warranty." The legislature's use of "including" plainly indicates that breach of implied warranty claims are to be considered a type of reasonable care claim, not a separate claim.

This conclusion is further supported by the last clause of § 600.2947(6)(a): "and that failure [to exercise reasonable care] was a proximate cause of the person's injuries." (emphasis added). The legislature did not use the language "and that failure or breach of implied warranty was a proximate cause of the person's injuries." Clearly, the only claim envisioned by the legislature in § 600.2947(6)(a) was failure to exercise reasonable care.

Plaintiff could argue that although § 600.2947(6)(a) does not allow for a separate claim of breach of implied warranty, the legislature intended for breach of implied warranty to be an alternative way to show the seller failed to exercise reasonable care, without any additional showing of fault. However, this argument is unpersuasive.

Traditionally, failure to exercise reasonable care was considered a "tort" claim, and breach of implied or express warranty was considered a "contract" claim. *Hollister v. Dayton Hudson Corp.*, 201 F.3d 731, 736 (6th Cir. 2000). § 600.2947(6)(b) allows for a plaintiff to recover under the contract theory of breach of express warranty, without a showing of fault. However, the legislature did not place the reference to breach of implied warranty in § 600.2947(6)(b), the "contract" clause of the section. Instead, the legislature placed the reference to breach of implied warranty in § 600.2947(6)(a), the "tort" clause of the section. This placement indicates that the legislature intended to add an element of fault to the traditional implied warranty claim. This conclusion is bolstered by the clause's emphasis on reasonable care. § 600.2947(6)(a) states that a plaintiff cannot recover unless the non-manufacturing seller's failure to use reasonable care "was a proximate cause of the person's injuries."

. . . .

[A]ccording to the Senate Fiscal Agency, the statute established a fault-based standard of liability for non-manufacturing product sellers. A plaintiff can only recover against a nonmanufacturing seller if the seller fails to exercise reasonable care, or breaches an express warranty. This statement of legislative intent clearly supports J.C. Penney's interpretation of the statute.

J.C. Penney's interpretation also best comports with other sections of the statute. Prior to the passage of the Tort Reform Act, a defendant in a products liability action could be required to pay damages "greater than his or her percentage of fault." *Senate Fiscal Agency Analysis of S.B. 344* at 6. However, M.C.L. § 600.6304(4) now provides that "a person shall not be required to pay damages in an amount greater than his or her percentage of fault." . . .

The Court finds that both the language of § 600.2947(6) and the legislative intent behind the statute show that non-manufacturing sellers cannot be held liable for damages due to breach of implied warranty, unless they failed to exercise reasonable care. As discussed above, Plaintiff stated that the allegedly defective shoe appeared to be in perfect condition when she purchased it. Plaintiff has failed to produce any evidence showing that J.C. Penney was negligent in failing to detect the defect in the shoe. Thus, Plaintiff's claim against J.C. Penney fails as a matter of law.

. . . .

For the above reasons, Plaintiff's motion for summary judgment is DENIED. J.C. Penney's motion for summary judgment is GRANTED.

NOTES AND QUESTIONS

1.   Are cases like *Coleman* driven by a desire to avoid the unfair imposition of fault and concomitant liability on innocent third person or is there a broader agenda? In the end, is this about narrowing the courthouse door—or improving the quality and value of the cases litigated within?[9]

2.   Beyond an endorsement of fault-based liability, *Coleman* echoes a common theme in tort reform: liability must be based on wrongdoing, and only to the percent or share that wrongdoing contributes to the plaintiff's injuries. Stated another way, one should not be liable for harms they did not cause, regardless of the chain of distribution, or, for that matter, the nature of the activity or product in question. In this context, a plaintiff's uncompensated loss is a lesser injustice than imposing on a defendant money damages for harms not attributable to the defendant's misconduct. Hence, joint and several liability has been a prime target of tort reform. For a comprehensive discussion of the topic, *see* Nancy C. Marcus, *Phantom Parties and Other Practical Problems with the Attempted Abolition of Joint and Several Liability*, 60 ARK. L. REV. 437 (2007). For an interesting review of a case involving a number of defendants and the effects of tort reform, see *Viera v. Cohen*, 283 Conn. 412, 927 A.2d 843 (2007) (reciting the history of tort reform in Connecticut before getting to the problem of multiple defendants).

---

[9]   Sandra F. Gavin, *Stealth Tort Reform,* 42 VAL. U.L. REV. 431 (2008); Lee Harris, *Tort Reform as a Carrot-and-Stick*, 46 HARV. J. LEGIS. 163, 171 (2009); Conference, Center for Democratic Culture at UNLV, *The Law and Politics of Tort Reform,* 4 NEV. L.J. 377 (2003).

CONCLUSION

■ ■ ■

Some years ago, Connecticut Supreme Court Justice Shea wrote that Connecticut tort reform "represents a complex web of interdependent concessions and bargains struck by hostile interest groups and individuals of opposing philosophical positions."[1] It is by no means the only attempt to capture the field in a single sentence.[2] As much as one might be tempted to boil down the field to some digestible singularity, at this point, such distillations may not resonate with you.

Having read the essays, articles, interest group statements, and walked briefly in the shoes of Devon Armstrong, Dr. Bernard Starling, or Miranda Daine, are you content with the notion that tort reform is simply a somewhat civil battlefield on which the inherently contradictory positions (business interests vs. consumer interests) collide?

As you sort through the cases and literature and begin to refine your own ideas, a final thought on this wonderfully challenging field. As stated at the outset of this text, there is no doubt about the depth of belief, passion, and intensity evident in those involved in the tort reform discourse. Powerfully held beliefs take on an emotional quality—and it is fair to ask whether emotion should be central to this discourse.

As you look at the literature in the field, how should you take into account the partisan nature of the debate[3]—and 'partisan' may be an understatement. Notice the title of Stephen J. Werber's 1997 article on the subject: *Ohio Tort Reform in 1998: The War Continues.*[4] War? In an article by Deborah Goldberg, *et. al., The Best Defense: Why Elected Courts Should Lead Recusal Reform,*[5] participants in the tort reform debate are referred

---

[1]   *Sanzone v. Board of Police Commissioners,* 219 CONN. 179, 185, 592 A.2d 912, 917 (1991).

[2]   Gregory B. Westfall from *The Nature of This Debate: A Look at the Texas Foreign Corporation Venue Rule and a Method for Analyzing the Premises and Promises of Tort Reform*, 26 TEX. TECH L. REV. 903, 925 (1995) ("The tort reform debate really boils down to a simple policy question: Do we favor the interests of business over the interests of those harmed thereby, or vice versa."); Nancy C. Marcus, *Phantom Parties and Other Practical Problems with the Attempted Abolition of Joint and Several Liability*, 60 ARK. L. REV. 437, 438 (2007) ("[T]he doctrine of joint and several liability has been a frequent target of tort reform efforts."); Jonathan Todres, *Toward Healing and Restoration for All: Reframing Medical Malpractice Reform*, 39 CONN. L. REV. 667, 693 (2006) ("Non-economic damages are a favorite target of tort reform. . . .")

[3]   Ashley L. Thompson, *Note: The Unintended Consequences of Tort Reform in Michigan: An Argument for Reinstating Retailer Product Liability*, 42 U. MICH. J.L. REFORM 961, 970 (2009) (characterizing tort reform as partisan).

[4]   45 CLEV. ST. L. REV. 539 (1997).

[5]   46 WASHBURN L.J. 503, 509 (2007).

to as "combatants." How does one sort out a problem this complex given the charged or, perhaps more to the point, bellicose nature of the discourse?

Finding meaningful common ground between those supporting tort reform and those opposed becomes an almost impossible task when the identity of the advocate and the content of the argument are merged.[6]

It may be that participants in the tort reform discourse are not just effectively and zealously representing a position—the position they take has become ingrained, central to their sense of self.[7] For lawyers, this is risky territory:

> To empathize with a client and identify with her . . . cause can provide an energy and enthusiasm that can prove invaluable. . . . That kind of alliance with the client can be a benefit to the attorney-client relationship; it can bolster the clients' morale and spirits during long and difficult litigation. [However, such] alliances also can have drawbacks. Attorneys can "over-identify" . . . and assume they know exactly what the client wants or needs. . . . Moreover, objectivity is vitally important. The empathetic attorney must be wary of too complete an identification with the client. You will need to *step back from the client's situation*, in ways that the client often cannot, in order to provide the critical eye and assessments that are part of your obligation. . . .

Robert Dinerstein, Stephen Ellmann, Isabelle Gunning & Ann Shalleck, Connection, Capacity and Morality in Lawyer-Client Relationships: Dialogues and Commentary, 10 CLINICAL L. REV. 755, 766–767 (2004) [emphasis added]

For some involved in the tort reform debate, it may be difficult to follow the sage advice of Professors Dinerstein, Ellmann, Gunning, and Shalleck. Tort reform touches on some of our most treasured institutions as well as our fundamental individual rights and entitlements. It is at once both an elegant legal and public policy challenge and a complex personal and (at times) emotional issue. Given the dimensions of the field, detachment is no small task.

The hope of this text, both for those who have labored in the trenches for years and those new to the field, is for a few moments of detached, objective thinking about the civil justice system. Who knows—maybe you will be the first to see the obvious and apparent solutions, the first to define the common ground.

---

[6]   Norman W. Spaulding, *Reinterpreting Professional Identity*, 74 U. COLO. L. REV. 1 (2003) (a good discussion of issues of attorneys identifying—or over-identifying—with clients).

[7]   Gerald J. Postema, *Moral Responsibility in Professional Ethics*, 55 N.Y.U. L. REV. 63, 77 (1980) (discussing the risks of the lawyer becoming "an extension of the legal, and to an extent the moral, personality of the client. . . .").

INDEX

References are to Pages

ABUSE OF LEGAL SYSTEM
See Fraud and Abuse of Legal System, this
  index

ACCESS TO JUSTICE
Benefits and burdens of tort reform, 108
Center for Justice and Democracy position,
  106
Corporate power imbalances, 107
Discriminatory effects of damage caps, 34,
  255
Legal aid access, 38
Medical malpractice reforms, expert
  reports requirements, 295, 301
State legislation infringing, 107

ADVERTISING
Insurance industry marketing of tort
  reform, 46

AIRCRAFT INDUSTRY
Statute of repose, 70, 239

**AMERICAN ASSOCIATION FOR
  JUSTICE (AAJ)**
ATRA criticism of, 212
Medical malpractice, 245
Policy position, 90
Tactics and goals, 69

**AMERICAN MEDICAL ASSOCIATION
  (AMA)**
Health care reform, 176
Medical malpractice reform, 33, 246s

**AMERICAN TORT REFORM
  ASSOCIATION (ATRA) [103]**
Agenda, 208
Americans with Disabilities Act litigation,
  211
ATRA criticism of, 212
Attorneys general as plaintiffs, 104
Business-oriented advocacy, 216
Consumer protection laws, 217
Founding, 207
Judicial Hellholes Report, 210
Marketing of tort reform, 46
Medical malpractice costs study, 158
Membership, 207
Mission, 207
Pet litigation, 213, 220
Plaintiffs' trial bar criticisms, 214
Policy position, 104, 207, 254
Pro-reform organization, 14

Qui tam litigation, 212, 216
Separation of powers position, 103
Statutes of limitation and repose, 221
Success of, 68
Trespasser defenses, 105
Wrongful death damages, 218

**AMERICANS WITH DISABILITIES
  ACT LITIGATION**
ATRA position, 211

ANECDOTAL EVIDENCE
  See also Empirical Evidence, this
    index
Distortions, marketing, 45, 185
Hot Coffee Litigation, this index
Internet circulation, 192
Power of, 200
Public opinion effects, 43, 185
Runaway jury tales, 37, 43, 201
Spurious and fabricated, 192

ANESTHESIA LITIGATION
Safety measures resulting from, 68

ARBITRATION
Class action restrictions, 168
Politically motivated judicial support, 28

ASBESTOS LITIGATION
  Generally, 35
Bankruptcies resulting from, 75
Fraud and abuse problems, 75
Mass tort lawsuits, growth of, 75
Plaintiff recruitment, 76
Publicity attending, 12

**ASSOCIATION OF TRIAL LAWYERS
  OF AMERICA (ATLA)**
  Generally, 86
See also American Association for Justice,
  this index

ATTORNEY AND CLIENT
Contingent Fee Caps, this index
Defense Bar, this index
Doctor/lawyer dichotomy, 9, 165
Empathy dangers, 305
Narrative of a plaintiff's attorney, 127
Plaintiff Recruitment, this index
Plaintiffs' Trial Bar, this index

**ATTORNEYS GENERAL AS
  PLAINTIFFS**
ATRA position, 104, 215

Litigation-specific state laws, 112
Police power, outsourcing of, 77
Separation of powers issues, 77, 104, 111

AUTOMOBILE ACCIDENT LITIGATION
No-Fault Regimes, this index
Safety measures resulting from, 68

BANKRUPTCY
Asbestos litigation caused bankruptcies, 75

BAR ASSOCIATIONS
Judicial influence, 41

BENEFITS AND BURDENS OF TORT REFORM
Generally, 107, 108
Costs of Tort Law Regime, this index
Costs of Tort Reform, this index
Safety and Tort Law, this index
Vulnerable Victims, this index

BENZENE LITIGATION
Generally, 35

BEST PRACTICES, LITIGATION PROMOTING
See Safety and Tort Law, this index

BIFURCATION
Punitive damages bifurcation statutes, 169

BIOMATERIALS INDUSTRY
Immunity statutes, 169

BRAIN INJURIES
Narratives, 127, 131

BUSINESS INTERESTS
Pro reform, 5

BUSINESS ROUNDTABLE
Business-oriented advocacy, 67
Marketing of tort reform, 49

BUSINESS TORTS
Consumer torts distinguished, 38

CALIFORNIA
Medical Injury Compensation Reform Act (MICRA), 166, 263

CASELAW
Generally, 267 et seq.

CATO INSTITUTE
Business-oriented advocacy, 67

CENTER FOR JUSTICE AND DEMOCRACY (CJD)
Access to justice, 106
Anecdotal evidence, debunking of, 188
Goals, 187
Health court proposal, 98
Lobbying activities, 56
Medical malpractice costs study, 159

Medical malpractice limitations and insurance rates, 262
No fault regimes, 250
Policy position, 13, 106
Web site, 186

CHAMBER OF COMMERCE
Business-oriented advocacy, 67
Class Action Fairness Act, support for, 73
Elected judiciary position, 73
Institute for Legal Reform (ILR), 73
Marketing of tort reform, 47
Policy position, 74

CHAMPERTY
See also Plaintiff Recruitment, this index
Investor financing of litigation, 81

CHEMICAL MANUFACTURERS ASSOCIATION
Marketing of tort reform, 47

CHILDREN
Damage caps, adverse effects, 255

CITIZENS' SUITS
See Qui Tam Litigation, this index

CIVIL CALENDAR DELAYS
Generally, 38

CIVIL JUSTICE SYSTEM
See also Access to Justice, this index
Benefits and burdens of tort reform, 107, 108
Democracy, fundamental principles of, 121
Difficulties of either changing or defending, 117
Fraud and Abuse of Legal System, this index
Tort reform within, 1

CIVIL RIGHTS LITIGATION
Tort law based remedies, 108

CLASS ACTION FAIRNESS ACT OF 2005
Generally, 168
Chamber of Commerce support, 73

CLASS ACTIONS
See also Mass Torts, this index
Arbitration restrictions, 169
Class Action Fairness Act 2, 41, 103, 168, 240,
Control of litigation, lawyer vs client power, 80
Epidemic of litigation, 5
Law and economics view of venue choices, 265

COALITION FOR UNIFORM PRODUCT LIABILITY LAWS
Marketing of tort reform, 47

COLLATERAL SOURCE RULE
Congressional Budget Office, 18, 229
Federal legislative proposals, 54
Law and economics movement, insurance
    analysis, 72
Successes of limitation advocates, 53

COMMON GROUND
Advocates vs issues, 309
Elusive nature of, 309
Irreconcilable disputes and, 71 et seq.
Narratives, search for common ground in, 6

COMMON LAW
See Judge-Made Law, this index

COMPARATIVE FAULT
    See also Comparative Negligence,
        this index
Proportional allocation alternatives to joint
    and several liability, 230

COMPARATIVE NEGLIGENCE
Hot coffee litigation, 37
Joint and several liability rule and,
    inconsistency of joint acceptance, 115
Judge-made law, 116
Judicial acceptance of, 53
Reformation of harsh contributory
    negligence rules, 20

CONGRESSIONAL BUDGET OFFICE
    (CBO)
2004 study, 18
2009 study, 158
Collateral source rule, 229, 230
Contingent fee caps, 249
Costs incident to medical malpractice
    litigation, 19, 159
Damages study, 18
Economics of tort reform, 225
Joint and several liability elimination
    proposals, 229
Liquidated products liability damages
    proposals, 227
Medical malpractice costs of tort law
    system, 158
Medical malpractice report, 245, 261
Nonpecuniary damages caps, 228
Settlement reform proposals, 228
Transaction costs of tort law, 225

CONSTITUTIONAL LAW
Damage caps challenges
        Generally, 118, 157
        Equal protection, 167
Due process
        Punitive Damages, this index
        Supreme Court, this index
Federal Employers' Liability Act,
    constitutionality, 175
Medical malpractice affidavit challenges,
    294
Remedy rights, tort reform laws infringing
    on, 299

CONSUMER EXPECTATIONS TEST
Generally, 93
Narrative, 137

CONSUMER FRAUD STATUTES
ATRA position, 104

CONSUMER PROTECTION LAWS
ATRA criticism, 217
Medical malpractice claims based on, 299

CONSUMER RIGHTS MOVEMENT
Plaintiffs' trial bar, 223

CONSUMER VS BUSINESS
    INTERESTS
Generally, 6

CONTINGENT FEE CAPS
Congressional Budget Office report, 18, 34,
    225
Lawsuit Abuse Reduction Act of 2017, 90
Mechanics of contingent fee system, 249
Medical malpractice, 248
Settled case limitations, 250
Sliding scale limitations, 250
State law caps, 29, 167, 168, 249
Unintended consequences, 250

CONTRIBUTORY NEGLIGENCE
    See also Comparative Negligence,
        this index
History of, 53, 115
Judicially developed exceptions, 115, 117
Last clear chance exception, 116
Reckless or wanton conduct exception, 116
Reformation of harsh rules, 116

CORPORATE POWER IMBALANCES
Access to justice effects, 106

COSTS OF HEALTH CARE
See Health Care Reform, this index

COSTS OF TORT LAW REGIME
    Generally, 39, 52, 180
Congressional Budget Office stud, 225
Expert testimony costs, 98, 249, 265
Medical Malpractice, this index
Transaction Costs, this index

COSTS OF TORT REFORM
    See also Economics of Tort Reform,
        this index
Consumers' burdens, 41
Loser-pays rules, 50
Marketing of loser-pays rules, 50
Medical Malpractice, this index
Medical malpractice reform proposals, 33
Transaction Costs, this index

CRIMINAL SENTENCING
Cruel and unusual punishment, 27

CRISES AND CALLS FOR REFORM
    Generally, 13, 96, 183, 186 et seq.
Causation disputes, 264

Medical malpractice crisis of 1960s, 96
Products liability crisis of 1970s, 96

CRUISE SHIP INDUSTRY
Federal legislative protections, 68

DALKON SHIELD LITIGATION
Generally, 35, 99

DAMAGES
Cap laws
    Congressional Budget Office 2004
        study, 18
    Constitutional restrictions, 171
    Constitutionality, 118, 157
    Empirical studies of effects of, 34
    Equal protection challenges, 167
    Marketing of, 51
    Medical malpractice caps, below
    Plaintiff groups adversely affected, 33
    Successes of limitation advocates, 53
General damages, terminology, 33
Lost earnings damages, race and gender
    bias, 110
Marketing of caps laws, 47
Medical malpractice caps
    Generally, 245
    Good provider standards, 247
Noneconomic Damages, this index
Pain and Suffering Damages, this index
Punitive Damages, this index
Race and gender bias in tort awards, 110

DEFAMATION LITIGATION
Punitive damage awards, 11

DEFENDANTS' PERSPECTIVES
Lawyer/doctor dichotomy, 9, 165
Narratives
    Generally, 122
    Punitive damages, 141

DEFENSE BAR
Lobbying power of, 111
Tort reform interests and attitudes, 40

DEFENSIVE MEDICINE
See Medical Malpractice, this index

DEFINITIONS OF TORT REFORM
    Generally, 95, 118
ATRA position, 103
Latin derivation, 164
Pendulum analysis of reform movements,
    96
Plaintiff-favoring reform eras, 108
Restriction vs reform, 113, 114
Semantic strategies, 113

DEMOCRACY
Strengthening through tort reform, 83

DES LITIGATION
Generally, 35

DESIGN DEFECTS
Narratives, 134, 137

DISTORTED JOURNALISM
Hot coffee litigation, 36

DOCTORS
See Physicians, this index

DRUG LITIGATION
See Pharmaceutical Litigation, this index

DUE PROCESS
Punitive Damages, this index
Supreme Court, this index

DYSPHASIA
Narrative, 131

EARLY OFFERS PROPOSAL
Settlements, 65

EARLY REFORM MOVEMENTS
No-fault automobile insurance, 53

ECONOMIC DAMAGES
Non-economic damages distinguished, 56

ECONOMICS OF TORT REFORM
    Generally, 69
    See also Costs of Tort Reform, this
        index; Law and Economics
        Movement, this index
Congressional Budget Office report, 225
Judge Posner's views, 264

ELDERLY PERSONS
Damage caps, adverse effects, 34

ELECTED JUDGES
Chamber of Commerce position, 73
Federal vs state systems, 83
Public opinion pressures, 41

EMERGENCY ROOM TREATMENT
Narrative, 124

EMOTIONAL DISTRESS
See Noneconomic Damages, this index

EMPIRICAL EVIDENCE
    See also Anecdotal Evidence, this
        index
Congressional Budget Office, this index
Death rates, correlation to medical
    malpractice tort reforms, 258
Frivolous litigation, 204
Insurance premiums correlation with
    medical malpractice tort reforms, 261
Judges' tort reform opinions, 201
Jury awards, empirical vs anecdotal
    evidence, 200
Medical cost reductions associated with
    tort reforms, 255
Medical malpractice reforms
    Correlation to death rates, 258
    Effects on health care, 249, 265

Insurance premium correlation with, 261

ENTERPRISE LIABILITY THEORY
Generally, 53

EVIDENCE
Anecdotal Evidence, this index
Empirical Evidence, this index

EVOLUTION OF TORT LAW
Generally, 20
Tort reform legal issues, 15,16

EXPERT TESTIMONY
Costs, 97–98, 249, 265
Epidemic of litigation charges, 4
Medical malpractice expert report
    requirements, 294–95, 301
Narrative, 134
Neutral expert proposals, 97–98
Questionable expert testimony and the
    litigation epidemic, 4
Reforms limiting, 35

**FEDERAL EMPLOYERS' LIABILITY
ACT**
Constitutionality, 175

FEDERAL LEGISLATION
    See also Federalism Questions, this
        index
Aircraft industry statute of repose, 239
Collateral source rule proposals, 244
Cruise ship industry protections, 68
Gun manufacturer protections, 68, 169, 199
Health care reform proposals, medical
    malpractice elements, 105
Health insurance proposals, 67
Non-economic damage cap proposals, 54, 56
State vs federal approaches to reform
        Generally, 16, 60
        See also Federalism Questions, this
            index

FEDERAL PREEMPTION
Medical malpractice reform, 30–31
Pharmaceutical litigation, 277
Politics of preemption, 284
Supreme Court decisions, 277

FEDERALISM QUESTIONS
        Generally, 224
Class Action Fairness Act of 2005, 240
Interstate commerce effects of legislation,
    60–61, 87
Mass tort cases in state courts, 90
Medical malpractice reform as state vs
    federal issue, 264–65
Preemption decisions, 224
Product liability, federal legislation
    proposals, 99
Punitive damages award reviews, 270
States' rights issues, 60
Tort tax effect of state court litigation, 86

FELLOW SERVANT RULE
Constitutional prohibitions, 171, 175

**FLEXIBLE TORT REFORM
PROPOSAL**
Generally, 245

FORUM SHOPPING
        Generally, 210
        See also Venue, this index
Judicial Hellholes Report, 80, 210

**FRAUD AND ABUSE OF LEGAL
SYSTEM**
Asbestos litigation, 235, 241
Insurance fraud schemes, 147
Investor financing of litigation, 80
Silicosis litigation, 235
State attorneys general, co-opting of, 76,
    103

FRIVOLOUS LITIGATION
        Generally, 187
        See also Anecdotal Evidence, this
            index
Judicial survey, 205

GENDER BIAS
See Women, this index

GOALS OF TORT LAW
Generally, 181

GOALS OF TORT REFORM
Generally, 164

GROUPTHINK
Marketing strategies, 42

GUN INDUSTRY
Federal legislation, 68, 169

HEAD INJURIES
Narratives, 123, 127

HEALTH CARE REFORM
American Medical Association position, 176
Federal legislative proposals
        Generally, 54
        Medical malpractice elements, 105
Narrative, health care costs, 128
Offensive and defensive medicine costs, 30
Public opinion, 176–77
Quid pro quo tort reform tradeoffs, 177
Tort reform aspects of proposals, 29, 178

HEALTH COURT PROPOSAL
        Generally, 97
Center for Justice and Democracy, 158

HERITAGE INSTITUTE
Business-oriented advocacy, 67

**HISTORICAL DEVELOPMENT OF
TORT LAW**
Contributory negligence rule, 115
Democratic Expansionary Era, 167

Insurance liability premium increases, 183
Joint and several liability rule, 115
Legal realist movement, 109
Legislative reform activity, 11
Medical malpractice, 165
Pro- and anti-plaintiff eras, 95
Progressive Era of 20th century, 170
Progressive movement of 19th century, 12
Reform movements generally, 4
Strict liability, 63
Workers compensation legislation, 12, 170

HOT COFFEE LITIGATION
　　　　Generally, 43
　　　　See also Anecdotal Evidence, this
　　　　　　index
Comparative fault, 37
Distorted journalism, 36
Jackpot justice charges, 43
Public opinion, 29, 36

HUMAN FACE OF TORT REFORM
Generally, 55

IMMUNITIES
Biomaterials industry, 169
Charitable immunity, repudiation of, 45
Family immunity doctrine, erosion of, 46
Gun industry, 169
Judicial immunity, 83
Medical provider immunity proposals, 247
Safe harbor guidelines, 31
Spousal immunity doctrine, erosion of, 46
Tort reform legal issues, 15

IMPACT OF THE TORT REFORM
　　　　MOVEMENT
Generally, 178

INCOME EQUALIZATION
Insurance principles, 70

INDUSTRY SAFE HARBOR
　　　　GUIDELINES
Private reform proposals, 31

INFANTS
Damage caps, adverse effects, 34

INFORMED CONSENT
Battery claims, 300
Narrative, 131

INSTITUTE FOR LEGAL REFORM
　　　　(ILR)
Generally, 73
See also Chamber of Commerce, this index

INSURANCE INDUSTRY
Adverse selection, 70
Advertising, marketing of tort reform
　　　　through, 46
Bad faith litigation, punitive damages, 271
Excess liability coverage, 155, 272
Federal health insurance legislation, 54
Income equalization, 70

Moral hazard, 70
Narrative, health insurance limitations,
　　　　131
No-Fault Regimes, this index
Premiums
　　　　History of tort reform, 13
　　　　Medical malpractice tort reforms
　　　　　　correlation, 260–61
　　　　Obstetrics practice, prohibitive
　　　　　　insurance premiums, 94
　　　　Practice inhibiting insurance
　　　　　　premiums, 133
Strict liability, insurance effect of, 69
Tort law, insurance alternatives, 226
Tort reform interests and attitudes, 41, 120

INTEREST GROUPS
　　　　Generally, 51 et seq., 163 et seq.
Lobbying practices, 155
Narrow tailoring of reforms by, 41
Positions of, 176

INVESTOR FINANCING OF
　　　　LITIGATION
Generally, 80

IRRECONCILABLE DISPUTES
Common ground, search for, 72 et seq.

JACKPOT JUSTICE CHARGES
Marketing of tort reform, 42

JOINT AND SEVERAL LIABILITY
　　　　Generally, 57, 116
Aiders and abettors of securities fraud
　　　　liabilities, 58
Comparative negligence rule and,
　　　　inconsistency of joint acceptance, 116
Congressional Budget Office
　　　　Generally, 18
　　　　Elimination proposals, 50, 229
Epidemic of litigation, 5
History of, 115
Law and economics movement, insurance
　　　　analysis, 71
Litigation epidemic, 5
Marketing of limitations on, 50
Phantom party problems, 230
Products liability, 306
Proportional allocation alternatives, 230
Reform proposals, 115
Restatement of Torts, 231
Successes of limitation advocates, 53
Tort reform legal issues, 15

JOURNALISTS
　　　　See also Anecdotal Evidence, this
　　　　　　index
Hot coffee litigation, distorted reports, 43
Indolent failure, 44
Tort reform coverage, 67

JUDGE-MADE LAW
  See also Legislative Solutions, this
    index; Separation of Powers
    Issues, this index
Activism and tort reform, 66
Charitable immunity, repudiation of, 45
Comparative fault, 53
Comparative negligence rule, 116
Contributory negligence rule exceptions,
  116
Cost/benefits analyses, 21
Decisionmaking, public policy influences,
  21
Legislative vs judicial approaches to tort
  reform, 16
Public policy considerations, 21
Strict liability, 96
Tort law developments, 20
Unintended consequences, 21

JUDGES
Bar association influences on, 40
Elected Judges, this index
Immunity, judicial, 83
Tort reform opinions, 14, 201

JUDICIAL HELLHOLES REPORT
American Tort Reform Association, 105,
  210

JURIES
Anecdotal evidence of runaway jury tales,
  37
Attractive plaintiffs and sympathetic
  juries, 247
Empirical vs anecdotal evidence of awards,
  201
Skepticism, medical malpractice claims, 34
Sympathies
  Generally, 116, 149
  Attractive plaintiffs, 246–47
  Narrative, 140

JURISDICTION
Class Action Fairness Act of 2005, 168
Forum Shopping, this index
Magic jurisdiction, 73, 82

LAW AND ECONOMICS MOVEMENT
Class action venue choices, 265–66
Collateral source rule, insurance analysis,
  71
Conservative approach of, 53
Economic case for tort reform, 69
Joint and several liability, insurance
  analysis, 70
Judge Posner on tort reform, 264
Pain and suffering damages, insurance
  analysis, 71
Strict liability as insurance principle, 69

LAW SCHOOLS
Teaching of tort reform, 35

LEAD LITIGATION
Litigation-specific state laws, separation of
  powers criticisms, 112
Proximate cause rules, 111

LEGAL AID ACCESS
Generally, 38

**LEGAL FORMALISM AND LEGAL
  REALISTS**
Reform doctrines, 108

LEGISLATIVE SOLUTIONS
  See also Judge-Made Law, this index
Class Action Fairness Act 2, 41, 103, 168,
  240,
Constitutional challenges to tort reform
  legislation, results of, 103
Federal Legislation, this index
Fraudulent Joinder Prevention Act of 2017,
  2, 17, 24, 91, 243
History of, 11
Judge-made law compared
          Generally, 59
          See also Judge-Made Law, this
            index; Separation of
            Powers Issues, this index
  Legislative correction, 21
Judicial approaches to tort reform, 16
Lawsuit Abuse Reduction Act (LARA) of
  2017, 90
Perspectives of legislators, narratives, 142,
  150
Retroactive tort law changes, 155
Separation of Powers Reduction Act of
  2017, 2, 78, 86, 213, 268
State Legislation, this index

LITIGATION INDUSTRY
Manhattan Institute characterization, 67

LOBBYISTS AND LOBBYING
Interest groups' lobbying practices, 155–56
Narratives, lobbyists' perspectives, 144,
  148, 154
Regulation, 156

MAGIC JURISDICTION
Generally, 73, 82

MAINTENANCE
  See also Plaintiff Recruitment, this
    index
Investor financing of litigation, 80

MALPRACTICE TAX
Generally, 69

MANHATTAN INSTITUTE
Business-oriented advocacy, 67

MANUFACTURERS
Tort reform interests and attitudes, 40

MARKETING OF TORT REFORM
  Generally, 42
American Tort Reform Association, 47
Anecdotal tales, distorted, 44, 184
Business Roundtable, 47
Chamber of Commerce, 47
Chemical Manufacturers Association, 47
Coalition for Uniform Product Liability
  Laws, 47
Damages caps, 50
Groupthink, 44
Insurance industry, 46
Jackpot justice charges, 43
Joint and several liability, limitations on,
  50
Loser-pays rules, 50
National Association of Manufacturers, 47
National Federation of Independent
  Businesses, 47
Product Liability Alliance, 47
Product Liability Coordinating Committee,
  47
Reformer, co-opting of term, 45

MASS TORTS
  See also Class Actions, this index
Federalism concerns as to mass tort cases
  in state courts, 86
Growth of, 76
Police power, outsourcing of, 77

MEANING OF TORT REFORM
See Definitions of Tort Reform, this index

**MEDICAL INJURY COMPENSATION
  REFORM ACT (MICRA)**
Generally, 166, 263

MEDICAL MALPRACTICE
  Generally, 245 et seq.
Affidavit requirements of reform statutes,
  294, 298
American Association for Justice position,
  245
American Medical Association position, 33,
  245
American Tort Reform Association costs
  study, 159
Assumptions of reform movements, 175
Attractive plaintiffs and sympathetic
  juries, 247
Award costs, Congressional Budget Office
  study, 19, 158
Battery claims, 300
Best practices, litigation promoting, 37
California, 166, 263
Carrot-and-stick approach to reforms, 251
Center for Justice & Democracy costs
  study, 158
Center for Justice and Democracy, medical
  malpractice limitations and
  insurance rates, 262
Common Good proposal, 97

Congressional Budget Office costs study,
  158
Constitutionality challenges to affidavit
  requirements, 294
Consumer protection law claims against
  providers, 299
Contingent fee caps, 248
Cost impacts of reform proposals, 34
Costs of tort law system, 158
Damage caps
  Generally, 246
  Good providers standards for, 248
Death rates, correlation to tort reforms,
  258
Defensive medicine, good and bad, 34, 201
Defensive medicine costs, 30, 39, 104
Dysphasia narrative, 131
Elective surgery narrative, 132
Expert reports, reform requirements, 295,
  302
Expert testimony, neutral experts, 98
Federal preemption of reforms, 30
Federal vs state reforms, 265
Good and bad defensive medicine, 34
Good providers standards for damage caps,
  248
Harvard study, 9
Health care costs, effects on, 247
Health care reform proposals, tort reform
  components, 29, 105, 178
Health court proposal, 97
High-risk practice area liabilities, 159
History of tort reform, 165
Hospital entity liability proposals, 252
Informed consent
  Battery claims, 300
  Narrative, 132
Insurance costs inhibiting practice, 94, 133
Insurance crisis of 1960s, 95
Insurance liability premium increases, 13
Insurance premiums correlation with tort
  reforms, 260
Juror skepticism, 34
Legislative proposals aspects of health care
  reform, 105
Managed care organizations, 252
Migration to reform states, 33
Narratives
  Dysphasia, 131
  Elective surgery decisions, 132
  Informed consent, 132
  Practitioners, impacts of awards on,
    133
  Testing negligence, 132
Neutral expert proposals, 98
No-fault compensation proposals, 245, 252
Noneconomic damage caps
  Generally, 54
Obstetrics practice, prohibitive insurance
  premiums, 94
Offensive and defensive medicine costs, 30
Pain and suffering damage cap, 33
Physicians, this index

Politics of reform, 253
Practitioners, impacts of awards on
    Generally, 159
    Narratives, 132
Private reform proposals, 31
Procedural reforms
    Generally, 294
    Expert reports requirements, 301
Procedural requirements of reform
    statutes, 294, 301
Professional competence effects of
    litigation, 165
Provider immunity proposals, 247
Public opinion, 253
Safe harbor guidelines, 31
Safety protocols resulting from litigation,
    45
State law damage caps, 30
State legislative reforms, 68
State vs federal reforms, 265
Statutes of limitation,166, 171, 302
Testing negligence narrative, 132

MINORITIES
Damage caps, adverse effects, 255

MISUSED PRODUCTS
Tort reform legal issues, 15 et seq.

NARRATIVES
    Generally, 9, 122 et seq.
Brain injuries, 131, 142
Common ground search, 6
Consumer expectations test, 93
Defendants' perspectives
    Generally, 122
    Punitive damages, 141
Design defects, 93, 199
Dysphasia, 131
Elective surgery, 132
Fundamental, 4
Head injuries, 125
Health care costs, 39, 176 et seq.
Health insurance limitations, 130
Juror sympathies, 107, 116, 149
Legislators' perspectives, 111 et seq., 118 et
    seq.
Lobbyists' perspectives, 148
Physicians impacted by malpractice
    awards, 152, 159
Plaintiff's attorney, 111
Products liability, 93, 99
Punitive damages, defendants'
    perspectives, 141
Settlement pressures on plaintiffs
    Financial, 134
    Legal, 136
Tort reform, 103

NARROW TAILORING OF REFORMS
Interest groups pressure effects, 118, 176

**NATIONAL ASSOCIATION OF
MANUFACTURERS**
Marketing of tort reform, 42, 47

**NATIONAL FEDERATION OF
INDEPENDENT BUSINESSES**
Marketing of tort reform, 47

**NATURE OF THE TORT REFORM
MOVEMENT**
Generally, 179

NERVE INJURIES
Narrative, 126

NEW ZEALAND
No-fault automobile insurance, 53

NO-FAULT REGIMES
Automobile insurance
    Generally, 179
    Early reform movements, 53
    New Zealand, 54
    Quid pro quo reforms, 108
Center for Justice and Democracy position,
    13, 187, 206
Health court proposal, 97 et seq.
Medical malpractice proposals, 247, 252
Vaccine industry, 16, 239
Workers' Compensation, this index

NONECONOMIC DAMAGES
    See also Pain and Suffering
        Damages, this index
Congressional Budget Office, 18
Economic damages distinguished, 56
Emotional distress, 109, 220
Federal legislative proposals, 54, 243
Litigation epidemic, 5
Medical malpractice
    Generally, 56
Reality of injury compensated for, 45, 220,
    255
Vulnerable groups, 255
Windfall characterizations, 118

ORIGINS OF TORT REFORM
Generally, 15

PAIN AND SUFFERING DAMAGES
    See also Noneconomic Damages, this
        index
Federal legislative proposals, 52, 54
Insurance principle of income equalization
    compared, 70
Law and economics movement, insurance
    analysis, 71
Medical malpractice, 33
Successes of limitation advocates, 42, 48
Terminology, 33

PANTSUIT LITIGATION
Generally, 104

PENDULUM ANALYSIS OF TORT REFORM MOVEMENTS
Generally, 10, 96, 170

PERSONAL INJURY BAR
Generally, 208 et seq., 218
See also Plaintiffs' Trial Bar, this index

PERSPECTIVES ON TORT REFORM
Generally, 4

PET LITIGATION
ATRA position, 174
Emotional distress damages, 174
Loss of companionship damages, 17

PHANTOM PARTY PROBLEMS
Generally, 190

PHARMACEUTICAL LITIGATION
Bendectin, 16
Federal preemption, 193, 278, 284, 293
Industry marketing of tort reform, 45

PHYSICIANS
Lawyer/doctor dichotomy, 9, 245
Medical Malpractice, this index
Political power, 175, 253
Tort reform interests and attitudes, 176

PLAINTIFF RECRUITMENT
Asbestos litigation, 75
Attorneys General as Plaintiffs, this index
Class Actions, this index
Control of litigation, lawyer vs client power, 74, 80

PLAINTIFFS' TRIAL BAR
ATRA criticisms, 209
Consumer rights movement lobbying, 188
Contingent fee caps, 166, 168, 197
Lobbying power of, 111, 213
Michigan litigation lobbying, 218
Narrative of a plaintiff's attorney, 111
Political contributions to judges, 184
Public opinion, 165
State attorneys general involvement in mass tort cases, 79, 104
Stereotypes, 48
Tort reform interests and attitudes, 39

POLICE POWER
Outsourcing by state attorneys general, 77

POLICY POSITIONS
American Association of Justice, 90, 236
American Tort Reform Association, 13, 33, 103, 207
Center for Justice and Democracy, 13, 187
Chamber of Commerce, 17, 92

POLITICS OF TORT REFORM
Generally, 27
Medical malpractice, 253

PRECEDENTIAL BASES OF TORT LAW
Generally, 18

PRIVATE REFORM PROPOSALS
Medical malpractice, 31

PRIVITY DOCTRINE
Reform of, 46, 114

PRO REFORM BUSINESS INTERESTS
Generally, 5

PRODUCT LIABILITY ALLIANCE
Marketing of tort reform, 47

PRODUCT LIABILITY COORDINATING COMMITTEE (PLCC)
Marketing of tort reform, 47

PRODUCTS LIABILITY
Absolute liability theories, 62
Congressional Budget Office report, 18, 187
Consumer Expectations Test, this index
Corporate interests, power of, 47, 61
Design defects rules, 93
Federalism objections to proposed federal legislation, 88
Insurance crisis of 1970s, 95
Insurance effect of strict liability recoveries, 69
Insurance liability premium increases, 13
Manufacturers' interests and attitudes towards tort reforms, 40
Narratives, 136, 145
Privity doctrine, reform of, 46, 114
Reasonable alternative design proposal, 93
Retailers, liability of, 158, 238, 304
Risk-utility balancing, 93
Spoliation, 303
Statutes of repose, 63, 199, 222, 238
Strict Liability, this index

PROGRESSIVE AND REGRESSIVE REFORMS
Generally, 46

PROGRESSIVE MOVEMENTS
19th century, 12
20th century, 12, 46, 170 et seq.

PRO-PLAINTIFF REFORMS
Generally, 114

PROPORTIONAL ALLOCATION
Joint and several liability alternatives, 230 et seq.

PROXIMATE CAUSE RULES
Lead litigation, 111
State law modification proposals, 111

PUBLIC OPINION
Generally, 35
Anecdotal evidence affecting, 14, 185, 200
Asbestos litigation publicity, 35

Elected judge pressures, 40
Health care reform, 176
Hot coffee litigation, 37, 43
Jackpot justice charges, 43
Law school teaching impacts, 35
Medical malpractice, 254
Plaintiff's trial bar, 165
Tobacco litigation publicity, 12

PUBLIC POLICY
Legislative vs judicial law changes
reflecting, 16, 59

PUNITIVE DAMAGES
Bifurcation statutes, 169
Congressional Budget Office 2004 study, 18
Defamation litigation, 11
Defendants' perspectives, narrative, 141
Due process standards
Generally, 19, 157, 237, 274
See also Supreme Court, this index
Economic vs physical injury, 273
Empirical research of awards, 49, 277
Epidemic of litigation, 5
Goals of tort law served by, 181
Growth in size of awards, effects of, 11, 14
Hot coffee litigation, 43
Insurance bad faith litigation, 91, 272
Litigation epidemic, 5
Misrepresentations as to size and number
of awards, 49
Narratives, defendants' perspectives, 141
Out-of-state conduct influencing awards,
275
Proportionality review, 237, 275
Ratio analyses, 68, 254, 268 et seq.
State law caps, 29, 167, 169
Substantive due process analyses, 234, 270
Supreme Court, this index
Tort reform legal issues, 15

PURPOSE OF TORT REFORM
Generally, 164

**QUESTIONABLE EXPERT
TESTIMONY**
Litigation epidemic, 5

QUI TAM LITIGATION
See also Attorneys General as
Plaintiffs, this index
ATRA position, 212

QUID PRO QUO REFORMS
Generally, 177
Health care reform tradeoffs, 177
No-fault automobile insurance, 108
Workers' compensation, 108

RACE BIAS
Tort awards reflecting, 110

REASONS FOR TORT REFORM
Generally, 4

REFORMER
Marketing use of term, 35, 42

REGULATORY LAW
Safe harbors for approved products, 227

RESTATEMENT OF TORTS
Joint and several liability, 231
Strict liability, 63, 233

RETROACTIVITY
Legislative changes, 136, 223

SAFE HARBORS
Guidelines, medical malpractice
immunities, 31
Regulatory
Approved products, 227
Punitive damages, 16

SAFETY AND TORT LAW
Generally, 3, 38
Economic theory, 53
Medical safety, 98, 265, 300
Product safety, 55

SCOPE OF PROBLEM
Generally, 1

SEMANTICS
See Definitions of Tort Reform, this index

SEPARATION OF POWERS ISSUES
See also Judge-Made Law, this index;
Legislative Solutions, this
index
ATRA position, 213
Constitutional challenges to tort reform
legislation, results of, 87, 298
Lead litigation, state laws affecting, 111
Legislation, Separation of Powers
Reduction Act of 2017, 2, 17
Litigation-specific legislation, policy
criticisms, 101, 111
Medical malpractice, statutory affidavit
requirements, 295
Police power outsourcing by state attorneys
general, 78
Privity doctrine, judicial reform of, 114
Public policy, changes reflecting, 86
Separation of Powers Restoration Act of
2017, 2, 78, 86, 213, 268
State attorneys general, involvement in
mass tort cases, 78, 104
Tobacco litigation, state laws affecting, 104
Tort reform as a check and balance
influence, 86

SETTLEMENTS
Congressional Budget Office report on
reform proposals, 225
Contingent fee caps for settled cases, 249
Control of litigation, lawyer vs client
power, 80
Early offers proposal, 65
Financial pressures narrative, 134

Government officials, mass tort settlements
        benefiting, 78
Legal pressures narrative, 139

SEVERELY INJURED PERSONS
Damage caps adversely affecting, 33

SILICA LITIGATION
        Generally, 22
See also Asbestos Litigation, this index

SOCIAL JUSTICE PRINCIPLES
Tort law based remedies, 109

SPOLIATION
Products liability, 303

STATE LEGISLATION
        See also Federalism Questions, this
                index
Access to justice infringements, 2, 106
Caps
        Contingent fees, 250
        Medical malpractice damages, 31, 68,
                166, 254
        Punitive damages, 68, 167, 254
Constitutionality challenges, 17, 87, 267
Consumer fraud statutes, 104
Federal vs state approaches to tort reform,
        16
Litigation-specific separation of powers
        criticisms, 111
Medical malpractice tort reform, 68
Michigan legislation, 218
Tobacco litigation and legislative changes
        favoring recovery, 111

STATES' RIGHTS
        Generally, 61
See also Federalism Questions, this index

STATISTICS
        See also Empirical Evidence, this
                index
Problems with statistical approaches to tort
        reform, 18

STATUTES OF LIMITATION
ATRA position, 221
Constitutional restrictions, 170

STATUTES OF REPOSE
Adoption of, 63
Aircraft industry, 239
ATRA position, 221

STEREOTYPES
Damage computations rules, 110
Trial lawyers, 48, 54

STRICT LIABILITY
Epidemic of litigation, 5
Historical development, 63
Insurance effect of, 70
Judge-made law, 69, 72
Litigation epidemic, 5

Restatement Second of Torts, 63, 303
Tort reform legal issues, 15

SUPREME COURT
Arbitration decisions, 28
Federal Employers' Liability Act, 175
Federal preemption
        Generally, 193
        Pharmaceutical litigation, 195, 278
Political influences, 27
Punitive damages
        Generally, 187, 234, 268 et seq.
        Economic vs physical injury, 273
        Guideposts, 272 et seq.
        Insurance bad faith litigation, 272
        Limitations, 18, 276
        Product liability, 234
        Proportionality review, 237, 277
        Ratio analyses, 68, 268 et seq., 274
        Standard of review, 272
        Substantive due process analyses,
                157
        Substantive due process challenges,
                268
        Third-party harms influencing
                awards, 241

TARGETS OF REFORM
Generally, 51

TEACHING TORT REFORM
Generally, 35

**THIRD-PARTY FUNDING OF
        LITIGATION**
Generally, 81, 241

TOBACCO LITIGATION
Fraudulent concealment theories, 94
Government officials, mass tort settlements
        benefiting, 104
Industry marketing of tort reform, 45
Litigation-specific state laws, separation of
        powers criticisms, 86
Plaintiff blaming, 38
Police power, outsourcing of, 62
Publicity attending, 8
Separation of powers criticisms of
        litigation-specific state laws, 112
State attorneys general as plaintiffs, 77,
        104
State law changes favoring recovery, 111

TORT LAW
Civil rights litigation based on tort law
        remedies, 109
Congressional Budget Office costs report,
        158, 225
Costs of Tort Law Regime, this index
Goals of tort law, 164
Historical Development of Tort Law, this
        index
Insurance alternatives to tort remedies,
        226
Precedential bases of, 18

Transaction Costs, this index

TORT TAX
Generally, 69
Federalism issues, 89

TRANSACTION COSTS
Congressional Budget Office, 225 et seq.
Early offers proposal, 65
Uncertain law and, 64
Workers' compensation systems compared,
173

TRESPASSER DEFENSES
ATRA position, 105

TRIAL LAWYERS ASSOCIATION
Generally, 212, 236, 254
See also American Association for Justice,
this index

VACCINE INDUSTRY
No fault regime, 239

VENUE
See also Forum Shopping, this index
Class actions, law and economics view of
venue choices, 240, 266
Nexus rules, reform proposals, 106

VICTIMS
Pro-victim tort reform pressures, 114
Vulnerable Victims, this index

VULNERABLE VICTIMS
Disparate tort reform impacts, 107, 118,
197
Human face of tort reform, 55
Lost earnings damages, race and gender
bias, 110
Narratives, this index
Non-economic damage caps, 33, 109, 255
Settlement pressures
Financial, 134
Legal, 136
Tort reforms disadvantaging, 107, 255

WASHINGTON LEGAL FOUNDATION
Business-oriented advocacy, 67

WHAT SHOULD CHANGE
Generally, 224

WOMEN
Damage caps, adverse effects, 33, 57, 109,
255
Lost earnings damages, race and gender
bias, 110

WORKERS' COMPENSATION
Generally, 12, 170
Opt-out provisions, 173
Quid pro quo reforms, 108
Transaction costs, 170, 173

WRONGFUL DEATH DAMAGES
ATRA position, 218